FATHERS AND
DAUGHTERS
IN ROMAN SOCIETY

JUDITH P. HALLETT

FATHERS AND DAUGHTERS IN ROMAN SOCIETY

Women and the Elite Family

PRINCETON UNIVERSITY PRESS

PRINCETON, NEW JERSEY

Published by Princeton University Press, 41 William Street,
Princeton, New Jersey 08540
In the United Kingdom: Princeton University Press,
Guildford, Surrey

Library of Congress Cataloging in Publication Data will be
found on the last printed page of this book

ISBN 0-691-03570-9
ISBN 0-691-10160-4 (pbk.)

This book has been composed in Linotron Bembo

Clothbound editions of Princeton University Press books are
printed on acid-free paper, and binding materials are
chosen for strength and durability. Paperbacks, although satisfactory
for personal collections, are not usually suitable for library rebinding

Printed in the United States of America by
Princeton University Press
Princeton, New Jersey

For Dory

QUAE
ME SCRIBENDI
TAM VASTUM MITTIS
IN AEQUOR

CONTENTS

Preface and
Acknowledgments

THE STUDY of women's role in the ancient family, and in ancient society generally, began as a collaborative effort between classicists and anthropologists. As S. C. Humphreys points out, during the mid-nineteenth century such European, American, and British scholars as H. S. Maine, J. J. Bachofen, N. D. Fustel de Coulanges, J. F. McLennan, and L. H. Morgan sought to reconstruct early stages of Greek and Roman society out of their shared belief that all societies had passed through parallel stages of evolution; such scholars postulated as identical the successive phases of Greek and Roman cultural development and assumed these to constitute a universal social experience.[1] Central to this collaboration between classicists and anthropologists, moreover, stood a concern with the relative, familial and political, importance of males and females in successive stages of social evolution. Thus ancient Greek and Roman authors were closely scrutinized and frequently cited in the heated nineteenth-century debate over whether or not matriarchy preceded patriarchy in primitive social organization.

After World War I—as Humphreys also observes—the relationship between classicists and anthropologists cooled, largely due to a growing distrust of the very social evolutionary schemes which participants in the earlier collaborative effort had regarded as an article of faith. Nevertheless, since World War II a sympathetic

[1] S. C. Humphreys, "Anthropology and the Classics," in *Anthropology and the Greeks* (London, 1978) 17-18; see also C. Kluckhohn, *Anthropology and the Classics* (Providence, 1961) 9-11.

attitude between classicists and anthropologists has been returning. The benefits of this sympathy and renewed collaboration are evident in work on Greek society by such European, American, and British scholars as L. Gernet, J. Redfield, and Humphreys herself.[2] They are no less apparent in work on women in Greek family and society by F. I. Zeitlin, C. P. Segal, and H. P. Foley.[3] The articles of the latter, American, scholars owe a special debt to various essays in *Woman, Culture, and Society*, a volume of immense value to my own thinking in this study.[4]

Scholarship on Roman society, and on women's role within it, has employed the theories, categories, and insights of modern social anthropology to a lesser degree. Yet M. Beard's pioneering, exemplary essay on the Vestal Virgins quite clearly points up the advantages of doing so.[5] The present study of women in the elite Roman family has been written in the hope of enriching our understanding of both women and the elite Roman

[2] See, e.g., L. Gernet, *Anthropologie de la Grèce antique* (Paris, 1968) as well as Humphreys' own survey of "The work of Louis Gernet" in *Anthropology*, 76-106; J. Redfield, *Nature and Culture in the Iliad: The Tragedy of Hector* (Chicago, 1975); Humphreys, *Anthropology* and "Foreword, Part II." to N. D. Fustel de Coulanges, *The Ancient City: A Study on the Religion, Laws, and Institutions of Greece and Rome* (Baltimore and London, 1980) xv-xxiii.

[3] See, e.g., F. I. Zeitlin, "The Dynamics of Misogyny: Myth and Mythmaking in the *Oresteia*," and C. P. Segal, "The Menace of Dionysus: Sex Roles and Reversals in Euripides' *Bacchae*," *Arethusa* 11 (1978) 149-184 and 185-202, respectively; H. P. Foley, "The Conception of Women in Athenian Drama," *Reflections of Women in Antiquity*, ed. H. P. Foley (London, 1981) 127-168, and "The 'Female Intruder' Reconsidered: Women in Aristophanes' *Lysistrata* and *Ecclesiazusae*," *CP* 77 (1982) 1-21.

[4] I would like to thank S. K. Dickison and F. I. Zeitlin for first calling my attention to this volume.

[5] M. Beard, "The Sexual Status of Vestal Virgins," *JRS* 70 (1980) 12-27.

family through various ideas contributed by recent work in social anthropology. It thus seeks to expand the collaborative endeavors between classicists and anthropologists. For this reason I have chosen to make use of anthropological terminology unfamiliar to many classicists (e.g. "structural centrality") in referring to certain social phenomena investigated and analyzed by anthropological scholarship (and hence theoretically defined as well as described by such technical labels). Similarly, and perhaps more unorthodoxly, I have presumed upon my classicist's training in the ancient tongues from which scientific terminology is minted and have coined, for this study, "filiafocality," an anthropological term of my own.

Several classicist colleagues have taken umbrage at my decision to use and especially to invent such (in their phrase) "jargon"; this decision thus necessitates some further defense. I would not only invoke, in the name of improved mutual understanding, the cause of collaboration between classics and an important, often neglected, cognate field. I would also like to substitute a more accurate descriptive term for the Roman social phenomenon I document than the loaded words of classical provenance invented by an earlier generation of classically trained scholars: namely "matriarchy" and "matriliny." These words themselves bear substantial responsibility for classicists' mistrust of anthropological theorizing on the ancient family, and might well continue to be misapplied to various aspects of Roman kinship and society discussed in my study if no other terms exist.

I have not, however, adopted the standard anthropological terms (e.g. EGO) and abbreviations (e.g. MoBro, SiSo) for kinship roles. My reasons are not so much aesthetic as practical. Precise Latin words, used by our classical Roman sources themselves, comprehensible even to many non-classicists through their English derivatives (e.g. *avunculus* for mother's brother) serve just as well. For the benefit of the Latinless, and those somewhat unfamiliar with what amounts to a fairly specialized branch of Latin vocabulary, these words and other relevant technical terms (e.g. *cognomen*) are translated when they first appear in the text, and also in the index. For the Latinless I have also translated (or at least paraphrased) the Latin phrases and passages it seemed important to quote. Although I use traditional, Latinized, transliterations of ancient Greek names (e.g. Herodotus), I have transliterated actual Greek words (e.g. *kyrios*).

My approach to Roman kinship relies heavily on what modern anthropologists would term the "biographical" method: that is, I am concerned with the way in which elite Romans themselves behaved in and viewed various kinship roles. The limited nature of my data, consisting as they do to a large extent of literary and other testimony for general cultural notions about different male and female familial roles, has required this focus. I have tried, insofar as possible, to examine different relationships involving specific kinship roles from the perspective of *both* participants (e.g. mother's brother and sister's son), often by looking at cultural generalizations, in ideological and realistic literature, about this relationship; admittedly, our lack of any evidence from elite Roman women themselves, lamented in my final chapter, makes such examinations extremely difficult. The findings I offer in this study, however, may be of interest in formulating larger theories about, and abstract categories for analyzing, the elite Roman family and women's place within it.

I have not attempted to be exhaustive in citing and

discussing ancient evidence on elite Roman notions about and conduct in female and male familial roles. On the contrary, I have tried to concentrate on a limited group of families, some fictive but most historical. In so doing I have purposely used the same pieces of evidence about various of these families (e.g. those portrayed in certain Plautine comedies; those of late republican luminaries such as the younger Cato) when making different points about different familial roles in different chapters. My rationale here is twofold. First, the non-specialist, and even the professional Latinist or Roman historian who does not engage in intense research on Roman prosopography, might find less selective documentation bewildering and difficult to follow. Hoping to avoid such confusion, I have additionally provided readers with a "scorecard for following the players" by introducing them to the families most frequently discussed in my second chapter, and by furnishing genealogical tables in my appendix. Second, the evidence on several of the families I have selected for study not only illustrates more than one aspect of elite Roman notions about and conduct in female and male familial roles but also testifies to the behavior exhibited by the same individual in different familial roles (e.g. the younger Agrippina as daughter, sister, wife, and mother; Atticus as son, brother, maternal uncle, and father). Such evidence is, accordingly, essential to my argument that elite Roman women's "apprenticeship" in their early familial roles as daughter and sister enabled them to behave more assertively, and command increasing respect, as they matured and assumed maternal roles. I have tried to be as comprehensive as possible in my choice of sources themselves, particularly those reporting on the behavior and attitude of historical personages. I have sought evidence from a wide variety of Roman authors so as not to misconstrue and misrepresent the actions and views of, e.g. Cicero, as typical of all elite Romans throughout the classical era.

This study evolved out of several interdisciplinary teaching efforts, first in undergraduate courses on women in classical antiquity and Roman civilization, then as a course combining the two topics entitled "Women in Ancient Rome" which was given as the Spring 1980 Blegen Lectures at Vassar College. To my predecessor in the Blegen post at Vassar, Virginia J. Hunter of York University, to my chairman at Vassar, Robert L. Pounder, and to the Blegen fund itself I owe an incalculable debt; the support I received and the collegiality I enjoyed at and from Vassar have been invaluable and inspirational in sustaining me through this project. My interest in both the major texts mined by and the issues confronted in this particular undertaking nonetheless ranks as a longtime concern, dating back to my undergraduate course work at Wellesley College with Katherine A. Geffcken, Mary R. Lefkowitz, Barbara P. McCarthy, and the late Margaret E. Taylor. For their introduction to both these ancient works and their cultural background I wish to express my appreciation as well.

This study was also made possible by the past decade of solid and innovative scholarship and teaching on women in classical antiquity here in the United States. Two fellow participants in this intellectually exhilarating and rewarding endeavor of "recovering women" in the ancient Greek and Roman world deserve special commendation for their T.L.C. (*tempus, labor, cura*, as another Latinist once put it) to both author and manuscript: Sheila K. Dickison and my dedicatee Dorothea S. Wender. Needless to say, this study could not have been brought into the shores of light without the contributions of

Sarah B. Pomeroy; the work of Keith Hopkins has proven no less indispensable. To those *duo fulmina* of republican Roman historical studies in North America, Ernst Badian and Erich S. Gruen, belongs my warmest gratitude for wise and informed succor to one with but shaky Roman historical training as well as for incisive criticism and indefatigable nurturance. The linguistic expertise of Jaan Puhvel and D. Gary Miller enabled me to utilize with greater confidence a body of material generally neglected by scholars on Roman women and the family; the encyclopedic bibliographical acquaintance of Jan Bremmer eased my research in numerous unfamiliar areas; Jane M. Cody's helpful explanations elucidated for me various complexities of republican Roman coinage; Allen Ward enlightened me on various complexities of Roman prosopography. An hour-long conversation with Froma Zeitlin stimulates and illuminates far more than many weighty volumes: I would like to thank her for several such hours, and the clarification of my thinking on sundry matters which they provided.

During its incubation this study profited greatly from the presentation of its major tenets and observations in papers delivered at a wide range of scholarly gatherings and institutions, and from the comments of colleagues in attendance on those occasions. The former include the Fall 1976 meeting of the Classical Association of the Atlantic States; the 1977 Conference on the History of Women in St. Paul, Minnesota; a seminar on "Perspectives on Greek and Roman Kinship" at the 1981 meeting of the American Philological Association; and the 1982 meeting of the Association of Ancient Historians. The latter include Bard College, Classical Studies and Women's Studies faculty seminars at Boston University, the University of California at Santa Barbara and Los Angeles, California State University at Los Angeles, the

University of Missouri at Columbia, the State University of New York at Albany, Haverford College, Wheaton College (Mass.), the University of Maryland at College Park, and the University of Colorado at Boulder. An invited seminar on the topic of this study at the Center for Hellenic Studies in Washington, D.C., eventuated in many fruitful ideas and associations; for these, and for his own sagacious remarks at that time, I am grateful to the director of the Center, Bernard M.W. Knox.[6]

Several individuals also merit my sincerest thanks for their patient lucubrations over my manuscript in its various stages and their criticisms and advice: Thomas W. Africa, William S. Anderson, Charles R. Beye, Jan Bremmer, Jean D'Amato, Walter Donlan, Joseph Geiger, Sally Humphreys, Barton Kunstler, Eleanor W. Leach, Jerzy Linderski, Daniel McCall, Jorgen Mejer, Ronald Mellor, Kurt Raaflaub, Jennifer Tolbert Roberts, Reinhold Schumann, Kristine Gilmartin Wallace, James E.G. Zetzel. Their assistance does not imply assent to all (or any) of the views voiced in my study; in accordance with the author's *mos maiorum*, I claim full and sole responsibility. Sincerest thanks, too, go to those whose care and helpfulness saw this manuscript through its last stages: my typist Ronit Shevach Sucoff; my professional *sodalitas emerita*, the Classical Association of New England (who added to the Blegen Fund's generous subsidy for typing with a Discretionary Fund grant); the General Research Board of the University of Maryland at College Park; my Princeton University Press editors, Joanna

---

[6] The title for these presentations, first delivered in 1976, has varied somewhat, but invariably included my title phrase for this study, "Fathers and Daughters." The choice of the same phrase by Dr. William Appleton for his 1981 case-based study of contemporary psychodynamics is entirely coincidental.

Hitchcock, Gail Ullman, Rita Gentry, and Judith May. Finally, I would like to thank my husband, son, and daughter for their unfailing display of understanding and love. They serve as a constant reminder that kinship, by blood and by marriage, is as vitally important to the heart and the spirit as it is to an intensely engaged mind.

ABBREVIATIONS

Africa	T. W. Africa, "The Mask of an Assassin: A Psychohistorical Study of Marcus Brutus," *Journal of Interdisciplinary History* 8 (1978) 599-626.
AJA	*American Journal of Archaeology*
AJAH	*American Journal of Ancient History*
AJP	*American Journal of Philology*
Balsdon	J.P.V.D. Balsdon, *Roman Women: Their History and Habits* (London, 1962).
CIL	*Corpus Inscriptionum Latinarum*
CJ	*Classical Journal*
CP	*Classical Philology*
CQ	*The Classical Quarterly*
CR	*The Classical Review*
CW	*The Classical World*
Ernout-Meillet	A. Ernout and A. Meillet, *Dictionnaire étymologique de la langue latine*[4] (Paris, 1967).
G and R	*Greece and Rome*
Herrmann	C. Herrmann, *Le rôle judiciaire et politique des femmes sous la république romaine* (Brussels, 1964).
IG	*Inscriptiones Graecae*
ILS	H. Dessau, *Inscriptiones Latinae Selectae* (Berlin, 1892-1916).
JHS	*Journal of Hellenic Studies*

JIS	Journal of Indo-European Studies
JRS	Journal of Roman Studies
Lacey	W. K. Lacey, The Family in Classical Greece (London, 1968).
Ogilvie	R. M. Ogilvie, A Commentary on Livy Books I-V (Oxford, 1965).
OLD	Oxford Latin Dictionary, ed. P. W. Glare (Oxford, 1968-1982).
ORF	Oratorum Romanorum Fragmenta³, ed. H. Malcovati (Turin, 1967).
Origines	Les origines de la république romaine. Entretiens Hardt 13 (Geneva, 1967).
Pomeroy, GWWS	S. B. Pomeroy, Goddesses, Whores, Wives and Slaves: Women in Classical Antiquity (New York, 1975).
RE	Real-Encyclopädie der klassischen Altertumswissenschaft (1893-), ed. A. Pauly, G. Wissowa, and W. Kroll.
RhM	Rheinisches Museum für Philologie
Syme, The Roman Revolution	R. Syme, The Roman Revolution (Oxford, 1939).
Szemerényi	O. Szemerényi, Studies in the Kinship Terminology of the Indo-European Languages with special reference to Indian, Iranian, Greek. Acta Iranica 16 (Tehran-Liege, 1977).
TAPA	Transactions and Proceedings of the American Philological Association
Woman, Culture, and Society	Woman, Culture, and Society, eds. M. Z. Rosaldo and L. Lamphere (Stanford, 1974).

FATHERS AND
DAUGHTERS
IN ROMAN SOCIETY

I

THE PARADOX OF ELITE
ROMAN WOMEN: PATRIARCHAL
SOCIETY AND FEMALE
FORMIDABILITY

THE women's movement of the 1970s has heightened a
long-standing scholarly interest in the women of the
Roman elite during the classical era—a period extending
from the late third century B.C. through the early second
century A.D. Yet this newly heightened interest has done
little to connect the study of elite Roman women with
the study of the elite Roman family during the same
period. The separation of Roman women's history and
Roman family history into two fairly discrete areas of
research mirrors a separation between women's history
and family history generally, a separation which the
distinguished American historian Carl N. Degler has
recently documented and attempted to explain in his
own field. Degler refers to this separation as particularly
surprising and regrettable. For, he asserts, "To any casual observer, it would seem natural that the two fields
should be related if only because historically women
have been active primarily in the family, and therefore
might be thought to be of central importance in explaining the history of that institution."[1]

[1] C. N. Degler, "Women and the Family," in *The Past Before Us*.

To be sure, major studies of women's position in elite
Roman society during the classical period tend to remark
upon women's rights and activities within the upper-
class family.[2] Various discussions point out that by the
mid-fifth century B.C. Roman law empowered women
to inherit, own, and bequeath property (albeit under the
tutelage of a male guardian, customarily a blood kinsman or a husband, who formally represented them and
presumably protected their financial interests). So, too,
scholars are fond of noting that well-born Roman women

Contemporary Historical Writing in the U.S., ed. M. Kammen (Ithaca,
N.Y., 1980) 310. The chapter on "Classical Antiquity" in *History of
the Family and Kinship: A Select International Bibliography*, ed. G. L.
Soliday, with T. K. Hareven, R. Vann, and R. Wheaton (Millwood,
N.Y., 1980) 159-167, has separate headings for "ROME," "Kinship,
the Family, Law and Politics" therein, and "WOMEN." Of its seven
selections representing Roman kinship, the family, law, and politics,
only one—Pomeroy's "The Relationship of the Married Woman to
Her Blood Relatives in Rome," *Ancient Society* 7 (1976) 215-227—
contains the word "woman" in its title. Like Syme's *The Roman
Revolution*, another of these seven selections, most scholarship on
the elite Roman family has been generally prosopographical; unlike
the work on U.S. family history cited by Degler, it tends not to be
quantitatively based. Although its concern has chiefly been with
family membership and connections through marriage, it has not
been particularly interested in the (amply documented) behavior of
individuals in their familial roles. For some general criticisms of
prosopographical writing on elite families and the assumptions about
kinship it makes see L. Stone, "Prosopography," *Daedalus* 10 (1971)
58-60. See also T. F. Carney, "Prosopography: Payoffs and Pitfalls,"
Phoenix 27 (1973) 156-179, which focuses specifically on prosopographical interpretation of Roman republican history. Whatever the
shortcomings of prosopographical analysis, its findings have been
of great benefit to this study.

[2] The most accessible studies of women in classical Roman society
are the important theoretical discussion by S. de Beauvoir, *The Second Sex*, transl. and ed. H. M. Parshley (New York, 1952) 84-89,
Balsdon, Herrmann, and Pomeroy, *GWWS*, 149-189. Other major
studies of ancient Roman women include those listed by Herrmann,
124-125, under "Bibliographie spéciale," and enumerated, along with
a brief summary of their contents, by L. Goodwater, *Women in
Antiquity: An Annotated Bibliography* (Metuchen, N.J., 1975) 107-151.

played a crucial part in their children's education and marriage arrangements. What is more, work on Roman women emphasizes that certain female members of Rome's most illustrious houses at times acted on their entire family's behalf and determined the outcomes of significant family matters.[3] In fact, their active and important role in family affairs would establish elite Roman women as what anthropologists would call "structurally central" family members: that is, members having some degree of control over their family's economic resources and being critically involved in its decision-making processes.[4] Women's extensive involvement in family affairs also marks the upper-class Roman family of the classical period as an unusual Roman institution, in integrating women as fully as it did men. Nevertheless, by merely noting that women were involved so extensively in the affairs of the elite Roman family, our studies imply that additional research on that institution might be of importance in illuminating the position of elite Roman women and render the separation between Roman women's history and Roman family history even more surprising.

[3] On Roman women's property rights and guardianship, see the general discussions of J. Crook, *Law and Life of Rome* (Ithaca, N.Y., 1967) 103-104, 113-116, 119-120, A. Watson, *Roman Private Law Around 200 B.C.* (Edinburgh, 1971) 39-41, and Pomeroy, *GWWS*, 161-163; see, too, Herrmann, 12-13, 33. For the involvement of various Roman women in the education and marital choices of their children, see Balsdon, 203; Herrmann, 96; E. E. Best, Jr., "Cicero, Livy and Educated Roman Women," *CJ* 65 (1970) 199-204; J. E. Phillips, "Roman Mothers and the Lives of Their Adult Daughters," *Helios* 6.1 (1978) 70-73; and T. Carp, "Two Matrons of the Late Republic," *Women's Studies* 8 (1981) 197-198. For Roman women who publicly represented their distinguished families and wielded authority in settling important family matters, see, for example, Balsdon, 49-53, 58-59, and Herrmann, 90-91.

[4] For the term "structural centrality" and its definition, see N. Tanner, "Matrifocality in Indonesia and in Africa and Among Black Americans," *Woman, Culture, and Society*, 131-132.

A further and striking phenomenon of elite Roman female existence renders this separation between the history of Roman women and that of the Roman family more surprising still. Merely a superficial inquiry into the position of women among the Roman upper classes reveals what scholars appear to regard as a paradoxical fact: that many well-born women are remembered as possessing forceful personalities and exerting a substantial impact on men's public affairs, despite their society's extolling of domesticity as women's only proper concern, and despite their own legal disabilities and formal exclusion from political participation.[5] This paradoxical formidability is imputed to well-born Roman women both as individuals and en masse; it is imputed as a result of both actual conduct by female members of Rome's classical elite and contemporary perceptions of how elite Roman women were capable of acting. Various aspects and effects of this formidability warrant immediate note in their own right before we consider the scholarly treatment and explanation of such a phenomenon.

Throughout Rome's history, its ideological literature glorified women's conscientious attendance to household responsibilities. Its laws required that all but a few exceptional women be legally subject to male guardians. Its government denied all women the right to take formal and active part—as voters, officeholders, and members of political assemblies—in civil life, although such participation was a right automatically claimed by its male citizens. Roman glorification of the upper-class

---

[5] Cf. Herrmann, who speaks, on p. 6, of "La situation paradoxale de la femme romaine, toute-puissante mais incapable"; see also, more recently, M. B. Arthur, " 'Liberated' Women: The Classical Era," in *Becoming Visible: Women in European History*, eds. R. Bridenthal and C. Koonz (Boston, 1977) 79, which describes the position of Roman women specifically as a "paradox." A similar concern with this paradox informs the discussions of Beauvoir, *The Second Sex*, 84-89, and Pomeroy, *GWWS*, 185-189.

woman wholly devoted to domestic duties appears most memorably at chapter 28 of Tacitus' *Dialogus de Oratoribus*, a work written in the early years of the second century A.D., but set in A.D. 75. Here Tacitus portrays Vipstanus Messala, an admirer of Rome's republican past, as fondly recalling the well-born women of the second and first centuries B.C. Such women, Messala says, deemed it a special source of praise to watch over their homes and dedicate themselves to their children (particularly their sons); with no less fondness Messala goes on to recall the virtuous elderly kinswomen who assisted such matrons in educating their offspring, and whose mere presence banished all unseemly talk and behavior from the household:

For the son of each citizen, child of a virtuous female parent as well, was from the start brought up not in the cubicle of a hired nurse, but in the lap and bosom of his mother, whose special praise it was to look after her home and devote herself to her children. What is more, there was an elder kinswoman appointed so that every child of this same family might be entrusted to her approved and admired character; in her presence it was not right to utter any seemingly shameful expression or commit any seemingly shameful act. And she, with a certain piety and modesty, regulated not only the endeavors and concerns, but also the relaxations and pastimes of boys. Thus we learn that Cornelia, mother of Tiberius and Gaius Gracchus, Aurelia, mother of Julius Caesar, and Atia, mother of Augustus Caesar, took charge of their children's educations and produced sons who led the Roman state. This training and strictness brought it about that each man's nature—untainted and honest and warped by no perversions—would, with his total commitment, seize upon honorable undertakings at once. Be it an interest in military matters or legal learning, be it an interest in the pursuit of eloquence, he devoted himself exclusively to it, he steeped himself entirely in it.[6]

[6] On the *Dialogus*, and its dating, see Syme, *Tacitus* (Oxford, 1958) I.104-113. Similar idealization and glorification of female domesticity may be found at Livy 1.57.9-10; it describes Lucretia's victory over

The complete exclusion of Roman women from formal involvement and leadership in the political sphere ranked as a similarly long-lived and hallowed tradition. Not only do we find the later jurist Ulpian proclaiming matter-of-factly at *Digest* 50.17.2: "Women are debarred from all duties whether civil or public, and thus cannot be judges or hold magistracies."[7] This exclusion even seems a traditional point of Roman male pride. Cicero, one of the greatest Roman statesmen of the first century B.C., reportedly contemplated with utter dismay a society which "included women in assemblies" and which allowed women "soldiery and magistracies and commands." His precise words bear quotation: "How great will be the misfortune of that city, in which women will assume the public duties of men."[8]

Nevertheless, in the face of this popular ideal of female domesticity, and in the face of these prevailing constraints on female public activity, some Roman women of the upper classes proved formidable, politically influential figures in the late republic and early empire—Cicero's and Tacitus' own times. It is with such women, and the paradoxical nature of their formidability and political influence, that those who study women in the classical Roman elite chiefly concern themselves. Ancient sources report that several women from Rome's leading houses wielded substantial clout during the forties B.C., a decade rife with civil war and political tur-

---

several Etruscan princesses in a contest to determine female excellence after a surprise visit had found her spinning rather than partying at night.

[7] Significantly, Ulpian goes on to add, "likewise a young man not fully grown should abstain from all civil duties," thereby equating women in general with immature male youths. I owe this observation to E. Badian.

[8] Lactantius, *Epitomes* 33 [38] 1-5, ascribed to *De Re Publica* 4.5 by K. Ziegler in his Teubner edition.

moil. They encourage modern scholars to accord special attention to such females as Marcus Brutus' mother Servilia and Mark Antony's wife Fulvia, who are portrayed by classical authors as staging summit conferences, commanding armies, implementing political proscriptions, and thereby controlling men's affairs.[9] Tacitus and Suetonius vividly document the powerful roles played by shrewd and redoubtable female kin in the reigns of Rome's Julio-Claudian emperors; their accounts have attracted, and deserve, no less notice.[10] Ancient sources, moreover, regard politically powerful women as a time-honored element of Rome's heritage. Both the historian Livy, writing in the final quarter of the first century B.C., and the biographer Plutarch, a century and a half later, give serious consideration to a legend which credits a woman, the nymph Egeria, with advising Rome's second king, Numa Pompilius, on weighty matters of state: their assumptions about Rome in the eighth century B.C., may well derive from their observations of Roman politics in later, historical, eras.[11]

Perhaps more importantly, even upper-class Roman women who did not possess special political influence nor concern themselves deeply with the workings of

[9] See, for example, Balsdon, 49-53, as well as Africa, *passim*, on this Servilia; C. Babcock, "The Early Career of Fulvia," *AJP* 86 (1965) 1-32, as well as J. P. Hallett, "*Perusinae Glandes* and the Changing Image of Augustus," *AJAH* 2 (1977) 151-171, on Fulvia. See, too, B. Fortsch, *Die politische Rolle der Frau in der römischen Republik* (Stuttgart, 1935).

[10] See, for example, Balsdon's lengthy section on the women of the Julio-Claudian household, 63-130, which quotes liberally from Tacitus and frequently cites the testimony of Suetonius, as well as Syme, "Princesses and Others in Tacitus," *G and R* 28 (1981) 40-52.

[11] Livy 1.19, 21.3-4; Plutarch, *Numa* 4. See also Herrmann, 23; the discussion of Egeria by Ogilvie, 102-103, and the article by Samter in *RE* 5 (1905) 1980-1981.

Roman government seem to have been perceived by politically experienced and aware Roman males as disturbances and even threats to Roman political order. Accounts summarizing an oration delivered in the early second century B.C. by the elder Cato serve as a case in point: in this oration, Cato is said to have justified the prohibition against young boys' attending the Roman senate as protecting young boys, and the senate, against the rapidly mobilized forces of their inquisitive and gossipy mothers.[12] Livy, moreover, attributes to the elder Cato a speech expressing outrage at a group of wellborn women who demonstrated against inequitable legislation restricting their personal adornment. This rendition of Cato's supposed remarks characterizes these women as not merely riotous but actually in the process of overthrowing male rule.[13] By Livy's time, however, other men had joined Cato in regarding women with the most minimal political involvements as nonetheless capable of having considerable political impact. Sallust, writing in the decade before Livy launched his lengthy history and in the years immediately following his own retirement from political life, assigned a character sketch of the aristocratic matron Sempronia a featured place when chronicling the Catilinarian conspiracy of 63 B.C. Yet it is clear from all of our evidence, much of it supplied by Sallust himself, that Sempronia played no part in the conspiracy whatever and was at most deemed a possible influence on various men.[14] By the first century

---

[12] Aulus Gellius 1.23 and Macrobius, *Saturnalia* 1.6.19 = *ORF*, pp. 67-69; the speech is also discussed by Balsdon, 203-204, Herrmann, 48-49, and in chapter five below.

[13] Livy 34.2-4, discussed by Balsdon, 33-35, Herrmann, 60-62, and Pomeroy *GWWS*, 180.

[14] Sallust, *Bellum Catilinae* 24.3-25.5; see also Balsdon, 47-48, and Syme, "No Son for Caesar," *Historia* 39 (1980) 428-431. Herrmann, however, refers, on 103, to Sempronia as "l'âme de la conspiration" and to her political role in the conspiracy as "pas négligeable."

A.D., apprehensions about the political potential of women altogether removed from public life had become more commonplace. During the emperor Nero's reign of terror in the early sixties A.D., the female relations of his male victims routinely suffered persecution at Nero's hands. Even Nero's adoptive half-sister Claudia Antonia, whom Tacitus pointedly depicts as a quiet and unassertive woman, appears to have met her death because Nero harbored political suspicions about her.[15]

Indeed, the assumption that women, especially those of high birth, were instrumental in affecting the course of Roman republican and imperial politics manifests itself frequently and strongly enough in our ancient Roman male sources to render it impossible for scholars today to distinguish clearly between women's actual influence and women's imagined influence in political matters.[16] Whatever the true extent of Roman women's political involvement, it is indisputable that the political impact attributed to certain of them reflects a general

[15] For the female victims of Nero's reign of terror, see Tacitus, *Annales* 15.71ff. We may infer that Claudia Antonia was not a woman known for seeking attention or power from Tacitus' statement, at *Annales* 15.53.3-4, that an account by the elder Pliny—of Claudia's plans to support the conspiracy of Piso by publicly accompanying him to Rome's military headquarters "so as to elicit the approval of the populace"—may seem ridiculous (*quamvis absurdum videretur*). Furthermore, Claudia Antonia figures in the *Annales* only in connection with her role as the emperor Claudius' daughter by Aelia Paetina (12.2.1), her unprotested ill-treatment by her stepmother Agrippina (12.68.3), and her marriage to Faustus Cornelius Sulla Felix (13.23.1), who was executed by Nero in 62 (so *Annales* 14.57). For her execution, see Suetonius, *Nero* 35.4.

[16] See, for example, Balsdon, 45, who is so confused as to generalize, prior to describing a small number of influential women in the later republic, ". . . the New Woman has arrived. Her interests lie outside the four walls of her home. In politics she is a power in her own right." He tends, however to credit Roman republican women with less political influence than does Herrmann, as is illustrated by their disagreement over the role of Sempronia in the Catilinarian conspiracy (note 14 above).

image of Roman women as socially significant and often highly visible individuals. Such an image of course differs radically from that of well-born women in the society to which later republican and early imperial Rome is sometimes likened, that of fifth century B.C. Athens. "Citizen women" of the classical Athenian era barely figure in accounts of political history and are not represented as integrally involved in male social concerns; their social invisibility has created difficulties for generations of scholars merely interested in determining their social status.[17]

In the light of scholars' readiness to note Roman women's paradoxical, real and imagined, political influence and social significance during classical times and to acknowledge Roman women's structurally central, and hence influential and significant, position within the elite family, one might therefore expect scholarship to connect this familial structural centrality and this paradoxical formidability with one another. At the very least one would expect a strong scholarly interest in the dynamics of Roman women's involvement in the politically influential, socially significant, upper-class family itself. Yet the behavior thought appropriate to and the behavior actually evinced by women in their various roles within the elite Roman family—of mother, sister, wife, daughter—are only beginning to undergo examination; the same holds true for the patterns of bonding with and among female family members.[18] Even in re-

[17] For Athenian women of the fifth century B.C. and the scholarly controversy surrounding their status, see Lacey, 151-176; Pomeroy, *GWWS*, 58-60, 67-68, 74, 93ff.; R. Just, "The Conception of Women in Classical Athens," *Journal of the Anthropological Society of Oxford* 6 (1975) 153-170; J. Gould, "Law, Custom and Myth: Aspects of the Social Position of Women in Classical Athens," *JHS* 100 (1980) 38-59.

[18] E.g. by Phillips, "Roman Mothers and Daughters"; K. G. Wal-

cent investigations into these matters, Anglo-American scholars have not made much of an effort to consider the relationship between the paradox of Roman women and women's conduct in their role, or roles, within the upper-class Roman family.

This lack of effort need not, however, be ascribed to scholarly obtuseness. For generations a theory of Roman social development based on the views of the nineteenth-century jurist Bachofen and his followers has been invoked, largely in European studies, to account for the paradox of Roman women. This theory pointedly assumes an impact of early Roman family structure and sentiment on women's position in much later elite Roman society. The theory and its explanation for the paradox of Roman women deserve special scrutiny and detailed refutation for two reasons. Most obviously, its understandable failure to convince most Anglo-American scholars may help elucidate the failure of recent studies to link upper-class Roman women's familial position to their social significance and political influence.[19] More importantly, its shortcomings make clear various

---

lace, "Kinship Terms in Tacitus," delivered at the meeting of the Women's Classical Caucus held in conjunction with the American Philological Association, December 29, 1976; Africa; A. C. Bush, *Studies in Roman Social Structure* (Washington, D.C., 1982) 65ff. The last of these, by defining a woman's brothers and sons-in-law as "equivalent in status to her husband," sees marriage as the crucial link to men's holding of political office; he does not consider any connections which might exist between women in familial roles other than that of wife and *women's* political impact generally.

[19] By way of contrast, Herrmann, 10, subscribes to "l'opinion généralement admise" that there exists a system more primitive than patriarchy which accords women "une prééminence inconnue des civilisations patriarcales"; she believes that many legends related to the Roman monarchic era "semblent rappeler une période matriarcale." Beauvoir, *The Second Sex*, 84, also maintains that "it is probable that in the time of the monarchy Rome still practiced exogamy under a matrilineal regime."

problems to be encountered in seeking to relate the paradox of Roman women to their structural centrality in the elite family of classical times.

Bachofen and more recent supporters of his theory such as G. D. Thomson maintain that a matriarchal or matrilineal order prevailed in Rome's monarchic era (which, by Roman reckoning, extended from 753 to 510 B.C.). They suppose as well that this matriarchal or matrilineal order was first associated with Rome's Sabine component and reached its peak during the Etruscan domination of Rome in the late seventh and sixth centuries B.C. According to such a view, therefore, the esteem granted and formidability attributed to so many well-born women of the republican and early imperial periods, the very opposite of what one might expect from their lack of formal civil rights, constitutes a survival of early "mother right," Sabine and Etruscan in provenance.[20]

Yet the hypothesis that matriarchal or matrilineal elements in Sabine, and in particular Etruscan, culture were absorbed into Roman civilization, though a convenient means of accounting for certain seemingly incongruous features of later republican and early imperial Roman society, poses certain problems. In the first place, the identification and isolation of purely Sabine and Etrus-

[20] See J. J. Bachofen, *Die Sage von Tanaquil: eine Untersuchung über den Orientalismus in Rom und Italien* (Heidelberg, 1870), most recently available as Vol. VI of his *Gesammelte Werke*, ed. K. Meuli (Basel, 1943); G. D. Thomson, *Studies in Ancient Greek Society: The Prehistoric Aegean* (New York, 1949) 92-101, 171-177; and, among others, R. Briffault, *The Mothers: A Study of the Origins of Sentiments and Institutions* (New York, 1927) 343ff.; H. Diner, *Mothers and Amazons: The First Feminine History of Culture*, ed. and transl. J. P. Lundin (Garden City, N.Y., 1973) 193-201. For some vigorous challenges to Bachofen's view, see H. J. Rose, "Mother Right in Ancient Italy," *Folklore* 31 (1920) 93-108, and L. Eving, *Die Sage von Tanaquil* (Frankfurt, 1933).

can components in pre-republican Roman culture are not only difficult, but fraught with complications. Scholars differ strongly over when Sabine and Etruscan influence was felt in early, "Latin," Rome, and thus where a particular early Roman practice originated.[21] One must also consider why many practices, if indeed non-Roman in origin, were adopted. For if Roman society of the monarchic period is to be attributed with its own, native, Latin, practices and institutions, which it gradually combined with those of non-Latin (Sabine) and non-Indo-European (Etruscan) peoples, it presumably incorporated solely those foreign elements which fitted its existing needs and adapted those elements to conform with its own pre-existing attitudes and usages.[22] In fact, two of the so-called Sabine and Etruscan practices which

[21] Indeed, J. Poucet, *Recherches sur la légende sabine des origines de Rome* (Louvain, 1967) denies altogether the Sabine element in Rome's early history. For a refutation of his argument, see Ogilvie, *CR* 18 (1968) 237-239; for another explanation of the early Sabine presence, see M. Pallottino, "The Origins of Rome," in D. and F. R. Ridgway, eds., *Italy Before the Romans: The Iron Age, Orientalizing and Etruscan Periods* (New York, 1979) 214-215. On 156-157 and 194-195 of his Livy commentary, moreover, Ogilvie contends that the reign of Rome's sixth king, Servius Tullius, "confirms a Latin interruption in the Etruscan domination of Rome as represented by the Tarquins." He thus places little credence in the identification of Servius Tullius by the Roman emperor Claudius with the Etruscan Mastarna (so CIL XIII.1668 = ILS 212), and the Roman view of Servius' reign as part of Rome's "Etruscan" phase. T. N. Gantz, "The Tarquin Dynasty," *Historia* 24 (1975) 539-554, also thinks the identification of Servius Tullius and Mastarna unlikely, but claims that Servius, "Latin or not . . . ruled Rome as a member of an Etruscan dynasty, and presumably ruled accordingly" (547).

[22] On evidence for Rome's pre-urban epoch (i.e. prior to a Sabine synoecism) and for the pre-Etruscan phase of the following epoch, that of the "archaic city," see E. Gjerstad, *Origines* 3-18. For a criticism of Gjerstad's "down-dating" and contraction of Rome's pre-Etruscan era, which would view 575 B.C. as "seeing the culmination of the process of urbanization carried out by the Etruscan kings," see Pallottino, "Origins of Rome," 204-208.

Thomson himself remarks upon as significant "matriarchal" features of monarchic Rome as it is portrayed by classical authors such as Livy—royal succession by a son-in-law and by a daughter's son—are also said, by Livy himself, to have first obtained among the Latins. At 1.1.9-11 Livy depicts Rome's Trojan forefather Aeneas as able to claim the throne of Latium only after wedding the daughter of its king, Latinus; Livy later represents Aeneas' descendant Romulus and his twin brother Remus as claiming their monarchic rights to found a new city because their mother was daughter of Numitor, rightful king of the Latin city Alba Longa.[23] Thus it would seem likely that if the social importance and political influence ascribed to Roman women of the classical period are survivals from the years of Sabine and especially Etruscan hegemony at Rome, then the Romans of those early eras must have found the general Sabine and Etruscan view of women as significant individuals compatible with their own. Furthermore, the fact that a practice based on widespread human familial sentiment (such as the respect for motherhood in monarchic Rome discerned by Bachofen and his adherents) "survives" from an earlier period should imply that the sentiment still obtains to some extent in the later period.

[23] Thomson, *Studies*, 97-99; for Aeneas and Lavinia, see also chapter three below, n. 61; for Numitor and his maternal grandsons, see Livy 1.3.10-11,5.5-6, Plutarch, *Romulus* 2-3, and Dionysius of Halicarnassus 1.76.3-84 (also cited in chapter three below, n. 53). That both types of succession, actually found among the Julio-Claudian emperors as well as ascribed to the early monarchy, should be regarded as "matrilineal" was earlier argued by M. Murray, "Royal Marriage and Matrilineal Descent," *Journal of the Royal Anthropological Institute of Great Britain and Ireland* 45 (1915) 317-325, and refuted by Rose, "Mother Right in Ancient Italy," 104-105, and "Patricians and Plebeians at Rome," *JRS* 12 (1922) 114. On Murray's argument, and Rose's refutation, see also Bush, *Studies in Roman Social Structure*, 83ff.

Concern for the origins of women's social significance and political influence in classical Roman times does not, therefore, in itself suffice: the reasons why women continued to be regarded as socially significant and politically influential after the monarchic, and through the classical, era deserve equal attention.

Although we have relatively little knowledge of earliest Sabine society outside our later Roman literary sources,[24] we do have a large body of independent evidence on the Etruscans in the late seventh and sixth centuries B.C. and in the several centuries thereafter. Many Etruscan works of art and inscriptions, largely from their grave goods and cemetery decorations, still exist and reveal much about the Etruscans' life style and values. This evidence, moreover, also calls the theory of Bachofen and his adherents seriously into question: it does not suggest that the Etruscans ever exalted older women by ceding to them positions of political leadership denied to men, or that the Etruscans ever reckoned descent solely through the female line.[25] In other words, the terms "matriarchy," signifying rule by mothers, and "matriliny," meaning the reckoning of ancestral descent through mothers, do not accurately represent the Etruscans' political organization or kinship

[24] A bibliography of works providing archaeological and linguistic evidence for the Sabine element in early Rome is given by Ogilvie, 65-66; see also Pallottino, "Origins of Rome," 214-215, and the bibliography furnished by Ridgway on 195 of the same volume.

[25] On this point, see F. Slotty, "Zur Frage des Matriarchates bei den Etruskern," *Archiv Orientální* 18 (1950) 262-285; for the misunderstanding and misrepresentation of Etruscan women by ancient Greek and Roman writers (which in turn encourage modern misrepresentations of Etruscan society), see L. Bonfante Warren, "Etruscan Women: A Question of Interpretation," *Archaeology* 26 (October 1973) 242-249, and "The Women of Etruria," *Arethusa* 6 (1973) 91-101.

structure in any period.[26] Indeed, the term "matriarchy" has no descriptive relevance to the political or the kinship structure of any society in which women do not monopolize (or significantly control) government, but have available to them opportunities for political involvement and influence also open (and in some societies only open) to males. The term "matriliny" is similarly uninformative about any society which values maternal lineage, and mothers themselves, but not to the degree that it discounts or devalues paternal lineage and fathers. Etruscan society seems to have provided women with opportunities for public involvement and to have assigned great value to maternal lineage.[27] The social importance the Etruscans accorded women and the Etruscan emphasis on maternal ancestry have even been, as we have noted, enough to earn them a reputation among certain scholars for belief in the principle of "mother right." But as this discussion has observed and will continue to

[26] For the misinterpretation of the former term, as well as its erroneous confusion with matriliny and matrilocality, in recent studies of ancient societies, see S. K. Dickison, "Forum," *Arethusa* 9 (1976) 119-120. Dickison would, for example, dispute Herrmann's general definition of matriarchy (10) as a community of women who ultimately place their children under the authority of their maternal uncles rather than their fathers (owing to doubts over their paternity). Since women do not necessarily possess political power under such a system, she would merely view it as matriliny. For Bachofen's own confusion between loving mothers and matriarchs, and for the inapplicability of the term "matriarchy" to any historical society, see J. Bamberger, "The Myth of Matriarchy: Why Men Rule in Primitive Society," *Woman, Culture, and Society*, 263-280. Bamberger's thesis that the existence of matriarchy myths in a given culture is significant evidence for the society's larger preoccupations does, of course, have some bearing on this study of women in the elite Roman family, although Rome's major myths about women center, as we will see, on women in their role as daughters.

[27] As is concluded by J. Heurgon, "Valeurs féminines et masculines dans la civilisation étrusque," *Mélanges d'archéologie et d'histoire de l'École Française de Rome* 73 (1961) 139-160.

demonstrate, elite Roman society of classical times displayed these very features as well.

Admittedly, the Etruscans differed considerably from the classical Romans in their mode of identifying women and in their definition of acceptable female behavior. Unlike their Roman counterparts, well-born Etruscan women were given individuating names and often commemorated by indications of both their fathers' and their mothers' names. Tomb paintings and objects document that affluent Etruscan women took part in dancing and athletic exercise and indulged themselves at lavish parties and with elaborate attire, behavior which contrasts with that of Roman women. Such artifacts imply, too, that Etruscan women of high birth, in contrast to aristocratic Roman matrons, were not celebrated for wool-spinning and domestic administration.[28] These differences between Etruscan and classical Roman women are not to be dismissed. They warrant investigation and explanation—through study of each larger society and its values and, more specifically, of how women were integrated into each entire culture and its institutions and beliefs.[29]

[28] On these details of Etruscan vs. Roman female existence, see again Slotty, "Zur Frage des Matriarchates," and Bonfante Warren, "Etruscan Women" and "Women of Etruria," as well as Bonfante, "Etruscan Couples," *Women's Studies* 8 (1981) 157-187.

[29] M. Arthur, "Review Essay," "Classics," *Signs* 2 (1976) 384, notes that "the correlation between the forms of the family, of economics, of authority and of ideological systems" is insisted upon by the Centre d'Études et de Recherches Marxistes in Paris. Bonfante, "Etruscan Couples," 168-169, and V. Hunter, "Review of M. Lefkowitz and M. Fant, *Women in Greece and Rome*," *Helios* 7.1 (1979-80) 82-95, also stress the need to understand the institutions and values of a society itself and how women were integrated into both; Hunter in particular regards material from other, comparable and better known, societies as vital in helping scholars systematize random evidence about the workings of ancient cultures. This study does not, needless to say, attempt any such large-scale analysis of the Romans, or even the Roman upper classes; its reliance on com-

But these differences should not be exaggerated, particularly by those who would explain the formidable behavior and image of elite Roman women in the classical era as a survival of early "mother right" connected with the Etruscans.[30] By the same token, superficial similarities between later Roman and earlier Etruscan beliefs and practices relating to women do not automatically establish the former as "Etruscan legacies," nor should they be used to account for other features of republican and imperial Roman civilization; rather, they must be understood in the context of their own culture and its entire social structure.

The argument that behavioral patterns associated with early Roman "mother right" survived into the classical era is most thoroughly demolished, however, by actual examination of Roman society during its earliest years, including those in which Sabine and Etruscan culture would have exerted their greatest influence; such an examination reveals the thoroughly and overwhelmingly patriarchal nature of Roman society of that time. The patriarchal nature of earliest Roman society, moreover, seems to have had its roots in the organization of the Roman family. Testimony about the earliest Romans

parative materials is kept to a minimum (and restricted to other ancient cultures kindred with and familiar to the Romans themselves). This study does, however, seek to establish the similarities between Roman upper-class family structure and family-related economic institutions, patterns of political behavior, language, and legends—especially those related, by such authors as Livy, Plutarch, and their sources, with a moralistic, "ideological," purpose—in their emphasis on certain female roles, and to argue for the cultural centrality of one, primal, female familial role to explain these similarities.

[30] And cf. the well-taken observation of Bonfante, "Etruscan Couples," 168-169, which implicitly likens women's prominent public position in the aristocratic society of southern Etruscan cities to women's position in Rome by the mid-republican era, when the latter was "at its most aristocratic."

consists of sundry data: laws attributed by the Romans themselves to the monarchic era and a legal code securely datable to the mid-fifth century B.C.; later legends about Rome's monarchic and early republican past; cultic and linguistic survivals from pre-republican and early republican times which corroborate the implications of monarchic law and legendary lore. Yet from this body of evidence one can have little doubt that *patres*, fathers, and hence older males generally, functioned as figures of supreme authority from the first moments of Rome's existence, and that these *patres* became even more powerful in both the Roman family and state after an aristocratic form of representative government, the republic, replaced the monarchy.

The *Leges Regiae*, royal laws attributed to Rome's period of monarchic rule by various classical Roman sources, were supposedly codified during the reign of Rome's last, Etruscan, king. While many scholars feel that these laws, or at least the form in which ancient authors have recorded them, date from a somewhat later period, the *Leges Regiae* do, as we shall see, represent Roman monarchic society in much the same way as do other significantly more reliable sources.[31] They, moreover, give fathers tremendous powers over the lives of

---

[31] For these *Leges Regiae*, see S. Riccobono, ed., *Fontes Iuris Romani Antejustiniani*[2] (Florence, 1941) 3-18. So pronounced is their patriarchal nature that Herrmann, an evolutionist and believer in monarchic-era matriarchy, feels obliged to assign them a post-monarchic date (10-11). Post-monarchic dating for the collection on more credible grounds is also implied by E. Gabba, *Origines*, 161-163, 170, and suggested by A. Momigliano, 170, although one contributor to the same volume, F. Wieacker, 327-328, sidesteps the issue of dating by ascribing the *Leges Regiae* to sacral authority (such as the *rex sacrorum*) and another, K. Hanell, 360, apparently accepts monarchic dating. On the scholarly controversy over the dating and authenticity of the *Leges Regiae*, see the article "*Ius Papirianum*" by Steinwenter in *RE* 10 (1919) 1285.

their children and use the father-son relationship as a model for the sociopolitical bond to obtain between the male heads of the privileged, propertied kin groups, also called *patres*, and their dependent *clientes*. For these royal laws require that a father raise only his first-born female offspring, and, while stipulating that he must rear all his male children, grant him almost total control over his sons for as long as he lives. These laws bestow upon *patres* full legal responsibility for their *clientes*, and demand that the *clientes* compensate their protectors by providing them with whatever financial support they request. By way of contrast, these laws state that an adult woman may not institute divorce proceedings against her husband and, in circumstances where her acceptability as a wife lies in question, must submit to the judgment of her husband and male blood kinfolk: while a wife divorced for any reason other than injuring her husband's property or lineage could, under this legislation, claim half of his estate, the children are defined as the husband's and not her own.[32]

The Twelve Tables, traditionally codified in 451-450 B.C., only half a century after the alleged departure of Rome's last Etruscan king, also accord a father extensive powers. One of these powers, the right to sell a son thrice into bondage, is originally attributed to the *Leges Regiae* by one source; that the Twelve Tables' general emphasis on father-right is consistent with that of the

---

[32] For the law requiring a *paterfamilias* to rear all of his sons but only the first-born daughter (quoted by Dionysius of Halicarnassus 2.15.2 and 27), see also the discussion of Herrmann, 14, and Pomeroy, *GWWS*, 164-165. The law detailing a client's obligations to his patron is noted by Dionysius of Halicarnassus at 2.10. For discussions of regulations on women—ascribed by our sources for them, Dionysius of Halicarnassus 2.25 and Plutarch, *Romulus* 22.3-4, to Rome's first king Romulus—see Herrmann, 12-14, and Pomeroy, "Relationship of the Married Woman," 67-69.

Leges Regiae renders it plausible that the royal laws contain provisions from an early, and perhaps an earlier, period.[33] Other paternal powers assigned by the Twelve Tables—to kill, quickly, a deformed child; to have claimed automatically as offspring any child born to one's wife up until ten months after one's death—additionally warrant notice in this context.[34] What is more, the Twelve Tables would seem to have strengthened the position of the father, and elder males generally, by reportedly instituting the principle of agnate guardianship and succession. According to this principle, kindred related to an individual through males were assigned responsibility for administering that individual's property should said individual die or be incapable, and were awarded priority—after that individual's offspring and siblings—in inheriting it. By way of contrast, the Twelve Tables affirm that all females, save for Vestal Virgins, must remain in the guardianship of a male father figure as long as they live.[35]

[33] On the dating of the Twelve Tables, see Ogilvie, 452ff., and Wieacker, *Origines*, 293-356. It is, again, Dionysius of Halicarnassus who, at 2.27, credits Romulus with the law entitling a father to sell his son thrice into slavery, and who states that the Romans' high regard for this law led it to be recorded on the fourth of the Twelve Tables; the law is also ascribed to the Twelve Tables by Ulpian, *Tituli* 10.1. The consistency between provisions of the *Leges Regiae* and Twelve Tables may, however, merely point to an effort by classical Romans, who knew the Twelve Tables by heart, to invent royal laws of a similar nature: cultic and linguistic survivals from pre-republican times, therefore, are more reliable confirmation that the royal laws represent the reality of the monarchic era.

[34] For these laws, see Cicero, *De Legibus* 3.8.19, Aulus Gellius 3.6.12, and Ulpian, *Digest* 38.16, 3, 9, 11.

[35] For the implication that the Twelve Tables *instituted* agnate succession, argued on the basis of Ulpian, *Fr.* 11.3 and 27 (or 26?).5, see E. H. Warmington, *Remains of Old Latin III: Lucilius, Laws of the Twelve Tables* (Cambridge, Mass., 1967) 448-449; this view is also accepted by Watson, *Rome of the Twelve Tables* (Princeton, 1975) 68. For guardianship of females in the Twelve Tables, see also Gaius,

Legends concerning Rome's foundation, its subsequent adjustment to Etruscan domination, and the eventual establishment of a more representative form of government also depict the role of father as prominent and "father-right" as persistent throughout early Roman society. Rome's supposed parent city, Alba Longa, is said to have been ruled by a dynasty of males, first among them Ascanius, son of *pater* Aeneas. Nascent Rome herself is said to have been ruled solely by a series of mature male monarchs and never (unlike some other ancient Mediterranean powers) by a queen.[36] The murder of one father,. Servius Tullius, and the bereavement of another, Spurius Lucretius Tricipitinus, are remarked upon for contributing to the agitation for the Etruscans' overthrow. For Lucius Junius Brutus, celebrated for rousing the Romans to liberate themselves from Etruscan tyranny and to found a republican government, is said by Livy to have inspired such action in a moving speech: it recalled how the wife of the current Tarquin ruler,

---

Institutes 1.144-145 and the discussions of Herrmann, 31-32, and Pomeroy, *GWWS*, 150-155.

[36] For a defense of these legends and their dramatis personae as representing "at least a core of historical truth" according to most scholars, see Pallottino, "Origins of Rome," 216ff. For the Alban king list itself, see Ogilvie, 34, 43-45. On 17-18 Herrmann interprets Livy's statement at 1.3.1. that after Aeneas' death the kingdom was placed in the guardianship of his widow Lavinia until her stepson (or, according to another tradition, son) Ascanius came of age as "une reminiscence" of a matriarchal order. Our findings, however, would encourage one to impart less significance to the fact that this unique responsibility was supposedly accorded a woman in a maternal relationship to the heir apparent (as the precise nature of their relationship is uncertain) than to the fact that it was assigned to the only daughter of the region's former king. In any event, Lavinia is not regarded by Livy as a true ruler of her people—whereas such a figure as Artemisia of Halicarnassus is so regarded by Herodotus at 7.99ff. That Rome was never reportedly ruled by a woman is also remarked upon by Balsdon, 13.

Servius Tullius' daughter, had driven her carriage over her father's corpse; it also brought to mind the grief of another father—Lucretius, whose daughter had taken her own life after being raped by the king's son.[37] Even Brutus himself was remembered by later generations specifically as a harsh father, for inflicting capital punishment on his sons when they conspired to overthrow the republic he had helped institute and to reinstate the Tarquins he had helped oust.[38]

As the sources for these legends postdate the monarchic and early republican eras by several centuries, these tales—like the *Leges Regiae*—cannot enjoin immediate credence as accurate portrayals of monarchic and early republican practice and sentiment. But religious and linguistic survivals from this, archaic, period of Rome's past impart the same impression. The Vestal Virgins are thought by many scholars to have originated as the daughters of Rome's priest-king, *rex*.[39] An array of evidence points to the existence and cultural importance of this priest-king (and arguably symbolic father-

---

[37] Livy 1.59.8-13. The account of this speech by Dionysius of Halicarnassus at 4.77-83 does not refer to Tullia's role in the death of Servius Tullius (although Dionysius himself makes much of it at 4.39); it does, however, stress Lucretius' suffering at his daughter's treatment and suicide.

[38] Cf., for example, Polybius 6.54; Vergil, *Aeneid* 6.817-823; Livy 2.5.8.; Valerius Maximus 5.8.1. For the differences between Livy's and others' accounts see Ogilvie, 242-243.

[39] The classical articles expounding this view are H. J. Rose, *"De Virginibus Vestalibus,"* Mnemosyne 2nd ser. 54 (1926) 440-448, and *"Iterum de Virginibus Vestalibus,"* Mnemosyne 2nd ser. 56 (1928) 79-80; see, too, the article in *RE*²8 (1958) 1732-1753 by Reidinger, H. Hommel, "Vesta und die frührömische Religion," *Aufstieg und Niedergang der Römischen Welt* I.2 (1972) 397-420, and M. Beard, "The Sexual Status of Vestal Virgins," *JRS* 70 (1980) 12-27. On the later, paternal, role occupied by the *pontifex maximus* in relation to the Vestals, see also Herrmann, 32 and 43. The Vestals will be discussed further in chapter three below.

figure) in pre-republican times: the appearance of the words, *sacer*, "holy," and *rex*, "king," on the *Lapis Niger*, the oldest Roman stone inscription as yet discovered; the remains of the *Regia*, supposed dwelling of Rome's king and later the quarters of the *pontifex maximus*, her chief priest; the title *rex sacrorum*, king of sacred duties, which was held in the classical period by Rome's second highest priest.[40] The application in archaic formulae of the term *pater* to Rome's most venerable and ancient gods, such as Janus, Mars and Jupiter (the last of these ultimately incorporating this title into the nominative form of his name)—deserves notice as well.[41] The title *mater* is employed to nowhere near as great an extent in addresses to the major Roman goddesses, suggesting that the idea of fatherhood was invested with more religious awe by the early Romans than was motherhood and that these masculine deities were revered more than those conceived of as feminine.[42]

[40] On the *Lapis Niger*, see, for example, A. Ernout, *Recueil de textes latins archaïques*[2] (Paris, 1973) 4-7. On the *Regia*, see F. E. Brown, *Origines*, 47-60, and E. Nash's article on Rome in *The Princeton Encyclopedia of Classical Sites*, ed. R. Stillwell, W. L. MacDonald, and M. H. McAllister (Princeton, 1976) 764, both of which date the building to the late sixth century B.C. Brown has since expressed different views on the chronology of the *Regia* in "La protostoria della Regia," *Rendiconti della Pontificia Accademia di Archeologia* 47 (1974-75) 15, as a result of new findings dating back to the late seventh century B.C.; an earlier date of construction, however, may merely strengthen the argument for the pre-republican importance of the *rex*. On the *rex sacrorum* himself, see Ogilvie, 237-238.

[41] On *pater* as epithet of Rome's major male gods, see L. A. Holland, *Janus and the Bridge* (Rome, 1961) 109, and the fragment from Lucilius (19-22 Marx) which she cites: it alludes to Neptune, Liber, Saturnus, Mars, and Janus Quirinus (or Janus and Quirites) as *patres*. On the Indo-European heritage of this phenomenon see Ernout-Meillet, 487-488; on the derivation of Juppiter from *dies* and *pater*, see Ernout-Meillet, 329.

[42] Although, as Ernout-Meillet remark on 389, *mater* is used in addresses to Terra, the earth, and Vesta, spirit of the hearth (in the

Additional substantiation for the early Romans' high valuation of fatherhood and for their cultural elaboration of the familial paternal role into a social model and metaphor for supreme authority and advantage is afforded by the complex of Latin words which derive from *pater*, words either of archaic vintage themselves or associated with archaic institutions. Several such words describe people who wield political control and influence: *patronus*, a term found in the Twelve Tables, denotes the male protector of a *cliens*, a "leaning" and hence a weaker man; *patres*, the council of elders (or *senatus*, group of older men) who constituted Rome's governing assembly, and who originally represented, as individual heads of household (*patres familiae*), her wealthiest kin groups; *patricii*, those having the rank and dignity of the *patres*, and hence the Roman aristocracy.[43] Yet others designate impressive possessions: *patrimonium*, the legal status of fatherhood, comes to mean that which a father would legally bequeath his children, and hence becomes the term for property inherited from a father; *patria potestas*, a father's power of life and death over his offspring. The Romans resembled the Greeks in calling the homeland to which they were deeply committed their *patria*, father country. The Romans even had a denominative verb *patrare*, literally meaning "to act like a father." Its antiquity may be inferred from its appearance in the title *pater patratus*, applied to a priestly official who conducted international relations, and whose ritual conduct bears

case of the latter indicating that the idea of maternity itself was not necessarily implied by this appellation); the Roman respect for motherhood revealed by such a usage tallies with other evidence to be discussed in chapter five below.

[43] On these terms, see Ernout-Meillet, 487; for *patronus* in the Twelve Tables, see Servius, *ad Aeneidem* 6.609; of the distinction between *patres* and *patricii*, see R.E.A. Palmer, *The Archaic Community of the Romans* (Cambridge, 1970) 273.

a distinctly archaic stamp; the power granted Roman fathers of earliest times seems clear from the fact that *patrare* comes to signify "bring to completion" and "achieve one's wishes" (and satirically, "reach orgasm"). No analogy for such linguistic formations, which associate the word *pater* with power, ownership, and achievement, may be adduced among the Latin words built from *mater*, mother.[44]

One cannot, therefore, accurately and adequately explain upper-class Roman women's actual and perceived public influence, or their social significance, in the classical era as vestiges of pre-republican matriarchy. One must, instead, account for the paradoxical presence of this influence and significance in a staunchly and traditionally patriarchal system. Concomitantly, surveying the testimony for the traditionally patriarchal nature of this system points up the need for fuller study of the patriarchal upper-class family during the mid- and late republican, and early imperial, periods. For this and other evidence reminds us that the elite Roman family did not merely possess political influence and social significance. It also ranked as a major and stable social, economic, and political institution. Its political function was most important in republican times, when the elite family's socialization of its male members endeavored to prepare them for governing and serving the state, when its alliances with other houses through marriage facilitated its public achievements, and when these achievements were themselves regarded as measure-

[44] On *patrimonium* and *patria potestas*, see Ernout-Meillet, 487; for the latter, see also Crook, "*Patria Potestas*," *CQ* n.s. 17 (1967) 113-122. On *patrare*, see Ernout-Meillet, 488-489; for the *pater patratus*, see Ogilvie, 111, and Palmer, *The Archaic Community*, 186. For similar words from *mater* (e.g. *matrona*, *matrimonium*) and their failure to connote the possession of power or property, see chapter five below.

ments of its own worth; nevertheless, these republican family traditions were quickly adapted to the conditions of imperial rule and bureaucracy.[45] Due to the patriarchal nature of Roman society, and to the elite family's role as a major, if not the main, political unit therein, the structural centrality of female members in the upper-class Roman family would seem inextricably related to women's ascribed political significance: the elite family, its patriarchal nature notwithstanding, was able to furnish its womenfolk with what modern political scientists label a "power base." What is more, the elite family's own central role in Roman political life resulted in the lack of a clear differentiation between what anthropologists would define (and the classical Romans themselves apparently did define) as domestic and public spheres in ancient Roman society; this blurring of these two spheres would tend to create a state of social affairs thought by various scholars to accord women more power and esteem than a distinct separation.[46]

[45] For the Roman upper-class family as a republican political institution, see, for example, D. C. Earl, *The Moral and Political Tradition of Rome* (Ithaca, N.Y., 1970) 26ff.; E. S. Gruen, *The Last Generation of the Roman Republic* (Berkeley, Los Angeles, and London, 1974) 47-82; and Syme, *The Roman Revolution*, 10-27, 490ff.; for the adaptation of this family tradition to the conditions of imperial rule and bureaucracy, see Syme, *Tacitus*, II.570-584.

[46] For the theory that societies firmly differentiating between public and domestic spheres, isolating women from one another and placing them under a single man's control (the situation in classical Athens), accord women far less power and value than those which blur this distinction and encourage female bonding (the situation, as we shall see repeatedly, prevailing in upper-class Rome as well as in other ancient Indo-European societies to be surveyed in chapter six), see M. Z. Rosaldo, "Woman, Culture, and Society: A Theoretical Overview," in *Woman, Culture, and Society*, 36ff. For a criticism of this theory as based on a false, oversimplifying, ethnocentrically biased dichotomy, see R. Rapp, "Review Essay, Anthropology," *Signs* 4 (1979) 508ff.; for a re-evaluation and defense of the theory, stressing that different social systems express the domestic/public

Yet rejection of pre-republican matriarchy in favor of patriarchy as the primordial and persevering Roman familial and social scheme does not necessitate abandoning altogether the notion of "archaic survivals," institutional or sentimental, as a means of accounting for Roman practices and attitudes of the classical period. A special and much remarked upon trait of the classical Romans was their adherence to tradition. "On the customs and men of old the Roman state is founded," proclaimed the poet Ennius in the second century B.C., to be quoted a century later by Cicero and still evoked more than one hundred and fifty years after that by Tacitus; the Romans constantly looked to the *mos maiorum*, ancestral custom, to justify and indeed sanctify their actions and feelings.[47] As this discussion will illustrate, the Roman upper-class family seems to have been particularly tradition-minded, at least in its assumptions about its members' various obligations and ties to one another. An investigation into these and other traditional aspects of elite Roman kinship—the idealized images and actual behavior associ-

---

dichotomy differently, see Rosaldo, "The Use and Abuse of Anthropology: Reflections on Feminism and Cross-cultural Understanding," *Signs* 5 (1980) 389-417. That the classical Romans themselves perceived a dichotomy between female/domestic and male/public realms of special interest, a perception much acknowledged by literary and epigraphic texts, is illustrated by the quotations from Cicero and Tacitus that appeared earlier in this chapter. It is also illustrated by such prescriptive remarks as Plautus, *Menaechmi* 796-797, discussed in chapter two below, and by such statements as Cicero's apparently critical description of his own wife, Terentia, as "more inclined to share in his political concerns than to allow him a share in her domestic ones" (Plutarch, *Cicero* 20.2). The public, and often political, influence of many elite Roman women and the domestically based power of their menfolk are thus all the more noteworthy and hence amendable to elucidation by this theory.

[47] Ennius 500 Vahlen, quoted by Cicero, *De Re Publica* 5.1; for Tacitus on Roman tradition-mindedness, see *Annales* 3.55, and 11.23-24. See also the discussion of Earl, *Moral and Political Tradition*, 28ff.

ated with female and male roles within the upper-class
family as well as the relationships of these roles to one
another—is particularly warranted, in part because it has
not been previously undertaken, in part because it can
place these female roles into both their familial and larger
social context.

The main purpose of this study is to examine women's
roles within the upper-class Roman family of the classical period; by so doing, we will attempt to account
for women's paradoxical public influence and esteem in
a society where patriarchal traditions and the traditionally patriarchal family possessed immense cultural importance. Our first task will be to establish that women's
political influence and social significance are not merely
linked with, but virtually inseparable from, their structural centrality in the Roman upper-class family. Consequently, the next chapter will survey varied ancient
testimony—much of which also figures prominently in
other studies of Roman women—with this aim in mind.
We will maintain that political and social significance
were accorded women not merely in connection with
their membership in politically influential and significant
Roman families but also in connection with their occupancy of certain familial roles. Evidence adduced in
this chapter will suggest that, although upper-class women
exerted the greatest social and political impact, and elic-
ited the most esteem from men, in *maternal* roles (a
phenomenon which does much to explain the genesis
of the aforementioned "matriarchal survival" theory),
they also commanded respect from, and because of, ties
with the male blood kin who were their approximate
contemporaries, and were assigned value from infancy
as daughters of their fathers.

Subsequent chapters will examine the sentimental and
behavioral dimensions of what appear to be the three

major female roles in the upper-class Roman family during the classical period: first, that of father's daughter (the first familial role a Roman woman technically ocupied), then that of mature sister, and finally that of mother. In other words, these chapters will consider, from different kinds of ancient testimony, several closely connected matters: how the classical Roman elite generally defined and assigned affective value to each role (both individually and relative to other familial roles); in what ways the Roman elite expressed their assessment of each role in their social institutions and literary traditions; what sort of conduct was viewed as normative to, and actually exhibited in, each role. From evidence adduced in these chapters, moreover, this discussion will seek to provide an explanation for the paradox of Roman women by positing elite women's increasing influence over, and esteem by, their male kinfolk as they matured and assumed different familial roles; the evidence for such an assumption would suggest that the initial valuation of Roman women as their fathers' supposedly deferential daughters underlies the respect they later command as self-assertive sisters to their fathers' sons, and the reverence they ultimately receive as demanding mothers and maternal figures.

These chapters will establish that substantial significance and sentiment were lavished upon Roman women in their role as their fathers' daughters, to the extent that Roman society elaborated the daughter role, just as it did the paternal role, into a social metaphor for culturally valued female behavior (although behavior antithetical to that thought fitting for a father). Significantly, the first of these chapters will also show that the daughter role was not of particular cultural interest to, and that daughters were not particularly cherished by, the Etruscans and classical Athenians, Rome's most culturally prestigious and imitated neighbors. It is thus not surprising that both Etruscans and Athenians allotted upper-class women images and familial existences quite different from those of their Roman counterparts. More speculatively, these later chapters will argue that various aspects of Roman kinship—the valuation of women as dependent daughters and the cultural elaboration of the daughter role, the ensuing respect given sisters and the importance placed upon their role, the reverence bestowed upon mother figures and the esteem for the maternal role—in classical times may well survive from Rome's monarchic era. While it is impossible to prove the precise age of such general Roman sentiments and practices, there is some reason to believe, as the classical Romans themselves did, that they are long-lived traditions completely compatible with primitive monarchic, aristocratically based, patriarchy as well as with later and different kinds of Roman, aristocratically based, patriarchal government.

As part of its investigation into these three female familial roles—and the male-female and female-female bonds whose particular strengths would seem closely associated with the emphasis these roles received in elite Roman culture—this study will also explore major male familial roles. It will additionally investigate the bonds between males which help explain, or are explained by, the cultural prominence assigned the roles and the major family ties of the Roman daughter, sister, and mother. A concluding chapter will reflect upon the important kinship patterns which emerge from such a study of Roman upper-class familial roles and bonds. After comparing these patterns of kinship to similar ones in other, related, ancient societies with which the classical Romans were acquainted we will try to account for these patterns of kinship by considering the general cultural factors which may have contributed to their articulation. We will, however, contend that the intense affect with which the elite Romans seem to have invested the father-daughter bond lacks parallels in these kindred cultures; we will maintain that this affect can best be attributed to circumstances peculiar to the Roman *pater*, and to the brand of patriarchal culture peculiar to the ancient Romans.

II

WOMEN OF ELITE FAMILIES
AND ROMAN SOCIETY

WHEN investigating the political involvement and social
significance of women in ancient Rome during the republican and early imperial eras, one can easily accord
insufficient importance to a basic fact:[1] women did not
generally become politically involved, or even bulk large,
in Roman society unless they belonged from birth to
upper-class Roman families, families whose male members held positions of public authority and prestige, and
families which often possessed sizable fortunes as well.
To be sure, ancient sources at times also downplay this
fact, de-emphasizing a woman's family connections while
stressing her sex, and the technical incongruity of its
entry into the male realm of political affairs. Sallust's
account of the Catilinarian conspiracy, for example, notes
that Catiline's followers included a number of sexually
profligate women driven to desperation by huge debts.
He then describes one of their number, Sempronia, as

[1] One might be led to minimize this fact by such scholars as Pomeroy, who, at *GWWS* 185-189, uses as her paradigms of "Women
in Politics" only the non-Roman Cleopatra and Antony's wives,
Fulvia and Octavia. She does not even mention in this section Antony's mother Julia (on whom see chapters four and five below),
despite an earlier reference to her on 175, in a discussion of the appeals
to Julia, Fulvia, and Octavia by wealthy women whom the triumvirs
had taxed in 42 B.C. Pomeroy also makes no effort to generalize
about the family backgrounds or familial roles of politically active
and publicly valued Roman women.

having committed crimes of "masculine daring"; only thereafter, and vaguely, does he refer to her pedigreed family background.[2]

Membership in a politically prominent and prosperous house did not, moreover, ensure a Roman woman's political or social importance: our ancient sources say nothing about the female kin of many powerful Roman men. So, too, women of the lower orders in classical Rome did at times gain and wield public influence, and did so in an extra-familial capacity: through first attracting a powerful man sexually and then advising him on important matters or controlling access to him by other men. One finds such instances of female sexual allure turned to political profit in Plutarch's picture of Praecia, mistress of Cethegus, and in Cicero's characterization of Chelidon, mistress of Verres.[3] But powerful Roman males appear to have furnished women of their own social station with a much greater potential for political influence and social eminence, substantial influence and eminence which had relatively little to do with their sexual appeal. What is more, elite Roman women's potential for influence and eminence seems not only to have stemmed from their kindred bonds with powerful, wellborn Roman men, but to have been rooted deeply and specifically in their occupancy of certain roles within the Roman family.

This consideration of the political impact and social significance ascribed to elite Roman women in various familial roles will survey an assortment of evidence from the Roman republic and early empire, and from Roman fantasy as well as reality. Admittedly, portrayals of well-

[2] Sallust, *Bellum Catilinae* 24.3-25.5 (also discussed in chapter one above).

[3] For Praecia, see Plutarch, *Lucullus* 6.2-4; for Chelidon, see Cicero, *In Verrem* 2.1.104, 106, 120, 136ff.; 2.25; 3.78; 5.34, 38.

born women in relatively fanciful literary settings—the exaggerated and Hellenized situational comedy of Plautus, the idealizing and moralistic narratives about Rome's remote past by such authors as Livy and Plutarch—often derive from other, imaginative, literary models. Thus they may not seem as trustworthy testimony to the actual workings of the politically influential Roman elite family as do closely contemporary, factual documents on and accounts of interactions within elite Roman families of the classical era. Nevertheless, the general picture which these imaginative works provide of women's conduct and larger social impact in different familial roles is virtually identical to that which emerges from more realistic reportage. Both kinds of evidence, therefore, qualify equally well as illustrations of the connection between a well-born Roman woman's specific kinship role in her own family and the larger social political significance which she—and what she did or desired—could claim in the eyes of Roman, and ostensibly male-controlled, society. A survey of this evidence will also furnish a valuable background to our later examination of the different female roles within the Roman upper-class family, of the images traditionally assigned to and the behavior generally displayed in these roles, and of the relation between these familial roles and those occupied by Roman men.

It stands to reason that a society which is ruled by its male senior citizens through the control of younger and less powerful men would instill reverence for the wisdom of advancing age in its male youth. The Romans, we might observe, referred to previous generations as *maiores*, greater individuals, and employed the adjective *magnus*, great, in the kinship terms for parents' close male and female ascendants (a practice the English language has adopted with its use of the adjective "great" for kin of earlier generations); such a practice testifies to the Roman equation of seniority with superiority, and to the inclusion of women among its superior seniors.[4] Thus it should come as no surprise that older women seem to command more respect, inspire more awe, and have (or be perceived as having) greater social and political influence than do younger ones. In addition, Roman women along in years were more likely to have young male relatives who were eager to prove themselves worthy of and to their elders, and who were mindful of the nurturance they had recently received from mothers and older kinswomen; such young men were under special pressure to manifest their respect and awe for their female *maiores* through publicly visible gestures.

We have already examined the idealization in Tacitus' *Dialogus* of the moral instruction and intellectual sustenance provided for an eternally indebted Roman male youth committed to a life of public service by his upstanding female relatives; this picture is far from unique in Roman writings. Such a vision of an older Roman matron's function, and of Roman mother-son relations, seems the parodic point of Plautus' *Casina*. The play, composed immediately before the playwright's death in 184 B.C., was popular enough to be revived in the next generation. In it, the *materfamilias* Cleostrata intimidates her elderly and socially powerful husband both through proving herself his moral superior and, as her son's ally and abettor, by ingeniously securing for this son the sexual favors of a slave girl his father also covets. By cleverly rendering her presumably grateful son such services, attracting admiration for her capable handling

---

[4] For *maiores* as "ancestors" and *magnus* in Latin kinship terms, see the *OLD*, fasc. V (1976) 1065.

of this complex affair, but nonetheless setting herself up as a moral example in the process, she evidently travesties the Roman concept of a wise, righteous, and exemplary mother.[5]

This same vision, however, is reproduced as part of a serious moral and political *exemplum* in Livy's narrative on the Bacchanalian scandal, an episode which profoundly shook Roman society shortly before the *Casina* was first performed.[6] Livy's young male protagonist Aebutius and his reluctantly influential courtesan mis-

---

[5] For the dates of the *Casina* and its revival, see W. T. MacCary and M. M. Willcock, *Plautus' Casina* (Cambridge, 1976) 11, 98-99; the introduction, 19-20, discusses the comic purpose of Cleostrata's (and other Plautine matrons') characterization, and its relation to the activities of Roman matrons when the play was first produced. The admiration accorded Cleostrata is most clearly evinced at lines 1004-1006, when she represents Plautus himself in saying that she will forgive her husband so as not to lengthen the play. Throughout this study, Plautine comedy will be adduced, often as our earliest surviving evidence from the classical period, to document elite Roman attitudes and assumptions about conduct in various familial roles. Although members of all social classes attended comic performances, and all of Plautus' plays are set in the Greek world, members of the Roman elite presided over public dramatic presentations: a popular and successful playwright such as Plautus must, therefore, have composed his representations of family life with their views and experiences especially in mind. For Plautine comedy as sarcastic reflection upon and humorous reversal of Roman notions and customs generally, see D. C. Earl, *The Moral and Political Tradition of Rome* (Ithaca, N.Y., 1970) 25-26, and "Political Terminology in Plautus," *Historia* 9 (1960) 235ff., as well as E. Segal, *Roman Laughter* (Cambridge, Mass., 1968), *passim*. For Plautus' comic reflection—in the *Poenulus*—on contemporary matters specifically concerning (elite) Roman women, see P. A. Johnston, "*Poenulus* 1, 2, and Roman Women," *TAPA* 110 (1980) 143-159.

[6] Livy 39.9ff. Livy's account is translated and subsequently discussed by Balsdon, 37-43; the Bacchanalian scandal is also treated in a separate chapter by Herrmann, 68-79. On the role of women in the Bacchanalian scandal, see J. A. North, "Religious Toleration in Republican Rome," *Proceedings of the Cambridge Philological Society* 25 (1979) 85-103.

tress Hispala Fecinia manage to bring the matter to the
consul Postumius' attention, and Postumius proceeds to
bring the malefactors to justice, solely through the aid
of Aebutia, *amita* (father's sister), to Aebutius, and Postumius' venerable mother-in-law Sulpicia. These two
older women—depicted as virtuous, beneficent, sagacious, deserving of male reverence and hence, by Livy's
implication, truly "maternal"—are contrasted with two,
far less admirable, matronly counterparts: Aebutius' own
mother Duronia, whose devotion to both her second
husband and his interest in depriving Aebutius of his
patrimony led her to seek her son's undoing by having
him initiated into Bacchic worship; the Campanian
priestess Paculla Annia, who began the Bacchic cult's
corrupting influence by initiating its first men, her own
sons. Livy's account, at 39.11ff., of Postumius' efforts
to ascertain, through Sulpicia, the character of Aebutia,
warrants special notice since here he treats these two
nurturant and publicly influential mother figures in a
sympathetic and sentimentalizing fashion: he refers to
the former woman as dignified, a *gravis* (and later a
gravissima) *femina*, to the latter as morally upright and
of old-fashioned ways, *probam et antiqui moris*;[7] he even
describes Aebutia as moved to tears by the dreadful
treatment of her brother's son (*filius eius fratris*), also
morally upright (*probus*), by those who should have been
the last to do so.

Another, doubtlessly romanticized, moralizing tale
also attests to both the esteem in which a young Roman

---

[7] Perhaps not uncoincidentally, Tacitus uses the same phrase, *antiqui moris*, which Livy applies to Aebutia, when he is praising the
mother of Vitellius at *Historiae* 2.64.2 for her public support of her
son; should Tacitus have wished to evoke this Livian model here,
he would then provide further evidence for Aebutia's characterization
as a maternal figure.

male was to hold his elder kinswomen's judgment and moral authority and to the public display and political impact of such esteem, namely the story of Gnaeus Marcius Coriolanus. Set in the mid-fifth century B.C., the story achieved great popularity in the classical period: a lost book by Cicero's closest friend Titus Pomponius Atticus featured Coriolanus prominently; Livy, Valerius Maximus, and Plutarch all treat his tragedy. Coriolanus has recently been called the "Roman archetype" of the "perpetual mama's boy" in a provocative psychoanalytic study of the Roman mother-son relationship, and for good reason: he allegedly valued his widowed mother so highly that he abandoned a traitorous march on Rome at the head of an enemy force only after she demanded that he desist.[8]

There are less dramatic, and probably somewhat more reliable, pieces of ancient Roman testimony to the reverential regard of young Roman men for the older, maternal female members of their families, to their—and others'—experience of these women as significant and influential individuals, and to the frequent exhibition of both this regard and this experience in a larger sociopolitical context. Several *laudationes funebres*, orations delivered by aristocratic Roman men (and usually youthful ones) to honor a deceased relative of political distinction, belong in this category. Cicero reports that the first such speech in commemoration of a woman was given in 102 B.C. by the consul Quintus Lutatius Catulus to honor his mother Popilia; no young woman received this same recognition until over thirty years later, when Julius

---

[8] For Atticus' book, see Cicero, *Brutus* 42. For the story of Coriolanus and his mother, see Livy 2.40; Valerius Maximus 5.2.1 and 4.1; Plutarch, *Coriolanus* 1.2, 4.3-4, 34-36; and Appian, *Roman History* 2.5. For the archetypal function of the legend and its psychoanalytical implications, see Africa, 602ff.

Caesar's second wife, Cornelia, was buried amid her husband's public praises.[9] That same year, however, Caesar made a more memorable, or at least better remembered, contribution to funeral oratory with his laudation of his father's sister Julia, wife of the military and political leader Marius. Caesar's words first proclaimed the glory of this aunt's, and hence his own father's, maternal ancestry:

The maternal lineage of my paternal aunt Julia descended from kings, the paternal is connected with the immortal gods. For the Marcii Reges go back to Ancus Marcius, Marcia being the name of her mother, and the Julii, to which clan our family belongs, are offspring of Venus. There is, therefore, in her lineage both the holiness of kings, who have the greatest power among humans, and the religious quality of gods, in whose power are the kings themselves.

Perhaps not insignificantly, Ancus Marcius, the early king from whom Julia's maternal Marcii traced their lineage, supposedly inherited Rome's throne through his maternal grandfather; so, too, the divinity from whom her (and her nephew's) paternal Julii avowed their descent was Venus, mother of the Trojan hero Aeneas.[10]

A later, and also elderly, Julia, Caesar's sister, was hailed in the funeral *laudatio* upon her death in 51 B.C. by the twelve-year-old Octavius, whose mother Atia was Julia's daughter; through this maternal grandmother Octavius, later the emperor Augustus, could claim de-

[9] For the *laudatio* on Popilia, Catulus' mother, see Cicero, *De Oratore* 2.11.44; for Caesar's *laudatio* of Cornelia (mother of his daughter and only child, Julia), see Suetonius, *Divus Julius* 6.1 and Plutarch, *Caesar* 5.2.

[10] For Caesar's words on his *amita*, see Suetonius, *Divus Julius* 6.1. On Ancus and the Marcii (among whom was numbered the mother-fearing Coriolanus), see Cicero, *De Re Publica* 2.33, Livy 1.32.1-2, and the article by Münzer in *RE* 28 (1930) 1535ff.; on the Julii, see Münzer's article in *RE* 10 (1918) 106-107. For the family of Julius and Augustus Caesar, see Table I.

scent by blood, as well as adoption, from Venus and
the Julian clan. The *laudatio* delivered in 42 B.C. to
honor the nonagenarian Caecilia by her son Atticus, a
man whose attraction to the Coriolanus legend we have
already noted, stirred comment as providing proof of
Atticus' familial devotion (*pietas*): said to be sixty-seven
at the time, he pointed out that he had never once needed
to apologize to his mother, nor quarreled with his sister,
who was almost the same age as he. One might also
consider in this context an inscription generally dated
to the early empire, the *laudatio* of a noble matron Murdia. It is dedicated by a son of the woman's first marriage, despite the fact that her second husband seems to
have been numbered among her survivors. She is, moreover, identified only with the words *Murdiae L(ucii)
F(iliae) Matris*, "Murdia, Lucius' daughter and my
mother"; she is acclaimed by this son as "most precious
to me" (*carissima mihi*), although he says nothing about
affection between her and either husband. Along with
citing her modesty (*modestia*), upright character (*probitas*,
an attribute we have seen noted in Livy's Aebutia and
Aebutius), chastity (*pudicitia*), compliant nature (*opse-
quium*), wool-spinning (*lanificium*), conscientiousness, and
trustworthiness (*diligentia* and *fides*), he cites her wisdom
(*sapientia*); what is more, he accords her special praise
for treating all of her sons equally in her will.[11]

[11] For this Julia's *laudatio*, see, for example, Suetonius, *Divus Augustus* 8.1, and Quintilian 12.6.1; for Caecilia's see Nepos, *Atticus*
17. For Murdia's, see CIL VI. 10230 = ILS 8394. On this inscription,
see also the discussion and text by F. Vollmer, *Laudationum funebrium
Romanorum historia et reliquiarum editio, Jahrbücher für classische Philologie*, Supplement-Band 18 (1892) 484ff.; see, too, W. Kierdorf, *Laudatio Funebris. Interpretationen und Untersuchungen zur Entwicklung der
römischen Leichenrede, Beiträge zur Klassischen Philologie* 106 (Meisenheim am Glan, 1980) 112 and 145-146, as well as the discussion by
Balsdon, 206-207.

Both *mater* and *amita* also figure prominently in another, fairly early and important source for the public reverence awarded and sociopolitical significance clearly and justifiably ascribed to older Roman women of the upper classes by their younger male relatives. This is Polybius' nearly contemporary recollection of how, as a young man, his friend Scipio Aemilianus attained the highest reputation of any male in second-century B.C. Rome. Polybius' account relates several events following the death of Aemilia, sister of Scipio's biological father Lucius Aemilius Paullus—and, as wife of the great Scipio Africanus, mother of his adoptive father, Publius Cornelius Scipio. Polybius first notes that Scipio inherited the splendid clothes, carriage decorations, gold and silver sacrificial utensils, and numerous slaves which Aemilia had conspicuously displayed at women's ceremonies. These, Polybius reports, young Scipio promptly gave to his biological mother Papiria, whose impoverished state had previously kept her from taking part in public functions. Then, once Papiria drove out in Aemilia's adornment, "the women who looked on were dazzled by Scipio's moral excellence" and (according to Polybius, most un-Roman) generosity: "with uplifted hands, they prayed that he might obtain all the glorious objectives he sought." To this episode, moreover, Polybius assigns the beginnings of Scipio's renown for nobility of character, because "women are by nature talkative, and once they have gotten something started never have too much of it."[12]

[12] Polybius 31.23-26, discussed by Pomeroy, *GWWS*, 162-163, 177, 181. The goings-on at these women's ceremonies, we should note, are portrayed here as affecting developments in the Roman male political establishment; this episode thus supports the theory, discussed in the previous chapter, that a connection exists between a society's blurring of its public and domestic spheres and its promotion of female associations on the one hand, and its according of

Polybius next describes how young Scipio finished payment on the dowries of Aemilia's daughters, his adoptive father's sisters (and hence his adoptive *amitae* as well as his biological *amita*'s offspring), surprising and impressing their husbands, Tiberius Gracchus and Scipio Nasica, by handing over the whole sum due in ten months. Further generosity to the women of his family two years later added, Polybius claims, to Scipio's reputation for family loyalty, and hence his public renown: upon Papiria's death, Scipio's simply gave his own sisters all of her property, largely consisting of their *amita* Aemilia's former possessions, to which they had no legal right.[13] The younger of Scipio's adoptive *amitae*, Gracchus' wife Cornelia, eventually became Scipio's mother-in-law; Scipio's violent political opposition to her son Tiberius Gracchus drove her, one source asserts, to have him murdered in 129 B.C.[14] The intensity of a virtuous and nurturant Roman mother's attachment, which caused her to disregard her bonds with and considerate personal treatment by one of her own blood kinsmen out of

larger significance to women on the other. For the family of Scipio Aemilianus, see Table II.

[13] Polybius 31.27-28, discussed by Balsdon, 187, and Pomeroy, *GWWS*, 163. See also the comments of F. W. Walbank, *A Historical Commentary on Polybius* III (Oxford, 1979) 505-512. Cicero additionally cites Scipio's generosity to his sisters at *De Amicitia* 11.

[14] So Appian, *Bella Civilia* 1.20, discussed by Herrmann, 91 (who sees this deed as more likely to have been wholly Sempronia's doing and idea, vengeance by a sister on behalf of her brothers; she does not consider the possibility of Cornelia's masterminding a vendetta on behalf of her avowedly precious sons, the younger still alive and victimized by Scipio's anti-Gracchan activity), and Pomeroy, *GWWS*, 150. See also A. E. Astin, *Scipio Aemilianus* (Oxford, 1967) 241, for other ancient sources suspicious of Sempronia. Astin also regards Scipio's disposition to his own mother and sisters of property belonging to Aemilia, Cornelia's mother, as potentially displeasing to Cornelia and as contributory to later family and political tensions (36).

devotion to her male offspring, is notable. It may help further to elucidate why other young Roman men of the upper classes regarded their elder female relations, their own and other men's mothers, so seriously, looking upon them as socially and politically powerful figures deserving publicly visible homage.[15]

Atticus' sister of sixty-odd, Aemilia, the dowager sister of Lucius Aemilius Paullus, and the matrons who were sisters of Aemilia's son Publius Cornelius Scipio (and hence enjoyed the magnanimity of his adoptive son) obviously rank among older women, whether by age or by relation to their devoted male kin.[16] But the concern publicly evinced for other, younger, women of high birth by their brothers, such as that displayed by Scipio in his munificence to his sisters, indicates that

[15] The theme of the mother ready to murder her own kinfolk for the political advancement of her son occurs in several other Latin authors of the classical period. Probably its most memorable appearance is at Tacitus, *Annales* 12.1ff., with its portrayal of Nero's mother Agrippina (as willing to die as well as kill to ensure that her son rule). We also find these circumstances at Livy 40.37, detailing an event which antedated Scipio Aemilianus' death by half a century, the demise of C. Calpurnius Piso, consul in 180 B.C. According to Livy, Piso's wife, Hostilia Quarta, promised her son by an earlier marriage, A. Fulvius Flaccus, that he would succeed to the post in two months; when he did succeed, she therefore was suspected of (and convicted for) poisoning her husband. For the significance of this motif, see chapter five below.

[16] Herrmann, 87, dates the younger Cornelia's birth to around 191 B.C., which would make her six years Scipio's senior. Yet a claim that Herrmann herself makes—that Cornelia did not bear the first of her children until 165 B.C.—suggests a later birthdate. For, as M. K. Hopkins, "The Age of Roman Girls at Marriage," *Population Studies* 18 (1965) 309-327, argues, Roman women were generally wed in their early teens; thus a decade of childlessness followed by the twelve full-term pregnancies that the elder Pliny attributed to Cornelia (*Natural History* 7.57) hardly seems likely. In any event, both Corneliae were not much older than Scipio Aemilianus, even though they were his adoptive *amitae*, and the younger of the two was his mother-in-law.

sisters in Roman elite society were also highly, and publicly, esteemed by their brothers. Evidence from Roman
comedy merits special note in this context. A lengthy
passage from Plautus' *Aulularia* generalizes on the feelings and duties of brothers and sisters to one another:
it depicts Roman brothers and sisters as partaking of a
close relationship, sharing the same concerns, and looking to one another for advice; it depicts one particular
sister, moreover, as expecting her advice to be followed.
At lines 120ff. Eunomia speaks of her sincere commitment to her brother Megadorus' best interests as "be-
fitting a sister of the same parents" (122 *ut aequom est
germanam sororem*). While acknowledging that brothers
find sisters bothersome (123 *nos odiosas haberi*), she points
out their mutual obligation to counsel and admonish
one another, and even demands that Megadorus do what
she orders; she justifies these demands on the grounds
that she is closest to him and he to her (128 *tibi proxumam
me mihique esse item te*). More importantly, both Roman
legend and Roman historical writing concur in their
depiction of this fraternal esteem for sisters, and fraternal
compliance with sisters' wishes, as having a substantial
public impact among the Roman elite. They suggest that
a Roman sister, though likely to be regarded with respect
rather than veneration, and subtly complimented rather
than eulogized, by her brother, often exerted influence
of a political nature both on and through him; they
indicate that various sisters publicly reflected in—and
often actually benefited from—their brothers' social and
political prestige.

In several accounts of the Coriolanus legend, it is
Valeria, sister of the late consul Valerius Publicola, who
heads the delegation of women to Coriolanus' wife and
mother and successfully urges them to make their personal appeal: Plutarch's version states that Valeria en-

joyed great honor and respect in Rome after her brother's death, and implies that her brother's public achievements had gained Valeria her position of female leadership.[17] One Claudia, sister of a mid-third-century B.C. consul who was vanquished in a naval battle at Drepanum, is even remembered by several ancient sources for perversely recalling her brother's public *disgrace* as a means of publicly asserting her own special status. Annoyed with the congestion of Roman streets, she shouted out—in the middle of a traffic jam—"If only my brother were alive to lose another fleet! That would thin out the population a little"; as a result of this wrong-headed outburst, she is said to have been the first Roman woman to stand trial for treason.[18] The list of women in the late republic and early empire who became publicly respected, and at times politically formidable, figures because of their supportiveness to, or strong support from, powerful male siblings includes the sisters of Julius and Augustus Caesar and of the demagogue Clodius; the last of these women was acerbically assailed by Cicero in his oration on behalf of her ex-lover Caelius in part so as to discredit her younger brother.[19]

[17] Plutarch, *Coriolanus* 33; Dionysius of Halicarnassus 8.39, 40, 43, 55; Appian, *Roman History* 5.3. See also Herrmann, 28.

[18] Suetonius, *Tiberius* 2.3. See also Livy, *Periochae* 19, Valerius Maximus 8.1 *Damnatae* 4, Aulus Gellius 10.6 and the discussions by Balsdon, 43, and Herrmann, 49–50.

[19] For Caesar's sisters and their support to and from their brother, see Suetonius, *Divus Julius* 74.2 and *Divus Augustus* 8 as well as M. Deutsch, "The Women of Caesar's Family," *CJ* 13 (1918) 502–514. For Octavia and her brother, see, *inter alios, L'année épigraphique* (1928) no. 2, identifying her solely as "Augustus' sister" (*soror Augusti*) on her tombstone; Suetonius, *Divus Augustus* 29.4 (the naming of the *Porticus Octaviae* in her honor); Seneca, *Ad Polybium De Consolatione* 15.3 (her preciousness to her brother); Plutarch, *Antony* 35 (her role in the peace arrangements of 37 B.C.); Valerius Maximus 9.15.2 (Augustus' punishment of a man claiming to be her discarded son). See also the discussions of Balsdon, 69–70; Pomeroy, *GWWS,*

This roster also, and most importantly, includes Servilia, better remembered as mother of Julius Caesar's assassin, Brutus, and mistress of Caesar himself. Born in about 100 B.C., she soon lost her stepfather and mother in short order; she, her brother and sister, and her mother's son and daughter by the second marriage were reared together in the house of their *avunculus* (mother's brother), the tribune M. Livius Drusus. The special closeness between their late mother and this brother—since under Roman law a man's agnate kin held priority of succession, one would have expected the male relations of the children's respective fathers to have assumed responsibility for their upbringing—obtained among Servilia and her siblings as well.[20] For after the death of Servilia's

---

183-187; M. W. Singer, "Octavia Minor, Sister of Augustus: A Historical and Biographical Study," unpublished Ph.D. dissertation, Duke University, 1945; and K. P. Erhart, "A New Portrait Type of Octavia Minor?" *The J. Paul Getty Museum Journal* 8 (1980) 117-128. The last of these notes the exceptional privileges, including the erection of statues, obtained by Augustus for her and his wife Livia through senatorial decrees; more importantly, it points out that Octavia was the first woman to be honored with her portrait on Roman coins (an exceptional distinction "undoubtedly" granted because of her political role in the events of 40-36 B.C.) (125 n. 29). For Clodia and the Clodiae, see, for example, Cicero, *Ad Atticum* 2.1.5, *De Domo Sua* 92, *Pro Milone* 73, and *Pro Caelio, passim*; Plutarch, *Cicero* 29.4-5 and *Lucullus* 34.1 and 38.1. See also the discussions of W. C. McDermott, "The Sisters of P. Clodius," *Phoenix* 24 (1970) 39-47; T. P. Wiseman, *Cinna the Poet and Other Essays* (Leicester, 1974) 111-114; and M. B. Skinner, "Pretty Lesbius," *TAPA* 112 (1982) 204-208. For Clodius' family and their relation to the Metelli, see Table III. The view that Cicero attacked Clodia in the *Pro Caelio* (and delivered the speech itself) largely to ridicule and discredit his enemy Clodius has most recently been advanced by S. Dixon, "The Family Business: Women and Politics in the Late Republic," *Classica et Medievalia* 34 (1983) 91-112 and M. B. Skinner, "*Amica Populi*: Clodia Metelli and the Politics of Prostitution," paper delivered at the fifth Berkshire Conference on the History of Women, Vassar College, June 17, 1981.

[20] For the childhood of Servilia and her siblings, see Plutarch, *Cato*

first husband Marcus Junius Brutus in 78 B.C., her brother
Quintus Servilius Caepio may have legally adopted her
only son.[21] Furthermore, Servilia's half-brother Marcus
Porcius Cato the younger, later known as Uticensis and
always known as a champion of reactionary republican-
ism, seems to have provided young Brutus with paternal
nurturance of a more spiritually substantial nature. Plutarch tells us that Brutus esteemed Cato more highly
than any other Roman: as a youth Brutus joined this
avunculus on an important mission to Cyprus, where he
earned Cato's praise for helping him sort out problem-
atic administrative affairs; as a mature man, he passion-
ately took up his uncle's political mission after Cato's
suicide in 46 B.C., first wedding Cato's daughter Porcia,

Minor 1, Valerius Maximus 3.1.2, and Africa, 607. On the expectation of agnate succession among the Romans, see Watson, *Roman
Private Law Around 200 B.C.* (Edinburgh, 1971) 35-36. On Livius
Drusus, see the article by Münzer in *RE* 13 (1926) 859ff.; that, as
will be noted several times in this study, Drusus predeceased the
male agnate kin of his former brothers-in-law makes his assumption
of this responsibility all the more striking. For the family of Servilia,
Cato, and Brutus, see Table IV; a different reconstruction of this
family, making the "younger" Servilia the "elder" Servilia's niece
rather than her sister, is suggested by J. Geiger, "The Last Servilii
Caepiones of the Republic," *Ancient Society* 4 (1973) 143-156.

[21] As has been argued by Münzer, *Römische Adelsparteien und Adelsfamilien* (Stuttgart, 1920) 338ff.; Syme, *The Roman Revolution*, 34 n.
7; and now Africa, 609, and D. R. Shackleton Bailey, *Two Studies
in Roman Nomenclature* (New York, 1976) 129-131. Geiger, "The
Last Servilii Caepiones," 148ff., presents various arguments against
Brutus' adoption by this particular *avunculus* (e.g. Plutarch's failure
to mention an adoptive son when recounting the death of this man
in his *Cato Minor*). Evidence for this adoption, however, includes
Brutus' own apparent use of the name Q. Caepio Brutus on coins
he issued following Caesar's assassination as well as a Greek inscription from Oropus (IG VII. 383) referring to him as Quintus Caepio
Brutus, son of Quintus; on the former, see M. Crawford, *Roman
Republican Coinage* (Cambridge, 1974) I.514-516 (nos. 501-505). Furthermore, even according to Geiger's hypothesis, making Brutus'
adoptive father a son of Servilia's father by an earlier marriage,
Brutus' adoptive father would still be his mother's half-brother.

then penning an encomium in his uncle's honor, and finally slaying his uncle's enemy Caesar at the head of an illustrious conspiracy. Cato's eagerness to please his half-sister helps explain his solicitude for her son; Servilia's need to repay Cato appears to be behind her promotion of the relationship between the two. After all, ancient sources not only report that Servilia wielded immense—indeed a mother's—influence on Cato (*maternam obtinebat auctoritatem*), they note that he had once spared her second husband Silanus from prosecution for electoral bribery. Cato's other half-siblings, however, also exerted strong claims on him: Cato's adoration for his elder half-brother Caepio was proverbial; his second half-sister, the younger Servilia, appears to have turned to him for aid to herself and her son after she was widowed by Lucullus—and to have redeemed herself from a reputation for unchastity by becoming Cato's ward, and sharing his wanderings and life style.[22]

The elder Servilia's liaison with Caesar, authorities avow, brought embarrassment and disgrace to Cato, a man conspicuous for moral rectitude and contemptuous of Caesar's panache and demagoguery. Curiously, Cato's suicide follows closely upon Servilia's first blatant, and successful, attempt to exploit her lover for the sake of her son, a maneuver which estranged Brutus from

[22] For Brutus and Cato, see Plutarch, *Brutus* 2-3, 13 and *Caesar* 46; see also Cicero, *Ad Atticum* 12.21, 13.46; Syme, *The Roman Revolution*, 58; and Africa, 609-610, 614-623. For the elder Servilia and Cato, see Asconius 17 K-S and Plutarch, *Cato Minor* 21.2-3. For Cato, Caepio, and the younger Servilia, see Plutarch, *Cato Minor* 3.5-6, 8.1, 11, 15.4 (Caepio), 24.3, 54.1-2 (Servilia). Geiger's reconstruction of this family in "The Last Servilii Caepiones" makes this younger Servilia Cato's niece. His argument on 155, however—that Cato's brother, born ca. 98 B.C., would have married ca. 80 B.C. and promptly sired this Servilia (who wed Lucullus in the midsixties)—seems improbable in the light of Hopkins' findings in "The Age of Roman Girls": one would not expect a Roman man to wed until he had reached his early twenties.

his *avunculus* when the latter needed him most: because of Servilia's entreaties, Caesar granted Brutus safety at Pharsalus, and Brutus offered Caesar his services in recompense. In the year after Cato's death, Servilia seems to have opposed the marriage between his daughter and her son, fearing that it portended the cessation of Caesar's patronage to Brutus. But, after Caesar's assassination, Servilia reasserted her loyalties to her blood family and displayed a strong commitment to the cause of her late half-brother and living son over that of her paramour. In June of 44 B.C. she tampered with a decree of the Roman senate which irked Cato's political heirs, Brutus and his co-conspirator Cassius, the latter husband of Servilia's daughter (and Brutus' half-sister) Junia Tertia. By way of contrast, her other son-in-law Lepidus, who had taken Antony's side, does not appear to have obtained her *political* support: when he was declared a public enemy, and his property seemed at risk of being confiscated, she worked both through Brutus and alone only to protect the financial interests of her daughter and her grandchildren. Additionally, Servilia's power in this second triumviral period—her ability to exert influence on behalf of her son Brutus and son-in-law Cassius, and with the leaders of the Roman senate—surely emanates from her position as sister of the admired Cato. In 42 B.C., needing protection herself, she took refuge with Atticus, son and brother of formidable older women, best friend to Cato's most eloquent supporter Cicero, guardian to Cato's son, and immensely fond of her own son. As she had been aided by her brother, and his political connections, in his lifetime, so she continued to profit from them—while furthering his political cause—after his death.[23]

[23] For Cato's well-known moral rectitude, see Valerius Maximus

The political achievements of her brother also seem to have brought public distinction to another matron of Scipionic ancestry, one born in these very years and dead in 16 B.C. Propertius 4.11, the first-person funeral *laudatio* of the noble Cornelia, portrays her as not merely taking pride in her brother's occupancy of Rome's highest political office, but even as listing her brother's political successes as a crowning reward of her own life. The kinship terms for both brother and sister, *frater* and *soror*, resound prominently among her words: "We have also seen my brother (*fratrem*) hold a second distinguished office; he was made consul at the time his sister (*soror*) was taken away." Although Cornelia's husband Lucius Aemilius Paullus, to whom she first addresses her speech, served as consul suffectus in 34 B.C., she does not allude to this distinction—and only, in passing, refers to his censorship of 22 B.C.[24] Of further interest

---

2.10.8, 4.1.14, and 3.2, as well as Plutarch, *Cato Minor, passim*; for his opposition to Caesar, and his embarrassment over the elder Servilia's liaison with him, see Valerius Maximus 2.10.7, Plutarch, *Cato Minor* 23-24, 27, 33, 51ff., and *Brutus* 5 as well as Africa, 608-613. For Caesar's grant of safety to Brutus, and Brutus' offer of his services to Caesar, see Plutarch, *Brutus* 4-6 and *Caesar* 46; Appian, *Bella Civilia* 2.112. For Servilia's apparent opposition to Brutus' and Porcia's marriage, see Cicero, *Ad Atticum* 13.22, and Africa, 614; for Servilia's intervention against this senatorial decree, see Cicero, *Ad Atticum* 15.11 and 12; see, too, Syme, *The Roman Revolution*, 58 and 116, and Africa, 609, 614-615. For Servilia's (and Brutus') activities in the interests of her daughter and grandchildren (though not of Lepidus), see Cicero, *Ad Brutum* 1.12, 13, 15, 18; see also Phillips, "Roman Mothers and the Lives of Their Adult Daughters," *Helios* 6.1 (1978) 74, and chapter four below. For Servilia's influence on Brutus' and Cassius' behalf, see Cicero, *Ad Familiares* 12.7 (asking Cassius' apologies for acting in contravention of his mother-in-law) and *Ad Brutum* 1.18. For her refuge with Atticus, Atticus' guardianship of Cato's son, and Atticus' intimacy with Brutus, see Nepos, *Atticus* 8-11 and 15-16.

[24] I follow H. E. Butler and E. A. Barber, *The Elegies of Propertius* (Oxford, 1933) 149, and the manuscripts of Propertius in placing

is Cornelia's expressed pride in her relation—through her mother, Augustus' second wife Scribonia—to the *princeps'* daughter, and only child, Julia; in line 59, she asserts that Augustus mourned her as a sister worthy of his own daughter (*sua nata dignam . . . sororem*). Scribonia's brief union with Octavian, moreover, resulted from the fact that *she* was sister to L. Scribonius Libo, the father-in-law of Sextus Pompeius: by this marriage Octavian helped strengthen the pact of Misenum with young Pompey.[25] This pact itself—we should also observe—was sealed through the mediating efforts of Sextus' mother Mucia, a woman whose own political influence may be viewed as having originated from her powerful consular half-brothers, the Metelli.[26]

Yet in addition to revering their older, maternal, kinswomen as socially and politically powerful figures, and to conferring the special benefits and burdens of their own political involvement upon their respected sisters, Roman men of the upper classes during the republican

the couplet on the consulship of Cornelia's brother at lines 65-66. That the couplet interrupts Cornelia's farewell to her children has, as Butler and Barber observe on 384, so disturbed several editors as to provoke sundry transpositions. That these, however, prove unsatisfactory and that Cornelia seems to cite, after addressing her sons, the achievement of their politically prominent *avunculus* as an inspiring example to them support the manuscripts' arrangement. For this Cornelia, her mother Scribonia's family, and the family of the Aemilii Lepidi into which she married, see Tables V and VI. For the censorship of Cornelia's husband, to which Propertius has her refer in lines 41-42 and 67, see Cassius Dio 54.2 and Velleius Paterculus 2.95.3; for his consulship, see Cassius Dio 49.42.

[25] On Scribonia, see Appian, *Bella Civilia* 5.53; Suetonius, *Divus Augustus* 62.2, 69.1, and E. F. Leon, "Scribonia and her Daughters," *TAPA* 82 (1951) 168-175.

[26] Cicero, *Ad Familiares* 5.2 (to Mucia's half-brother Metellus Celer, dealing with their brother Metellus Nepos, and attesting to the role played by Mucia, then wed to Pompey the Great, as liaison between them and her husband). On Mucia, see also Balsdon, 52-53, and Herrmann, 106-107; see Tables III and V as well.

and early imperial periods also seem to have bestowed
social and political significance upon their daughters.
The Romans themselves thought that a daughter's interests had been of major importance to her father even
in pre-republican times. For the *Leges Regiae* do not
merely insist that a male rear at least the first of the
female children born to him, but also require *clientes* to
furnish their protectors' daughters with dowries if funds
are not otherwise available.[27] Literary and historical
sources also make it clear that paternal concern for
daughters' welfare was assumed, and resulted in the special, public recognition of these women among the classical Roman elite; some of this varied testimony now
merits examination.

Roman comedy, in its topsy-turvy way, suggests a
reliance by daughters, especially those whose husbands
prove inadequate to their needs, on powerful, prosperous or merely protective fathers; it implies that *generi*,
sons-in-law, like *clientes*, were obliged to please influential *patres* by adequately and visibly providing for their
daughters' well-being. A scene in Plautus' *Menaechmi*,
for example, depicts a wronged wife summoning her
father to punish her errant husband. This father, in typ-
ically Plautine fashion, first lambasts all women who
"arrogantly relying upon their handsome dowries, demand subordination from their husbands" (*viros subser-
vire / sibi postulant dote fretae feroces*). But eventually he
acknowledges, in generalizing terms, that "a daughter
never summons her father unless . . . she has 'good
reason' " (*nec pol filia unquam patrem accersit ad se, / nisi aut
. . . iurgi est iusta causa*). What is more, the aged father
later decides to confront his son-in-law with the charge
that he has given his wife's clothes and jewelry to his

[27] See Dionysius of Halicarnassus 2.10.

mistress. In true comic fashion, however, the old man restricts himself to this charge alone and responds to his daughter's complaints by praising her husband for consorting with the courtesan next door; so, too, he blames his daughter for insisting that men be her slaves, and for virtually expecting her husband to card wool with the maids (*servire tibi / postulas viros? dare una opera pensum postules, / inter ancillas sedere iubeas, lanam carere?*). Plautus' *Stichus* begins by portraying the anxiety of a publicly admired older gentleman over the three-year absence of his two daughters' husbands; it emphasizes his disquietude at popular pressures to take the women back to his own home and make new matches for them. The apparent comic twist here, however, is the father's refusal to reclaim his daughters—after they remind him that they are only obeying his orders in standing by their spouses.[28]

Furthermore, ancient historical testimony, some of which we have previously discussed as evidence for the esteem accorded republican and imperial Roman mothers, maternal elder kinswomen, and sisters, clearly indicates that such women commanded additional and simultaneous respect as daughters of powerful men. Classical authors and a classical artifact refer to the younger of the two Corneliae—whose rapid and generous dowering by Scipio Aemilianus so dazzled her own and her sister's husbands—as the daughter of the great Scipio Africanus, and as publicly identified in that way long after her death.[29] Tacitus relates that Nero's mother, the

---

[28] Plautus, *Menaechmi* 766-767, 770-771, 790-797, 803-810; *Stichus* 10-23, 75-87, 126ff. See also Segal, *Roman Laughter*, 46, on this passage in the *Menaechmi* and on the comic sympathy displayed by the father-in-law for his errant son-in-law.

[29] See, for example, Plutarch, *Gaius Gracchus* 19; ILS 68, the portrait statue of Cornelia in the Porticus Octaviae identifying her as *Africani filia, Gracchorum*; Pliny, *Natural History* 34.31, describing this

younger Agrippina, both before her marriage to the
emperor Claudius and after her falling out with her son,
depended upon her position as daughter of the beloved
Germanicus for her political influence.[30] The younger
Cato's daughter Porcia, Brutus' wife, is also most memorably represented as a credit to her father and his
political philosophy. Plutarch's life of Brutus describes,
in chapter 13, how Porcia once assured Brutus of her
eagerness to support his political endeavors by wound-
ing herself and thereby proving her superiority to pain.
Plutarch narrates that her first words on this occasion
were "I am Cato's daughter," and that she went on to
avow "I am fortunate to be the daughter of Cato and
the wife of Brutus." Plutarch's life of the younger Cato
even concludes with the statement that "the daughter
of Cato did not lack in either temperate wisdom or
manly courage," remarking that "her suicide was be-
fitting to her noble birth," and referring the reader to
his life of Brutus for further details. Porcia's devotion
to her late father may have in part been due to a feeling
of gratitude for his past kindnesses. For Porcia, Plutarch
reports, had been sought in marriage by Cato's intimate
Q. Hortensius while she was still wed to her first husband Bibulus. Eager for a close tie with Hortensius, but
terming it absurd to propose marriage with a *daughter*
who had been given to another, Cato refused; never-

statue as (to) *Corneliae Gracchorum matri, quae fuit Africani prioris filia*
("Cornelia, mother of the Gracchi, who was the daughter of the
elder Africanus").

[30] See Tacitus, *Annales* 12.1.2 (introducing Agrippina as *Germanico
genitam*); 2.3 (Pallas' claim that she would bring to a marriage with
Claudius "Germanicus' grandson," *Germanici nepotem*); 13.14.3
(Agrippina's self-definition as *Germanici filia* when raging at Nero);
14.7.4 (where Burrus tells Nero that the praetorians will not attempt
anything against Agrippina, *Germanici . . . progeniem*). For Germanicus and his children, see Table I.

theless, he subsequently agreed, with the permission of
his father-in-law Marcius Philippus, to let his present
wife Marcia wed Hortensius, thereby evincing a greater
solicitude for the stability of his daughter's domestic life
than for his own (and arguably a greater concern for her
than for his own wife).[31] Hortensius' own daughter Hortensia seems to have been the wife of Cato's half-brother
(and brother of the Serviliae and putative adoptive father
of Brutus) Quintus Servilius Caepio. Ancient sources,
however, do not, when discussing Hortensia, mention
her husband; rather, they stress Hortensia's oratorical
talents, brilliantly exercised in 42 B.C. on behalf of the
female kin of those men proscribed by Cato's and Bru-

---

[31] Porcia's self-wounding is also related by Valerius Maximus 3.2.15,
who introduces Porcia as Cato's daughter. In chapter 23 of *Brutus*,
Plutarch first remarks upon Porcia's obsession with a painting of
Hector's farewell to Andromache; he then describes Acilius' reci-
tation to Brutus of the Homeric lines (*Iliad* 6.429ff.) from the same
mythic episode, in which Andromache calls Hector her father and
brother as well as husband. He next asseverates, on the authority of
Porcia's son Bibulus, that Brutus dismissed Hector's words to Andromache, ordering her to her loom and disparaging her advice to
him on military strategy, as inappropriate to Porcia—since Porcia
had the spirit to fight as nobly for her country as any man. Plutarch
thus seems to imply that Porcia's fixation on Hector was thought
to signify a view of Brutus as a surrogate for her late father; furthermore, by characterizing Brutus as in this context terming Porcia
not a domestically defined wife, but a fellow fighting patriot, Plutarch seems to associate Porcia's devotion to her father with her
militant patriotism. On this episode, see also the discussions of Balsdon, 50-51, and Herrmann, 117. For Plutarch's praise of Porcia at
the conclusion to his life of Cato, see *Cato Minor* 73.4; Plutarch's
Brutus concludes with Porcia's death as well (53.4). Valerius Maximus also relates the details of Porcia's suicide at 4.6.5 (as noted in
chapter five below); even though he utilizes this episode as an instance
of conjugal love, he refers to Porcia here as M. Cato's daughter and
as imitating her father's death. For Cato's decision to dissolve his
own marriage rather than Porcia's, see Plutarch, *Cato Minor* 25.

tus' enemies, and much praised as bringing credit to her late father as well.[32]

A well-born Roman daughter might, upon marriage in her early teens, legally be under her husband's control, and would certainly reside with him: residence with and legal control by a husband would, of course, thereby remove a woman to some extent from her father's, and male agnates', sphere of influence.[33] By the time a daughter was married, a well-born Roman father might already have died, and thus deprived her of his support and protection: such was the case with the fathers of the Corneliae, Agrippina, Servilia, and Servilia's own daughters; this was a particularly strong likelihood in the war-torn and crisis-ridden periods of the classical era. But the fact that a Roman woman legally belonged to the household of her husband rather than that of her father (or brother or son or any other kindred male who served as her guardian) would not have necessarily distanced her greatly from any of her male blood kin.[34]

[32] For Hortensia, see Valerius Maximus 8.3.3; Appian, *Bella Civilia* 4.4.32; Quintilian 1.1.6; the article by Münzer in *RE* 8 (1913) 2481-2482; Balsdon, 56; Herrmann, 111-115; Pomeroy, *GWWS*, 175-176; and the discussion in chapter five below.

[33] For the age of Roman girls at marriage, see Hopkins, "The Age of Roman Girls"; on the Roman married woman's relations with her blood kin, see Pomeroy, "The Relationship of the Married Woman to her Blood Relatives in Rome," *Ancient Society* 7 (1976) 215-227. To be sure, by the late republic, marriage with *manus*, which placed a wife under her husband's control, had become less common than it seems to have been in earlier periods. Yet the fact that both the mother and sister of the matron honored in the so-called *Laudatio Turiae* of ca. 10 B.C.—as is observed by E. Wistrand, *The So-Called Laudatio Turiae* (Goteborg, 1976) 33—appear to have been wed *in manum* indicates that it was still very much in existence.

[34] As Pomeroy remarks at *GWWS*, 152, a Roman woman's guardian was not necessarily a relative. But the expectation was that he would be either a male kinsman or a friend of a male kinsman; such,

Upper-class Roman society of the republican and early imperial eras—the group and time span with which the historical, and for the most part anecdotal, evidence adduced in this discussion has dealt—consisted of a few families, connected by blood and marriage, and living within a relatively small urban area; ties of kinship, once formed, were thus easily maintained.[35] The evidence surveyed in this chapter for the importance of well-born women to the men of their natal families, their visibility in Roman society at large, and their impact on Roman political developments would also imply close and frequent contact between them and their male kin.

Furthermore, we shall soon see that during the classical period (and perhaps from earliest Roman times onward) a Roman father was expected to provide for his daughter even after his death. It should also become clear that a Roman father was buttressed socially in this commitment to his daughter by male blood kin and in-laws, in addition to being financially supported in this commitment by all of his dependents. So, too, an all-powerful Roman father's initial valuation of his daughter

---

at least, is Cicero's intimation when, in appealing to popular sentiment at *Pro Caecina* 5.14, he criticizes the choice by the late, mature widow Caesennia of her own friend Aebutius for such a position.

[35] See Pomeroy, "Relationship of the Married Woman," 220ff. Roman wives did not regularly accompany their husbands to provincial posts until the early empire and were discouraged from accompanying them thereafter; see Tacitus, *Annales* 3.33, chapter six below, and A. J. Marshall, "Roman Women and the Provinces," *Ancient Society* 6 (1975) 109-127. Roman men sent into exile—according to Marshall, 113—"preferred the reassurance of leaving their wives behind." Rome's wars, which involved the energies of so many aristocratic Roman males, were fought far from the capital. Thus Roman women of the upper classes were much more likely to be in Rome than were their husbands. This situation, as will be pointed out again in chapter five, would tend to strengthen such married women's ties with male blood kin who were either too old for war and administration or not old enough.

and initial concern with having his daughter provided for as long as she lived seem to have led other kindred males to follow suit; it is this valuation and this concern which demand our attention next, and which apparently furnished Roman women in other kinship roles—those of sister, mother, aunt and even wife—with their significance and political influence in both elite Roman families and elite Roman society.

III

FILIAE FAMILIAE

IN his second oration against Verres, delivered in 70 B.C., Cicero provides vivid testimony to the high emotional valuation of daughters, and the role of daughter, by Roman fathers, even fathers (like Cicero himself) with male children. "What," he asks the men assembled, "has nature wanted to be more pleasurable to us (*nobis iucundius*), what has nature wanted to be more dear to us (*carius*) than our daughters?" In the proemium to his *De Rerum Natura*, Cicero's contemporary Lucretius employs Agamemnon's slaying of his daughter Iphigenia to illustrate the unspeakable evils caused by religion; in so doing, he accentuates the horror felt by the blameless maiden when she sees her father preparing her slaughter. Writing a century after Cicero and Lucretius, the younger Seneca consoles Marcia on the death of her son by first recalling the deep affection felt for Marcia by her own late father, the historian Cremutius Cordus, and by later ascribing to Cordus in heaven a speech claiming that he and his grandson are together among the blessed. The younger Pliny, mourning the death of his friend Fundanus' younger daughter, excuses Fundanus' total absorption in his grief on the grounds that the girl was her father's exact image in appearance and ways, and recalls the father's and daughter's clinging embraces. Plutarch's "Advice to Bride and Groom" generalizes that "Mothers appear to have a greater affection for their sons because sons are thought better able to help them, whereas fathers have a greater affection for their daughters because daughters are thought in need of their help." And Juvenal's fifth satire, like Pliny's letters and Plutarch's essay a product of the early second century A.D., issues the following piece of advice to a prospective fortune-hunter: "If you want to become master of a household, and rule over its master, don't seek a household with a little male offspring playing in its halls, or a daughter more precious than the male child."[1]

The discussion to follow will place these six passages in their cultural context and explore the distinctly Roman cultural phenomenon to which they attest. For such indications of the cultural prominence assigned to the role of daughter, and especially to fond fatherly feeling for individual daughters, seem to lack parallels in our surviving testimony about Rome's two most culturally prestigious neighbors. An array of evidence from classical Roman sources will illustrate how the role of father's daughter was emphasized in various aspects of classical Roman culture: social institutions, literary representations of family interactions, actual public and private behavior by the Roman elite, patterns of bonding between upper-class men and kindred of younger generations. Testimony that deep paternal concern for

[1] For Cicero's remarks, see *In Verrem* 2.1.112; see also Cicero's similar remarks on Atticus' daughter at *Ad Atticum* 5.19.2, written in 51 B.C. (in which he again employs the adjectives *cara*, "dear," and *iucunda*, "pleasant"). For this other testimony to daughter-valuation by fathers as normative, and important, in elite Roman life, see Lucretius 1.80-101; Seneca, *Ad Marciam De Consolatione* 22, 26; Pliny, *Epistles* 5.16; Plutarch, *Coniugalia Praecepta* 36 (a passage also remarked upon by Pomeroy, "The Relationship of the Married Woman to Her Blood Relatives in Rome," *Ancient Society* 7 [1976], 215); Juvenal 5.137-139 (a humorous echo of Vergil, *Aeneid* 4.328-329). I am grateful to J. D. Moore for the observation on Lucretius' proemium; I owe the Juvenal reference to K. G. Wallace.

daughters, and the importance of the daughter role generally, remained a Roman cultural constant throughout the classical era will prompt us to consider another issue: whether this high valuation of women in their role as their fathers' daughters and the centrality of the daughter role itself in elite Roman kinship and society go back— as the Romans of the classical period themselves believed—to Rome's monarchic era. Last, the evidence on cultural elaboration and individual valuation of the daughter role to be amassed will allow us to examine what the occupancy of this role actually and ideally entailed: from this and other testimony, we may infer that well-born Roman women's initial valuation as their fathers' dependent and deferential daughters not only helped ensure their subsequent valuation in other roles but also allowed them to transcend the most obvious limitations of this one—indeed, to display increasing independence and self-assertiveness as they matured and assumed the "next" female familial role of sister.

Throughout this study, the high valuation of individual Roman daughters by their fathers, the elaboration of the daughter role in various Roman social institutions, and the Roman emphasis on ties of blood and marriage through and to men's female children will be regarded as the major attributes of a single phenomenon in the realm of elite Roman society and kinship; this phenomenon will be referred to by the term "filiafocality," "daughter-focus." The first element of this newly minted word, *filia*, Latin for daughter, needs no explanation or defense; the second element, borrowed from the modern anthropological term "matrifocality," perhaps may. "Matrifocality" was coined by an observer of the Negro family in British Guiana, and has since been employed by anthropologists to characterize numerous societies and their kinship systems and features the world over.[2] A recent study has stressed two "constructs" of "mother-focus" as especially significant: (1) kinship systems in which the role of the mother is structurally, culturally, and affectively central; (2) societies in which these features coexist, where the sexes enjoy a relatively egalitarian relationship, and both women and men are important actors in the economic and ritual spheres.[3]

We have already defined "structural centrality" in our opening chapter, and observed its general appropriateness as a term for the position occupied by all female members of the Roman upper-class family.[4] "Cultural centrality" derives, according to this recent study, from "questions of valuation," e.g. "what is the image of a given kinship role—and is it culturally elaborated and valued?" "Affective centrality" involves the "cultural valuation and patterning of the *emotions*" linked with a given kinship role.[5] As the passages just cited should indicate, and as evidence to be examined later will document, elite Roman society accorded the role of father's daughter a strikingly positive image: bestowing attention and value upon individual daughters; culturally emphasizing and elaborating the daughter's role within the family. So, too, we will see that our sources portray in a highly positive light the emotions aroused by individual daughters and associated with the role of father's

---

[2] For the term, coined by R. Smith, *The Negro Family in British Guiana* (London, 1956), see R. Randolph, "The 'Matrifocal Family' as a Comparative Category," *American Anthropologist* 66 (1964) 628-631; Smith, "The Matrifocal Family," in J. Goody, ed., *The Character of Kinship* (Cambridge, 1973); and N. Tanner, "Matrifocality in Indonesia and in Africa and Among Black Americans," *Woman, Culture, and Society*, 129-134.

[3] Tanner, "Matrifocality," 131.

[4] See chapter one above, n. 4.

[5] Tanner, "Matrifocality," 132.

daughter; this portrayal suggests that this role was affectively as well as culturally central in the Roman kinship system. Such facts further justify labeling the elite Roman cultural emphasis on and valuation of daughters "filiafocality."

One might reasonably argue, however, that the role of daughters and of all women in ancient, elite Roman society differs in crucial respects from that of mothers and of all women in a "classical" matrifocal kinship system and society; one might, therefore, maintain that "filiafocality" does not qualify as a suitable descriptive term for ancient Roman daughter valuation and the cultural centrality of the daughter role among the classical Roman elite. For one thing, the control of Roman women over family economic resources and the crucial involvement of Roman women in kin-related decision-making processes—the requisites of women's structural centrality—did not generally occur until women had reached maturity, and hence had come to occupy other familial roles—of sister, mother, wife, aunt—*besides* that of their fathers' daughters. Furthermore, it would be difficult to maintain that the sexes enjoyed a relatively egalitarian relationship in classical Roman elite society as a whole, or that upper-class Roman women were as important actors as their menfolk in the ritual and economic spheres. As we have seen, the formal exclusion of women from active participation and leadership in civil life, politically prestigious priestly bodies, and—by reason of their enforced guardianship—substantial business transactions sharply distinguished them from men.[6]

Nevertheless, even after Roman women had come to occupy other, more "mature," familial roles, they con-

[6] See chapter one above and, *inter alios*, Beauvoir, *The Second Sex*, transl. and ed. H. M. Parshley (New York, 1952) 84-88, and Pomeroy, *GWWS*, 150-152.

tinued to be symbolically and publicly defined as *daughters*. Just as the Romans employed the role of *pater* as a social metaphor for controlling, responsible male behavior in interactions with individuals other than one's offspring, so they made metaphoric use of the daughter role and its attributes in delineating the relationship between women and male kin other than their fathers. As we will see, upon marriage in her early teens, a Roman woman either passed into the control (*manus*) of her husband, with rights in respect to him of a daughter, or legally remained a daughter in her family of birth under her actual father's or another agnate kinsman's protection. As we will see, too, until the time of Augustus, and often even thereafter, a Roman woman was called by the feminine form of her father's family name, from the cradle through however many marriages to the grave; Roman society thus labeled her the daughter of her father for purposes of lifelong identification.[7] Additionally, Roman women's structural centrality in other, more "mature," familial roles seems, from evidence to be examined in this study, to result from their initial valuation as their fathers' daughters.

Just as significantly, the formal exclusion of women from active participation in civil life did not, as we noted in the previous chapter, prevent them from becoming involved in politics or from being perceived as politically influential figures. The all-female order of the Vestal Virgins was given an honored place in the Roman state, and may arguably be viewed as equal in prestige to the major (and more briefly held) male priesthoods. Roman males are said traditionally to have considered their wards,

[7] For a Roman wife's invariable legal status as a daughter and a Roman woman's lifelong identification by the feminine form of her father's name, see Pomeroy, *GWWS*, 152, 165, as well as the discussions below.

and the women for whom they served as guardians, their first obligation and priority; many well-born Roman women are known to have managed sizable fortunes with little or no assistance from male guardians. As a result, the institution of *tutela mulierum*, guardianship over women, could not have substantially affected Roman women's opportunities to determine the disposition of their property.[8]

One can, therefore, readily maintain that the relationship between the sexes in Roman elite society of classical times did not feature large disparities in power and privilege; one can also contend that women were not much less important actors than men in the Roman ritual and economic spheres. In other words, the standard attributes of a matrifocal society are not drastically

[8] On upper-class women's actual and perceived political significance, see chapters one and two above. As E. Badian has pointed out to me, the "priestly" status of Vestals is implied by Aulus Gellius when he says, at 1.12.11, that they are referred to as "taken," *capi*, just as are Rome's leading male priests, the *flamen Dialis* and augurs. By discussing the efforts of Tiberius to enhance "the prestige of priests" prior to mentioning an increase in the financial award to Vestals (and immediately after noting concerns voiced by Tiberius regarding the post of *flamen Dialis*), Tacitus also portrays the Vestal Virgins as no less distinguished than Rome's most venerated male priests (*Annales* 4.16). On the Vestals' lengthy terms of office and prestige, see the bibliography cited in n. 39 of chapter one above, the discussion below, and Pomeroy, *GWWS*, 210-214. Of particular interest in this connection is the contention of M. Beard, "The Sexual Status of Vestal Virgins," *JRS* 70 (1980) 17-18, that the Vestals "were regarded as playing a male role and were, in part, classified as masculine." On the priority traditionally shown by *tutores* or guardians to their wards, particularly their female ones, see the remarks of the jurist Masurius Sabinus quoted by Aulus Gellius 5.13.5 (most notably "other things being equal women were accorded preference to men, although a ward under age was shown preference to a grown woman"); on the independent management of large estates by such women as Cornelia and Terentia, see Pomeroy, *GWWS*, 151, and T. Carp, "Two Matrons of the Late Republic," *Women's Studies* 8 (1981) 193-195.

dissimilar to those of classical Roman elite society, despite the fact that Roman women's public interactions
with men, and ritual and economic endeavors, quite
often—as we shall observe—concerned them in or related to their valued initial role of daughter. What is
more, our later investigation of Roman women in their
"mature" roles as sisters and mothers may differentiate
Roman valuation of mothers from matrifocality, but
will also point up the presence of other, "classical,"
matrifocal features in the Roman kinship and social
structure: strong emphasis placed upon the mother-child
and sibling relationships; the expectation that the conjugal relationship will be less solidary and less affectively
intense.[9] But let us now turn to the cultural nature and
significance of Roman filiafocality itself.

DAUGHTERS IN ETRUSCAN AND CLASSICAL ATHENIAN SOCIETY

One fact about the high emotional valuation of Roman
daughters by their fathers and the cultural centrality of
the Roman role of daughter is particularly noteworthy.
Namely, this phenomenon did not apparently obtain in
the two advanced societies on which the Roman elite of
the classical period modeled so much of its culture: those
of the Etruscans and the fifth century B.C. Athenians.
Filiafocality thus differs from various other Roman sociocultural phenomena in that it was not merely a "bor-
rowing" from one or both of these societies. Rather, its
emphasis on daughters and the role of daughter enabled
Roman culture to distinguish itself from both Athenian
and Etruscan civilizations in a major regard.

Both Greek and Roman authors characterize Etruscan

[9] Smith, "The Matrifocal Family," 140-141.

woman as hedonistic, luxury-loving, and morally abandoned. Contemporary artistic representations of Etruscan life, which we adduced as evidence in our earlier discussion of women in archaic Etruscan society, confirm the first two of these impressions, although not the third: they merely suggest that Etruscan women socialized, and socialized with males, to an extent impossible for a respectable Greek, and unthinkable for a respectable Roman, woman. Nonetheless, this "freedom" of Etruscan women seems mainly to have rendered them more compatible and dynamic public companions for their spouses. Representations of affectionate, pleasure-loving couples abound in Etruscan art. Roman legends about Rome's early Etruscan rulers—Tarquinius Priscus and his inspiring wife Tanaquil; Tullia, the ambitious daughter of Servius Tullius, and her goaded husband Tarquinius Superbus—also appear to furnish testimony to the cultural emphasis placed by the Etruscans on the bond between, and mutual support of, husband and wife. Furthermore, an Etruscan woman was, as noted previously, given a "name of her own," rather than a feminine form of her father's. And Etruscan inscriptions will generally identify a woman not only by this name but also by the names of her husband, mother, and father: what evidently mattered to Etruscan society were the married couple of which she was a member and the married couple which produced her.[10]

[10] For the hedonistic image of Etruscan women, the implications of Etruscan art about women's conduct and Etruscan couples, see L. Bonfante Warren, "The Women of Etruria," *Arethusa* 6 (1973) 92ff., and "Etruscan Couples," *Women's Studies* 8 (1981) 157-187; see, too, J. Heurgon, *Daily Life of the Etruscans*, transl. from the French by J. Kirkup (New York, 1964) 32-39, 74-96, and E. Richardson, *The Etruscans: Their Art and Civilization* (Chicago and London, 1964) 102, 143-146 (and plates XLIII-XLIV). For Tanaquil and Tullia, see Livy 1.34.4-9, 41, 46ff., Dionysius of Halicarnassus 3.47.4;

Ties between an Etruscan woman and her father, to judge from Etruscan sources, do not seem to have mattered much at all. Roman sources, moreover, indicate that Etruscans' notions about this particular bond stood in absolute antithesis to their own. Several Roman writers make much of King Servius Tullius' assassination at his daughter's hands. Livy characterizes Tullia as, like the Greek male mother-slayer Orestes, deserving the vengeance of the Furies for desecrating hallowed blood ties. The late republican scholar Varro is reported to have declared the detestable Tullia wholly unlike another king's daughter of legendary lore, the Greek Antigone.[11]

4.4-7, 28-30.6, 39, as well as the discussions of Bonfante Warren, "Women of Etruria," 96, and Heurgon, 80-83, 86-88. For the identification of Etruscan women, see Heurgon, 75-76, who points out that Etruscan inscriptions will give both father's and mother's names of men as well. As an example, one might cite figure 188 of C. Vermeule III and M. B. Comstock, *Greek, Etruscan and Roman Art. The Classical Collections of the Museum of Fine Arts, Boston* (Boston, 1972), discussed by Heurgon on 192-193. On a stone cinerary urn from the city of Chiusi, this inscription is dated to the third century B.C. (thus, though late as an Etruscan artifact, it is roughly contemporary with the beginning of Rome's classical period and some of our earliest sources for it): it identifies its occupant, a wealthy, athletic, and pleasure-loving woman—for the urn contains dice, a strigil, and a large quantity of jewelry—as Fastia, "daughter of a Velsi and of Larza, and wife of a Vel." H. Rix, "Zum Ursprung des römische-mittelitalischen Gentilnamen-systems," *Aufstieg und Niedergang der römischen Welt* 1.2 (1972) 754, observes that the formation of women's names in the Etruscan system ranks as the strongest linguistic argument against an Etruscan origin of the Roman naming system.

[11] Livy 1.59.13, "Tullia fled from her house, with men and women cursing her wherever she went and calling down the furies of her parents against her"; at 1.47.7 he refers to her husband as *muliebribus instinctus furiis*, "inspired by a woman's furies." As Ogilvie, 190, notes, this image of the Furies is wholly absent from the account of Dionysius of Halicarnassus, and evokes the plight of Orestes at Aeschylus, *Eumenides* 46ff. For Varro on Tullia and Antigone, see Aulus Gellius 18.12.9-10; see also the discussion in the third section of this chapter.

Indeed, so strong was the opposition in the Roman mind between Etruscans and dutiful, beloved daughters that Vergil and Dionysius of Halicarnassus, in relating stories about early Rome, portray two native daughters, Camilla and Cloelia, as both objects of paternal pride and courageous foes of Etruscan fighters.[12]

Athenian drama may have represented Antigone as noble in her devotion to her father Oedipus, and in her commitment to ties of blood—her brother and the rites owed his corpse. Yet it also casts her as a tragic and alien figure. Her uncompromising commitment to ties of blood of course brings about her death in Sophocles' play.[13] More significantly, in Sophocles' later *Oedipus at Colonus*, Antigone's public devotion to her father prompts Oedipus' baffled comparison of his supportive daughters and stay-at-home sons to exotic Egyptians, who completely reverse the roles of the sexes.[14] Other Attic trag-

[12] For Camilla as cherished daughter and Etruscan foe, see Vergil, *Aeneid* 11. 532-896; for Cloelia, see Dionysius of Halicarnassus 5.33-35 as well as Pliny, *Natural History* 34.28.29. These passages are also discussed below, in the third section of this chapter.

[13] For the strength of this commitment, see in particular Sophocles, *Antigone* 905-912, a passage similar in sentiment to Herodotus 3.119, on the Persian wife of Intaphrenes: both women stress their ties to their brothers over those to spouses and offspring on the grounds that they can get other husbands and children but—with their parents dead—never another brother. Pomeroy, *GWWS*, 100-101, discusses both Sophoclean and Herodotean passages, provides the suggestive parallel of Octavia in Shakespeare's *Antony and Cleopatra*, and aptly reminds us that various Sophoclean scholars—offended by Antigone's notions of important kinship ties—would delete the speech as unworthy of the heroine.

[14] Sophocles, *Oedipus at Colonus* 337ff., again evoking Herodotus (2.35). For the relationship between the two men and their work, see the bibliography provided by H. R. Immerwahr, *Form and Thought in Herodotus* (Cleveland, 1966) 1 n. 1. See also the discussion of C. M. Bowra, *Sophoclean Tragedy* (Oxford, 1944) 322ff., who asserts that the Egyptian comparison "shows how unwomanly Antigone and Ismene are if judged by Greek standards" (323).

edies may portray daughters and unmarried sisters as figures men can comfortably trust, and therefore different from mothers and female sexual partners: one thinks of Electra, and the way in which Aeschylus, Sophocles, and Euripides contrast her nature and conduct with those of her mother, Clytemnestra.[15] But the death of Electra's sister Iphigenia at her father's hands, though provoking sorrow and outrage from chorus and characters in various plays by all three leading tragedians, is depicted as a far less heinous act than Clytemnestra's murder of her husband, and far less consequential than Orestes' slaying of his mother.[16] As far as one

[15] E.g. Aeschylus, *The Libation Bearers* 84-245; Sophocles, *Electra* 254-659; Euripides, *Electra* 998-1232.

[16] Indeed, the Attic tragedians tend to portray the slaying of Iphigenia by her father as almost entirely the grievance of her mother Clytemnestra—and to portray Clytemnestra herself in a generally unsympathetic manner. At *Electra* 1027-1050, for example, Euripides' Clytemnestra hypocritically claims that she murdered her husband not for killing their daughter, but out of jealous rage when he brought home a captive mistress (though she proceeds to complain that men's sexual transgressions—unlike women's—do not lead to wars and sacrificing offspring of the transgressor's sex). At 558-576 of Sophocles' *Electra*, Electra actually justifies her father's slaughter of her sister; the chorus in Euripides' *Electra* reminds Clytemnestra—when she criticizes Agamemnon for killing "what was hers"—that a wife should yield to her husband in all matters (1051-1054). In Euripides' *Iphigenia at Aulis*, Iphigenia herself patriotically rationalizes and gladly accepts her death at her father's hands (1368-1401). For an interpretation of Sophocles' *Antigone* and *Electra* as pointing out the contradictions between Athenian women's shifting family roles and the stability of the family itself, see C. E. Sorum, "The Family in Sophocles' *Antigone* and *Electra*," *CW* 75 (1982) 201-211; Sorum sees Antigone and Electra as thwarted in and thwarted by performing their daughterly obligations, and hence the Athenian role of daughter as itself conflicting and conflicted. On the helpfulness of young women in Athenian tragedy, the perversion of the "benign father-daughter relationship" in Euripides' *Iphigenia at Aulis*, and women's general image in mythically based Greek (and for the most part Athenian) literature, see P. Slater, *The Glory of Hera* (Boston, 1968); see also Pomeroy, *GWWS*, 93-112.

can tell, it took Lucretius, a Roman poet, to raise this Greek mythic episode to a paradigm for culturally inspired barbarity.

Other evidence from and about fifth-century B.C. Athenian society confirms the implications of Attic tragedy and provides more reliable proof that Athenian men did not assign much value to female children or cultural emphasis to their role. In classical Athens daughters could not—as could their Roman counterparts—inherit their fathers' property in their own right. Brotherless daughters were reckoned *epiklēroi*, "women included in the paternal estate." Upon her father's death, an *epiklēros* was ordinarily expected to become the ward of, and marry, her father's *anchisteus*, closest living male relative; such marriages between *epiklēroi* and their fathers' kinsmen often necessitated divorces between *epiklēroi* and their present husbands. The male offspring of an *epiklēros* and this new husband (the closest approximation genetically to a son his late maternal grandfather could have sired) would then inherit the dead man's estate.[17] All Athenian women, moreover, automatically became wards of their husbands upon marriage (although the *kyrios*, guardian, of a widow or divorcee was merely her closest living male relative, and might be her father, brother or son). This phenomenon, combined with upper-class women's segregation from men's affairs, allowed for little contact between a well-born woman and a male relative other than a *kyrios*; it hence militated

[17] On the epiclerate, see A.R.W. Harrison, *The Law of Athens I: The Family and Property* (Oxford, 1968) 9-12, 23; Lacey, 139-145; Pomeroy, *GWWS*, 60-62; D. Schaps, *Economic Rights of Women in Ancient Greece* (Edinburgh, 1979) 25-47. On 39-42 Schaps advances the theory that the intention of the epiclerate was to ensure that fatherless and brotherless daughters were married, and hence guarantee that their father's *anchisteus* who became their *kyrios* not seek to profit from the estate by keeping them unwed. I am grateful to S. G. Cole for elucidation of Schaps' study.

against much contact between a well-born woman in the *kyrieia* of a husband and her father or brother.[18] Additionally, when speaking in law courts about respectable and respected women, the Athenians tended to identify them not by their given names, but in terms of their current *kyrios*—e.g. Spudias' wife, Onetor's sister—reinforcing their lack of legal personhood and their dependence on the man who served as their guardian.[19]

The potential of the institution of *kyrieia* to distance Athenian daughters from fathers may also help explain a linguistic convention prominent in the writings of Herodotus, who displays—for a male writing in fifth-century B.C. Athens—a remarkably high assessment of women's capabilities and social significance elsewhere in his work. Twice he calls a man *apais*, which literally means "without children," and then adds that this man left one or more daughters.[20] This convention is, how-

[18] On guardianship of Athenian "citizen women," see Lacey, 138-139, 151-152; Pomeroy, *GWWS*, 62-64; Harrison, *The Law of Athens*, 30-32; Schaps, *Economic Rights*, 48-60. On their seclusion, see Lacey, 158-162, and Pomeroy, *GWWS*, 79-84. In " 'The Female Intruder' Reconsidered: Women in Aristophanes' *Lysistrata* and *Ecclesiazusae*," *CP* 77 (1982) 1-21, H. P. Foley observes that both sexes shared in the public religious life of classical Athens and that men had both an interest and certain involvement in the household. Nevertheless, male and female activities even in these shared realms of concern tended to be of a very different nature. Foley herself makes this point in "The Concept of Women in Athenian Drama," *Reflections on Women in Antiquity*, ed. H. P. Foley (London, 1981) 149: there, citing J. P. Vernant, "Hestia-Hermès: sur l'expression religieuse de l'espace et du mouvement chez les Grecs," *Mythe et pensée chez les Grecs* (Paris, 1969) 97-158, she observes that the "sexualization of space" within the Athenian domestic sphere pervades the organization of space in public religious and political life as well.

[19] See Schaps, "The Woman Least Mentioned: Etiquette and Women's Names," *CQ* n.s. 27 (1977) 323-330, and A. Sommerstein, "The Naming of Women in Greek and Roman Comedy," *Quaderni di Storia* 11 (1980) 393-409.

[20] Herodotus 5.48, 67.4. For Herodotus' relatively high assessment of female capabilities, see his description of Artemisia at 7.99ff., Semiramis and Nitocris at 1.184ff., and Tomyris at 1.205ff. These

ever, by no means unique to Herodotus' work. The early
Greek poet Hesiod apparently uses the word *pais*, "child,"
at *Works and Days* 376-380, when he can only be referring
to a son. The later Greek emigré Polybius, admirer of
and participant in republican Roman society, observer
of kindred women's significance in the political fortunes
of his good friend Scipio Aemilianus, even employs a
compound of the term *teknon*, "child," to exclude females as well. At 31.28, when noting that Scipio's biological (and, by Roman laws of adoption, ex-) father
Lucius Aemilius Paullus was predeceased by the two
young sons still in his *potestas*, Polybius asserts that Paullus died *ateknos*, childless; in fact, Paullus was survived
by two daughters (and perhaps three, since one is remembered as Tertia, "the third daughter"), one the wife
of the elder Cato's son, another married to Aelius Tubero.[21] In so doing, Polybius stands in stark contrast to
native Romans on the child-status of female issue. As
we have seen and will continue to see, the Romans viewed
their daughters as important offspring, and expressed
this view both individually and collectively; these
expressions merit our attention next.

THE ROMAN DAUGHTER'S PLACE AND VALUE

A wide array of ancient source material attests to the
central role in kinship and society assigned as well as

and other Herodotean women are now discussed by C. Dewald,
"Women and Culture in Herodotus' *Histories*," *Women's Studies* 8
(1981) 93-127.

[21] For Scipio's (and his brother Fabius') legal relationship to Lucius
Aemilius Paullus, who had given both to be adopted by other fam-
ilies, see A. Watson, *Roman Private Law Around 200 B.C.* (Edinburgh,
1971) 32-33; for Paullus' daughters, see Polybius 31.28.9; Plutarch,
Cato Major 20.8 and *Aemilius Paullus* 5.4-5 and 10.3-4; Cicero, *De
Divinatione* 1.46.103, *De Amicitia* 11, and *De Senectute* 15; Valerius
Maximus 1.5.3.

the high emotional valuation accorded to the upper-class Roman daughter; in so doing, it points to several major cultural manifestations of filiafocality among the Roman elite. We will examine first evidence for the importance of daughters and the role of daughter in various ancient Roman practices and institutions: the public identification of individuals; the immensely revered state religious cult of the Vestal Virgins; laws involving property ownership and succession. After surveying this testimony to the general, culture-wide, elaboration of the Roman daughter's role, and hence to general daughter valuation, we will turn to literary accounts of individual, and for the most part historical, Roman fathers' concern and affection for individual elite Roman daughters. Third, we will document the close ties of Roman elite males with kindred related to them through daughters; such evidence on men's close bonding with such in-laws and blood relations makes it clear that daughters were even central figures in Roman male kinship networks, albeit often as "links" between men and other kindred rather than as valuable individuals in their own right. Yet the notion of elite Roman daughter's interests as subordinate to those of the males they linked tallies with widely voiced Roman notions of proper daughterly conduct; thus it helps to explain certain expectations and observations made of Roman daughters which we will note later.

The Romans of the classical period called immediate public attention to the blood relationship between a father and his daughter—whom he had, according to Roman tradition, chosen to rear and accept as he would any son—by their mode of identifying daughters. As noted earlier, in classical times a well-born Roman woman was never known by anything other than the name given her on the eighth day after her birth. This was the feminine form of her father's or (occasionally, later and for reasons to be explored further in subsequent discussions) her mother's father's family name, *nomen*; at times she also might use his hereditary "third name," *cognomen*. Although her brother would also receive, on the ninth day after his birth, his father's *nomen*, or *gentilicium* as it is technically called, he generally took his hereditary *cognomen* as well, and was further distinguished from other brothers by an individuating first name, *praenomen*. Thus, to recall some obvious examples, Marcus Tullius Cicero's daughter was called simply Tullia; the daughter of Gaius Poppaeus Sabinus' daughter, Poppaea Sabina; Tiberius Sempronius Gracchus' daughter and sons were Sempronia, Tiberius Sempronius Gracchus, and Gaius Sempronius Gracchus, respectively. Fathers who chose to rear more than one daughter were forced to use comparative or ordinal adjectives—the elder and younger (*Major* and *Minor*), the third, fourth and fifth (*Tertia, Quarta*, and *Quinta*)—to differentiate among them. Diminutives of such epithets, and of women's proper names (e.g. Tertulla for Servilia's daughter Junia Tertia, Tulliola for Cicero's daughter), presumably affectionate in their purpose, seem to have been in informal use.[22]

Admittedly, an upper-class father's culturally prescribed failure to give a female child any name of her

---

[22] For the conventions of Roman naming and the complications of *cognomina*, see I. Kajanto, "On the First Appearance of Women's Cognomina," *Acts of the Sixth International Congress on Greek and Latin Epigraphy* (Munich, 1972) 402-404; "On the Chronology of the Cognomen in the Republican Period" and "On the Peculiarities of Women's Nomenclature," *L'onomastique latine*, Colloques Internationaux du Centre National de la Recherche Scientifique (Paris, 1977) 63-70, 147-158. For the time of naming Roman offspring, see Plutarch, *Quaestiones Romanae* 102. For the names distinguishing different daughters of the same father, see Kajanto, "On the Peculiarities of Women's Nomenclature," 149-150, and "Women's Praenomina Reconsidered," *Arctos* 7 (1972) 13-30.

own might be construed as indicating a culture-wide desire to rob daughters of personhood and to advertise an individual daughter as nothing more than her father's, and his family's, possession. Even well-born women in classical Athens had individual names, and names often descriptive of attributes and ideas esteemed by Athenian males, despite the fact that propriety seems to have dictated that women's names not be mentioned in certain public contexts. Plutarch relates, for example, that Cimon was married to a woman called Isodice, "Equal Justice," and that Alcibiades was son of Deinomache, "Fearsome in Battle."[23] But a Roman father's culturally prescribed situation of being, and having his blood family, associated with his daughter publicly, even after his death, regardless of who happened to be her husband or formal guardian, is significant in and of itself. For it appears to imply a symbolic pledge to his daughter's welfare on a father's part, and on the part of those men who also bore his *nomen*, most notably his sons. At least a pledge of this sort, and the use of the same name in masculine and feminine forms to symbolize it, was also evidently required of a well-born woman's husband, who customarily succeeded her father in providing her with a home and often in according her a daughter's inheritance rights. When conducted to her new husband's house, a Roman bride uttered the ritual formula, "Where you are Gaius, I am Gaia." As these words liken the husband-wife relationship to that of a man and woman with masculine and feminine forms of the same name,

[23] On the deliberate avoidance of women's names by the Athenian orators and their reasons for so doing, see Schaps, "The Woman Least Mentioned"; see also J. Bremmer, "Plutarch and the Naming of Greek Women," *AJP* 102 (1981) 425-426, who observes that the Athenian Xenophon shrank from mentioning even the name of a dead Spartan woman, daughter of King Agesilaus. For Isodice and Deinomache, see Plutarch, *Cimon* 4.9 and *Alcibiades* 1.1.

they would seem to equate a husband's obligations to his wife with those of the males who shared her given name, her father and brothers; they thus furnish another example of the metaphoric extension of the daughter role to another female familial situation.[24]

The practice of assigning daughters *praenomina* in addition to the feminine form of their father's name(s) was thought to have flourished in earliest Rome by later onomatological authority; it occurred regularly in neighboring parts of Italy from early republican times, and was even adopted by a few Romans of the classical period themselves (e.g. the dictator Lucius Cornelius Sulla, who bestowed the names Faustus and Fausta, "Fortunate," upon his twins, and several imperial aristocrats).[25] There must, therefore, be some reason why it did not generally prevail among the leading families in Rome of the classical era. The general Roman disregard for this practice may, of course, merely point to a Roman preference for originally limiting the number of daughters, sanctioned by the *Leges Regiae* at some

---

[24] On this ritual formula, see Plutarch, *Quaestiones Romanae* 30, and Cicero, *Pro Murena* 12.27; for a slightly different interpretation of its significance—i.e. that the shared *nomen* Gaius/Gaia symbolizes the *gentilicium* of the husband and the wife's entry (with daughter-status) into his family under his *manus*—see C. W. Westrup, *Recherches sur les formes antiques de mariage dans l'ancien droit romain* (Copenhagen 1943) 26. To be sure, Gaius/Gaia is apparently not a *gentilicium* at all, and hence not the sort of name a Roman woman would share with her father and brothers; if anything, it is a *praenomen*. Nevertheless, Gaia was also the *praenomen* regularly ascribed to former female owners by Roman freedom, and regarded—according to the Roman *liber de praenominibus* 7—as the most common female *praenomen* in Rome's remote past. One may hence judge it a symbolic, generalized *nomen* for all Roman women and for this reason used as the feminine form of the common male *praenomen* Gaius in a pledge of familial solidarity by bride and groom.

[25] See the *liber de praenominibus* 7, and Kajanto, "Women's Praenomina Reconsidered"; see also Valerius Maximus 8.3.2, who speaks of a first-century-B.C. female orator as Gaia Afrania.

moment in Roman history, and obviating the necessity to distinguish among female children as one did among sons; so, too, it may solely reflect a Roman belief that women, though significant representatives of their blood family, were not as self-reliant, socially visible, or politically important as men, and thus did not require the same specific individuation. But if the former assertion holds true, it also suggests that aristocratic Roman males reared only "wanted" second and subsequent female children, whom they were committed to protect, and therefore cared for and perhaps about them in a way they could not always care for their sons. Should the latter contention prove correct, we may assume that Roman fathers symbolically acknowledged and perhaps (as Plutarch alleges) even liked a daughter's vulnerability and greater need for male protection than a son's.[26]

In addition, Roman documents tend to identify both

[26] That the Romans preferred more than one male offspring may be inferred from various passages in ancient authors: e.g. the depiction of Lucius Aemilius Paullus, at Polybius 31.28 and Valerius Maximus 5.10.2, as deciding to retain two sons as heirs when giving his other male children to be adopted by other families; Valerius Maximus' portrayal, at 7.1.1, of the supremely fortunate Q. Caecilius Metellus Macedonicus as having three consular sons and buried by several *filii*. A connection between Roman female naming convention and the royal law exempting fathers from rearing more than one daughter (and later attitudes compatible with that law) is posited by Pomeroy, *GWWS*, 165; the view that well-born Roman women were identified by their *gentilicia* alone because of the increasing importance of the *gens*, extended family, in aristocratic Rome of the mid-republic, and because of their own home-bound (vs. their brothers' more public) existences is advanced by Kajanto, "Peculiarities of Women's Nomenclature," 149, and "Women's Praenomina," 28ff. It may be significant that various Roman authors note the affection felt for *younger* daughters by Roman men. At 6.34 Livy depicts the affection of (the early republican and presumably fabled) Fabius Ambustus for Fabia Minor; Cicero, *De Divinatione* 1.46.103, Valerius Maximus 1.5.3, and Plutarch, *Aemilius Paullus* 10.3-4, all cite the affection of Lucius Aemilius Paullus for Tertia; Pliny, *Epistles* 5.16, describes the affection for Fundanus for Minicia Marcella.

women and men by listing their fathers' *praenomina* as
well as the individuals' "own" names: Murdia, we should
recall, is termed "L.f.," Lucius' *filia*. In fact, the entry
under *filia* in the *Thesaurus Linguae Latinae* states, in
regard to Roman nomenclature, not only that "from
earliest times her father's *praenomen* is added to a woman's name" along with *f(ilia)* but also that omitting *f(ilia)*
is a most un-Roman characteristic ("*apud barbaros . . .*").
By way of contrast, the comparable entry for *filius*, son,
avows that in the more ancient Roman sources the word
f(ilius) was not added to the genitive of the father's *praenomen*. To be sure, a woman's identification as *f(ilia)*
may merely serve to establish that she was not the similarly named freedwoman or sister of the man in question; it need not imply that the word *filia*, or the role
of daughter, carried affective connotations which their
masculine counterparts lacked. But that Roman culture
habitually endeavored to specify that a woman stood in
the relationship of daughter—rather than freedwoman
or sister—to a given man is alone noteworthy. What is
more, the practice of providing paternal *praenomina* for
both sons and daughters signifies the existence of equal
pride, on the part of a Roman father and of Roman
patriarchal society, in female and male offspring, and a
view that a man should be publicly identified with his
daughter and her generally domestic achievements as
well as with his son and his accomplishments in the
public sphere. The notion that Roman fathers were expected to feel equal pride in their children of both sexes
receives strong support from the mere fact that the Romans used *filia* and *(g)nata*, the feminine forms of the
Latin nouns for son, *filius* and *(g)natus*, as their standard
words for daughter. This concept of male and female
children as similar and equivalent in the eyes of their
parents is not, significantly, expressed in other Indo-

European languages, inasmuch as they generally employ totally different words for offspring of different sexes.[27]

Roman religion also furnishes important testimony to the Roman valuation of daughters and to the cultural elaboration of the daughter role. We have already alluded to the Vestal Virgins in connection with the amply documented theory that a priest-king functioned as a dominant figure in earliest Rome. Other facts about Vestals themselves are pertinent at this juncture: that the latter-day head of the Roman state religion, the *pontifex maximus*, greeted a new Vestal with the address *amata*, presumably from *amare* (to love), and meaning "cherished one"; that a Vestal was chosen when she was between the ages of six and ten; that a novice Vestal needed to have both parents living.[28] Such data corroborate the related theory that the Vestals had originated as the pre-

---

[27] For *filia* in Roman nomenclature, see *TLL* 6 (1912-1926) 747-748, *pater additur pleno mulieris nomine inde ab antiquissimis . . .*; for *filius*, see *TLL* 6, 753, *de usu antiquiore et Graecorum et Oscorum, quo genitivo patris non additur*, citing a study by F. Bücheler, *RhM* 39 (1884) 410ff. On standard Indo-European words for son and daughter, see Szemerényi, 10-22.

[28] For the address of the *pontifex maximus* to the new Vestal, see Aulus Gellius 1.12.14, 19. Both Reidinger, *RE*²8 (1958) 1746, and K. Latte, *Römische Religionsgeschichte* (Munich, 1960) 108 n. 4, interpret the address "Amata" quite differently. Beard, "Vestal Virgins," 15, also expresses uncertainty about the translation "Beloved." For the age and family background of new Vestals, see Aulus Gellius 1.12.1-9. Gellius states at 1.12.9 and 13 that the new Vestal was led away from the parent under whose control she was, and passed from his *potestas* upon her delivery to the pontiffs; this observation would support the theory of Herrmann, 32 and 45, that the *pontifex maximus* functioned as the Vestals' father surrogate (although Vestals, to reiterate, had no actual guardian). As Beard observes, on 14, one may also liken the right of punishment exercised by the *pontifex maximus* to the disciplinary powers of a Roman husband over his wife; on 15, however, Beard rightly adds that a Roman husband's control over a wife in *manus* would have been almost identical to the control of a father over his daughter.

marriageable daughters of Rome's priest-king; the symbolic association, by several Roman sources, of fire with the male procreative force allows the additional inference that the Vestals were initially entrusted with the keeping of a flame because fire represented the power to create and sustain life which their father possessed and they had not yet personally encountered. The tasks and privileges assigned in classical times to these apparently archetypal *filiae*, daughter-figures for the entire Roman community, warrant attention next. Because the Latin word for the hearth which Vestals guarded, an object which came to symbolize the Roman people no less than it did Roman male procreative power, is *focus*, the important cultural role played by the Vestals stands as perhaps the most etymologically apposite illustration of Rome's filiafocality.[29]

[29] For the Roman association of fire and the male procreative force, see the passages cited by Beard, "Vestal Virgins," 24 n. 98, 99, 100, 101: e.g. Varro, *De Lingua Latina* 5.61; Dionysius of Halicarnassus 4.2; Pliny, *Natural History* 36.204; Plutarch, *Romulus* 2.3-5ff. The last of these well illustrates the specific connection of Vesta and the Vestal cult to stories associating the hearth flame with a phallus. Other ancient sources also imply a link between fire and male procreative potential. Livy 1.39 joins Dionysius of Halicarnassus 4.2 in telling of the flames that leapt from the head of the boy who became King Servius Tullius. Although Livy does not, as does Dionysius, relate that Servius' mother had previously conceived him by having intercourse with a phallus on the hearth, Livy does maintain that Tanaquil interpreted the flames as a sign that Servius Tullius would prove of aid and importance to the Tarquins' house, and concludes by observing that Tarquin thus wed his daughter to this promising young man. At *Fasti* 4.788ff., Ovid explains the fire employed at the ancient pastoral festival of the Parilia by recalling that fire and water, together the source of life (*vitae causa*), are given to a bride as she enters her new home. The flames which leap from Ascanius' head at *Aeneid* 2.681ff. may additionally be of relevance, since he is thought by some—e.g. Livy, at 1.3—to be the forefather of the Alban kings. On the association of phallus and hearth, see further U. W. Scholz, *Studien zum altitalischen und altrömischen Marskult und Marsmythos* (Heidelberg, 1970) 126ff. For general discussions of the Vestals and the fire they guarded, see Ogilvie, 97-98; Balsdon, 235-242;

Various duties and attributes of the Vestals seem more appropriate to archetypal wife- than to daughter-figures. Such "wifely" duties and attributes include preparing the *mola salsa*, sacrificial cake, and cleansing the temple of Vesta, their involvement in state festivals which originated in fertility rites, and their matronal costume. But the Vestals' paradoxical combination of these wifely and their distinctly daughterly aspects—multiplicity, virginal status, early admission to and limited term in the order, white veil—has a parallel in the daughterly attributes assigned a Roman married woman. Her name still identified her as her father's daughter; her nuptial pledge to be Gaia to her husband's Gaius symbolically obligated him to adopt a paternal role towards her; her legal status relative to her husband—were theirs a marriage with *manus*—was that of daughter to father. In other words, the Vestal cult demonstrates not only the metaphoric extension of the daughter role to female conduct in another, state religious and extra-familial realm, but also shows the ability of the role to coexist with that which daughters were expected to assume literally (and hence the Vestals assumed symbolically). Additionally, the fact that the Vestals were defined symbolically as *both* unmarried daughters and more mature wives helps to clarify why their membership in the order benefited their blood families in the way that it seems to have done.[30]

Pomeroy, *GWWS*, 210-214; Beard, 24-25. Beard's treatment of the fire's symbolic ambiguity as a parallel to the ambiguity of the Vestal's sexual status is excellent, although (as she acknowledges on 26) the Romans themselves did not regard the priestesses and their flame as "symbolically mediational." On the *focus* as symbolic of the Roman people, see, for example, Ovid, *Fasti* 6.417ff., which points out that Vesta's temple not only contains Rome's Trojan hearth, but guards the sacred image of Pallas Athene supposedly brought from Troy itself.

[30] For the combination of wifely and daughterly features displayed

A Vestal was unique among Roman women in that, under the laws of the Twelve Tables, she required (and hence burdened) no legal guardian. Like a woman who had passed into her husband's *manus* upon marriage, she passed out of her father's *potestas* and personal responsibility upon admission to the order. But even though Vestals could not for this reason inherit from an intestate kinsman, they, unlike other women, could make wills, and thus bequeath to others the sum—which by the early first century A.D. was a handsome one—they routinely received when they joined the order. To be sure, the Vestal herself was technically given this money; it may, however, have been ultimately intended to compensate her family of birth for taking away their daughter. After all, ancient sources also assert that after the cult's establishment the number of Vestals increased, the terms of the Vestals' tenure lengthened, and consequently the order in the classical era numbered nubile girls and grown women as well as those who had not yet reached the age of marriage. While one finds scholarly skepticism about this assertion, its antique authority demands that we at least account for the change in the order such sources describe. And we may best account for the expansion of the order and extension of the members' tenure by considering how these two developments would have affected the actual and prospective Vestals' families of birth, and why these families might have entered their daughters in the order to begin with.[31]

---

by the Vestals, see Beard, "Vestal Virgins," 13ff., and the sources she there cites; for Roman wives' daughterly attributes, see also the discussion earlier in this chapter.

[31] For the Vestals' guardian-less state, see Aulus Gellius 1.12.9; Gaius, *Institutes* 1.145; Plutarch, *Numa* 10.3. For the Vestals' testamentary rights, see Aulus Gellius 1.12.9 and 18; Cicero, *De Re Publica* 3.10. Beard, "Vestal Virgins," 17-18, regards these privileges and the Vestals' right to a lictor's services as indices of a third, masculine,

For it is plausible, though by no means provable, that a connection exists between these two developments in the cult's history and the frequency in early Roman republican times of periods when war or economic crisis diminished the available number of suitable husbands for daughters of leading houses. In such circumstances, of course, families unable to find large dowries for one or more daughters were at a special disadvantage. More reliable testimony on later periods of Roman history merits special note in this context: namely, accounts that after the disaster at Cannae in 216 B.C. two of the six Vestals were executed for unchastity, and that in the midst of a similarly tense period a century later three of the Vestals were condemned to death. The timing of these historical episodes suggests that this large-scale public scapegoating may in part have been sanctioned because well-born and powerfully situated families coveted for their own prepubescent daughters the places that would be left vacant by such executions—due to circumstances which rendered them unable to wed these daughters to husbands of their station. If social and economic factors of this sort influenced admission to and duration of stay in the cult during the mid-republic, they may well have done so earlier: the order may, therefore, have originally been enlarged and the length of service in it protracted so as also to relieve elite families of the matchmaking difficulties and financial burdens entailed in contracting marriages for their female children during

---

aspect of their status. For the sum given the Vestals, see Livy 1.20.3 and Tacitus, *Annales* 4.16.4; for their wealth see also Plutarch, *Crassus* 1.2. The increase in the Vestals' number (from two to six) and length of tenure (from five to thirty years) is maintained by Plutarch, *Numa* 10.1 and Dionysius of Halicarnassus 1.76.3 and 2.67.1. Although their testimony commands the credence of Rose, *De Virginibus Vestalibus,"* *Mnemosyne* 2nd ser. 54 (1926) 440-448, Beard, "Vestal Virgins," 14 n. 21, regards it, and Rose's defense of it, as suspect.

a manpower shortage; the monetary award, too, may have been meant to ease such families' financial difficulties—perhaps even allowing them to dower another daughter.[32]

However one explains these alleged changes in the order and its membership, and even if the benefits accrued by a family whose daughter became a Vestal did not invariably include the sum she was herself awarded, the mere fact that marriage on the part of a former Vestal was deemed inadvisable documents the pressure placed on the individual Vestal to leave her estate to her family of birth rather than to a husband or children later acquired on her own. Such pressure would encourage her to regard herself throughout her life as first and foremost a member of her blood family: as an exemplary daughter, and eventually (after her parents' death) a sister and aunt. The evidence of late republican coinage would indicate that various Vestals were themselves regarded posthumously as important and exemplary antecedents by subsequent generations of similarly named kin from their natal families. A coin of 41 B.C. minted by one Gaius Clodius Vestalis pays tribute to the Vestal Claudia, daughter of Appius Claudius Pulcher, consul in 143

---

[32] For the execution of Opimia and Floronia after Cannae, see, e.g. Livy 22.57.2. For the sources on the condemnation in 114 B.C. of Aemilia, Licina, and Marcia, see, e.g. Livy, *Periochae* 63, the article by Münzer on Licinia in *RE* 13 (1926) 497, and E. Gruen, *Roman Politics and the Criminal Courts, 149-78 B.C.* (Cambridge, Mass., 1968) 127-132. See also Herrmann, 52-53, on other measures affecting women and reflecting economic difficulties immediately after Cannae; see, too, H. H. Scullard, *From the Gracchi to Nero*[3] (London, 1970) 47-48, for the "strain" of Roman life from 119 to 109 B.C. At 2.42.11 Livy reports that in 483 B.C. a Vestal named Oppia was put to death for unchastity; at 4.44.11 he relates that in 420 B.C. a Vestal named Postumia was accused of conduct unbecoming a member of the order (but acquitted). Both episodes, we should observe, occurred in periods of wartime and general tension as well.

B.C.; a year earlier the triumvir Marcus Aemilius Lepidus was honored by the issue of a coin representing Aemilia, a legendary Vestal from Rome's monarchic era. What is more, an allusion to admirable female conduct by Cicero at *Pro Caelio* 34, and a story related by later Roman authors as well, implies the actual feeling of such blood familial loyalties by the first of these two Vestals (whom we should perhaps also remember as sister to the wife of the tribune Tiberius Gracchus). During her father's triumph in the year of his consulship, we are told, this Claudia kept a tribune from intervening to stop the celebration by throwing herself into her father's arms, clinging to him tenaciously, and thus affording him her sacred protection as he occupied his chariot in the procession. It is perhaps also worth noting that Cicero himself publicly acknowledges and exploits a Vestal's emotional ties to her family of birth and self-definition in terms of her brother at *Pro Fonteio* 46-47. There he attempts to win sympathy for his client M. Fonteius by referring to the embraces and emotional needs of Fonteius' mother and Vestal sister; he claims that the latter—unlike other women who can have the protection of sons and companionship of husbands—has nothing else but her brother that is "dear" or "delightful" (*iucundum* and *carum*, the very words we have seen Cicero use elsewhere when acknowledging the sentimental value of daughters to their fathers).[33]

[33] On the "superstitious fears" about marriage inspired in Vestals of the classical era—by emphasis on the unfortunate experiences of the few former Vestals who had married—see Dionysius of Halicarnassus 2.67.2 and Plutarch, *Numa* 10.2. Inasmuch as Vestals were exempt from guardianship, post-retirement marriage (at least with *manus*) would have, by subjugating them to a husband's control, meant a reduction in their autonomy and authority; adjustment to these circumstances might have been difficult. I owe this observation to E. Badian. For the coins depicting this Claudia and Aemilia, see

The role of daughter also figured prominently in Roman laws and practices involving ownership of and succession to property. Fifth-century B.C. Roman law provided for a daughter still in her father's *potestas* to inherit his estate (albeit under the tutelage of another male guardian). The Twelve Tables also define male and female children as equals by granting them the same rights of succession, at least in cases of a father's intestacy.[34] These render a Roman daughter's economic position and role within both her family and society immediately and altogether dissimilar from those of her classical Athenian counterpart, who could not have such

---

the discussions of M. Crawford, *Roman Republic Coinage* (Cambridge, 1974) I.521 (pl. 512) and 502 (pl. 494.1). The story of this Claudia is also found in Valerius Maximus 5.4.6 and Suetonius, *Tiberius* 2.5; the latter, in fact, portrays Claudia's wronged and triumphant kinsman as her brother. For *iucundus* and *carus*, and their earlier application by Cicero to daughters, see above, n. 1. That accusations of and hence efforts to discredit Vestals were often "politically" motivated, aimed actually at discrediting their similarly named male agnate kin, is maintained by Ogilvie, 602, and Herrmann, 42-43, à propos of Postumia as well as by Münzer (above, n. 32) and Gruen, *Roman Politics*, 127ff. à propos of Licinia, Aemilia, and Marcia. Gruen in fact notes Licinia's defense by her first cousin L. Licinius Crassus and suggests that enmity between her putative father C. Licinius Crassus, controversial tribune of 145 B.C., and the Scipionic faction may have engendered ill will against her; he also observes the hostility between the Vestals' inquisitor L. Cassius Ravilla and Marcus Aemilius Porcinna. This, too, would argue for public identification of a Vestal with her family of birth, and pressure to regard herself as having strong attachments to them.

[34] See Justinian, *Institutes* 2.13.5, and Pomeroy, *GWWS*, 162. As Pomeroy notes, both here and in "The Relationship of the Married Woman to Her Blood Relatives in Rome," *Ancient Society* 7 (1976) 225-226, the Senatus Consultum Orfitianum of A.D. 178 enabled children to inherit from intestate mothers as well. This and related legislation, however, helped to redefine a woman as belonging to the same family as her husband and children by the late empire (a period beyond the concerns of this study); it differed from earlier laws—identifying a woman as a member of her father's family—in so doing.

claims made on her behalf, and who even in the absence
of brothers merely belonged to her father's estate as an
epiklēros. As a matter of fact, in a passage from one of
Cicero's letters, composed soon after his beloved daughter Tullia's death, though well within his son Marcus'
lifetime, he laments that, with Tullia gone, the lack of
someone to whom he can bequeath his possessions causes
him more sorrow than the sufficiency of his worldly
goods brings him pleasure. Furthermore, lines 137-139
of Juvenal's fifth satire, quoted earlier in this chapter,
indicate that Cicero's preference for his daughter over
his son as an heir is not unparalleled within classical
Roman society, although his fondness for Tullia does,
at times, run to extremes.[35]

A Roman daughter's right to inherit, however, complicated the financial plight of even those fathers who
did not wish to accord female children preferential treatment in inheritance over their brothers. The decision
whether or not to give a daughter in *manus*-marriage,
as a result of which she would become one of her husband's heirs and thus relinquish automatic rights to her
father's property, was surely affected by both the father's
ability to fund her testamentary portion if she continued

[35] For Cicero's lament, see *Ad Atticum* 13.23.3, "I swear to you
with all my heart, and I sincerely hope you believe me, that my
meager earthly goods cause me more annoyance than pleasure. For
I grieve more that I have no one to leave them to than I rejoice that
I have them for my own enjoyment," I owe this reference to
E. Rawson. Plutarch may also testify to another Roman's preference
for a daughter over a son as heir at *Cato Minor* 11.4, where he claims
that the estate of Cato's half-brother Caepio fell to Cato and Caepio's
daughter. Should Caepio have, as some scholars assume (chapter
two above, n. 21) adopted his sister's son M. Junius Brutus, then
he must have decided to exclude this son from his will in favor of
his daughter and half-brother. For Cicero's extreme fondness for
Tullia, see Carp, "Two Matrons," 197, and the quote from Lactantius she provides.

as his heir and his need for those assets which he could distribute elsewhere if she did not. On the other hand, choosing *manus*-marriage may have necessitated providing in the form of a dowry a sum comparable to that which a daughter would have inherited and may have occasioned difficulties connected with its payment. We remember Polybius' account of Scipio Aemilianus' financial maneuvers, and the fact that half the dowries promised the husbands of Scipio's adoptive aunts could not be provided until after the death of Aemilia, the women's mother. Social considerations figure no less prominently than do monetary ones in such a system. Well-born daughters who did end up inheriting an "offspring's" portion of a wealthy father's estate stood, of course, in a strong position to make decisions regarding their families' private, and even public, expenditures—and thus to influence their families' interactions with and image in Roman society.[36]

We may assume that some well-born daughters not only made such decisions, and had such influence, but also were regarded for this reason and at one time as a

[36] On the legal ramifications of *manus*-marriage, see Pomeroy, *GWWS*, 152ff., and CIL VI.1527, 31670, and 37053 (= ILS 8393, the so-called *Laudatio Turiae*) 16, which states that the subject's sister would have been left without any share in their intestate father's property since she had been given in *manus*-marriage. On this passage, and the inscription itself (to be discussed in greater detail below), see E. Wistrand, *The So-Called Laudatio Turiae* (Goteborg, 1976) 33, and the bibliography cited there; the inscription is also discussed by W. Kierdorf, *Laudatio Funebris. Interpretationen und Untersuchungen zur Entwicklung der römischen Leichenrede. Beiträge zur Klassischen Philologie* 106 (Meisenheim am Glan, 1980) 33-48, who provides a full text on 139-145. For Roman dowries in general, see the discussions of Balsdon, 186-189, and J. Crook, *Law and Life of Rome* (Ithaca, N.Y., 1967) 104-105; for Roman patrician dowries and the possible difficulties of meeting them out of liquid assets, see F. W. Walbank, *A Historical Commentary on Polybius*, III (Oxford, 1979) 507.

threat to the Roman patriarchal social structure, from the passage of the Lex Voconia in 169 B.C. The law limited the right of inheritance by certain women of the highest propertied class. Although sisters of a dead man could succeed in cases of intestacy, a woman could not be designated as heir to a large patrimony, and any legacy left to a woman could not exceed what was left to the (male) heir or heirs.[37] Certain pieces of evidence about the law—Cicero's paraphrase of its text as forbidding any maiden (*virgo*) or woman (*mulier*) "from being named heir" after it had passed; a passage from Catullus 68 portraying a previously heirless old man as ecstatically joyful over the birth of his daughter's son—are particularly worth noting. For these statements allow one to infer that the law was specifically aimed at daughters of wealthy men; with Rome's manpower losses in the Second Punic and Macedonian Wars, many such women must have found themselves unexpectedly brotherless, or somehow the sole remaining heirs to their family fortune. The elder Cato is said to have heartily approved of this law and spoken to urge its passage; the surviving fragments of this speech deplore the insubordination to, and harassment of, husbands by wives who inherit large sums.[38]

[37] For recent discussions of the Lex Voconia, see, for example, A. E. Astin, *Cato the Censor* (Oxford, 1978) 113-118; Herrmann, 82-85; Pomeroy, *GWWS*, 162, and "Relationship of the Married Woman," 222ff. I agree with Pomeroy's assertion in the latter (223) that the law was intended "to inhibit not only men but women from leaving large sums to other women"; thus I join her in interpreting Aemilia's institution of Scipio Aemilianus as "her heir" as a dodge to evade the law.

[38] For Cicero's paraphrase of the Lex Voconia, see *In Verrem* 2.1.107 (*nequis heredem virginem neve mulierem faceret*); for Catullus' allusion, see 68.119-123. Cf. also the wording of the law by Augustine, *De Civitate Dei* 3.21 (*nequis heredem faceret, nec unicam filiam*), "that no one make . . . an only daughter an heir." For Rome's manpower

Yet the impact of newly acquired wealth on well-born women in the early second century B.C. did not restrict itself to their marital affairs. One might recall the situation of Aemilia, whose fortune was clearly obtained from her late husband but arguably in her legal capacity as a wife, in a *manus*-marriage, with the inheritance rights of a daughter. Aemilia is reported to have left more money upon her death, seven years after the Lex Voconia went into effect (and therefore to have left this money to Scipio Aemilianus), than her brother Lucius Aemilius Paullus bequeathed when he died two years later. Aemilia's affluence surely accounts for her influence in this illustrious brother's household, enabling her to enlist one of his sons, the most politically promising of his four, to manage her children's financial affairs (as adopted son of her own son). Papiria's acquisition

---

losses in the second century B.C. and their impact see Pomeroy, *GWWS*, 177ff., and "Relationship of the Married Woman," 222ff. In the latter study Pomeroy espouses the view that the acquisition of wealth by women in the early second century B.C. was proving a threat to the Roman tax structure and the military service predicated upon it, since husbandless women and orphaned children were exempted from paying the *tributum*, which supported the military establishment; the need for stronger support of the Roman military was, she contends, the principal motive for the law's passage. But she also observes that two years after the law was proposed, Roman citizens were made no longer liable for the *tributum*: this suggests that other sources of funding (most recently the spoils of L. Aemilius Paullus' victory over the Greeks in 168 B.C., but surely the fruits of earlier conquests and further forms of taxation as well) were available for Roman military expenditures, and that women's use of their funds rather than a national Roman need for them was the issue behind the Lex Voconia. For further discussion of the Romans' (and Italians') release from the *tributum*, and its explanation, see Gruen, "Macedonia and the Settlement of 167 B.C.," *Philip II, Alexander the Great and the Macedonian Heritage*, ed. W. L. Adams and E. N. Borza (Washington, D.C., 1982) 266ff. For the elder Cato's support of the Lex Voconia, see Aulus Gellius 17.6.1; Festus p. 356 Lindsay; Servius, *ad Aeneidem* 1.573 = *ORF* pp. 60-61.

and display of Aemilia's possessions attracted a veritable
fan club of females for this son and subsequently advanced his political career; Scipio's gift of these possessions to his sisters redounded to his political credit still
further. We may better understand Cato's resentment
of independently wealthy women, kindred to the men
of Rome's highest census class, if we assume that the
resources belonging to many of them were used to fi-
nance, or at least to promote, the political careers of
their male kin—Cato's rivals for political office; Polybius' testimony to the wealth of Aemilia and her female
kin may then illuminate Cato's arrangement of a marriage between one such woman, Scipio's sister and ben-
eficiary of his largesse, and Cato's own son.[39]

[39] Walbank, *Polybius*, 503 and 506, also infers from Polybius' remarks in 31.26-27 that Aemilia had inherited her fortune from her
late husband, Scipio Africanus, though he merely states that Africanus had made her his heir, and does not speculate on the legal
nature of their marriage. Valerius Maximus 6.7.1 may suggest that
slaves came into Aemilia's possession as part of her inheritance from
Africanus in addition to the large sum from which she paid the first,
and Scipio Aemilianus the second, half of her daughters' dowries (so
Polybius 31.27.2). On Aemilia's estate and its size relative to that of
her brother, see also Polybius 31.22, 28; Pomeroy, *GWWS*, 163; and
Walbank, *Polybius*, 503. On Lucius Aemilius Paullus' high hopes for
and high valuation of Scipio Aemilianus, see Plutarch, *Aemilius Paullus* 22. For the marriage of Cato's son to Paullus' daughter, see
Plutarch, *Cato Major* 20.8 and Table II. Of relevance is the observation by Walbank, *Polybius*, 511, that Papiria's property would not
have reverted solely to Scipio Aemilianus—to the exclusion of his
elder brother Fabius and his sisters—unless he alone had been named
as her heir. Walbank suggests that perhaps she was grateful for
Scipio's generosity; it is plausible, too, that she perceived him as
more politically promising than Fabius, and hence thought such a
bequest better able to profit him in his career. One might also consider relevant in this context Valerius Maximus 7.8.2, a passage
which will be discussed further in chapter four below. It deals with
one Aebutia, apparently of the early second century B.C. (and possibly the *amita* of that name in Livy's account of the Bacchanalian
scandal). Valerius reports that although she had two daughters of

Nevertheless, the effort of the Lex Voconia to channel private wealth away from rich men's daughters and into the hands of males encountered substantial and eventually total opposition. The passage in Cicero's second oration against Verres cited above, in which Cicero waxes rhapsodic about the joy imparted by daughters to fathers, in fact concludes a story of one P. Annius Asellus, who died leaving an *unica filia* in 75 B.C. In order to leave this only child as his heir, he simply failed to register at the census, and thereby exempted himself from the Lex Voconia. His behavior, according to Cicero, was identical to that of many other men who wished their estates to pass to female children. And his conduct, according to Cicero, was only natural. For, Cicero says, *quid est dignius in quo omnis nostra diligentia indulgentiaque consumatur?*, "what is a more worthy object on which to lavish all our care and tenderness," than a daughter?[40]

---

very similar upright character (*simillimae probitatis*), Pletonia and Afronia, she made Pletonia alone her heir and merely left Afronia's sons twenty *nummi* out of a still ample "paternal estate." Valerius lists this episode in his chapter on those legal settlements which could have justly been disputed but were not. Nevertheless, by also noting that Afronia had sons, and by specifying that they inherited only a small portion of their maternal grandmother's wealth at the same time that he cites Afronia for her high-minded acceptance of the inequitable will, he implies that these males were ultimately defrauded no less than their mother and that they should have been able to count more heavily on the financial support of her kin. Needless to say, I would take issue with Astin, *Cato the Censor*, 116 n. 41, who argues—on the matter of the law's motivation—that wealth could not have given "political power" to women owing to their "unquestioned exclusion from political office, deliberative bodies and voting assemblies"; at the least I would assert that wealth gave Roman women of this period "political significance and influence."

[40] Cicero relates Asellus' circumstances at *In Verrem* 2.1.104ff. and justifies his conduct as natural at 2.1.112. The provision, under the ratio Voconiana (on which see Gaius, *Institutes* 3.14) for sisters, but not daughters, of the deceased to succeed in cases of intestacy seems

We have already looked at several statements by classical Roman authors, not all of them fathers of daughters, attesting to the fond feelings stirred in well-born Roman fathers for daughters, and expected to arise in Roman fathers for daughters. Like our evidence for the significance and elaboration of the daughter role in various Roman institutions and practices, these statements also point to the Roman cultural valuation of daughters. Other expressions and indications of both individual Romans' paternal sentiment for daughters and general Roman cultural emphasis on the role of daughter may additionally be adduced. They, too, represent a wide range of sources spread over the years from ca. 220 B.C. to ca. A.D. 130: thus they show that both this sentiment and the centrality of the daughter role remained cultural constants among the Roman elite throughout the classical period.

Two literary works from the late third and early second centuries B.C. which feature individual fathers' displays of concern for their daughters were examined in

---

to have arisen because men subject to the Lex Voconia were deliberately failing to write wills, and thus managing to leave their estates to brotherless female offspring, in the years immediately after the Lex Voconia was passed. Such, at least, may be the implication of Cicero, *De Re Publica* 3.10, set in 129 B.C. Its speaker here, Lucius Furius Philus, refers to the Lex Voconia as "passed for men's advantage, and full of injustice to women"; he asks "why should a woman not have money of her own?"; he questions the limitation on the amount a woman could possess, since the daughter of Publius Crassus, her father's only child, could inherit a grandiose sum (presumably because her father had died intestate) whereas his own daughter was debarred from inheriting one-fiftieth as much (in his will). Another effort by a father to dodge the Lex Voconia and leave his estate to his daughter is noted by Cicero at *De Finibus* 2.55; here Cicero also criticizes the instituted heir (and his advisers) for thwarting the dead man's wishes. On the restriction of inheritance rights to a sister born of the same father (*consanguinea*), see Pomeroy, "The Relationship of the Married Woman," 216.

the preceding chapter: namely, Plautus' *Menaechmi* and *Stichus*, whose comic portrayals of paternal protectiveness presumably present situations related to contemporary elite Roman reality. We should note as well Naevius' somewhat earlier epic depiction, in his *Bellum Punicum*, of Jupiter's solicitous reaction to his daughter Venus' appeal on her son Aeneas' behalf. Not only does it concur with the Plautine picture of concerned and caring paternal conduct as the expected response to a daughter in distress; it also represents a major transformation by Naevius of rather different material from his Greek literary sources. For Zeus and Achilles' mother Thetis, the main Homeric models for Vergil's later, and thus apparently Naevius' earlier, Jupiter and Venus are not, of course, father and daughter at all. It would therefore seem significant that a work, albeit an imaginative one, which was composed for educated, and hence elite, Romans characterized the Homeric Zeus' susceptibility to and affection for Thetis, a former ally in combat (and object of thwarted lust) as operative in Jupiter's relationship with his daughter. Significant, too, is the fact that this poem even characterized Venus as similar to Thetis in her claims upon the king of the gods—claims which Jupiter, like Homer's Zeus, views as stronger than those of his own wife.[41]

---

[41] For fathers and daughters in the *Menaechmi* and *Stichus*, see chapter two above. For Jupiter and Venus in Naevius' *Bellum Punicum*, see the testimony of Macrobius, *Saturnalia* 6.2.31. Macrobius claims that Venus' speech at 1.223-296 of Vergil's *Aeneid* is taken entirely from the first book of Naevius' *Bellum Punicum*, since Naevius' Venus also complains to her father, and Naevius' Jupiter also comforts his daughter with hope of the future. For the appeal of Thetis to Zeus at *Iliad* 1.500-530 as a model for Venus' interactions with Jupiter in *Aeneid* 1, see G. Knauer, *Die Aeneis und Homer. Hypomnemata* 7 (Göttingen, 1964) 374; as C. R. Beye has pointed out to me, the interchange between Zeus and his daughter Athene in *Odyssey* 1 serves as a model for this Vergilian scene, too.

Historical anecdotes reported by later authors about well-born individuals during this mid-republican period also depict protection, affection, and attention lavished on daughters by fathers as culturally prescribed and approved conduct. Valerius Maximus tells of the request made to the Roman senate during the Second Punic War by Gnaeus Cornelius Scipio. Consul in 222 B.C., Scipio was then fighting, and later fell, in Spain. He asked that another commander be sent to replace him, since he had a daughter of marriageable age, and her dowry could not be arranged without him. The senate, however, was unwilling to part with the services of a good general, and consequently funded this Cornelia's dowry itself— as Valerius claims it had done earlier for the daughters of other military leaders. Both Cicero and Plutarch as well as Valerius Maximus report that Lucius Aemilius Paullus so prized his small daughter's tearful reaction to the death of her dog Perseus as to assume correctly that this omened his victory over the Greek king by that name. Plutarch even maintains that the daughter-less elder Cato, during his celebrated censorship of 184 B.C., justified his expulsion of one Manilius from the senate on the grounds that this man had embraced his wife in broad daylight while his daughter looked on.[42]

The first century B.C. offers ample evidence, in the reported conduct of its key personages and descriptions of its major poets, that Cicero and Lucretius were not alone in the importance they placed upon the bond between father and daughter, and in the caring they felt the latter could or at least should be able to count upon

[42] For this Scipio and his daughter, see Valerius Maximus 4.4.10. For Paullus and his daughter, see Cicero, *De Divinatione* 1.46.103; Plutarch, *Aemilius Paullus* 10.3-4; Valerius Maximus 1.5.3. For Cato's punishment of Manilius (and his failure to observe proprieties in his daughter's presence), see Plutarch, *Cato Major* 17.7.

from the former. Suetonius claims that Julius Caesar broke all precedent in mourning the death of his daughter Julia by holding magnificent funeral games in her memory. Valerius Maximus states that the sight of Pompey's severed head caused Caesar to shed tears not only for his former son-in-law, but also for his late daughter, Pompey's one-time wife. Catullus' depiction in poem 68 of the joy afforded an aging father by his daughter's giving birth to a son is followed, at lines 142-144, by the apparent reflection that fond paternal sentiments are inappropriate in his own feeling for his beloved Lesbia, since her father's hand did not give her in wedlock to him. The younger Cato's previously mentioned unwillingness to dissolve his daughter's union with Bibulus and decision to dissolve his own marriage instead might be recalled as well, as might the proud remark, assigned by Propertius to Cornelia, that her stepfather Augustus had mourned her as a worthy sister to his own daughter.[43]

Early imperial literary and historical sources continue to depict the Roman father-daughter tie as extremely important to both father and daughter, and individual upper-class Roman fathers as honoring it. A few illus-

---

[43] For Caesar and his daughter, see Suetonius, *Divus Julius* 26.2, and Valerius Maximus 5.1.10. Cf. also Plutarch, *Caesar* 14.4-5, 23.4. For Cato and Porcia, see Plutarch, *Cato Minor* 25.2-4; for Augustus and Cornelia, see Propertius 4.11.59-60 (both also cited in chapter two above). We might additionally note Plutarch's remark, at *Cicero* 10.2, that Cicero's foe Catiline had been accused of taking his own daughter's virginity, a remark intended to characterize Catiline as extremely depraved and corrupt. So, too, T. P. Wiseman, *Cinna the Poet and Other Essays* (Leicester, 1974) 113ff., calls attention to the base of an honorary statue of "Licinia, the daughter of Lucius Licinius Lucullus" (IG.III²4233) erected by the people of Athens during the exodus of Roman aristocrats to join Pompey in 49 B.C. The reference to this woman's dead father rather than her apparent (and present) husband L. Metellus on this inscription warrants special notice.

trations should suffice. At *Fasti* 6.219ff., written in the first years of the first century A.D., the Augustan poet Ovid begins his discussion of why the first part of June is unpropitious for weddings by saying,

I have a daughter (and may she, I pray, live longer than my span of years); with her safe and sound, I will always be happy. When I wished to give her to a son-in-law, I sought to find out which times were suitable for weddings and which were to be avoided. . . .

A few years later, at *Tristia* 3.7.18, Ovid refers to his encouragement of the young girl Perilla's poetic efforts as like a father's leadership and companionship to his daughter (*utque pater natae duxque comesque fui*). A letter by the younger Seneca, whose poignant representation of the love felt for Marcia by her father has been noted above, speaks of a father's characteristic anxiety over his daughter's giving birth, and his eager efforts to bring the midwife. The sixteenth book of Tacitus' *Annales* tells of two daughters, Antistia Pollitta and Servilia, who repaid paternal affection by sharing death with their fathers under Nero's reign of terror: Tacitus describes Servilia's father, Barea Soranus, as pleading at his trial to separate his daughter's case from his own—on the grounds that her only crime was too much family affection—and unsuccessfully trying to embrace her. Last, just as the younger Pliny expresses sympathy for Fundanus on his daughter's passing, so he mourns the death of his friend Julius Avitus by observing that Avitus left a daughter whom he had only a short time before begun to rear, and who now was left "without experience of her father" (*ignaram patris*).[44]

---

[44] Seneca, *Epistles* 117.30; Tacitus, *Annales* 16.10-11, 30-32.2; Pliny, *Epistles* 5.16, 8.23.7-8. I owe the Seneca and second Pliny reference to V. French. Of interest, too, is Tacitus' account, at *Annales* 4.22.1, of Lucius Apronius' prosecution of his son-in-law Plautius Silvanus

Further proof of the importance persistently ascribed to the role of elite Roman daughter during the classical period may be discerned in the value accorded daughters' husbands—often by fathers with sons of their own—throughout this same span of time. Valerius Maximus' account of how seriously Julius Caesar viewed his relationship of father-in-law to Pompey belongs to a wealth of passages by Latin authors attesting to the general Roman acknowledgment that the marriage of Caesar's daughter to Pompey had forged a special bond between the two men—one which they shamefully desecrated by their eventual clash in civil conflict. Probably the earliest of these passages occurs in the last line of Catullus 29, where the two, both at this time alive, are addressed as "father-in-law and son-in-law" (*socer generque*) and asked why they have "destroyed everything." Probably the best known appears in the sixth book of Vergil's *Aeneid*: there Vergil also has Anchises refer to the two, long dead by the time of the *Aeneid*'s composition, as *socer* and *gener* when adumbrating the details of the civil war they were to wage a millennium after their sighting by Aeneas in the underworld.[45] Caesar, moreover, was himself greatly valued as *gener* by his final father-in-law Calpurnius Piso. While lashing out in invective against Piso, Cicero even assumed Piso's support of his daugh-

---

after the violent death of his daughter Apronia; Tacitus later notes (6.30.2) that Apronius' army in Germany was warmly disposed toward another son-in-law, Gnaeus Cornelius Lentulus Gaetulicus, presumably because he had proven a better husband to Apronius' daughter.

[45] Catullus 29.24; Vergil, *Aeneid* 6.830-831; cf. also Propertius 3.11.33-38; Lucan 1.289-290; and Martial 9.70.3-4. As Gruen, *The Last Generation of the Roman Republic* (Berkeley, Los Angeles, and London, 1974) 453, reminds us, when Pompey wed Julia in 59 B.C., Caesar named him as principal heir to his estate; Julia's death provoked no change in the contract, and Caesar did not cut Pompey out of his will until the outbreak of civil war.

ter's husband to justify cruelly casting Caesar's conduct in Piso's teeth. Piso's esteem for Caesar was, however, most vividly displayed after Caesar's assassination, when Piso insisted on a public funeral for his son-in-law.[46]

At 62.58 Catullus notes that marriage at the proper season makes a girl not only more dear to a husband but also less burdensome to a parent; he thus joins Ovid in pointing up the importance elite Roman fathers placed on obtaining husbands for their daughters. Indeed, when Cicero enumerates—at *De Oratore* 3.33.133—various concerns and business matters about which an orator might, because of his worldly knowledge, be asked for advice, he first cites finding a husband for a daughter, then purchasing and running a farm. Yet, at the same time, sources testify to the existence of a general Roman paternal concern about daughters' husbands and their personal welfare: by the late first century B.C., it would seem, display of solicitude for *generi* had been elevated to a time-honored tradition by the behavior of many earlier Roman *soceri*. The father of the "grass widows" in Plautus' *Stichus* frets over the long absence of his sons-in-law and welcomes them fondly on their return. Plutarch and Valerius Maximus report that Lucius Aemilius Paullus so prized the military efforts of his son-in-law Q. Aelius Tubero in the fighting against Perseus as to reward him with a heavy bowl of precious metal— whereas he only permitted his own sons to take the king's books. Plutarch also reports close ties between

---

[46] For Caesar and Piso, see in particular Appian, *Bella Civilia* 2.135-136; Suetonius, *Divus Julius* 21-22.1, 83.1; R. Nisbet, *Cicero: In L. Calpurnium Pisonem* (Oxford, 1961) vi, xiv-xvii (which argues that Cicero's "uncontrolled onslaught on Piso is in part a calculated thrust at Caesar") and chapters 59-61 (especially 59, with its *apud generum soceri*); Plutarch, *Caesar* 14.4-5. For a similar alliance between Pompey and his final father-in-law Q. Metellus Scipio, see Gruen, *Last Generation*, 154-155.

Tiberius Gracchus and his father-in-law Appius Claudius Pulcher; Valerius Maximus describes his model of
supreme Roman felicity, Q. Caecilius Metellus Macedonicus, consul in 146 and 143 B.C., as laid to rest by
his *filii* and *generi*, and cites his daughters' fruitful marriages along with his three consular sons as crowning
rewards of his life. The existence of a taboo enjoining
Roman fathers from bathing naked with their sons or
sons-in-law, and of a ban on gift-giving between Roman
fathers–in-law and sons-in-law should not escape our
attention either. No less importantly, Catullus' statement at 72.4 that he loves his mistress Lesbia "not as a
casual girlfriend, but as a father cherishes his sons and
sons-in-law" clearly points to the affection generally
presumed to exist for daughters' husbands among the
classical Roman elite in the republican era.[47]

Testimony about the early imperial period documents
the importance accorded the tie of father-in-law and son-

[47] For Cicero's list, see S. M. Treggiari, "Consent to Roman Marriage: Some Aspects of Law and Reality," *Classical Views* 26, n.s.1
(1982) 34-44. On Antipho's fretting over his *generi*, see *Stichus* 137-
138; for his welcome to them, *Stichus* 505-565. For Paullus and
Tubero, see Plutarch, *Aemilius Paullus* 28.6-7 and Valerius Maximus
4.4.9; for Paullus and his other son-in-law Cato, also an admired
co-fighter in the battle against Perseus (after which he wed Paullus'
daughter), see Plutarch, *Cato Major* 20.7-8. For Appius Claudius
Pulcher and Tiberius Gracchus, see Plutarch, *Tiberius Gracchus* 4.1-
3, 9.1, 13.1. For Metellus Macedonicus, see Valerius Maximus 7.1.1;
for his descendants, see Table III. For the taboo on nude bathing by
men with sons and sons-in-law, see Plutarch, *Cato Major* 20.6, and
Quaestiones Romanae 40 as well as Cicero, *De Officiis* 1.35.129. For
the ban on gift-giving between fathers-in-law and sons-in-law, see
Plutarch, *Quaestiones Romanae* 8. That the classical Latin language
declined, and persisted in declining, the nouns *socer* and *gener* iden-
tically might also suggest a fixed view of these two familial roles as
closely related and complementary (versus, for example, those of
father-in-law and daughter-in-law, or like those of mother-in-law
and daughter-in-law, *socrus* and *nurus*); for an unsuccessful effort to
update *socer* into *socerus*, see Plautus, *Menaechmi* 957.

in-law in that era. Augustus managed to make his chosen successors—Marcellus, Agrippa, and Tiberius—his
daughter's husbands, and the later Claudius married his
daughter Octavia to his adopted son and successor Nero.
One should note, too, Tacitus' description of the condemned Thrasea Paetus as rejoicing immediately before
his death because his son-in-law Helvidius Priscus was
merely banned from Italy, and as leading Helvidius into
his bedroom to witness the slashing of his veins. Although at *Annales* 15.3-25 Tacitus characterizes Caesennius Paetus as a poor general in the east under Nero,
this Paetus became Vespasian's first governor of Syria—
presumably because he had wed Vespasian's daughter;
at *Historiae* 1.13 Tacitus reports that rumors had accounted for the consul Vinius' support of Otho by naming them as prospective *gener ac socer*. Tacitus' own tribute to his father-in-law, Agricola, is notable in this context,
as Tacitus represents himself as no less bereaved than
his wife on her father's death, and as no less grieved
than she over her separation from Agricola during the
four years which preceded it. Finally, the younger Pliny's letter recommending the philosopher Euphrates to
Attius Clemens (1.10.8) notes to the credit of Euphrates'
father-in-law Pompeius Julianus that he chose a *gener*
outstanding for learning rather than rank; Pliny's letter
to Julius Genitor, 3.11, refers to Artemidorus' honor in
being chosen as a son-in-law by Gaius Musonius.[48]

[48] For Augustus and his *generi*, see *Res Gestae Divi Augusti* 21.1
(Marcellus); *Consolatio ad Liviam* 67-68 (Marcellus and Agrippa);
Velleius Paterculus 2.99.2; and chapter six below. For Nero as *gener*,
see Tacitus, *Annales* 12.3.2, 9, 58.1; Suetonius, *Divus Claudius* 27.2
and *Nero* 7.2. For Thrasea Paetus and Helvidius Priscus, see Tacitus,
Annales 16.34-35. Both E. Weinrib, "The Family Connections of
M. Livius Drusus Libo," *Harvard Studies in Classical Philology* 72
(1967) 263, and Syme, "The Historian Servilius Nonianus," *Hermes*
92 (1964) 416 = *Ten Studies in Tacitus* (Oxford, 1970) 100, also

Our sources do not represent close bonds between Roman father-in-law and son-in-law as invariably accompanied by paternal solicitude for the woman who linked the two men. But that the woman even served as a kindred link in such circumstances points to the centrality of her role, if not the importance of her person, to this bond; this central role, moreover, may well have encouraged her father to value her more highly. As sources do not speak of Caesar's fondness for his daughter before her marriage to Pompey, one gets the impression that Caesar's emotional attachments to Julia intensified after the union, and Julia's childbirth-related death. The birth of offspring to daughters as a result of their marriages may well have played no small part in intensifying paternal solicitude, love, and pride: such is implied by Catullus 68.119, referring to the daughter's long awaited child as *carum* to his maternal grandfather; by Seneca's portrayal of the father anxious about his daughter's parturition; and by Valerius Maximus' juxtaposed references to the marriages and offspring of the blessed Metellus Macedonicus' daughters. Were special affection for daughter by father to have been evinced before her marriage, the centrality of her role to the *socer-gener* bond would have been expected to help strengthen that, affinal, bond emotionally: Hortensius may have had such

suggest that Thrasea had taken the *cognomen* of his own father-in-law, Caecina Paetus, as his *agnomen* in a signal act of *pietas*. For Caesennius Paetus as governor of Syria in A.D. 70-72, see Josephus, *Jewish Wars* 7.59; for his marriage to Flavia Sabina, ILS 995. For Tacitus and Agricola, see *Agricola* 45.3-5. I owe the observation on Caesennius Paetus to K. G. Wallace; she has also called to my notice a suggestion made by G. B. Townend in "Some Flavian Connections," *JRS* 51 (1961) 54-61: namely, that Q. Petillius Cerealis, characterized by Tacitus at *Historiae* 4.71-79, 5.14-26, as insufficiently attentive to his military responsibilities, and yet consul in A.D. 70 and 74, was Vespasian's *gener* as well.

an expectation when he asked the younger Cato for Porcia's hand; its desired outcome is fictively dramatized in Antipho's warm wishes for his *generi* at lines 505ff. of Plautus' *Stichus*. The fact remains, however, that in this situation an elite daughter merely served as a link, whose interests and needs might well be ignored and submerged in favor of her father's and husband's; it will warrant further consideration later, in connection with Roman ideals of daughterly conduct toward fathers.[49]

Last, Catullus' use of an aged man's reaction when his daughter gives birth to a son as an illustration of profound human joy and Valerius Maximus' citation of Metellus Macedonicus' good fortune for merely having held his daughters' offspring in his arms indicate that Roman elite fathers highly valued the children of their daughters—and thus point to the centrality of the daughter role to yet another, blood rather than affinal, bond.

[49] For the argument that elite Roman men tended to regard the kinswomen whom they married to (and to cement alliances with) political associates as mere "political assets" and evinced "no concern for any feelings they might have," see, for example, J. P. Hallett, "The Role of Women in Roman Elegy: Counter Cultural Feminism," *Arethusa* 6 (1973) 107, 110. That our ancient sources so rarely concern themselves with the feelings of the women in question is itself strong support for such a view. At the same time the customary silence of ancient authors on this matter militates against much knowledge about men such as Cicero who might at times take their kinswomen's feelings into account. For Cicero's sensitivity to Tullia's wishes in the choice of her third husband, see Carp, "Two Matrons," 196-197, and Treggiari, "Consent to Roman Marriage," 41. Treggiari also argues, on 40, that by the second century B.C. the consent of a dependent child was legally necessary to a father's arrangement of a marriage of that child. Yet she additionally observes, on 39, that a daughter's willingness to abide by her father's decision does not prove that she was consulted (or her feelings considered) in the first place. And on 36 Treggiari remarks that the language describing marriage "emphasises the woman's inactive role. Her father betrothes her, *despondet*; she is *desponsa* or *desponsata* . . . A woman is given in marriage—*in matrimonium collocare*"—by someone else.

These two passages additionally serve as a reminder that
upper-class Roman males were lucky to live long enough
for their daughters to make them grandfathers, particularly during the upheavals and carnage of the late republican era. Sources tell of few aristocratic men in this
period who witnessed their daughters' motherhood.
Cicero does, however, report at *Brutus* 212 that the orator L. Crassus, consul in 95 B.C., adopted one of his
daughter's sons by P. Cornelius Scipio Nasica. At 239
of the same work he remarks that Manius Acilius Glabrio, consul in 95 B.C., was trained expertly in oratory
by his maternal grandfather Quintus Mucius Scaevola;
at 263 he identifies Gaius Sicinius, tribune of the plebs
in 76 B.C., as a grandson through the daughter (*ex filia
nepos*) of Quintus Pompeius the censor. Asconius states
that Cicero's supporter Titus Annius Milo was adopted
by his maternal grandfather as well. The tributes paid
maternal grandfathers and ascendants on late republican
coins—such as Q. Pompeius Rufus' celebration of his
mother's father Sulla as well as his paternal grandfather,
Sulla's co-consul in 88 B.C.—warrant notice too. For
they also testify to a Roman cultural emphasis at this
time on these blood ties through daughters and to the
fact that these ties were important to the descendants as
well as to their maternal kinsmen.[50]

[50] For Milo's adoption, see Asconius 47 K-S. For the coinage issued
by Rufus, tribune of the plebs in 52 B.C., see Crawford, *Republican
Coinage*, 1.456 (n.434), who cites as parallels n. 480/1 (p. 487), also
celebrating Sulla, and the inscription of *C. Memmius C.f. Sullae Felicis
n.*, discussed by Wiseman, "Lucius Memmius and his Family," *CQ*
n.s. 17 (1967) 164-167. For other contemporary coins honoring maternal male antecedents, see Crawford, n. 346 (issued by C. Marcius
Censorinus to honor his putative paternal ancestor King Ancus Marcius and Marcius' maternal ancestor King Numa Pompilius) and n.
433 (p. 455) (Brutus' tribute in 54 B.C. to his maternal male antecedent
C. Servilius Ahala and paternal male ancestor Lucius Junius Brutus).
For the relationship between Numa and Ancus Marcius, see also

Evidence also suggests that several important figures
under the more peaceful empire sought to be closely
associated with their daughters' children, to the extent
that some of these children even received the *nomina* of
these maternal grandfathers rather than those of their
own fathers. The emperor Augustus adopted, and publicly took pride in, his daughter's two elder sons; his
daughter's elder daughter was given the name Julia, and
hence represented his Julian clan as had her mother before her. We might also in this context recall Poppaeus
Sabinus, consul in A.D. 9, whose daughter's daughter,
named Poppaea Sabina after him, married both a future
and current Roman emperor. One scholar deduces that
the Servilia condemned to death in A.D. 66, and so touch-
ingly portrayed by Tacitus in *Annales* 16, was named
after her mother's father, the historian Servilius Nonianus; consul in A.D. 35 and dead in A.D. 59, Servilius,
too, seems to have named his own daughter, Considia,
after her maternal grandfather. By portraying the deceased Cremutius Cordus as reassuring his daughter that
he and her son are together in heaven, Seneca also implies that the Roman elite of this era expected a woman's
father to care deeply for any of her children he might
have the good fortune to encounter.[51]

Probably the most striking testimony to the valuation

---

below, n. 53; for Brutus and Servilius Ahala, see chapter four below,
n. 14.

[51] For Augustus' pride in his daughter's (and Agrippa's) sons, Gaius
and Lucius Caesar, see, for example, *Res Gestae Divi Augusti* 14, 22;
for Poppaeus Sabinus and his daughter's daughter, see Tacitus, *Annales* 13.45.1 (*sed nomen materni avi sumpserat*, "but she took the name
of her maternal grandfather"). For this Servilia and Servilius, see
Syme, *Ten Studies*, 95-96, 100-101; for Cordus and Marcia, see Seneca, *Ad Marciam De Consolatione* 25.2-26. At *Epistles* 3.3.1-2 the
younger Pliny also expresses to Corellia Hispulla his desire that her
son take after her own father, although he does admit the excellence
of the boy's father, paternal uncle, and paternal grandfather.

of elite Roman daughters, the cultural centrality of the daughter role, and the emphasis on kin ties through daughters may, however, be found in the classical Romans' own accounts of their most remote and hallowed past. None of the writers who provide these accounts in fact antedates the classical period; hence the notions, values and conduct which they ascribe to the days of Rome's monarchy and early republic primarily constitute further evidence for filiafocality in classical Roman times. But that these stories purport to present the realities of Rome's first and formative years places them in another category of evidence as well, one deserving of separate discussion.

The Roots of Roman Filiafocality

We have characterized the Romans and the upper-class Roman family of the classical era as generally tradition-minded. We have, moreover, now seen that daughters, the role of daughter, and bonds between Roman men and kindred related to them through their daughters continued to be valued, and portrayed as valued, from the late third century B.C. to the early second century A.D.—a period in which Rome evolved into a cosmopolitan city at the head of a vast Mediterranean empire, and Rome's government evolved from a representative and increasingly unstable republic to a highly bureaucratized monarchy; the persistence of daughter valuation thus indicates the strength of another tradition through the classical period. Yet one might legitimately ask whether this particular tradition itself survives, as do so many Roman practices and beliefs, from such earlier, pre-classical times. We have seen earlier that thinkers of the matriarchalist persuasion would argue that certain aspects of well-born women's position in the classical period should be viewed as vestiges of Roman culture in the monarchic era; less tendentious scholars would also discern patriarchal survivals from Rome's monarchic past in her later culture.[52] More importantly, the Romans of classical times themselves assumed daughters to have been central figures in Roman society from its very start, and thus believed that their own valuation of daughters, the role of daughter, and ties of blood and marriage through daughters belonged to a long-standing cultural tradition.

For the traditions about this earliest period, the legends about Rome in the years from 753 to 510 B.C., accord the role of father's daughter immense emphasis. First of all, authors relating these legends uniformly describe daughters as crucial individuals in determining, and strengthening, royal succession. Both Livy and Ovid, for example, state that Romulus (and Remus) asserted claims to kingship because their mother, a Vestal Virgin named Rhea Silvia and/or Ilia, was daughter of Numitor, rightful ruler of Alba Longa, who had been wrongly deposed by his brother Amulius. Ennius apparently viewed this Ilia as Aeneas' own *filia*—and followed the earlier Naevius in this regard. Plutarch reports that Rome's second king, Numa Pompilius, was married to the daughter of the Sabine leader Titus Tatius, who joined his people with those of Romulus during the latter's reign. Several authors assert that Rome's fourth king, Ancus Marcius, who was later alleged to be the ancestor of Julius Caesar's paternal grandmother, was also son of Numa Pompilius' daughter and her husband.[53] We hear from Livy and Dionysius of Halicar-

52 E.g. R.E.A. Palmer, *The Archaic Community of the Romans* (Cambridge, 1970) 197-202.
53 For Romulus' (and Remus') claims to kingship through their maternal grandfather, see Livy 1.3.11 (*fratris filiae Rheae Silvia . . . spem partus ademit*, "he removed the hope of issue from his brother's daughter Rhea Silvia") and 6.2 (*cum avum regem salutassent*, "when they had hailed their grandfather as king"). For Ennius' and Naevius'

nassus that Rome's sixth king, Servius Tullius, married
the daughter of his predecessor, Tarquinius Priscus; the
same authors state that Rome's seventh king, Tarquinius
Superbus, obtained the monarchy as a result of efforts
by his own wife, Servius Tullius' daughter, who had
earlier disposed of her husband's former wife (her own
elder sister) and her former husband (Superbus' brother).[54]

No less importantly, various sources have it that the

depiction of Romulus' mother as Aeneas' daughter, see Servius, *ad
Aeneidem* 6.777, 1.273; the lines quoted by Cicero, *De Divinatione*,
1.20.40 = Ennius 35-51 Vahlen, especially 45 "o daughter" (*o gnata*);
the lines quoted by Charisius, *Grammatici Latini* 1.90.26K = Ennius
55 Vahlen, "Ilia bright granddaughter" (*Ilia dia nepos*). See, too,
Plutarch, *Romulus* 2-3, and Dionysius of Halicarnassus 1.76.3-84 (as
well as chapter one above, n. 23). Dionysius even claims at 1.79.2
that Ilia's paternal uncle Amulius spared her life only because his
own daughter, who loved her cousin (as her cousin loved her) like
a sister, begged him to do so. For Numa's claim to the throne
through his wife's father, see Plutarch, *Numa* 3.6-7. For Ancus Marcius and his claim, see Cicero, *De Re Publica* 2.18.33 (*Numae Pompilii
nepos ex filia* . . . , "grandson through a daughter of King Numa
Pompilius"); Livy 1.32.1; Plutarch, *Numa* 21 and *Coriolanus* 1.1;
Seneca, *Epistles* 108.30; Dionysius of Halicarnassus 3.35. See also
Table VII.

[54] For Servius Tullius' and Tarquinius' marriages to their predecessors' daughters, see Livy 1.39.4-5 (*cum quaereretur gener Tarquinio
. . . filiamque ei suam rex despondit*, "when a son-in-law was being
sought for Tarquin . . . the king betrothed his daughter to him"),
42.1, 46ff.; Dionysius of Halicarnassus 3.72.7, 4.3.4, 28. Cf. also
Livy 1.40, on the decision of Ancus Marcius' exiled sons to assassinate Tarquinius Priscus rather than his chosen successor, Servius
Tullius, on the grounds that—should Servius be killed—Tarquin
would certainly choose another son-in-law to be his heir. For the
genealogy of the Tarquins, see T. N. Gantz, "The Tarquin Dynasty," *Historia* 24 (1975) 539-554, and Table VIII. Gantz, arguing
that our sources consistently represent Rome's early Etruscan rulers
as a dynasty, who keep power within the family, postulates the early
death of Priscus' son to explain Servius Tullius' succession; he would
identify this son as the Cneve Tarchunies Rumach described on the
François tomb as killed by Marce Camitlnas (552ff.). On Servius
Tullius' daughter, see also chapter one, n. 37, this chapter, n. 10,
and below.

embryonic Roman nation itself managed to incorporate once-hostile Sabine elements only because a group of daughters (the raped Sabine women) and the appeal of common male descendants (their children by their Roman abductors) were able to reconcile warring fathers and sons-in-law. Livy's dramatic description at 1.13.1–4 of the women's attempts to stop a fierce battle between Romans and Sabines merits quotation as evidence for both the emotional dimensions with which the story invested the father-daughter bond and the larger, sociopolitical impact of this bond in these tales:

Then the Sabine women . . . dared to throw themselves amid the flying weapons . . . to quell angers, begging their fathers on one side, their husbands on the other, not to sprinkle themselves—as fathers-in-law and sons-in-law (*soceri generique*)—with impious blood, and not to besmirch, through the slaying of kinsmen, their issue, the grandsons of one group and the freeborn offspring of the other. "If you, fathers, regret the connections by marriage between you and the Romans, if you, husbands, regret the marriage itself, turn your anger against us; we are the cause of war, we are responsible for the wounds and deaths of our husbands and parents. We shall prefer to die rather than live without either of you, widowed or orphaned." The situation moved the men . . . there was silence and a sudden hush: thereupon the leaders proceeded to make a treaty.

At *Fasti* 3.215ff., Ovid concludes his even more dramatic description of this battle—as he portrays the toddler children of the Sabine women as calling out and running to their maternal grandfathers and thus stopping the fray—with no less memorable words: "They praise and embrace their daughters, and each grandfather carried his grandson on his shield: for a shield this was a sweeter use."

In several other stories about regal Rome, moreover, we encounter several daughters who betray fathers and male blood kin by siding against them with a male sexual partner, actual or potential: these women are characterized as politically important individuals meriting the worst punishments possible. The first of such daughters figures in the tales of Rome's struggles with the Sabines and is portrayed by Livy, Propertius, and other sources as the polar opposite of the raped, self-abnegating and conciliatory Sabine women: this is Tarpeia, maiden daughter of the Roman commander Spurius Tarpeius, and by some accounts a Vestal Virgin. Desire for gold that Titus Tatius offered, or for Titus Tatius himself, led her to treason against the Romans by handing over the Capitoline citadel to the Sabine forces; the Sabines themselves, however, slew her as soon as they had attained their object, perhaps—Livy states—as an example to all traitors.[55]

A similar figure is the maiden sister of the three Horatii, slain by her sole surviving brother after she had publicly mourned for her fiancé, one of the three Alban Curiatii whom her brothers had killed in single combat. To be sure, both Livy and Dionysius of Halicarnassus claim that this brother was compelled to atone for his act ritually by passing under a small beam, the so-called *sororium tigillum*. Nevertheless, Livy asserts that his own father movingly and affectively defended the son's sororicide on the grounds that "he judged his daughter to have been killed rightly: had things been otherwise he would have exercised his father's right and killed his son." Dionysius, moreover, relates that his father re-

---

[55] Livy 1.11.5-9 (*Huius filiam virginem auro corrumpit Tatius . . .* , "Tatius corrupted his maiden daughter with gold"); Propertius 4.4; Ovid, *Fasti* 1.261-262; Dionysius of Halicarnassus 2.38; Valerius Maximus 9.6.1. On the two versions of this legend, see Ogilvie, 74-75, and W. Burkert, *Structure and History in Greek Mythology and Ritual* (Berkeley and Los Angeles, 1979) 76ff.

garded his son's act as a glorious and becoming deed, refused to admit his daughter's corpse into his house and ancestral tomb, and, on the day of her death, entertained his relations at a splendid banquet. He goes on to state that this father spoke up at his son's trial to blame his daughter for provoking her brother and to declare himself the proper judge of his private misfortunes, since he was the father of both.[56]

Servius Tullius' daughter of course serves as a further illustration of this same motif. Livy does not merely motivate her departure from Rome, upon her husband's eventual overthrow, by having his hero Lucius Junius Brutus first recall, for the Roman people, her heinous behavior at her father's murder. He does so with a phrase—*invecta corpori patris nefandoque vehiculo filia*, "a daughter driven over her father's body in a sacrilegious carriage"—in which the kinship terms *pater* and *filia* resound prominently. Ovid also uses kinship terms with powerful dramatic effect in portraying Tullia's carriage ride on the street where her father's corpse lay: *filia carpento patrios initura penates*, "his daughter in a coach en route to her father's home." Livy, as we have seen, even concludes his account of the Tarquins' expulsion from Rome by depicting how Tullia fled from her house amid curses, which invoked the furies of parents, uttered by both men and women.[57]

[56] Livy 1.24ff.; Dionysius of Halicarnassus 3.7ff. At 3.13.4 Dionysius also portrays the Horatii and Curiatii triplets as first cousins, whose maternal grandfather, an Alban named Sicinius, had wed his twin daughters to a Roman Horatius and an Alban Curiatius: hence his Horatia is also torn between agnate and cognate blood ties. See also Ogilvie, 114ff., and Pomeroy, *GWWS*, 152-153.

[57] Livy 1.59.10-13 (also discussed in chapter one above, n. 37); Ovid, *Fasti* 6.603ff. Cf. also Valerius Maximus 9.11.1, which cites Tullia's act as bringing eternal infamy not only upon herself but also upon the street which she befouled with her criminal deed. Cf., too,

Conversely, writers on this early monarchic period portray women's loyalty to fathers as heroic female conduct and assign great sociopolitical importance to such devoted daughters. The Sabine women are represented by Livy as willing to die themselves, taking the blame for their own rapes, rather than live without either their fathers or their husbands and as emphasizing their special bonds with the former by addressing them first and contemplating their loss last. But the most vivid and memorable example of such a daughter and her father occurs in the much-told story of Lucretia. According to Livy, Lucretia, when raped by Tarquinius Superbus' son at swordpoint, immediately sent a message to her father Spurius Lucretius Tricipitinus, in Rome, and her husband Lucius Tarquinius Collatinus, then at Ardea, in order to inform them that an unspeakable catastrophe had taken place. To be sure, the conversation which Livy claims ensued between her, these two men, and their two friends involves her admission of guilt initially to her husband; Livy immediately follows his description of her self-stabbing with the words: "her husband and father cried out." Still, Livy represents the speech delivered to the Roman people by Lucius Junius Brutus after Lucretia's death as stressing the bereavement of her *father* ("about Lucretius Tricipitinus' loss of a child, for whom the cause of his daughter's death was more unworthy and tragic than the death itself"); he describes the Romans who viewed her publicly displayed corpse as especially moved by her father's grief (*movet . . . patris maestitia*). Nothing is even said by Livy about the plight of, or about sympathy evinced for, Lucretia's husband. Indeed, Collatinus does not figure in Livy's narrative

---

Livy's description of Tullia as "maddened, with the furies of her husband and sister driving her on" when she drove over her father's corpse (1.48.7).

again after Lucretia's suicide until the last three words
of Book I, where Livy notes that he and Lucretia's avenger,
Lucius Junius Brutus, were named, in 509 B.C., Rome's
first two consuls.[58]

Other sources resemble Livy in stressing Lucretia's
father and in paying far less attention to Lucretia's husband. At *Fasti* 2.815 Ovid describes Lucretia as "summoning her aged father along with her faithful spouse,"
mentions her father before her husband again at 821 and
829, and in 831 depicts her falling at her father's feet
when she dies, bloodsoaked. At 4.66ff. Dionysius of
Halicarnassus claims that the raped Lucretia went straight
to her father's house in Rome, fell to her knees as a
suppliant, requested that he send for his friends and
kinsmen to hear her confession, and embraced and entreated him before dying. Her father's clasping of—and
attempts to revive—her corpse, Dionysius says, moved
those watching to vow their mortal enmity to Tarqui-
nian tyranny; although Dionysius acknowledges Collatinus' grief at 4.70, he accords it little notice elsewhere.

What is more, the works of Livy, Dionysius, and
others on the formative years of the Roman republic

[58] Livy 1.58-60. As Gantz, "The Tarquin Dynasty," 545-546, points
out, Lucretia's husband L. Tarquinius Collatinus is a great-grandson
of Demaratus (father of Tarquinius Priscus) and third cousin to
his wife's rapist Sextus (as well as the other Tarquin princes): hence
our sources may have minimized his involvement in this episode so
as to play down the fact that he is (agnatically) a Tarquin, "current
representative of the other side of the family." Yet Collatinus is,
through his membership in the Tarquin family, also third cousin to
his wife's defender (and his later co-consul) Lucius Junius Brutus,
himself son of Superbus' sister (and, according to Gantz' reconstruction of the family, grandson of Priscus' son). As these connections
are not used to explain Collatinus' alliance with Brutus, it appears
that Collatinus' lack of a blood tie to Lucretia rather than his blood
bond with the Tarquins accounts for his minor role in this drama.
For the Tarquin family, see Table VIII.

also contain stories about valued, virtuous, and heroic
daughters, stories similar to those on monarchic Rome
which portray such daughters as devoted as well as dear
to their fathers and as of substantial sociopolitical significance. Shortly after the beginning of Book II, for
example, Livy narrates the tale of Cloelia. A maiden
held captive by the Etruscans in 508 B.C., she led a
number of her fellow female hostages to safety by swim-
ming across the Tiber; her Etruscan captor Lars Porsenna ultimately rewarded her for her courage by granting her permission to choose other, male, hostages for
release. While daughterly virtue and fathers do not figure
in Livy's version of the legend, they do in that of Dionysius. He claims that the maidens managed their escape
by asking their male guards to withdraw while they
bathed and not look upon their nakedness; he portrays
the maidens as successfully countering a charge that they
had broken their fathers' former oaths by escaping with
the assertion that they had escaped without their fathers'
orders; he alleges that the maidens' fathers had subsequently honored Cloelia by erecting a bronze equestrian
statue on the Sacred Way.[59]

At *Natural History* 34.28ff., when ascribing an antique
origin to the practice of erecting equestrian statues at
Rome, the elder Pliny also remarks upon Cloelia's statue:
noting that it represented her as clad in a toga; observing
as well that statues were not voted to Lucretia and Lucius
Junius Brutus even though they had expelled the kings
on account of whom Cloelia had been taken hostage.
Yet Pliny then proceeds to consider how Cloelia's statue
had been funded; in so doing, he refers to a different

---

[59] Livy 2.13.6-11; Dionysius of Halicarnassus 5.32.4-35.2. The latter refers to Valeria, daughter of the consul Publicola, as merely one
of the female hostages: on this Valeria, see further below. For other
ancient treatments of this tale, see also Ogilvie, 267-268.

account of female heroism associated with this same, early republican episode and identifies the heroine in question as daughter of a distinguished father. For in this connection he cites Annius Fetialis' statement that an equestrian statue which had stood opposite the temple of Jupiter Stator in the forecourt of Tarquinius Superbus' palace had represented Valeria, daughter of the consul Publicola; he adds that she alone had escaped and swum across the Tiber, the other hostages having been sent to Porsenna and disposed of by Tarquin's treachery. At chapter 14 of his *De Muliebribus Virtutibus* (and at chapter 18 and following of his *Publicola*), Plutarch also refers to Valeria, daughter of this consul, as numbering among the Etruscans' female hostages and claims that she escaped from her captors; he, however, expresses uncertainty over whether an equestrian statue of a woman near the Sacred Way represents Cloelia or Valeria.

More memorably (and uniformly), several authors relate the story of the humble Verginius and his maiden daughter, whom Verginius slew rather than have her submit to the lust of the decemvir Appius Claudius, and whose death in 450 B.C., like Lucretia's a half-century earlier, ended the political tyranny her would-be seducer represented. Livy's account exploits the fact that Verginia, though still a schoolgirl, was betrothed to and defended by a popular ex-tribune named Lucius Icilius. Still, Livy places greater emphasis on the efforts made by her male blood kin to protect her honor. These men include her maternal grandfather (*avus*) and maternal uncle, both called P. Numitorius; both, however, yield center stage to her devoted father. Verginius is described, in a speech by his prospective son-in-law, as intending to raise the Roman army on behalf of his daughter and only child (*pro unica filia*). Livy depicts Verginius as clad in rags, and thronged by a group of wailing matrons, when guiding Verginia, herself dressed in mourning, to the tribunal. Verginius is later said to have cited a "father's grief" (*patrio dolore*) when requesting permission to remove Verginia from the crowd (and slay her); he is said to have cried, as he stabbed her, "In this one way which I am able, daughter, I make you free." So, too, Livy portrays Verginius' passionate speech to his fellow soldiers, in which he avowed that "his daughter's life would have been dearer to him than his own had she been able to live as a free and chaste woman," as ultimately inspiring the Romans to avenge him, and overthrow the *decemviri*. While Icilius and Verginia's *avunculus* P. Numitorius are reported by Livy to have joined Verginius on the next list of tribunes, Livy accords the former's bereavement no further mention. The sentimentality evinced at another point in Livy's narrative, presumably an effort to characterize Verginia's story as, like Tullia's, a tragedy, merits notice as well. At 3.58.11 he concludes his account of how all those guilty in Verginia's death suffered by stating that only after the punishment of these men did her ghost fully rest. Dionysius of Halicarnassus displays similar sentimentality at 11.37.4-5, where he says that Verginia clung closely to her father, fainting and sobbing before he led her off to a butcher's shop and plunged a knife into her vitals.[60]

Finally, at 6.34 Livy offers yet another daughter-doting father of early republican vintage, the patrician Fa-

[60] Livy 3.44ff.; Dionysius of Halicarnassus 11.28ff. See also Cicero, *De Re Publica* 2.63, and Diodorus Siculus 12.24. Dionysius of Halicarnassus' account also assigns a central role to Verginia's maternal uncle, P. Numitorius, and mentions Numitorius' son by the same name; since he says nothing about Verginia's maternal grandfather Numitorius, it is possible that Livy has confused Verginia's maternal grandfather and uncle with her maternal uncle and his son. See, too, Ogilvie, 476-479, 508-509.

bius Ambustus. According to Livy, Ambustus' role in supporting plebeian efforts to attain high political office had helped their cause succeed. Ambustus had become the plebeians' advocate in 377 B.C., Livy claims, because his younger daughter had wed Gaius Licinius Stolo, one of their number. For one day Fabia Minor's father, sensing that she was troubled, gently ascertained that she felt slighted at receiving inferior treatment to that accorded to her elder sister, who had married within their class. Ambustus thereupon determined to right this grievous wrong, and, comforting her, promised his daughter that she would soon enjoy the same honors as her sister.

Roman authors of the classical period, then, do not merely indicate that daughter valuation by fathers, the centrality of the daughter role, and the stress on kindred ties through daughters remained a cultural constant during the 350-odd, changeful years in which they lived and wrote. They also apparently imagined that these phenomena had abided no less persistently throughout the four hundred-odd and equally changeful years following 753 B.C., the traditional date of Rome's founding. Indeed, two stories narrated by Vergil paint filiafocal practice and sentiment as Roman phenomena long before that date: the legend that the Trojans had secured their foothold in Italy through Aeneas' union with King Latinus' daughter, and the tale that Aeneas' warrior-maiden Camilla owed her expertise at fighting to her devoted father's dedication of her in infancy to the goddess Diana.[61]

One cannot, however, simply accept Roman legends about the monarchy and early republic by themselves

[61] For the marriage between Aeneas and Lavinia, see Livy 1.1.9-11; Dionysius of Halicarnassus 1.64 and 70; as well as Vergil, *Aeneid* 7.71-106. For Camilla and her father, see Vergil, *Aeneid* 11.532-566.

as trustworthy evidence for that period. In the first place, the extant authors who retail these legends—unlike those from, and providing testimony on, the classical era cited elsewhere in this discussion—lived at a huge chronological remove from their subject. No authors extant actually witnessed the events and experienced the sentiments of those earliest times. The cultural continuity posited in filiafocal practice and feeling by the Latin literary tradition may therefore merely reflect a moralistic desire to depict Rome's most hallowed past as mirroring her present in one, admirable regard; after all, an author such as Livy explicitly claims, in sections 8-11 of his preface, to be treating Rome's origins in order to provide readers of his own day with examples of inspiring conduct for emulation.

What is more, literary analysis of these, filiafocal, stories alone renders their historicity suspect. Similarities in structure and message between the tale of Lucretia and that of Verginia, and the polar opposition between key details in the story of the traitorous Tarpeia and that of the heroic Cloelia (and/or Valeria) may even suggest that the fabled daughters of the monarchic age were consciously modeled on or against their less shadowy republican counterparts. Some scholars have argued that *all* of these stories are more fiction than fact, based heavily on fifth-century B.C. and Hellenistic Greek drama and romance, and used by Livy in particular merely as dramatic plot devices. Consequently we must look, as we did in our investigation of early Roman father-right, at the corroborative evidence of legal, cultic and linguistic survivals from earliest Roman times so as to determine if these legends even furnish a generally valid representation of the daughter role in the monarchic and early republican eras.[62]

[62] For the view that these legends about the monarchic and early

To be sure, provisions of the *Leges Regiae* guarantee that clients furnish dowries for their patrons' daughters in the event of their patrons' incapacity, and require that Roman fathers rear at least their first-born female children. But these regal laws cannot, as we observed earlier, be automatically accepted as indicative of attitudes from the monarchic era either, since uncertainties abound over their historicity; their testimony to daughter valuation, like the legends about daughters and the role of daughter in Rome's archaic past, may merely be the product of Roman legal imagination in the classical era and thus only reflect beliefs of classical Roman society. Furthermore, our surviving fragments of the more trustworthy Twelve Tables contain no explicit references to daughters or to the role of father's daughter. This body of legal evidence, therefore, appears at first glance to be less helpful on the topic of early Roman filiafocality than it has proven to be on early Roman patriarchy. Nevertheless, one of these laws does apply to women in their role as daughters by stating that the possessions of a woman in agnate guardianship could only be acquired

republican eras are not to be treated as reliable historical accounts, see, for example, E. Pais, *Ancient Legends of Roman History*, transl. M. E. Cosenza (Freeport, N.Y., 1971) 185ff., a work issued in 1905. Pais argues that the Lucretia and Verginia stories both arise out of cults from Rome's neighbor Ardea, cults transplanted to Rome in the second half of the fourth century B.C. (and hence that they merely represent the sentiments of the late fourth and early third centuries B.C.). See, too, A. Alföldi, *Early Rome and the Latins* (Ann Arbor, 1965) 147-153, and A. Momigliano, *Secondo contributo alla storia degli studi classici* (Rome, 1960) 84, cited with approval by Alföldi, 150-151. As noted in (chapter one, n. 36), M. Pallottino, "The Origins of Rome," in D. and F. Ridgway, eds., *Italy Before the Romans: The Iron Age, Orientalizing and Etruscan Periods* (New York, 1979) 216ff., claims that most scholars accept legends about Rome's protagonists and actors as containing at least a core of historical truth; "truthfulness" on this particular matter, however, does not necessarily prove the accuracy of the portrayal of early Rome as valuing daughters and emphasizing the role of daughters.

if she so wished and her guardian agreed; it thus allowed women not in their husbands' *manus* to control property they may have acquired from their fathers. As we have seen, the Twelve Tables' principles of succession also granted daughters and sons equal claims to the estate of an intestate father.[63]

Of additional interest may be the later jurist Gaius' remarks, at *Institutes* 1.111, on another provision in the Twelve Tables; known as the *trinoctium*, "three nights," it allowed a woman to avoid coming under her husband's *manus* by spending three nights each year away from him. Before describing this law, however, Gaius notes:

A wedded woman used to pass into *manus* by *usus* if she had lived with her husband for a year without interruption; because she was technically "held in use" by one year's possession, she passed into her husband's family and occupied the status of a daughter.

Gaius' reference to acquisition of "father's daughter-right" from a husband at this point in his discussion, immediately prior to relating how a woman could avoid her husband's *manus*, and hence the acquisition of "father's daughter right" from him, may well be significant. Such a juxtaposition of topics renders it not unlikely that the text of the actual law in the Twelve Tables on passing into a husband's *manus* through *usus* also acknowledged the "daughterly" legal status of a woman in her husband's *manus*. It is not improbable, either, that

---

[63] For these *Leges Regiae* (also cited in chapter one above, n. 32, and chapter two above, n. 27), see Dionysius of Halicarnassus 2.10.2 and 15.2. For provisions in the Twelve Tables prohibiting the husband of a woman in agnate guardianship from acquiring her possessions without her consent and her guardian's authority, see Gaius, *Institutes* 2.47; for provisions granting offspring of both sexes equal rights to inherit from an intestate father, see Justinian, *Institutes* 2.13.5.

this law also noted a woman's retention of "father's daughter-right" in her family of birth if she did avoid her husband's *manus*.[64]

Now if the mere practice of according a wife in *manus* "father's daughter right" does indeed date back to at least 451-450 B.C., when the Twelve Tables were published, and more probably (as these laws generally codified *existing* practice) even earlier, we may ascribe this practice to a belief of the earliest republican and perhaps late monarchic era in the significance of the father's daughter role. After all, such a law indicates that men's role relative to their female children was deemed important enough to be regarded the role appropriate for men who legally removed their wives from their families of birth, and thus deprived their wives of their rights as their fathers' daughters. We may also posit such a belief, at such a time, from the early republican, and arguably late monarchic, genesis of those practices codified in the Twelve Tables—entitling a woman to keep possessions that she acquired, and to claim inheritance rights, as a daughter. That these practices, and the beliefs apparently underlying them, date back to the late monarchic rather than the early republican era cannot, admittedly, be established. But the marriage formula "Where you are Gaius, I am Gaia," which, by employing the symbol of a common name, likens the role of a woman's husband to that of her father, would seem to warrant reconsideration in this context. For scholars place its origin in remote, monarchic times: should these words have been uttered in the Roman marriage ceremony as early as the regal period, they may indicate that paternal protection

---

[64] On the *trinoctium* see also Aulus Gellius 3.2.12ff.; on the daughter-status of a wife in *manus* see also the discussion of A. C. Bush, *Studies in Roman Social Structure* (Washington, D.C., 1982) 2 n. 15, 84 n. 7.

of daughters was already in that era so valued as to be judged a lifelong *desideratum* for all women; at least they suggest that regal Romans valued the role of father's daughter enough to utilize it as the appropriate model for that of a dependent wife.[65]

The Twelve Tables do make specific reference to the Vestal Virgins. As noted earlier, Gaius reports, at *Institutes* 1.144-145, that these laws exempted the Vestals from male guardianship; in so doing, Roman law rendered them unique among Roman women. It is, to reiterate, the general (and an eminently plausible) consensus of modern scholarship that the Vestals began as the daughters of Rome's priest-king and hence functioned as Rome's archetypal daughter figures. Not only analysis of the Vestal cult but also archaeological excavation of the Vestals' sanctuary points to an origin of the Vestal order before the end of the monarchic period, and hence well before the publication of the Twelve Tables. This legal privilege, therefore, suggests that the role of father's daughter possessed considerable cultural importance among earliest republican Romans, inasmuch as they assigned what were evidently their state's symbolic daughter figures a distinction which rendered these women wholly unlike ordinary Roman daughters in one particular regard. In view of the Vestals' putative beginnings in the monarchic era, such a privilege may even be regarded as a regal survival, perpetuating an earlier belief that the Vestals and their religious "daughterhood" merited public honor. One can, in consequence, securely judge the cult of the Vestals itself, with some

[65] The theory that the Twelve Tables introduced agnate succession (see chapter one above, n. 35) would, of course, make the provisions on agnate responsibility unusual in a body of laws which tend to codify established procedure. Scholars ascribing an origin in monarchic times to the Gaius/Gaia formula include Westrup, *Recherches*, 26; Kajanto, personal correspondence, July 1979.

certainty view the Twelve Tables' exemption of Vestals from guardianship, and tentatively look upon various provisions of the Twelve Tables as evidence for the Roman valuation of and emphasis on the daughter role by the final years of the monarchy. Accordingly, from evidence of this sort one may infer that the notions about daughterhood and its importance reflected in both legends about early Rome and the *Leges Regiae* may well be those of the period which these traditions purport to represent.[66]

Other, linguistic, evidence also allows this inference, Latin kinship terms which reflect notions of an era long before the Roman republic was founded. The most significant pieces of such evidence are the Latin word *avus*, grandfather, and its diminutive *avunculus*, maternal uncle. Romans of the classical era clearly perceived the two words as closely related: Festus even attempts to account for the resemblance between *avus* and *avunculus* by claiming that the latter may occupy the position of the former, and, owing to his consanguinity, be guardian to his sister's daughter. The fact that *avunculus* can only mean a mother's brother would indicate that the word from which it derives originally meant, at least to the earliest Romans, mother's father.[67]

[66] For the thesis that the Vestals originated as the daughters of Rome's early priest-king, see again the works cited above in chapter one, n. 39. The thesis is disputed by such scholars as Latte, *Religionsgeschichte*, and L. A. Holland, *Janus and the Bridge* (Rome, 1961) 304-305. Holland argues that "there was no hereditary kingship at Rome," that no two kings lived in the same place, and that no family could have its own cult imposed upon the whole, diverse, *populus*. Her view, however, rests on an overly literal interpretation and hence a misunderstanding of what early Roman "priest-kingship" is thought to entail. For the construction of the Vestals' sanctuary in pre-republican times, see, for example, the article in *RE*[2] by Reidinger and F. E. Brown, *Origines*, 57-59.

[67] For *avus, nepōs,* and *socer* as Latin forms of the Indo-European *awos (or *HauHos), *nepōs and *swekuros, see, for example, Szeme-

To be sure, some scholars committed to a rigid model of Proto-Indo-European patriarchy have proposed various ingenious and unconvincing explanations to prove that *avus* (and its Indo-European cognates) could only have signified father's father. Some have even endeavored to deny that *avus* initially designated a maternal grandfather by arguing, no more persuasively, for an additional original meaning of "mother's maternal uncle," "maternal grandmother's brother." But the fact that *avus* often refers to a maternal grandfather in classical Latin authors (and never refers to anything but a grandfather), suggests that there is nothing wrong with the more obvious etymology based on the meaning of *avunculus*: indeed, a new study would go so far as to contend that the linguistic ancestor of *avus*, Indo-European *HauHos, denoted both the maternal and paternal grandfathers and the maternal uncle as well.[68]

---

rényi, 47-53, 63-64; the similarity between such nouns and their Indo-European parents argues for their extreme antiquity. For Festus' derivation of *avunculus* from *avus*, see p. 13 Lindsay: *sive avunculus appellatur, quod avi locum obtineat et proximitate tueatur sororis filiam,* "whether he is called '*avunculus*' because he may occupy the place of a grandfather and owing to his close kinship serve as guardian to his sister's daughter."

[68] For the view that *avus* and its cognates referred to the father's father alone, see G. D. Thomson, *Studies in Ancient Greek Society: The Prehistoric Aegean* (New York, 1949) 79ff.; E. Benveniste, *Le vocabulaire des institutions indo-européennes* (Paris, 1969) I.223-235, and R.S.P. Beekes, "Uncle and Nephew," *JIS* 4 (1976) 43-63. For the view that it also signified maternal grandmother's brother (mother's *avunculus*), see most recently Thomson, 79; Benveniste, 226-227; and chapter six, below. For *avus* as maternal grandfather in classical Latin, see J. Bremmer, "Avunculate and Fosterage," *JIS* 4 (1976) 65-77, who points out on 69—with a reference to Livy 1.6.2, *cum avum regem salutassent*—that classical Romans *do* employ *avus* without the adjective *maternus* when referring to maternal grandfathers; with this observation he refutes Benveniste's claim on 226. For *avus* = *maternus avus*, see, for example, such other passages as Cicero, *De Finibus* 4.66 and *Brutus* 239, as well as Livy 1.32.2. Bremmer concludes that

The implications of this linguistic relationship for earliest Roman kinship attitudes are of major import. Most obviously, such a relationship would signify that the Roman maternal uncle was originally regarded as a lesser version of, and a surrogate for, his own father by his sister's—his father's daughter's—children. Furthermore, it allows one to conclude that Roman men were originally identified as special, paternal figures to their daughter's children and their father's daughter's children—not (or at least not merely) to offspring of sons and brothers. Such a formal identification, of course, bespeaks a situation we have already encountered in other Roman contexts: in the high valuation clearly given to daughters' children by, and by daughters' children to, men of the classical period; in that reportedly given to daughters' children by and by daughters' children to men of the monarchic era such as Numitor and the Sabine fathers. Corroboration for this same conclusion may be found, we should note, in other Latin kinship terms. *Nepos*, the Latin word for grandchild, is cognate with several Indo-European words for the offspring of one's daughter or sister: an original meaning of *nepos* as daughter's child would not only help confirm an (if not *the*) original meaning of Latin *avus* as mother's father, but further establish that the children of a Roman man's daughter—not (and at the least not only) those of his son—were deemed his important descendants. Although *nepos* and its feminine *neptis* do not come to mean an *avunculus'* nephew and niece until late in Latin linguistic history, the fact that *avus*—literal and linguistic

avus must have originally meant mother's father (73) and notes that this was also the view of Bachofen, *Gesammelte Werke, Vol. VIII. Antiquarische Briefe* (Basel, 1966). For Indo-European *HauHos as maternal and paternal grandfather and maternal uncle, see Szemerényi, 155.

parent of *avunculus*—apparently began as a term for maternal grandfather, *the* significant male ancestor of one labeled a *nepos*, helps explain why they do so, and how their application to a sister's children came about.[69]

That the Latin term *cognatus*, related by blood though not necessarily through a male, and *cognatio*, blood relationship though not necessarily through a male, carry positive, metaphorical, and affective connotations may perhaps be of relevance too. Classical authors regularly employ the adjective *cognatus* for valued individuals and things which closely resemble (and suit) one another; the phrase *cara cognatio* is in fact used for the *caristia*, the Romans' annual feast celebrating family ties and affection. Such connotations, however, are not to be found in the terms *agnatus* and *agnatio*, which denote relationship specifically and solely through males. These connotations may also, therefore, argue for the existence of publicly acknowledged and intimate ties between men

[69] For the etymology of *nepos* see Ernout-Meillet, 438, and Szemerényi, 156. For its connotations and history, see Szemerényi 156 n. 596, 166ff., and Beekes, "Uncle and Nephew," 49-50, who also observes that Latin *nepos* = nephew nearly always meant sister's son. The association of the word *nepos* with the blood kin of one's mother may be significant for another reason: maternal kin, after all, did not possess *potestas* over a woman's children (as opposed to these children's father and his father and possibly brothers). Thus they could behave more indulgently toward such children when they misbehaved, and in particular when such misbehavior involved overspending or mishandling of finances (or at least they were under no pressure and had no authority to be punitive; besides, their financial holdings would not ordinarily pass to these, non-agnate, relations unless they so chose). Consequently, the lesser expectations of maternal kin may explain the other Latin meaning of *nepos*, that of "spendthrift," "prodigal," "playboy." For this latter meaning, see, e.g. Plautus, *Miles Gloriosus* 1413, 1421 (the diminutive *nepotulum*); Cicero, *In Catilinam* 2.7, and Catullus 58.3 (*magnanimos Remi nepotes*, which plays on both senses of the word). See also Beekes, 51, the *OLD* fasc. 5 (1976) 1170, and Ernout-Meillet, 438, for this meaning of *nepos*.

of earliest Roman times and their daughters' (and fathers' daughters') children—or at least prove that men did not have such ties exclusively with children of sons (and brothers' sons).[70]

Of further interest are the Latin words *gener*, son-in-law, and *socer*, father-in-law. The ancient Romans seem to have regarded the former as derived from the same Indo-European root found in *gens*, family clan, and *genius*, continuative spirit of the family; while modern linguistic authority detects a different ultimate derivation (in order to connect the word with, *inter alia*, Greek *gambros*, "bridegroom" and "son-in-law"), there is still justification for considering *gener* an anomalous Indo-European form which would reflect, and attest to, a cultural peculiarity of the earliest Romans. An original sense of the term as denoting "he who perpetuates a male's blood line" not only accords with the view implicit in the etymologies of *avunculus* and *nepos*, that men in remote Roman times were defined as important ancestors of their daughters', and their daughters' husbands', children. It also has a striking counterpart in the special

---

[70] For *cognatio/cognatus*, see the *OLD* fasc. 2 (1969) 344-345. For the ancient definition (and contrast with *agnatus*) of *cognatus*, see *Digest* 38.10, 10,2: "cognates are also those whom the law of the Twelve Tables calls agnates, but agnates are kindred through a father from the same family, while those who are kindred through women are only called cognates." For *a(d)gnascor*, "to be born in addition to"/*a(d)gnatio/a(d)gnatus*, used metaphorically only of animals, plants, and bodily parts which are "later developments," see the *OLD* fasc. 1 (1968) 86-87. *Agnatus* is—unlike *cognatus*—attested as appearing several times in the Twelve Tables (e.g. by the *Auctor ad Herennium* 1.13.23, *lex est si furiosus escit, adgnatum gentiliumque in eo pecuniaque eius potestas esto*, "the law is that if a man is raving mad, authority over him and his goods shall belong to his agnates and relations"); it may owe its limited connotations to the fact that it was regarded as a legal and technical term, whereas *cognatus* was not. For further speculation on *cognatio/cognatus* and *agnatio/agnatus*, see the following chapter.

significance, discussed above, which men in the classical
era accorded sons-in-law; it may even help explain why
men in the classical era clung to primitive-sounding ta-
boos regarding the *socer-gener* bond. *Socer*, moreover,
would appear to derive from an Indo-European root
which means "of the same family group"; its etymology
would imply that a Roman married man originally perceived the maternal grandfather of his children as closely
kindred, and reciprocated his wife's father's feelings about
his daughter's husband.[71]

One has, therefore, some justification for taking seriously the classical Romans' claim that filiafocality characterized monarchic and early republican Roman society
no less than it did elite Rome of their own era, and that
their later, often moralistic narratives on Rome's first
centuries accurately represent this aspect of earliest Roman kinship practice and sentiment. Even if these accounts about Rome's remote past do not in any circumstances provide detailed documentation of actual historical
events, they deserve careful scrutiny for another reason;
namely, they supply some of our more specific evidence
for what Romans of classical times thought appropriate
conduct by a daughter toward her father and a father
toward his daughter. Along with accounts in imagina-

---

[71] For a new etymology of *gener*, see Szemerényi, 69-72, who
derives the word from *gem-er-*, "transformed to *gener* under the
influence of *genere*, the Old Latin byform of *gignere*, *genitor* etc.,"
and meaning "he who takes, buys or marries"; as such, the word
would be cognate not only with Greek *gambros* (metathetized from
gem-ə-ro-s to *gameros* under the influence of *gamos*, marriage) but
also Aryan jāmātā. On the etymology of *socer*, I take issue with Szemerényi, 34, and accept the view first voiced by Meringer in 1904 and
subsequently "of great favor with the French school," which regards
the first component of *socer* as *swe-* "one's own," "belonging to
the same family group." I am not, moreover, convinced by Szemerényi's explanation, in 65-67, of *-kuros* in *swekuros* as from *ker*,
the head.

tive literature and factual chronicles about the actual behavior of fathers and daughters toward one another during the classical period, they furnish proof that performing the role of daughter to one's father was thought to and did entail a large measure of self-abnegation. Yet they and our other evidence suggest that the role of father's daughter brought special status with it as well, status which seems to have permitted an increasing amount of female self-assertion in later familial roles.

ROMAN DAUGHTERHOOD: A FATHER'S VS. A BROTHER'S EXPECTATIONS AND ACTIONS

At *Ad Atticum* 12.1, in a letter from Arpinum written in November of 46 B.C., Cicero expresses his longing to hurry straight to his daughter Tullia's arms and the kisses of Atticus' own small daughter. In so doing, he equates the physical embraces of a thrice married woman of around thirty with those of a five-year-old girl; as he asks that Atticus write and tell him what Tullia is "chattering about," he leaves the impression of looking upon his mature—indeed, by Roman standards, virtually middle-aged—daughter as a childlike creature quite untouched by the experiences of adulthood, of "infantilizing" her. By way of contrast, the younger Pliny's *Epistles* 5.16, lamenting the recent death of his friend Fundanus' daughter, ascribes to the girl, who was barely into her teens, both "matronly dignity" (*gravitas*) and the wisdom of an old woman (*anilis prudentia*)—as if she had been a quasi-wife and mother to Fundanus as well. The emotional needs of Roman men surely differed from individual to individual, and from time to time: we should not be surprised, therefore, to discover Roman fathers making very different sorts of emotional demands on and harboring very different sorts of emotions toward their female children. What is significant is that Roman men apparently felt free to express their own feelings to and about their daughters, and no less free to elicit emotional reactions and shows of affection from their daughters, far freer than they did in regard to emotional interchange with their sons.

Cicero's adoration of Tullia arguably borders on obsessive fixation; thus a comparison between Cicero's more reserved conduct toward his son Marcus and his effusive outpourings on and toward Tullia may not prove particularly enlightening evidence for general Roman paternal behavior. It warrants attention, however, that the childless Pliny—who views his friend Fundanus' lavish display of grief over the loss of his younger daughter as completely natural and comprehensible—voices a very dissimilar reaction when writing about the orator Regulus' comportment after the no less untimely passing of his only child, a son. Admittedly, Pliny and Regulus were not on the best of terms; still, we should observe that Pliny utilizes Regulus' lavish display of grief as additional proof of Regulus' phoniness: clearly Pliny assumes, and expects others to assume, that no Roman man would sorrow so extravagantly over the loss of a son.[72]

---

[72] For Cicero on Tullia, see, for example, Cicero's intention of immortalizing his dead daughter with a shrine, expressed at *Ad Atticum* 12.18, 19, 20; in the last of these letters he requests details about the circumstances surrounding two earlier Roman parents, Caepio and Rutilia, both bereaved of sons, for a treatise on the alleviation of mourning which he is writing. See, too, *Ad Familiares* 4.5, Servius Sulpicius Rufus' consolation to the newly bereaved Cicero, which makes it clear that Cicero desperately needed to have his loss put into some perspective, and Cicero's response (at *Ad Familiares* 4.6), claiming that his personal plight renders this loss more painful than similar deaths of sons to others. As noted above (n. 35), Cicero's fixation on Tullia is treated by Carp, "Two Matrons," 197, who reminds us that their relationship was so close as to have led in

Lying behind Pliny's assumption may, of course, be
the Roman ideal that sons' deaths be borne by fathers
with tearless fortitude. Valerius Maximus' *Memorable
Deeds and Sayings* contains an entire chapter on fathers
who endured their sons' deaths with brave spirit, *forti
animo*; one thinks also of Plutarch's life of one such father,
Lucius Aemilius Paullus. Although elsewhere in this life
Plutarch notes this distinguished commander's concern
over his small daughter's tears, he, like Valerius Maximus, emphasizes that Paullus celebrated his triumph
immediately after the burial of his fourteen-year-old son
and despite the mortal illness of the boy's twelve-year-
old brother. Plutarch, moreover, relates that Paullus delivered an oration to the people pointing out the irony
in his captive Perseus' enjoyment of his own children,
while he, the conqueror, was deprived of his sons; Plutarch adds, though, that Paullus did so not as if seeking
comfort from his fellow citizens, but as if to console
them on their grief. But more closely connected to this
assumption that a father should not display extravagant
grief on his son's death may also be a Roman belief,
apparently based on emotional reality, that sons could
not relate to their fathers on an affective level to anywhere near the same extent that daughters did. Portrayals of actual and fictive Roman fathers sensitive to
and worried about their daughters' emotional states—
Plutarch's and Cicero's of Lucius Aemilius Paullus,
Plautus' of the *senex* in the *Menaechmi*, Livy's of Fabius
Ambustus, Seneca's of Cremutius Cordus—have no real
counterparts depicting paternal sensitivity to and anxiety
over (or even the acknowledgment of) a son's feelings.
Similarly, Cicero's conclusion to his *Pro Caelio* may stress

---

antiquity to baseless charges of incest. For Cicero on Marcus, see,
for example, *Ad Atticum* 12.7 and 8. For Pliny on Regulus' bereavement, see *Epistles* 4.2.

the loneliness and disgrace Caelius' aged father will suffer if his son is convicted, and cite the "pleasantness of children," but makes no reference to the general preciousness of sons. Cicero thus defines the overall emotional value of male children to fathers as rather different from the value he had ascribed to daughters in the passage with which this chapter began, from the second oration against Verres. [73]

Whatever the nature of a Roman father's emotional interactions with his own daughter, all elite Roman fathers appear to have expected—as the different emotional demands by such fathers as Cicero and Fundanus alone suggest—their daughters to act in accordance with their own wishes. Furthermore, fathers seem to have expected daughters to follow certain standard patterns of behavior and for the most part to have had these expectations met. These social dimensions of the daughter role in classical Roman times, both as idealized in fiction and experienced in actuality, next merit attention.

First, and most crucially, elite Roman fathers appear to have demanded deference and personal, often politically charged, allegiance from their female children. Two portrayals of this bond in imaginative literature particularly emphasize this aspect of father-daughter interaction—those by Plautus in his *Stichus* and *Menaechmi*. The former play represents the two sisters as conflicted between their duty to their absent but irresponsible husbands and their apparently greater obligation to obey their present if irritating father. It makes good comic

[73] For Paullus' remarkable conduct in this crisis, see Valerius Maximus 5.10.2 and Plutarch, *Aemilius Paullus* 35-36. Cf. also Seneca, *Ad Marciam De Consolatione* 12.3-15.3, especially 13.3-4 on Paullus, which claims that he actually congratulated himself on his bereavement. For Cicero's testimony, see *Pro Caelio* 79-80 (especially *vel recordatione parentum vestrorum vel liberorum iucunditate*).

capital out of the daughters' efforts to reassure their father of his authority over them: "who is more justly considered more powerful than you?" says one daughter at line 97. It similarly treats their endeavors to redefine "following their father's command" as refusing to abandon the spouses he gave them (141).[74] At 784ff., of the *Menaechmi* Plautus represents the *senex* as reminding his daughter, with a series of rhetorical questions, of his former instructions to her about how to keep in his own, and her husband's, good graces; he blames her present predicament on her failure to obey him.

Legends about father-daughter interactions during the monarchic and early republican periods impart the same impression about paternal expectations of daughterly deference; in such legends, moreover, we find several daughters who meet these expectations most memorably. One thinks first of the Sabine women, and Livy's assertion at 1.13.3-4 that they preferred to be punished, indeed to die, and thus suffer the consequences of willful disobedience rather than to be viewed as contributing to their fathers' and husbands' mutual enmity. Although in this particular speech these women are literally making demands of their own, they are described as doing so by emphasizing their eagerness to accommodate their male kinfolk. One thinks, too, of Livy's Verginia, following her father to the forum and later accompanying him from the tribunal to the butcher shop by the shrine of Cloacina, enduring his fatal stabbing without a murmur of pain or protest, or of Dionysius' Cloelia and her fellow hostage-maidens, with their exertions to disprove

---

[74] Though cf. also the evidently serious statement by the elder daughter Panegyris at 69 (in response to her sister's query on what to do if their father opposes them): "It is proper that we endure what he does, whose power (*potestas*) is more powerful (*plus potest*)," which plays on the technical term for a *pater*'s control.

that they had betrayed their fathers.[75] These attractively portrayed, deferential and politically loyal, daughter figures stand, as we have seen, in sharp antithesis to the self-assertive and politically disloyal Tarpeia, Horatia, and Tullia of monarchic legend. To be sure, the Sabine women—like the *matronae* of the *Stichus* and *Menaechmi*—are depicted as at pains to prove themselves good wives as well as devoted daughters. Yet the stories of these latter three daughters from the regal period, each of whose support to husband or lover resulted in traitorous treatment of her father and his concerns, point to a Roman belief that if a father's demands upon his daughter came into conflict with demands made on her by a sexual partner, the father's demands were supposed to receive precedence.

A major source on Roman moralistic thought in the classical era implies that most daughters did, as a rule, accord their fathers' demands not only preference but the fullest possible compliance. In his *Memorable Deeds and Sayings*, Valerius Maximus also has an entire chapter on "Fathers' Severity Toward Their Children" (5.8). It cites five examples of harsh fathers, moving chronologically from the early republican liberator Lucius Brutus to one A. Fulvius, father of a Catilinarian conspirator, who executed their offspring for disobedient or disloyal acts. All of these examples feature an impudent, or errant, and hence an executed son; none an impudent, errant, or executed daughter (indeed, sources concur that the one fabled daughter supposedly killed for disobedience and disloyalty to her blood family, Horatia, died at the hands of her *brother*). Correspondingly, a preceding chapter in Valerius Maximus on "Parents'

---

[75] For Livy on Verginia's deference to Verginius, see in particular 3.47.1 and 48.5-6. For Dionysius of Halicarnassus on Cloelia and the hostage maidens, see again 5.32.3-35.2.

Love and Indulgence Toward Their Children" (5.7), and a subsequent one on "Parents' Moderation Toward Children Under Suspicion" (5.9), restrict examples of singularly compassionate Roman parents and children benefiting from their extraordinary compassion to fathers and sons.

Anecdotes about actual instances of daughterly deference and allegiance to upper-class fathers in late republican and early imperial times depict various daughters as deeming their fathers' interests more important than those of their husbands. They also show that the heroic daughter figures of earliest Rome immortalized by Livy and the like resembled flesh-and-blood, albeit sentimentalized, women of the classical period, and were in fact imitated by such women as realistic role models. Additionally, these accounts allow us to contrast, and at times themselves contrast, the conduct of certain men's daughters with the less accommodating behavior of their female kin occupying other familial roles.

Tacitus' portrayal of Antistia Pollitta in *Annales* 16, for example, notes that she had seen her husband Rubellius Plautus assassinated and barely touched food in her mourning. Tacitus states, however, that it was on her condemned father's behalf that she went to Naples to plead with Nero; Tacitus reports that only after her womanly and unwomanly cries failed to move the emperor did Antistia join her father in death. Similarly, Tacitus remarks that Antistia's contemporary Servilia was inconsolable over the exile of her husband, Annius Pollio. Yet he had earlier observed that the two men exiled with Pollio—Decimus Novius Priscus and Glitius Gallus—had been, unlike Pollio, accompanied by their wives. Servilia's efforts to help her father, culminating in her appeal that Nero and the senate spare her father and punish her alone (on the unfounded charge of consulting magicians), surely explain her remaining in Rome no less than her father's supposed statement that she was "unimplicated in the accusations against her husband."[76]

Plutarch's *Lives* portray sundry daughters as more attentive to their fathers than were other female relations and as more closely attached—in the eyes of others as well as in their own circumstances—to fathers than to spouses. In his life of Cicero, Plutarch represents Cicero's daughter Tullia as displaying far more devotion to him when he returned from exile than did his wife, Terentia. Terentia, Plutarch maintains, "did not come to meet Cicero, although he stopped a long while in Brundisium, and when her daughter, though still a young girl [actually a married woman of at least eighteen], herself made the trip, she did not provide her with a proper escort or with means for travel." Later in the same chapter, when Plutarch describes Cicero's extreme grief at Tullia's death, he does not even correctly identify her husband of that time, Dolabella, though two chapters later he mentions Cicero's ties with the young man.[77]

Elsewhere Plutarch condemns Pompey's divorce from his first wife, Antistia, as dishonorable and pitiful, because Antistia had just lost her father on Pompey's account: Antistius, Plutarch remarks, had been killed in the senate house since he was thought to have supported

[76] For Antistia Pollitta, see again Tacitus, *Annales* 16.10.3-11; for Pollio's companions in exile, see *Annales* 15.71.3; for Servilia, see *Annales* 16.30.3-32.

[77] For Cicero's return from exile, see Plutarch, *Cicero* 41.2. For Tullia's age, see the article in *RE*² 14 (1943) 1329 by Groebe (who dates her birth to 79 B.C.) and, *inter alios*, D. R. Shackleton Bailey, *Cicero* (London, 1971) 23, who notes that she was in all probability wed in 63 (which allows her a slightly later birthdate—e.g. 76 B.C.—but nonetheless establishes her as fully grown and already married in 58, the year of her father's return from exile). For Plutarch's misidentification of Tullia's third husband as Lentulus and reference to the ties between Cicero and Dolabella, see *Cicero* 41.5, 43.2.

Sulla for Pompey's sake. Plutarch then adds that this divorce caused Antistia's own mother—Pompey's mother-in-law—to commit suicide; he does not, however, record any protest by Antistia herself, perhaps because her father's admiration for Pompey, and her acquiescence in Antistius' wishes, had brought about her marriage to Pompey in the first place. Nor does Plutarch mention any resistance on the part of Pompey's new wife, betrothed by her stepfather Sulla, although she was at the time pregnant by her current husband. Finally, as we have seen, Plutarch's life of the younger Cato and his life of Brutus stress the single-minded commitment of Cato's daughter to her late father's political mission. Yet in both the life of the younger Cato and that of Pompey Plutarch depicts Cato as under some pressure to placate his wife and sisters after he, against their wishes, rejected marital alliances between Pompey and one of Cato's nieces, and between Pompey's son and another. Furthermore, Plutarch does not even acknowledge the role played by one such sister, the elder Servilia, in perpetuating her brother's cause after his death.[78]

Our evidence about Roman daughters, idealized and real, also makes it clear that their fathers expected them to adhere to high standards of sexual comportment: virginity before their marriage, complete fidelity to their

[78] On Pompey's divorce from Antistia and remarriage to Sulla's stepdaughter, see *Pompey* 9; for Pompey's marriage to Antistia—due to her father's high regard for his courtroom conduct when accused, see *Pompey* 4.3. For Cato's devotion from Porcia, see *Cato Minor* 73.4 and references cited in n. 31 of chapter two above. For Cato's opposition from his sisters, see *Cato Minor* 30.3-5 and *Pompey* 44.2-4; see also the discussion by J. E. Phillips, "Roman Mothers and the Lives of their Adult Daughters," *Helios* 6.1 (1978) 71. I argue that the elder Servilia prominently furthered her brother's cause after his death in chapter two, above.

husbands. The decision by the raped Lucretia, in Dionysius' account, to take her own life after making confession to her father alone is certainly intended to indicate
that she had thoroughly internalized such paternal expectations. Verginius' decision to slay his own maiden
daughter rather than relinquish her to, as Livy puts it,
"slavery and unchastity," is intended to indicate that a
Roman father could and should feel quite strongly about
these expectations, and the prospect that they might not
be met. Although the *senex* of Plautus' *Menaechmi* may
upbraid his daughter for expecting total devotion from
her husband, and may even regard the extramarital dal-
liances of his son-in-law as completely understandable,
he does not suggest that she cope with this situation by
similar extramarital activity on her own part, and assumes her sexual fidelity while sympathizing with her
loss of material possessions. From the realm of Roman
reality, we might also recall Plutarch's assertion that the
elder Cato severely penalized one senator merely for
exposing his, presumably unwed, daughter to his and
his wife's embraces. Suetonius reports that Atticus dismissed his freedman Caecilius Epirota from the post of
teacher to his married daughter merely because he suspected Epirota of making advances toward her. The
emperor Augustus' moral legislation assigned a father
ultimate authority over an adulterous daughter, and considerably more authority than it assigned a woman's
husband: whereas it empowered a father to kill both his
daughter and her lover if he caught them having intercourse in his own or his son-in-law's house, it forbade
a man to kill a wife he caught in the act.[79]

[79] For Epirota's dismissal, reported at Suetonius, *De Grammaticis*
16, see A. Richlin, "Approaches to the Sources on Adultery at Rome,"
Women's Studies 8 (1981) 230; for Augustus' legislation on the rights
of an adulteress's father, see also Richlin, 227–228, discussing *Digest*

Last, Roman elite fathers appear to have expected their daughters to depend upon them for protection and support and not to have minded if they made this dependence manifest in various ways. Several of the passages we have discussed share Plutarch's perception that "fathers seem to have a great(er) affection for daughters because daughters are thought in need of their help." Some involve imaginary fathers and daughters: Livy's portrayal of Fabius Ambustus as not in the least annoyed at the disquietude of Fabia Minor over her husband's inferior social status, and as thereafter committed to assuring her a place in Roman society equal to that of her sister; Plautus' characterization of the *senex* in the *Menaechmi* as quick to come to his daughter's aid, and doing so with the remark "a daughter never summons her father unless . . . she has 'good reason'." But we might also note Seneca's choice of Cremutius Cordus as the obvious person in the world of the dead to offer, ungrudgingly and wholeheartedly, Marcia the reassurance that her son had earned a special place in eternity; we might recall, too, Valerius Maximus 4.4.10, on Gnaeus Scipio's willingness to relinquish his Spanish command in order to dower, and wed, his daughter.

Concomitantly, elite Roman fathers evidently did not welcome self-assertiveness or displays of independence from their daughters. Dionysius of Halicarnassus depicts Horatia's father as unforgiving in the face of such conduct; the presumably more realistic, if fictionalizing, Plautus represents the daughters in the *Stichus* as eager to masquerade their desire to defy their father's wishes; the total absence of daughters from Valerius Maximus' rolls of (for the most part actual) self-assertive children

---

48.5. See also Valerius Maximus 6.1.3,4, and 6, tales of fathers who harshly punished daughters for unchaste behavior.

punished and indulged by their fathers may be telling too, reflecting Roman perception if not reality. Indeed, one is struck by the characteristic failure of actual elite Roman fathers to consult daughters on matters of vital interest to them: one recalls the younger Cato's refusal to give the already-wed Porcia's hand to Hortensius without soliciting Porcia's opinion; one cannot help but notice the general tendency of Roman upper-class men (such as Pompey's first father-in-law Antistius) to select their daughters' husbands without soliciting the opinions of their daughters themselves (although they would apparently consult with their daughters' mothers and often aunts). Such culturally sanctioned disregard enabled fathers to avoid situations where daughters might reasonably question or protest their judgment, thereby pointing out that their lives and concerns were ultimately separate from their fathers. Such disregard, however, is altogether consistent with other paternal expectations of daughters, which allowed a father to deny his daughter's existence as an individual and thus, should he so choose, to sentimentalize her as a helpless and submissive creature.[80]

---

[80] For the exclusion of daughters—including Cato's wife Marcia when he gave her in marriage to Hortensius after consulting with her father—from this decision-making process, and the inclusion of the prospective bride's mother and aunt, see Plutarch, *Cato Minor* 25.4-5, and the passages cited by Phillips, "Roman Mothers," 70-73. These passages include Livy 38.57.6-8 and Plutarch, *Tiberius Gracchus* 4.1, on the engagements by their fathers, and to their mothers' annoyance, of Cornelia, *mater Gracchorum*, and her daughter-in-law Claudia, respectively; they also include accounts in Cicero, Valerius Maximus, the younger Seneca, and Aulus Gellius. Obtaining a daughter's consent to a husband chosen (by her parents) is not, to reiterate, the same thing as consulting a daughter before the choice is made; thus even Treggiari's findings ("Consent," 40) that by the second century B.C. consent of the dependent child was legally necessary do not allow dependent daughters much of a say in whom or when they wed. Besides, *Digest* 23.1.12 indicates that a woman

Legal, linguistic, and anecdotal evidence surveyed earlier attests that a Roman father could and did expect his male children to function as his surrogates in relation to his female children in the event of his death and as his supporters while he was still alive. There is symbolic evidence such as the linguistic relationship between the words *avus* and *avunculus*, and the fact that Roman fathers bestowed their own, masculine form of the *gentilicium* on their sons as well as bestowing its feminine form on their daughters; there is also factual testimony such as the Twelve Tables' provisions for (agnate) succession, whereby a father's obligations would pass to his sons after his death, and such as the actual assumption by fatherless brothers such as the younger Cato's *avunculus* Drusus and the younger Cato himself of paternal responsibility for their sisters' welfare (and in Cato's case his maternal half-sisters' as well as his full sister's welfare). Yet a well-born Roman woman evidently occupied a very different role in relationship to her brother than she did vis-à-vis her father and apparently possessed a very different image for her male siblings than she did for her male parent. Consequently, the differences between Roman fathers' expectations of and interactions with daughters and their sons' expectations of and interactions with their fathers' daughters seem to have been considerable and may be contrasted with profit.

For once a Roman *pater* had acknowledged and chosen to rear a female child, he accorded her essentially the same rights, and arguably more outward signs of affection, than he did his male offspring. Due to these circumstances and to the likelihood that a sister would be

---

was assumed to consent if she did not strongly oppose (*repugnat*) her father's wishes, and was not allowed to dissent unless the fiancé chosen was morally unworthy or "shameful."

fairly close in age to (and perhaps somewhat older than) her male siblings, a woman's brother would have grown up regarding her as a significant individual rather than as a helpless and submissive creature. That upper-class Roman women tended to marry, and thus assume their "adult" role in Roman society, almost a decade younger than men did would in particular tend to make sisters appear mature and worldly to their brothers of about the same age (or even older) during their brothers' adolescent years. Thus we should not be surprised to discover various sources portraying Roman sisters as self-assertive in their interactions with their brothers: because of their initial valuation by their fathers, Roman daughters would with good reason have been perceived by male siblings as having rights equal to their own, in and opinions as worthy as their own on many important matters—a sister's technical need for male "paternal" protection notwithstanding.[81]

In the first place, even if a Roman brother expected his sister to take pride in his accomplishments—which, for example, Propertius 4.11 depicts the noble Cornelia as doing—he could not, it would appear, expect from her the deference and unquestioning support she would have been expected to show her father. Self-assertive sisterly criticism of brothers' conduct, and the assumption that brothers must receive it graciously, figure in both Plautine comedy and monarchic legend. We should recall Eunomia in Plautus' *Aulularia*, and her brother's compliance with her overbearing ways. It is worth noting that the fabled Horatius, even after acquittal, was nonetheless forced to atone for his patriotic sororicide and, according to Livy, needed to be certified by his

---

[81] On the ages of Roman men and women at marriage, see again M. K. Hopkins, "The Age of Roman Girls at Marriage," *Population Studies* 18 (1965) 309-327.

father as his own surrogate before being let off as lightly
as he was for punishing a sister's self-assertiveness. Accounts of actual brother-sister dealings establish such
conduct as part of elite Roman reality. We have seen
how the younger Cato had to endure the elder Servilia's
liaison with his political foe Julius Caesar, and a(nother?)
sister's annoyance when he refused a marital alliance
between the daughters of his sister(s) and Pompey *père
et fils*; we will see, in the next chapter, how several other
Roman brothers—such as Atticus, Augustus, and Gnaeus
Domitius Ahenobarbus—are remembered for accommodating conduct toward their *sorores*.[82]

So, too, Roman brothers apparently did not demand
that their sisters be paragons of sexual virtue. Several
Roman brothers of late republican times are remembered for overlooking and tolerating their sisters' unchaste ways. The late republican demagogue Clodius'
acceptance of his sisters' loose-living habits earned him
a reputation as their lover—and the part, in Cicero's *Pro
Caelio*, of sympathetic adviser to one such sister on how
best to manage her wanton sexual escapades. Clodius'
contemporary, the younger Cato, renowned for his own
moral righteousness, is also reported to have stood by
and succored his two (half) sisters in spite of their adulterous conduct; the women's full brother, Quintus Servilius Caepio, seems to have been regarded as supportive
of them, or at least of their sons Brutus and Lucullus,
as well. At 37.49.3 Cassius Dio reports that Quintus
Metellus Celer, consul in 60 B.C., vigorously opposed

---

[82] For Cato and the elder Servilia's liaison, see Plutarch, *Cato Minor*
24.1-2 and *Brutus* 5; for Cato and the unsuccessful betrothal to the
Pompeii, see Plutarch, *Cato Minor* 30.3-5 and *Pompey* 44.2-4. For
Atticus' deference to Pomponia, see Nepos, *Atticus* 17, and Cicero,
Ad Atticum 13.42; for Augustus' to Octavia, see Plutarch, *Antony*
35 and 87.2; for Domitius' to his *soror*, see Suetonius, *Nero* 5.2: these
passages will be discussed in the following chapter.

Pompey in everything because Pompey had divorced
his half-sister Mucia even though he had had children
by her: as various authors, including Plutarch and Suetonius, ascribe Mucia's divorce to her adulterous conduct with none other than Pompey's ally at the time,
Julius Caesar, Metellus' readiness to blame Pompey for
this marital schism implies either his belief that the charge
against his sister was unfounded or a willingness to turn
a deaf ear to it.[83]

At 13.10.3 Aulus Gellius remarks that the Augustan
jurist Antistius Labeo derived the Latin word for sister,
soror, from *seorsum*, "outside," owing to a sister's trans-
fer by marriage from her home of birth to another family. Although the explanation is etymologically unten-
able, Labeo's implicit definition of a female sibling as
"she who becomes an outsider" deserves attention all
the same. It suggests that Roman brothers might have
looked upon their sisters as individuals with additional
bonds and bases outside their blood family, again doubtless because marriages of, and hence brothers' physical
separation from, sisters occurred fairly early in their
mutual lifetimes: brothers and sisters would spend a
greater proportion of the years in which both were alive
residing in different households than would father and
daughter. That Roman sisters generally bore children
soon after their early marriages, and thus assumed their

[83] For Clodius and his sisters, see the works cited in n. 19, chapter
two above, in particular Plutarch, *Cicero* 29.4-5 and *Lucullus* 34.1,38.1.
For the younger Cato and his sisters, see, Plutarch, *Cato Minor* 24.1-
3 and *Brutus* 5. Of relevance is the theory that Servilius Caepio had
adopted Brutus (see chapter two above, n. 21); cf. as well Cicero's
expression to Cato of his hopes that young Lucullus will grow up
to resemble both his kinsman Cato and the admired *Caepio noster* no
less than his father (*De Finibus* 3.8). For Metellus Celer and Mucia,
see Plutarch, *Pompey* 42.6-7; Suetonius, *Divus Julius* 50.1, and the
discussions of Gruen, *Last Generation*, 85, 130-131.

respected adult role of mother, might additionally invest sisters with an aura of "otherness." However one chooses to interpret this fanciful Roman connection of sisters with separation from their families of birth, evidence already adduced, and yet to be adduced, shows that Roman elite brothers, unlike Roman elite fathers, did not object to a sister's, particularly a married "maternal" sister's, independence, and indeed depended upon their sisters in certain important regards themselves.

A large body of evidence points to the high valuation of Roman "fathers' daughters" by their fathers' sons, chiefly but not solely fathers' daughters who had already become mothers of offspring. It also provides further testimony for the cultural importance of the father's daughter role, and the emphasis on kindred bonds through fathers' daughters, albeit from the perspective of daughters' siblings. The survey of this evidence to follow will in addition enable us to consider how the classical Roman elite viewed the bonds between siblings of the same sex; we may thus better ascertain how a sister's initial role as her father's valued daughter, and later role as mother to descendants of her father's blood line, helps account for her special status and independent image in her brother's eyes.

IV

Sorores Familiae

In attempting to provide an etymology for the word *amita*, "father's sister," the Roman scholar Festus far-fetchedly links it with *amare*, "to love": *amita dicta est, quia a patre meo amata est*, "she has been called *amita*, because she has been loved (*amata*) by my father." His explanation, however, deserves serious consideration. "For sisters are generally more cherished by brothers than brothers are cherished by one another, obviously because sisters are such different kinds of individuals— they are less prone to discord, and therefore to invidious competition."[1] In this chapter we will examine this bond which Festus perceived as so special to Roman males, that between brothers and sisters in elite Roman society. Both imaginative literature and accounts of actual behavior by Roman authors illuminate how Roman sisters were emotionally valued by their brothers, and how the role of Roman brother's sister (like that of sister's brother) was culturally emphasized during the classical period. In addition to exploring the Roman brother-sister bond, and some indices of its persistent emotional strength and cultural importance in classical times, we will also investigate Roman expectations about conduct in the roles of brother and sister as these roles are performed in interaction with same-sex siblings; we will thus look closely at what our sources say and imply about the

[1] Festus p. 13 Lindsay.

sister-sister and brother-brother bonds in classical Roman elite society.

The last of these sibling relationships was, of course, given far more cultural emphasis by upper-class Roman society than were the first two. The fact of agnate legal succession, coupled with men's legal responsibility for the guardianship of women and children, defined Roman brothers as virtual surrogates for one another, committed to assume their brothers' obligations in the event of their brothers' absences or deaths. The pressures on upper-class Roman males for political and military involvement also encouraged brothers to rely publicly upon and to identify with one another. Indeed, at 13.10.4 Aulus Gellius relates that one, highly imaginative, Roman etymologist, Publius Nigidius, derived the Latin term for brother, *frater*, from *fere*, "almost," and *alter*, "another," implying a view of brothers as not quite distinct individuals, as sharing a mutual identity.

Nevertheless, the bonds between Roman sister and brother, and Roman sister and sister, in upper-class families seem to have been emotionally stronger, or at least less strained, than those between Roman male siblings. Varied evidence supports Festus' observation, including evidence for expectations and actual affirmations of emotional ties to mothers' brothers (*avunculi*), fathers' sisters (*amitae*), mothers' sisters (*materterae*), and fathers' brothers (*patrui*). Furthermore, testimony to the high emotional valuation among the classical Roman elite accorded to the male and female siblings of a Roman mother and the sister of a Roman father and testimony on the cultural importance accorded to the roles of *avunculus, amita,* and *matertera* provide additional support for the overall thesis of this study: that a well-born Roman woman's initial valuation as her father's daughter contributed heavily to her esteem (and opportunities for self-assertive behavior) in the role of sister to her father's sons and other daughters, an esteem which would in turn increase after she and her siblings had become parents of their father's blood descendants. So, too, the importance of Roman sisters and the filiafocal kinship emphases of which this phenomenon was a part seem to have created another noteworthy situation among the classical Roman elite: the prominence and closeness of daughter-centered male ties in a society of intensely agnatic orientation.

SOROR FRATERQUE

Evidence on how the elite Romans of classical times defined the role and characterized the actual conduct of an *avunculus*, the brother of a sister with children, reveals elite Roman notions about, and behavior in, the role of brother to a sister. It thus testifies to the importance of the Roman sister as a link between her brother and her offspring. Certain facts about Roman *avunculi* also render more comprehensible the high valuation of a Roman *soror* by her brother and vice-versa. The maternal uncle's important role in the patriarchal family and society of elite Rome during the classical era, a phenomenon to which abundant testimony bears witness, is analogous to phenomena described and documented by anthropologists in other societies. The term employed by anthropologists for this phenomenon, the avunculate, derives from the Latin noun *avunculus* itself; the choice of this term is thus somewhat ironic in view of the limited scholarly attention paid to this phenomenon among the classical Roman elite. Indeed, the inadequate efforts by earlier studies of the Roman family to discern and document this phenomenon have long needed to be remedied, and make our initial concern with the elite Roman *avunculus* all the more justifiable.[2]

As we noted earlier, Festus terms an *avunculus* a father-figure to his sister's children of the female sex. *Avunculi* were also generally regarded as respected, paternal figures by sisters' male children, as is made clear both by Roman authors treating fictive but presumably familiar situations and by members of elite Roman families articulating their own attitudes and those of their milieu. In the first category, one might again cite Plautus' *Aulularia*, inasmuch as it is a very early piece of Roman testimony not only to general notions about the relationship between *soror* and *frater* but also to ideas about the bond between *avunculus* and *sororis filius*. Here Lyconides, son of Megadorus' imperious sister Eunomia, first expresses deep disquietude about not offending his *avunculus* over his request to wed the girl Megadorus has betrothed and he has himself impregnated. Later, when introducing himself to his father-in-law-elect, Lyconides implies Megadorus' paternal role toward himself by mentioning the name of this *avunculus* as well as that of his father. In the second category, one might cite

[2] The major studies of the maternal uncle in patri- and matrilineal societies, beginning with A. R. Radcliffe-Brown's 1924 article on "The Mother's Brother in South Africa," reprinted in *Structure and Function in Primitive Society* (London, 1952) 15-31, are summarized by J. Goody, "The Mother's Brother and the Sister's Son in West Africa," *Comparative Studies in Kinship* (Stanford, 1969) 39-90, and Szemerényi, 184ff. The latter notes on 187, citing E. Benveniste, *Le vocabulaire des institutions indo-européennes* I (Paris, 1969) 230ff., merely that "evidence of the close relation between maternal uncle and nephew is also found in the Celtic world and in Greece"; similarly, J. Bremmer's "Avunculate and Fosterage," *JIS* 4 (1976) 68, states, in its survey of various Indo-European societies, "For a special relationship among the Romans between MoBr and SiSo our data are scarce." I am grateful to Peter Rose for calling to my attention the paradoxical use of the Latin noun *avunculus* to describe a phenomenon whose existence in classical Rome itself has remained largely uninvestigated.

Cicero's attacks on Mark Antony for failing to model himself on his *avunculus* Lucius Julius Caesar and for emulating his stepfather instead.[3] We should, however, emphasize at this point that the paternal duties ascribed and thought appropriate to a Roman *avunculus* were not identical to the obligations ascribed and thought appropriate to a Roman *pater*. A Roman *avunculus* had no financial responsibility for his sister's children under the law, since these children technically belonged to their father and, upon their father's death, to their father's male agnate kin.[4] Rather, it was chiefly in the socializing

[3] For Lyconides' filial concern over Megadorus, see *Aulularia* 682–700; for his identification through *avunculus* and *pater*, see 777–780. Further republican literary testimony to the importance, and paternal role, of *avunculi* is found at Catullus 84.5–6: there Arrius is labeled as inveterate, and hopeless, in his speech defect on the grounds that his mother, *avunculus* and maternal grandparents share his phonetic peculiarity. At 1.1 of his life of Lucullus, moreover, Plutarch first notes that Lucullus' mother's brother was Metellus Numidicus, and then goes on to name Lucullus' father and cite his conviction for theft: clearly Plutarch judges Lucullus' politically prominent *avunculus* a more significant paternal exemplar than his *pater*.

For Cicero's attack on Antony's lack of proper imitative respect toward his *avunculus*, see *Philippics* 1.27, 2.14. As Velleius Paterculus 2.67; Plutarch, *Antony* 20.3 and *Comparison of Demetrius and Antony* 5.1; Appian, *Bella Civilia* 4.37 observe, Antony even had this *avunculus* placed on the proscription list later (although he was saved by his sister, Antony's mother Julia). As E. S. Gruen, *The Last Generation of the Roman Republic* (Berkeley, Los Angeles, and London, 1974) 60, points out, Antony did not include his *patruus* Hybrida among those he recalled from exile in 49 B.C. either; Cicero takes Antony to task for this conduct at *Philippics* 2.56. It may be significant, however, that Cicero merely speaks of this *patruus* as a good man worthy of his country, whereas he praises Antony's *avunculus* as a man you "ought to have as paradigm and mentor in all of your plans and all of your life"; Cicero's contrasting portrayals of the two men may also suggest, as argued below, a Roman view of *avunculi* as more highly valued than *patrui*.

[4] As observed in chapter two, n. 20, the responsibility taken for his sister's offspring by the tribune M. Livius Drusus is striking in the light of Roman law, inasmuch as male agnate kin of these off-

and social launching of her offspring that a well-born Roman woman would seem to have relied upon the assistance of her brother, especially if she had not passed into her husband's *manus*, legally remained a member of her paternal family, and (as appears to be the case with many of the Roman women depicted in our sources) had been bereaved of her father.

Stories about pre-republican Rome, such valuable evidence for classical Roman notions about the father-daughter bond, do not feature memorable portrayals of *avunculi*. To some extent this may be because they describe each generation of rulers as but tenuously linked to its predecessor, through apparently brotherless daughters. In fact, and for reasons to be proposed later in this chapter, several brothers who do figure in legends about the Roman monarchic period—Numitor's evil brother Amulius, Romulus and Remus, Tarquinius Superbus—are represented as threatening the ambitions of their male siblings and as meeting violent ends. Yet Livy does characterize Tarquinius Superbus as *avunculus* to Rome's legendary liberator Lucius Junius Brutus, and thereby explains Brutus' inclusion in a fateful embassy to the oracle at Delphi with two of Tarquin's sons. Livy reports that Brutus, after being told by the oracle that the highest authority at Rome would go to whoever of the youths first kissed his mother, immediately touched his lips to the earth; he consequently obtained the power which his cousins—one of whom kissed his biological mother upon returning to Rome—had vainly desired.[5]

spring survived Drusus himself: e.g. his sister's first husband Servilius Caepio and L. Cato, brother of his sister's second husband (so Livy, *Periochae* 75 and Aulus Gellius 12.20.13).

[5] For Amulius, who killed Numitor's son and conscripted his daughter into Vestal Virginity, see Livy 1.3.10-11, 5.7; Dionysius of Halicarnassus 1.71.4-5, 76ff.; Ovid, *Fasti* 3.35-54, 4.53-56. For Remus and his strife with Romulus over the foundation and lead-

Furthermore, it is to the influence of their *avunculi* the Vitellii that Livy and others ascribe the political rebelliousness of Brutus' own sons: their efforts to overthrow the republican form of government founded and headed by their father and to reinstate monarchic rule and the Tarquins. As a matter of fact, Dionysius of Halicarnassus' account of this episode pointedly contrasts Brutus' harshness towards his sons—condemning them to death and watching their execution as the only unmoved onlooker—with the leniency displayed by his consular colleague Collatinus to two of the youths' fellow conspirators, sons of Collatinus' own sister. Ultimately, and at the urging of his father-in-law Lucretius, Collatinus is said to have returned to Lavinium rather than allow the young men of whom he was *avunculus* to suffer the same fate as did those of whom Brutus was *pater*. Livy also makes much of the support provided Verginia by her

---

ership of a new colony, see Livy 1.6.3-7.3; Dionysius of Halicarnassus 1.85.4-87; Ovid, *Fasti* 3.69-70, 4.807-856; as well as the discussion of Ogilvie, 54. For Tarquinius Superbus and his brother Arruns, see Livy 1.46.4-47.6; Dionysius of Halicarnassus 4.28-30.3; and the discussion of Ogilvie, 184-190. For Tarquinius Priscus' disposal of, and disposal by, the sons of his predecessor Ancus Marcius, of whom he had been guardian and whom he had exiled when "running" for monarch, see Livy 1.34.12-35.2, 40, as well as Ogilvie, 144-146, 160-161.

For Tarquinius Superbus as *avunculus* to Lucius Brutus, see Livy 1.56.4-13; Valerius Maximus 7.3.2; Dionysius of Halicarnassus 4.68; T. N. Gantz, "The Tarquin Dynasty," *Historia* 24 (1985) 545ff., and Table VIII. All three ancient sources claim that Tarquin had slain Brutus' elder brother (explaining Brutus' half-witted behavior—and *cognomen*, which means "dim wit"—as a ploy to avoid appearing a threat to his *avunculus*). As such sources characterize the Etruscan Tullia as the Romans' notion of an evil *filia* and *soror*, and her husband the Romans' notion of a heinous *gener* and *frater*, it stands to reason that Tarquin also differs drastically in character from the kindly Roman *avunculus* we encounter elsewhere. See also the discussion later in this chapter on how the Tarquins are ascribed with violating all valued kinship ties.

own *avus* (Verginius' *socer*) and *avunculus*, perhaps even confusing the former with the latter and the latter with his son in the process.[6]

Nevertheless, more reliable evidence about the conduct of actual *avunculi* from early through later classical times suggests that many of them resembled Collatinus in their deep solicitude for the social welfare of their sisters' offspring—and that some of them even displayed concern for these children's financial well-being. Indeed, while testimony renders it plausible that Rome of the pre-classical era had, as legends imply, emphasized the role of mother's brother, we should judge these literary characterizations of Collatinus, Numitorius, and the Vitellii as, in the first instance, indicating the avuncular image during the period in which our sources on these legends lived. After all, we are told that Lucius Aemilius Paullus gave up one, and by one account the most promising, of his own sons to Scipio, the childless son of Paullus' sister Aemilia; Paullus thereby managed to ensure proper supervision of Aemilia's and her daughters' financial interests. Atticus, alone of his relatives, is said by Nepos to have won the good graces of his wealthy *avunculus* Caecilius: in Caecilius' will he adopted Atticus and left him the bulk of his estate; eventually Atticus was buried in his uncle's sepulcher. We have already noted the seriousness with which the tribune M. Livius Drusus, the *avunculus* of Servilia, the younger Cato, and

[6] For Brutus' sons and their *avunculi*, see in particular Livy 2.4.1 and Dionysius of Halicarnassus 5.6.4-12; see also Plutarch, *Publicola* 3.3-7. For Verginia and her *avunculus*, see Livy 3.44ff.; on the differences between his, and Dionysius', view of the relationship between Verginia and the two P. Numitorii, and the possibility that Livy has confused her *avus* and *avunculus* with her *avunculus* and his son, see chapter three above, n. 60; for another explanation of Livy's use of both *avus* and *avunculus* for P. Numitorius in his account, see Ogilvie, 484, 495.

their siblings, evidently took his responsibilities to them (although when adopting a son, he did not choose one of these nephews, but a Claudius, best remembered as father of the empress Livia). Drusus may have felt such deep concern for his sister's children because he had arranged her first marriage with Q. Servilius Caepio and had himself at that time wed Caepio's sister. Yet a few years later, when enmity arose between him and his "double" brother-in-law (over, among other things, a ring), both unions were dissolved, and Drusus' sister married M. Porcius Cato; the bad blood between Drusus and Caepio may account for Drusus' role in relieving Caepio's agnates from the task of rearing Caepio's children. Lastly, as we have seen, Drusus' two nephews, the younger Cato and Caepio, and Drusus' great-nephew Brutus emulated Drusus as model, influential, and re-marked-upon *avunculi*. When recording a conversation with Cato at *De Finibus* 3.8, Cicero speaks of the younger Servilia's son Lucullus as Cato's special responsibility, and expresses his wish that the youth be educated to resemble his father and "our Caepio" and Cato himself. Tacitus' obituary of the elder Servilia's daughter Junia Tertia, with which he closes book three of the *Annales*, even refers to her as "having Cato as maternal uncle," *Catone avunculo*, before noting that she was wife of Cassius and sister of Brutus. At *Ad Brutum* 13, Brutus appeals to Cicero on behalf of Lepidus' children, to whom he was *avunculus*, by asking to be regarded as having replaced their biological father and avowing that nothing he can do for his sister's children can satisfy his desire or duty.[7]

[7] For Paullus' relinquishing his son to his sister's son, see Polybius 31.26.1-4; Livy 44.44.1-3; Plutarch, *Aemilius Paullus* 5.3-4 (the last of these on the young man's exceptional promise). For Atticus' adoption by his *avunculus*, see Nepos, *Atticus* 5, 22.4, as well as Valerius

Scholars have contended that at least one Roman *avunculus* of the classical era married his sister's daughter: Scribonius Libo, son of the consul of 34 B.C., is viewed as the probable husband of Pompeia, daughter of Sextus Pompey and his wife (the consul's daughter) Scribonia. They postulate this union in the first instance to reconcile two descriptions: one by the younger Seneca, at *Epistles* 1.70.10, of how one Drusus Libo was upbraided by his *amita* Scribonia; the second by Tacitus, at *Annales* 2.27.2, of a Libo Drusus as having Pompey as his great-grand-father (*Pompeium proavum*) and Scribonia, "who had once been Augustus' wife, as his father's sister" (*amitam Scriboniam, quae quondam Augusti coniunx fuerat*). As sister of the consul of 34 B.C., however, this latter Scribonia would herself technically be *amita*, father's sister, to this former Scribonius (as well as *amita* to Sextus Pompey's wife). And although the word *amita* might mean *amita magna*, great aunt, in these two passages, and thus imply that Libo Drusus was Scribonius Libo's son, *amita* does so nowhere else in Latin: Tacitus may, therefore, have confused an actual nephew of Scribonia's with a great-great-nephew who was Sextus Pompey's grandson (and hence the great Pompey's great-grandson).[8]

Maximus 7.8.5. For Drusus' rearing of his sister's offspring and adoption of a Claudius, see the discussion above in chapter two, the article by Münzer in *RE* 13 (1926) 859ff., and Suetonius, *Tiberius* 3.1. For Drusus' earlier marriage to the sister of his former brother-in-law, see Cassius Dio Fr. 96.3 and Pliny, *Natural History* 33.20. For Junia as *Catone avunculo*, see Tacitus, *Annales* 3.76.1; for Brutus as *avunculus*, see also chapter two above, n. 23, and below. At *Brutus* 222, we might note, Cicero specifically refers to Livius Drusus as Brutus' *magnus avunculus*.

[8] For this family, see Table V; for the view that Pompeia had wed her *avunculus*, see the article on Pompeia by Miltner, *RE* 21 (1952) 2264, and the article on Scribonius Libo by Fluss, *RE* 2ª (1921) 885-887, as well as E. F. Leon, "Scribonia and her Daughters," *TAPA* 82 (1951) 174-175. For *amita*, see the article in the *TLL* I (1904) 1919. That Tacitus has confused the son of Scribonia's brother with the grandson of her brother's daughter is rendered more likely by the

The name Libo Drusus, moreover, need not even mark this man as *son* of a Scribonius Libo: he may simply have been named Libo after a maternal grandmother's brother who had adopted him (as e.g. Caesar had Augustus), or after his mother's (and perhaps even his father's) maternal grandfather, the consul of 34 B.C. himself. For the eldest son of M. Licinius Crassus Frugi, consul in A.D. 27, and his wife Scribonia (who is thought a grandchild of Sextus Pompey's daughter Pompeia and her *avunculus* Scribonius Libo by some scholars too) was named Cn. Pompeius Magnus after a maternal male ancestor, presumably the grandfather of his mother's grandmother. If Pompeia's granddaughter's son could

---

fact that he also attributes *consobrinos Caesares* to this Libo Drusus. As daughter of Scribonia, Augustus' daughter Julia would of course be the child of Libo's *amita* and hence his *consobrina*, child of a parent's sister or mother's brother. Since Libo's name "Drusus" also suggests a connection with Augustus' third wife Livia, daughter of a man adopted into the Drusi, one might posit Livia as an *amita* of Libo Drusus too (adoptive sister of his presumably adoptive father, M. Livius Drusus Libo, consul in 15 B.C., who was biological brother of the consul of 34 B.C., and hence also of Scribonia, Augustus' second wife; for Livia's "sisterly" relationship with this man and Scribonia, see, for example, A. C. Bush, *Studies in Roman Social Structure* [Washington, D.C., 1982] 5, 17). This would explain the plural *consobrinos*: under such circumstances Livia's son (and Augustus' adoptive son) Tiberius Caesar would be Libo Drusus' *consobrinus* as well. Significantly, Tacitus speaks of Libo Drusus specifically as *e familia Scriboniorum*, "out of the family of the Scribonii." See also the article on M. Livius Drusus Libo by Fluss, *RE* 13 (1926) 884, and E. Weinrib, "The Family Connections of M. Livius Drusus Libo," *Harvard Studies in Classical Philology* 72 (1967) 250ff. The latter postulates that M. Livius Drusus Libo, the consul of 15 B.C., was not the brother but rather a son of the consul of 34 B.C. as well as adopted son of the empress Livia's father; he also argues that the father of our Libo Drusus was another son of the consul of 34 B.C. whose existence must be postulated for purposes of stemma (this hypothesis would not, however, explain Tacitus' plural *consobrinos* nearly as well). According to Weinrib's theory, our Libo Drusus assumed the names of his paternal uncle as a form of tribute.

be named after her own paternal grandfather, her own
son might well have been named after her own maternal
grandfather; her granddaughter's name, Scribonia, may
have similarly honored Pompeia's maternal grandfather
rather than attest to a marriage between Pompeia and
her own *avunculus*.[9]

[9] For Scribonia, wife of Crassus Frugi and mother of Cn. Pompeius Magnus, see the article in *RE* 2ª (1921) 892. If, as Syme argues
at *The Roman Revolution*, 425 n. 2, her father L. Scribonius Libo and
patruus M. Scribonius Libo Drusus, consul and praetor, respectively,
in A.D. 16, were in fact grandsons of Sextus Pompeius, born in the
early part of Augustus' principate, they may well have been offspring
of Pompeius' rather than Scribonius' son. The decision to name them
after the family of Sextus Pompeius' wife, whose *amita* apparently
still identified herself as Augustus' wife years after their divorce—
on which point see Leon, "Scribonia," 170—rather than after Pompeius, Augustus' foe and foe to his adoptive father Caesar, might,
after all, be politically motivated. The possibility that Sextus Pompeius was their *paternal* grandfather is not considered by Weinrib,
"Family Connections," 252ff. Nevertheless, he disputes Mommsen's
hypothesis that the consul of 15 B.C. had derived the *agnomen* Libo
from his mother on the grounds that "such metronymics do not
become fashionable until later in the Julio-Claudian principate"; in
so doing, he observes that the earliest apparent example of the assumption of the maternal grandfather's *cognomen* is Cn. Cornelius
Cinna Magnus, consul in A.D. 5. In other words, Weinrib shows
that precedents as well as parallels may be adduced for the maternal
nomenclature of the praetor of A.D. 16. So, too, this precedent, like
the name given the son of M. Licinius Crassus Frugi, significantly
involves the leading republican family of the Pompeii, and thus
renders more likely a similar commemoration of the Libones, *adfines*
of the Pompeii, with prominent republican connections but also,
and more advantageously, the house of Augustus' second wife. Finally, Weinrib claims on 250 that the Pompeia married to the son
of the consul of 34 B.C. was not the daughter of Sextus Pompey but
of Sextus' sister, the Pompeia Magna who was also mother of Cn.
Cornelius Cinna Magnus. Yet under such circumstances Augustus'
wife Scribonia would still be our Libo's *amita magna* and her daughter
would not be his *consobrina*. Evidence for the existence of this Pompeia, however—an inscription (ILS 1946) on a slave and two freedmen belonging to her and her brother—reminds us again that under
the Augustan principate the naming of offspring after maternal

This effort to question scholarly consensus, in a complicated and speculative genealogical digression, stems from the fact that it does not appear to have been permissible under Roman law of any period for a man to marry his sister's daughter. We may ascertain this from the study of another, less tenacious, Roman legal prohibition. When the emperor Claudius decided to marry the younger Agrippina, daughter of his brother Germanicus, he was, according to Tacitus, *Annales* 12.7.2, forced to issue a decree which made "marriages between paternal uncles and their brothers' daughters legal" (*iustae inter patruos fratrumque filias nuptiae*). No precedents seem to have been found at Rome for such a union, merely the practices of "other peoples" (such as the Athenians). Yet Tacitus also states that one Roman knight followed Claudius' example at once. And although the jurist Gaius maintains, at least a century later, that Claudius' decree was then still in force, he adds, *sororis vero filiam uxorem ducere non licet*, "it is [still] illegal for a man to marry his sister's daughter."[10] Festus' definition of

---

grandfathers becomes fairly common; on this point, see also chapter six below.

[10] For Claudius' breaking with Roman precedent in wedding his brother's daughter and the decree authorizing his conduct see also Suetonius, *Divus Claudius* 26.3. Both H. Furneaux, *The Annales of Tacitus* XI-XVI (Oxford, 1907) II.69, and E. Koestermann, *Cornelius Tacitus Annalen* 11-13 (Heidelberg, 1967) III.118, assume that by "other peoples" Tacitus means the Spartans; they cite Herodotus 5.39.2. The Athenian institution of the epiclerate, however, must have led to many marriages between a brotherless daughter and her father's brother, since he had first claim to her hand; see, e.g. the discussions cited in n.17, chapter three above. On Claudius' imitators, see also Suetonius, *Divus Claudius* 26.3, which cites a freedman and a chief centurion who followed Claudius' example, the latter of whom had Claudius and Agrippina in attendence at his nuptials. At *Domitianus* 22 Suetonius relates that Domitian was offered the hand of his brother's daughter but refused; on their eventual liaison, see the discussion below.

an *avunculus* as a possible guardian to his sister's daughter may also reflect a Roman belief that a tie comparable to that of father and daughter existed between *avunculus* and *sororis filia* and thus further illuminate the illegality of a formal union between them: a view of a sister's children as one's father's, and hence one's own, blood line would additionally lie behind a taboo against wedding and siring offspring by a sister's daughter. The frequency with which we encounter well-born *avunculi* without sons who adopted their sisters' male issue certainly suggests that a special, paternal bond existed between themselves and these sisters' children. Such *avunculi* include the elder Servilia's brother Caepio, who may have adopted Brutus, and Caecilius, who adopted Atticus, during republican times. Also numbered among them are such figures of the imperial era as Augustus (who adopted his sister's son Marcellus) and the elder Pliny (whose sister's son is remembered by Pliny's own name and for immortalizing Pliny's heroic death).[11]

For Gaius' statement on the illegality of marriage between *avunculus* and *sororis filia*, see *Institutes* 1.62; this point is also made emphatically by Weinrib, "Family Connections," 249. At *Studies*, 108, however, Bush follows Münzer in postulating unions not only between Libo and his sister's daughter but also between D. Junius Brutus and his half-sister's daughter Sempronia. See also Plutarch, *Quaestiones Romanae* 6, who notes that "it has not been custom" for Romans to marry nearer kin than cousins.

[11] In his register of adoptions from roughly 130 to 43 B.C., D. R. Shackleton Bailey, *Two Studies in Roman Nomenclature* (New York, 1976) 122ff., notes the adoption of sisters' sons by the late republican dictator Marius, L. Minucius Basilus, one Sufenas and C. Rabirius. G. Alfs, *Adoptionen in der römischen Republik bis auf die des Caesar Octavianus* (Cologne dissertation, 1950) 88, goes so far as to say that in the republic the preferred relationship of adopter to adoptee was that between mother's brother and sister's son. For Augustus and Marcellus, see Plutarch, *Antony* 87.2; for the elder Pliny and his adoption of Pliny the Younger, see Pliny, *Epistles* 5.8.5. One might additionally cite the intention, reported by Valerius Maximus at 5.9.2, of the orator Hortensius to make his sister's son Messalla his

Tendencies for the nephews of an upper-class Roman *avunculus* to perform the public functions of or publicly evince the devotion expected from a Roman son merit notice as well. To cite an instance from the republican period, Quintus Aelius Tubero is credited with giving the funeral feast (and in one account the funeral *laudatio*) for his *avunculus* Scipio Aemilianus. From the early empire we might recall Tiberius' aide Sejanus, who used his influence with the emperor to obtain first a command and then a never-repeated honor (that of being hailed *imperator* by one's troops while still a private citizen) for his *avunculus* Q. Junius Blaesus.[12] These tendencies of sisters' sons to treat *avunculi* as fathers may merely be prompted by the paternal solicitude displayed by so many *avunculi* for the social welfare of their sisters' sons. Yet such acts may also have formally repaid *avunculi* for their

---

heir; the historian Sallust, according to Tacitus, *Annales* 3.30.2, adopted his sister's grandson (presumably in the years when the similarly adopted Augustus was rising to power).

[12] On Tubero, see Cicero, *Pro Murena* 75-76, Valerius Maximus 7.5.1, and the discussion of A. E. Astin, *Scipio Aemilianus* (Oxford, 1967) 243-244. Astin, however, disputes Cicero's claim at *De Oratore* 2.84.341 that Tubero presented the *laudatio*, and instead assigns it to Scipio's brother's son Fabius Maximus (on the evidence of other sources, including Cicero himself at *Pro Murena* 75). See also Gruen, *Last Generation*, 334, and T. P. Wiseman, *Cinna the Poet and Other Essays* (Leicester, 1974) 112ff. The former reminds us that M'. Acilius Glabrio and C. Memmius pleaded on behalf of M. Aemilius Scaurus at Scaurus' trial in 54 B.C.; Glabrio was son of Scaurus' sister Aemilia, Memmius son of Scaurus' maternal half-sister Fausta. The latter cites the completion of a monumental gateway at Eleusis, which had been begun in 54 B.C. by the consul Appius Claudius Pulcher, by Appius' sister's and brother's sons; Wiseman infers Appius' adoption of this *sororis filius* from the funeral games he held for the boy's late father, Q. Marcius Rex. For Sejanus and Blaesus, see Tacitus, *Annales* 3.35.3, 58, 72.3-4, 74.3-4. Both R.S.P. Beekes, "Uncle and Nephew," *JIS* 4 (1976) 50, and Bremmer, "Avunculate and Fosterage," 68, comment upon the frequency of *nepos fecit avunculo* on Roman imperial epitaphs.

out-and-out involvement in their nephews' training for aristocratic public life.

The involvement by mothers' brothers in preparing young men for the public arena is reported in various instances and may be inferred in several others. Cicero's letters, for example, clearly testify that his friend Atticus, father of a daughter but of no male children, had much to do with the education and upbringing of Quintus Cicero, son of his sister Pomponia by Cicero's own *frater*. At *Brutus* 108 and 115, moreover, Cicero seems to imply similar avuncular nurturance by two distinguished orators of the republican era. In the former passage Cicero notes the "moderate" oratorical achievements of one G. Cato and refers to this Cato not as grandson of the great censor and son of that censor's elder son Licinianus, but as the son of Scipio Aemilianus' sister. Cicero presumably does so because G. Cato's father had died when his son was quite young and Cato's *avunculus* had taken charge of his nephew's education in public speaking. In the latter passage Cicero describes a speech by the eloquent Publius Rutilius in his own defense and remarks that his sister's son G. Cotta added a few words *ut orator* as well. Cicero presumably remarks upon Cotta's performance on this occasion (and Cotta presumably performed) because Rutilius had played some part in Cotta's mastery of oratorical fundamentals.[13]

Later sources allow us to postulate political mentorship, or at least political inspiration, by *avunculi* in two families of the classical era renowned for their opposition

---

[13] For Atticus' role in educating Quintus Cicero, see Cicero, *Ad Atticum* 2.2.1, 4.7.1, 9.2; see also the article on Quintus by Münzer in *RE*² 7A.2 (1948) 1306-1311. For the early death of Gaius Cato's father, see Plutarch, *Cato Major* 24.6, 27.5; for Scipio Aemilianus' generosity to young Cato's mother, see (again) Polybius 31.28.8-9 and Cicero, *De Amicitia* 11. Velleius Paterculus 2.8.1 also identifies this Cato as *Africani sororis filius*.

to monarchic government. The impact of such *avunculi*, ironically, calls to mind that of the legendary Vitellii, under whose guidance the liberator Brutus' sons supposedly became supporters of the movement to restore monarchy in early Rome. Gnaeus Pompey, elder son of Julius Caesar's colleague-turned-enemy, became a leader of the anti-Caesarean cause after his father's death in 48 B.C., and was succeeded in this position—after his own death in 45—by his younger brother Sextus. Both Seneca and Cassius Dio report that Gaius Cornelius Cinna Magnus, son of Gnaeus' and Sextus' sister, made an attempt on the life of Caesar's heir Augustus; desire to avenge these two *avunculi*, and his *maternus avus* Pompey the Great, doubtless motivated Cinna's deed. More appositely, Velleius Paterculus furnishes some valuable information about Caesar's own slayer Marcus Junius Brutus, himself responsible for the survival of his *avunculus* Cato's pro-republican cause (and himself inspired to tyrannicide by the example of a maternal male ancestor, the early republican Servilius Ahala, no less than by Lucius Brutus the liberator): Velleius implies that Brutus provided his sister's children by Lepidus with political indoctrination as well as with paternal protection. For, Velleius reports, twelve years after Brutus' death young Lepidus also plotted unsuccessfully to assassinate Caesar's successor; significantly, Lepidus' execution was followed by the suicide of his wife, who claimed Brutus as *avunculus* and apparently espoused his political beliefs as well. *Avunculi* are remembered as affording sisters' sons opportunities for military experience too: the German military disaster of P. Quinctilius Varus in A.D. 9 was to some extent offset by the valor of his legate, L. Nonius Asprenas, son of Varus' sister. One *avunculus* may even have paved the way for his nephew's success in the field of literature: Pacuvius, the great tragic poet of the second century B.C., is noted as a disciple of Ennius, father of Latin literature and the brother to Pacuvius' mother.[14]

The responsibility taken, and regard shown, by an *avunculus* for his sister through solicitude for her children seems to have been reciprocated by similar solicitude on the part of a sister toward her brother's offspring; various sources characterize the Roman *amita* as a maternal and respected figure, the name she shares with her nieces and nephews perhaps symbolic of concern felt for, and esteem felt by, them. In Valerius Maximus' effusive praise, at 3.8.6, of Sempronia, sister of Tiberius and Gaius Gracchus and wife of Scipio Aemilianus, he observes that she was publicly and unsuccessfully pressured by one Equitius to recognize him as her brother Tiberius' son; Valerius hence suggests that *amitae* generally enjoyed authority among their agnates and might even represent such kindred in Roman society at large. Aebutius' grateful reliance upon his *amita* in Livy's account of the Bacchanalian scandal, Scipio Aemilianus' political (and his sisters' financial) profit from his own *amita* Aemilia's legacy, and Julius Caesar's rhetorical reflection on the glorious lineage of his *amita* Julia, all cited in chapter two, furnish testimony to the supportive posi-

---

[14] For Gnaeus and Sextus Pompeius, see, *inter alios*, Seneca, *Ad Polybium De Consolatione* 15.1-2; for Cornelius Cinna's plot against Augustus, see Seneca, *De Clementia* 1.9, and Cassius Dio 55.14ff.; for Cinna himself, see also above, n. 9. For Brutus' inspiration by both Servilius Ahala and Lucius Brutus, see Africa, 610, 616-617; Plutarch, *Brutus* 1; and chapter three above, n. 50. For young Lepidus' plot, see Livy, *Periochae* 133, and Velleius Paterculus 2.88. Lepidus' wife Servilia was daughter of P. Servilius Isauricus and Junia, another of Servilia's daughters; see Table IV. For the valor of Nonius Asprenas, see Velleius Paterculus 2.120.3. For Pacuvius as Ennius' *discipulus* and *sororis filius*, see Pomponius, *apud Nonium* 125 Lindsay, and Pliny, *Natural History* 35.19; I owe this observation to J. Bremmer.

tion often occupied by as well as the respect often accorded to fathers' sisters in the republican period. Similar
evidence remains about fathers' sisters in imperial times.
Octavia, *amita* (and mother-in-law) to Augustus' daughter Julia, is reported to have proposed the divorce of her
own daughter Marcella so that the recently widowed
Julia might wed Marcella's husband, Agrippa. Seneca's
anecdote about the sound and duly accepted advice proffered Drusus Libo by his *amita* Scribonia, called by Seneca a dignified woman, *gravis femina*, warrants mention
in this connection, as do the political machinations of
Domitia on her nephew Nero's behalf, and the care taken
of Nero by his other *amita* Domitia Lepida. Another
example of maternal concern for a brother's child is the
upbringing of the younger Pliny's wife, Calpurnia Hispulla, by her *amita*, to whom Calpurnia was devoted.[15]

An equality between Roman brother and sister in regard to responsibilities for one another's offspring follows logically from the aforementioned Roman defi-

[15] On Sempronia's confrontation with Equitius, see also the discussion of Herrmann, 90-91. For Octavia's initiation of Julia's marriage to Agrippa, see Plutarch, *Antony* 87.2; Suetonius, *Divus Augustus* 63.1, merely says that Octavia consented. See also J. E. Phillips,
"Roman Mothers and the Lives of their Adult Daughters," *Helios*
6.1 (1978) 73, and Balsdon, 73-74. For Scribonia and Drusus Libo,
see Seneca, *Epistles* 1.70.10. For Nero's *amitae* and their influence,
see Tacitus, *Annales* 12.64.2-3, 13, 19.4, 21.3; Suetonius, *Nero* 5.2,
6.3, 24.5; Balsdon 118-122. For the *amita* of Calpurnia Hispulla, see
Pliny, *Epistles* 4.19, 8.11, as well as the discussion of Phillips, "Roman Mothers," 74-75. At *De Oratore* 2.55.225ff. Cicero describes
how the death of an aged woman named Junia was oratorically
exploited to shame her kinsman Brutus. Brutus was asked in this
speech what news he wished the dead woman to convey to his father
and other deceased Junii Bruti; he was presented with a contrast
between his ancestors' glorious deeds and his own indolence, concluding "Don't you thoroughly tremble at the dead lady?" This Junia
would seem to be this Brutus' or his father's *amita*, and in any event
an immensely respected older female agnate.

nition—implied by the use of the same words in masculine and feminine forms to designate "sons" and "daughters"—of male and female children as equivalent offspring in the eyes of their parents. It also attests that sons and daughters were raised not only as individuals similarly valued by their fathers (and mothers) but as individuals with important mutual obligations to one another. Furthermore, an elite Roman brother's and sister's view of one another as equals regarding obligations to the others' children seems deeply rooted in the assumption of a brother's and sister's mutual affection.

Sundry sources suggest that a special and strong emotional bond was supposed to exist between an elite Roman sister and her brother throughout the classical era. Festus contends that brothers and sisters generally cherish each other. Plautus depicts Eunomia at *Aulularia* 120ff. as reminding Megadorus that she, like any sister, has his interests at heart, and that she is closest to him and he to her (128 *tibi proxumam me mihi esse item te*). We might also recall Cicero's courtroom description at *Pro Fonteio* 46-47 of Fonteius' preciousness to his Vestal sister, with its intimation that her embraces and appeals on his behalf bespeak her equal preciousness to him.

Evidence from the early empire reflects no less vividly this assumption about mutual brotherly and sisterly devotion. When Seneca refers to Augustus' profound sorrow over the death of his most precious sister (*carissimam*) Octavia, he a-chronologically lists this bereavement before all of Augustus' other losses and equates it with the loss (by the Greek freedman to whom he addresses this essay, and by other Roman upper-class men) of beloved brothers. In another consolatory essay, Seneca relates the reaction of Octavia to her son Marcellus' passing, remarking that "she did not even give a thought to her brother." Such a comment, coupled with the subsequent reference to Octavia's hatred of the good fortune gleaming around her from her brother's greatness, seems to imply emotional disturbance on Octavia's part; as Seneca assumes Octavia's own death to have been a painful blow to her brother, so he assumes that Augustus and his achievements should have afforded his sister comfort if not pleasure.[16] At *Annales* 14.64.1, Tacitus claims that Claudius' daughter Octavia appealed for mercy to her ex-husband and step-brother Nero on the grounds that she was "only a sister"; earlier, at 13.16-17, Tacitus had spoken of Octavia's suppressed grief and affection for her murdered brother Britannicus, and lamented that the dying youth had not even been given an opportunity to embrace his sisters. That a Roman brother was expected to feel strong emotional ties to his sister, and that he could expect affection of the same sort in return is also suggested by Martial in 2.4. By saying that one Ammianus so adores his mother that she calls him *frater* and he calls her *soror*, Martial imputes a strong affective resonance to both kinship terms.

That such mutual affection did exist between elite Roman brothers and sisters is implied by instances of their considerate and helpful conduct to one another. Elite Roman sisters, as we have seen, could often rely upon their brothers for various kinds of outright support, support resonating in Roman public life and sup-

[16] For Octavia's preciousness to Augustus, see Seneca, *Ad Polybium De Consolatione* 15.3. For Seneca on Octavia's (inappropriate) lack of concern for her brother, see *Ad Marciam De Consolatione* 2.4. At *Ad Polybium De Consolatione* 17.4ff., Seneca criticizes Caligula's lack of respect and princely decorum upon the deeply regretted death of his sister Drusilla (inasmuch as Caligula engrossed himself in gambling at his Alban villa rather than attend her funeral and cope appropriately with his grief); affection for sisters by brothers and vice versa was expected to be expressed through *constructive* public behavior.

port which redounded to their own, and not merely
their children's, benefit. Some of this support involved
distinctly paternal and protective behavior. Two inci-
dents discussed in earlier contexts spring first to mind:
the younger Cato's assumption of guardianship over the
younger Servilia after her divorce from Lucullus; Scipio
Aemilianus' display of generosity to his sisters after their
mother's death. Yet another warrants mention as well:
Plutarch reports that, after vainly dissuading her husband Gaius Gracchus from meeting certain death in the
forum, Licinia collapsed and was carried unconscious to
the house of her brother Crassus. Brothers are also remembered for using their political power in explicit accordance with their sisters' wishes. Cassius Dio relates
that one Tanusia and her proscribed husband, Titus Vinius, escaped the death penalty because of the intervention of Octavia—who arranged that her brother alone
of the triumvirs enter the theater at a popular festival,
hear Tanusia's account of how she had hidden Vinius
in a chest, and witness Vinius' actual emergence from
his hiding place. One may even attribute the ill will of
the younger Cato toward Pompey to the fact that Pompey had killed M. Brutus, husband of Cato's sister the
elder Servilia.[17]

One could additionally interpret Atticus' publicly
professed pride in the tranquillity of his relationship with
his sister Pomponia as a gesture of fraternal support.

[17] For Licinia's succor by Crassus, see Plutarch, *Gaius Gracchus*
15.4. For Octavian's efforts in response to Octavia's urging, see
Cassius Dio 47.7.4-5; I owe this reference to R. MacMullen. For the
younger Cato's hostility to Pompey and its causes—a point called
to my attention by E. Badian—see the article on M. Porcius Cato
Uticensis by Miltner in *RE* 22.1 (1953) 168ff.; Plutarch, *Pompey* 16.5-
6, 44, 52.5-6, 56.3; and *Cato Minor* 30.2-31, 41-45.2-4, 47 (as well
as *Brutus* 4.1, claiming that Brutus was expected to side with Caesar
rather than his father's slayer Pompey, but did not); Africa, 608.

After all, two years before Atticus delivered his famed *laudatio matris*, Pomponia's husband—and Cicero's brother—Quintus decided, after two and one half decades of marriage, that he could endure Pomponia's ill temper and imperiousness no longer; he arranged to repay her immense dowry and extolled the pleasures of a bachelor's bed. Perhaps Atticus wished to reassure his friends and acquaintances that Pomponia was not solely to blame for the rupture, and to do so by emphasizing the concord between Pomponia and her brother, a kinsman with whom she was expected to have strong differences of opinion. Whatever his motives for making this particular statement, Atticus clearly labored throughout his life to be of service to his sister. By alluding to his harmonious bond with her, implicitly representing her viewpoint on matters concerning him as one which he respected no less than she did his on those concerning her, he was also indisputably paying her a public compliment; in so doing, he appears to have acted in the publicly supportive manner that the Romans of his day and milieu deemed appropriate to a brother.[18]

Furthermore, Roman brothers of Atticus' day and the century and a half thereafter are, in turn, reported to have obtained various kinds of outright, publicly resonant support from their sisters. We might again recall

---

[18] For Pomponia's divorce, see Cicero, *Ad Atticum* 14.13.5, and Balsdon, 212; for Pomponia's ill temper and imperiousness, see Cicero, *Ad Atticum* 5.1.3-4. Plutarch's comments at *Cicero* 49.2, on Pomponia's alleged physical brutality to Philogogus, the freedman of Quintus who had betrayed Cicero to his assassins, may also be relevant here—testimony to her reputation for fierceness. For Atticus' services to his sister, see, for example, the letters cited in n. 13 above. One could, of course, interpret Atticus' public remarks about the concord between him and his sister in an oration about his newly dead mother quite differently—e.g. that he was claiming his family to be unusually harmonious—and not as necessarily reflecting upon Pomponia's divorce at all.

the interchange between Eunomia and Megadorus in the *Aulularia* on the obligations of male and female siblings to one another: numerous episodes of actual Roman behavior bear out its assertion that Roman sisters were no less liable to stand by their brothers than their brothers were to stand by them. Suetonius' account, at *Tiberius* 2.5, of the Vestal Claudia's heroism has her provide sacred protection for a triumphant *frater* rather than a *pater*. According to Suetonius, *Divus Julius* 74.2, Julius Caesar's sister Julia and mother testified in court to his wife Pompeia's adultery—and defiling of sacred ceremonies—with Publius Clodius; Caesar thereby managed to divorce Pompeia without having to give evidence on her conduct himself. Sources relate that Mark Antony's mother Julia managed to rescue her brother, Antony's disdained *avunculus* Lucius Caesar, when Antony had him proscribed in 43 B.C.: Caesar is said to have fled to his sister's house, and been saved by her harsh reminder to his persecutors that she had brought their commander Antony into this world and that they were not to slay her brother unless they killed her first. Correspondence between Marcus Brutus and Cicero in 43 B.C. portrays the former as relying upon his sister, wife of Cassius, as well as his mother to publicize Cassius' successes. At *Annales* 3.69.6 Tacitus tells how, in A.D. 22, the Vestal Junia Torquata appealed successfully to secure her brother Silanus a lighter sentence. Tacitus' *Annales* also cites several women in Julio-Claudian times who were outlawed or banished because of their brothers' political victimization—Sancia and Pompeia Macrina in A.D. 33, Junia Calvina in A.D. 49—and apparently treated thus lest they come to their brothers' aid. Finally, the younger Pliny's famed letter to Tacitus on the eruption of Vesuvius, 6.20, states that Pliny's mother refused to flee out of anxiety for her missing brother, claiming that she

and her son would not think of considering their own
safety as long as they were uncertain of his; an earlier
letter to Tacitus, 6.16, even credits her with initially
calling her brother's attention to an unusual cloud formation.[19]

Testimony to a general Roman cultural emphasis on
the role of brother's sister has previously been discerned
in the importance assigned, and attractive portrayals accorded, *amitae*. It may also be discerned in the close,
often politically expressed ties between many Roman
males of the upper classes and their sisters' husbands.
Such ties often seem to have been valued as much as
those between fathers-in-law and sons-in-law. Like *socer-gener* ties, of course, these brother-in-law bonds may
not necessarily have been forged with the individual
sister's wishes and interests in mind (particularly if her
father or another older male had arranged the match);
such unions, like those involving a daughter rather than
a sister of one male party, may merely have served economic or political purposes for the men so bonded. Still,
the elite Roman sister's role here, as link between her
brother and spouse, is a central one. What is more, were
she and her spouse to produce children, and thereby

[19] For Julia's rescue of her brother, see Plutarch, *Antony* 20.3, and
Appian, *Bella Civilia* 4.37; see also the article by Münzer in *RE* 10
(1918) 471 and Africa, 606. Testimony to Julia's reputation for intimidating and obtaining her way from males in fact begins Plutarch's
life of Antony: in chapter 1 she is reported to have extorted a confession and plea for forgiveness from her husband after she angrily
questioned the slaves as to the whereabouts of a silver bowl he had
given to a friend; in chapter 2 Antony is quoted as claiming that
Cicero would not hand over for burial the body of her second husband, one of Catiline's cohorts, until she prevailed upon him through
his wife. For Brutus' reliance upon Junia and his mother in this
connection, see *Ad Brutum* 2.3.3, 2.4.5. For Sancia, see Tacitus,
Annales 6.18.1; for Pompeia Macrina, *Annales* 6.18.2; for Junia Calvina, *Annales* 12.4, 8.

make her brother an *avunculus*, the involvement customary on his part with her offspring might have encouraged stronger bonding on his part with both her husband and herself.

Several major political alliances were created during the late republic through the marriage of one party to the other party's sister. To be sure, not all marriages uniting such men eventuated in issue; we thus cannot determine whether the birth of children brought brother and sister, and brother and sister's spouse, closer together in such cases. Yet it is possible that the apparent lack of offspring in the marriage of Cassius to the sister of his co-conspirator Brutus may have contributed to the documented tensions in the men's union: at least Brutus' devotion to the children of another sister suggests that he would have been a no less devoted and helpful *avunculus* in Cassius' household. The triumviral connection between Octavian and Antony, however, is said by Suetonius to have publicly foundered over the latter's intention of listing his children by Cleopatra as his heirs. By severing their alliance over this matter, Octavian may have thereby implied that Antony had somehow slighted not only his sister, Antony's wife Octavia, but also Antony's daughters by her. That this slight ranked to Octavian as—and evidently would have been judged by others—an unpardonable offense in turn implies that these children played and were expected to play a key role in his bonds with both Antony and his sister. And obviously children did play a key role in the previously cited and politically motivated "double bind" (with each man wed to the other's sister) between the tribune Drusus and Q. Servilius Caepio. After all, Drusus assumed care of Caepio's offspring by his sister Livia as well as those of this sister by her next husband Cato; Drusus thereby even continued to aid Caepio after each had divorced the other's sister (and had in fact become bitter political enemies) as well as managing to be of greater help to Livia herself.[20]

During the early imperial era sisters (and at times their children) also served to link brothers and spouses more closely, and with significant political impact. Various examples of elite brother-in-law bonding in the Julio-Claudian period illustrate that the role of brother's sister remained politically important despite the major transformation of Roman government from republic to imperial monarchy. Most notably, the marriage of Livilla, sister of Tiberius' adopted son Germanicus, to Tiberius' biological son Drusus was doubtless intended as a means of strengthening the bond between the two men. Although Germanicus died before Livilla gave birth to her twin sons, his own son and her (and Drusus') daughter were wed in A.D. 20, the year after Germanicus' death (and presumably betrothed well before that); we might recall this fact in connection with Tacitus' claim that *these* brothers were good friends, unaffected by the split in Tiberius' court between their respected partisans. Furthermore, according to Cassius Dio, another of Ger-

[20] For Brutus and Cassius, see, for example, Plutarch, *Brutus* 1.2, 6.3-10, 12.5, 16.3-4, 19.2-20.1, 28.3-30, 32, 34-35, 37-40, 42-46. For Octavian's rupture with Antony, see Suetonius, *Divus Augustus* 17. Plutarch does not, however, mention the provision for Cleopatra's children in his life of Antony. Yet he does claim at 31.1 that Octavian was immensely fond of his sister, and notes at 53.5 that she was reviled for having wed Antony not out of love but for politics and her brother's sake. For Drusus and Caepio, see above, n. 7. Other late republican—and politically important—brother-in-law bonds are discussed by Gruen, *Last Generation*, 47-82: e.g. the younger Cato's with Domitius Ahenobarbus (movingly described by Plutarch, *Cato Minor* 51.2ff.); Quintus Lutatius Catulus' with the orator Hortensius. The role played by sisters' children in strengthening ties of brother to sister, and brother-in-law, in these cases is not clear from our sources.

manicus' sons, the emperor Gaius Caligula, promised the succession to the husband of his sister Drusilla, only to have Lepidus executed after Drusilla's death for conspiring against him in A.D. 39. At *Annales* 13.53 Tacitus reports that one Pompeius Paulinus served as governor of Lower Germany early in the reign of Nero: Paulinus surely owed his occupation of this important post to Nero's tutor and counselor Seneca, wed to Paulinus' sister.[21]

We have observed that legends about earliest Rome also depict the bond between brother and sister, and the roles of brother's sister and sister's brother, as of great cultural importance during this remote era; they also characterize early Roman brother-sister bonding as exhibiting several behavioral features connected with that among the elite in the classical period. To wit, in these tales Horatius acts as his father's surrogate in regard to his sister (albeit without authorization at the time); Tarquinius Superbus provides his sister's son with valuable political training by including him in an important foreign mission; the Vitellii convert their sister's sons to their political cause; Collatinus offers his sister's sons indulgent political protection; Valeria acquires a position of political and moral leadership as a result of her consular brother's achievement.[22] Again, these legendary

---

[21] On the closeness of Drusus and Germanicus—an observation I owe to K. G. Wallace—see Tacitus, *Annales* 2.43.6. According to Tacitus, *Annales* 2.84.1, Drusus' twin sons were born immediately after his brother-in-law's death in A.D. 19. On the first marriage of Drusus' daughter to Germanicus' son, see Tacitus, *Annales* 3.29.4. For Caligula and Lepidus, see Cassius Dio 59.22.6ff.; Suetonius, *Caligula* 24.3; Balsdon, 117. For Paulinus, see Syme, *Tacitus* (Oxford, 1958) II. 591.

[22] For Horatius, see chapter three above, n. 56; for Tarquinius Superbus, the Vitellii and Collatinus, see above, nn. 5 and 6; for (Plutarch's) Valeria, see chapter 2, n. 17.

depictions of early Roman brother-sister bonding should
be regarded primarily as reflecting attitudes of the culture in and for which they were written, that of elite
Rome in the classical era. But evidence from earliest
Rome does render it plausible that both high valuation
of sisters by, and because of, their brothers and that a
cultural emphasis on the roles of brother's sister and
sister's brother obtained at that time too. Such a state
of family affairs would, of course, follow logically from
the high valuation initially accorded women by and because of their (and their brothers') fathers, and from the
cultural centrality of the daughter role; the preceding
chapter has, of course, posited the existence of both
phenomena during Rome's monarchic and early republican eras.

We have already discussed the testimony for early
Roman notions of kinship provided by the word *avunculus*, which points to a maternal uncle's original role of
special paternal figure to a sister's children as his father's
surrogate. No less significantly, the Latin term for sister,
soror, seems to derive from the same Indo-European root
as does *socer*. It seems to mean "the female with whom
one is most closely linked"; it thus implies that the female relation with whom a Roman man or woman originally was perceived as having the greatest common
interest was the daughter of his or her father; more
strikingly, it might also be construed as implying that
throughout his life a male member of earliest Roman
society, even a married man with his own children, was
to count his sister—even a married sister with her own
offspring—as his closest female kin.[23]

[23] See Szemerényi, 32-47, 150. As I did in the case of *socer* (chapter
three above, n. 71), I take issue with Szemerényi and accept the view
of Meringer and the French school, interpreting *soror* as from *swe-
and hence meaning "one's own woman," "the woman belonging

Under the Twelve Tables a wife who had passed into her husband's *manus* had the legal status of sister to her own children. Here, too, therefore, we encounter the modeling of a woman's formal role in a marital union upon the biological role of a woman in her family of birth, in this instance with the responsibilities assigned her male children implicitly defined as those undertaken by brothers. What is more, just as the symbolic extension of the daughter role beyond its biological confines to wives and Vestal Virgins bespeaks a larger cultural valuation of that role, this similar, metaphorical extension of the sister role implies that by the time of the Twelve Tables it was also valued in Roman culture at large. That from early times Roman women seem to have had the same *gentilicia nomina* as their fathers' sons merits attention in this context, since a Roman brother and sister were usually contemporaries, members of the same generation (whereas a Roman father and daughter were not): hence a Roman brother and sister would tend to be identified with one another longer than either would be with other similarly named kin.[24]

Admittedly, the longstanding Roman legal definition of a wife in *manus* as both *in loco filiae* to her husband and *in loco sororis* to her children, and the longstanding Roman linguistic practice of assigning a sister the female form of her father's, and hence her brother's, *gentilicium nomen*, merely rank as additional testimony to the importance of the role of sister to a brother and to the importance of the brother-sister bond in republican Ro-

---

to the same family group"; that the first Romans subscribed to this earlier Indo-European notion of sisterhood is suggested by both their naming practices and various legal and cultic details.

[24] For the "sister-status" occupied by a Roman wife married with *manus* relative to her own offspring, see Gaius, *Institutes* 1.148, and Pomeroy, "The Relationship of the Married Woman to her Blood Relatives in Rome," *Ancient Society* 7 (1976) 216.

man times; one cannot consider this definition and this
practice conclusive evidence about the monarchic era
(though we will presently examine testimony which
suggests that these bonding patterns did originate in the
monarchic period). Nonetheless, such data still indicate
that the Roman role of sister to a brother was regarded
as closely linked with, and indeed as the kindred successor to, the role of father's daughter. They thus permit
us to infer, as does much of the evidence surveyed so
far, that Roman sisters in large part owed their valuation
by brothers, just as brothers would in large part appear
to owe their valuation by sisters, to valuation from birth
by their fathers. Valuation *by* mothers of both female
and male offspring and valuation *of* mothers by both
male and female offspring also seem to have played a
large role in strengthening the bonds between upper-
class Roman siblings; the close ties between maternally
related half-siblings such as the younger Cato, Caepio,
and the Serviliae, or Mucia and the Metelli, alone imply
as much, as will other evidence to be studied in the
following chapter. But inasmuch as a Roman woman
could be sister to female as well as to male siblings, we
should now examine portrayals of the bond between
Roman sisters in our sources. Investigation of this bond,
moreover, further reveals that parenthood of offspring
descended from the same maternal grandfather was accorded special significance among the upper class Romans; it hence further accounts for the importance of
the "mature" familial roles of *avunculus* and *amita* to the
strong bond we have seen ascribed to, and existing between, the Roman *frater* and *soror*.

SOROR SORORQUE

Like the bond between a well-born Roman woman and
her brother, a Roman woman's bond with her sister

seems to have been strong, although the likelihood of a Roman woman's having a sister—in a society which supposedly required a father to rear all of his sons but only the first-born female child—was probably not as high as that of having male siblings. Several Latin literary sources idealize the mutual devotion of *sorores*. Perhaps Vergil's—and Ovid's—portrayal of the closeness between Queen Dido and her sister Anna may not be apposite in this connection, as these are Carthaginian and not Roman women. But a passage in Ennius' *Annales* assigned to Ilia, the Vestal mother of Romulus, seems to have influenced Dido's words to Anna in the *Aeneid*: here, in a moving address to her sister, Ilia begins by referring to this, *germana, soror*, as beloved by their father, and proceeds to recount a dream in which their late father Aeneas appeared to her and prophesied a favorable future. This passage, like other literary depictions of sisterly solidarity such as the lines which open Plautus' *Stichus* (1-154), thus links the intimacy between Roman sisters with their father's affection for them both. We find this same motif at lines 59-60 of the aforementioned Propertius 4.11, where Cornelia claims that Augustus mourned her as a worthy sister to his own daughter: to be sure, Augustus was not Cornelia's biological father, but his fond feelings for her, as his child Julia's female sibling, evidently were thought to validate her in this particular role.[25]

[25] For Dido and Anna, see Vergil, *Aeneid* 4.9-53, 416-440, 478-503, 675-687; Ovid, *Heroides* 7.191-192, and *Fasti* 3.559-566, 571, 597-599, 610, 623-624, 629-640. The traditional enmity between these sisters and their brother, Pygmalion, as we should and will again note, seems to characterize them as quite different from Roman sisters; for this emnity, see *Aeneid* 1.346-364, 4.21, 656; *Heroides* 7.113-118; *Fasti* 3.572-577. For Ennius' Ilia and her sister, see *Annales* 35-51 Vahlen, quoted by Cicero at *De Divinatione* 1.20.40; the opening of *Aeneid* 4, especially such phrases as *insomnia terrent*, *vestigia* and *effata*, suggests the influence of this passage and such phrases

Further and more reliable historical testimony to the strength of this particular bond in classical times appears in an episode related by Valerius Maximus. Set in the early second century B.C., the account describes how one Afronia refused to contest the will of her mother Aebutia and its appointment of her (half) sister Pletonia as heir so as not to wrangle with her sister in a lawsuit. More importantly, there is the evidence of the so-called *Laudatio Turiae*: this funerary inscription honoring a matron of the late first century B.C. was dedicated by the woman's husband of forty-one years. He describes how his wife and her sister jointly labored to avenge the murder of their parents, and how his wife's efforts to claim her rightful inheritance were directed on her sister's behalf no less than on her own; he hails his wife for *pietas* toward this sister, and remarks that she benefited from the aid of this sister (and her husband) when rescuing him from the proscriptions of 43 B.C. Significantly, he also relates that, after their union proved childless, she urged him to find another, fertile, wife and to regard herself henceforth as rendering him the duties and *pietas* of a sister or mother-in-law. While mainly furnishing additional evidence that the Roman elite of the classical period assumed mutual devotion to exist between brothers and sisters, this statement derives further poignancy from what we have already been told about the late woman's devotion toward her own sister; not surprisingly, she is also praised for devotion toward her own mother-in-law.[26]

---

therein as *exterrita somno, vestigare* and *ecfatus*.

[26] For Afronia, see Valerius Maximus 7.8.2. For the "*Laudatio Turiae*," its background and its text, see chapter three above, n. 36. *Fasti* 2.617-638, Ovid's passage on the *caristia*, Rome's ancient and annual festival for reaffirming family ties (as noted above, chapter three), lists several types of "harmful" relatives who should not be permitted to participate. These include the impious brother, the

Just as an *avunculus*, mother's brother, seems to have acted as a father of sorts toward his sister's children, so a *matertera*, mother's sister, seems to have been regarded and to have functioned as a maternal figure to them. Lines 31ff. of Persius' second satire speak of an *avia* (grandmother) or *matertera* taking a baby from his cradle and ritually averting evil spirits from him; such women— later labeled "nurses" by Persius—would seem to fit Tacitus' description at *Dialogus* 28 of the *propinquae* who assisted a Roman matron in childrearing. Cicero's writings furnish several examples of actual *materterae* from the republican period who were helpful to and respected by their sisters' children. At *De Divinatione* 1.47.104 he recounts the endeavors of one *matertera*, Caecilia, daughter of Metellus, to arrange a marriage for her sister's daughter. Having entered a shrine to receive an omen about this niece's prospects, the two women waited, Caecilia seated in a chair, the niece standing, for a long time without success. Finally the girl grew tired and asked her *matertera* if she might have her chair; Caecilia replied, "*Vero, mea puella, tibi concedo meas sedes*," "Certainly, dear girl, you may have my place"—and thus provided an omen with her words, since she herself died soon thereafter and the girl married Caecilia's husband. In two letters to Atticus of 45 B.C., 13.37 and 48, Cicero refers to a funeral oration which he himself had scripted to honor Porcia, sister of his late friend the younger Cato; he speaks in both letters of having this *laudatio* sent not only to Gnaeus Domitius Ahenobarbus, Porcia's son, but also to Brutus, son of Porcia's maternal half-sister Servilia. At *De Oratore* 2.1.2, Cicero also recalls his and his brother's own youthful studies with the

---

mother harsh to her offspring, the child who wishes his parents' death—but no women ill-disposed toward female siblings.

sons of their *matertera*; her marriage to Aculeo, esteemed friend of the distinguished orator Crassus, enabled the Cicerones as well as her own boys to be trained in those areas, and by those individuals, that Crassus valued.

One gets a similar impression of *materterae* from sources on the early imperial period. The marriage of Lucius Aemilius Paullus, son of the Cornelia celebrated in Propertius 4.11, to the daughter of Cornelia's half-sister Julia—a union bringing Paullus into the imperial family and helping him to a consulship in A.D. 1—cannot be unrelated to the fact that Julia was Paullus' *matertera*. When appealing to Augustus' mercy at *Epistulae Ex Ponto* 1.2.135ff., Ovid states that his own bride had come from Augustus' household and was once cherished by Atia Minor, Augustus' own *matertera*: he thereby implies that close ties of kinship connect him with the emperor and constitute all the more reason for extending forgiveness. Tacitus describes how Asinius Gallus proposed to Tiberius that he cease his dissimulation about the elder Agrippina and her offspring and notes that Gallus had Agrippina as *matertera* to his own children; Tacitus seems to have mentioned this relationship so as to emphasize Gallus' obligations to defend and protect her.[27]

---

[27] For Julia and Paullus, see Table I. At *Fasti* 6.809, Ovid also refers to Atia Minor, again as *matertera Caesaris*; in his discussion of the Matralia, at *Fasti* 6.481ff. Ovid additionally praises the mythic Ino, *matertera* of the god Bacchus, by terming her more serviceable to Bacchus than to her own children (562 *utilior Baccho quam fuit ipsa suis*). For Tacitus on Gallus and the elder Agrippina, see Tacitus, *Annales* 4.71.2, and A. B. Bosworth, "Tacitus and Asinius Gallus," *AJAH* 2 (1977) 173-192. An unpublished paper by S. Joshel notes Tiberius' later accusation, reported by Tacitus at *Annales* 6.25.2, that Agrippina and Gallus were themselves lovers. Such a charge may also be related to Agrippina's role toward Gallus' children: that these children's mother, Agrippina's half-sister Vipsania, was first Tiberius' own, and apparently beloved, wife (so *Annales* 1.12.4) might explain the emperor's sexual suspicions of Gallus; that these children

Festus defines a *matertera* as *matris soror quasi mater altera*, "a mother's sister, sort of a second mother." Etymologically, moreover, *matertera* means just that; such an original meaning allows the inference that the earliest Romans viewed sisters, who after all shared a common name, as actually obligated to share maternal responsibilities toward one another's children as well. The ritual details of the Matralia, a festival for women celebrated on June 11 and said to have originated in the days of Rome's second king Numa, allow the same inference: there the participants would pray for the children of their sisters and their brothers, but not for their own. It seems as if this annual vow began so as to formalize the commitment—manifestations of which we have already observed in a variety of sources—of *materterae* to live up to their names, and of *amitae* to claim an equal responsibility for the welfare of nephews and nieces.[28]

---

had been motherless since A.D. 20 (so *Annales* 3.19.3) and presumably looked to their *matertera* as Vipsania's surrogate could be construed to imply that Gallus so regarded her as well.

[28] For *matertera*, see Festus p. 121 Lindsay; Ernout-Meillet, 389-390; A. Walde-J. Hofmann, *Lateinisches Etymologisches Wörterbuch*[3] (Heidelberg, 1954) II.52. For the prayer at the Matralia, see Ovid, *Fasti* 6.559: "Let an affectionate mother not pray to (Mater Matuta) on behalf of her offspring" (which follows the description of nurturance given Bacchus by his *matertera* cited at n. 27 above), and 561: "You will do better to commend to the care (of Mater Matuta) the children of another"; Plutarch, *Quaestiones Romanae* 17 and *De Fraterno Amore* 21. I am indebted to Pomeroy, *GWWS*, 207, for interpreting Plutarch's Greek term *adelphōn* as meaning "of brothers" (*adelphoi*) as well as "of sisters" (*adelphai*), and thus maintaining, quite plausibly, that the prayer was on behalf of both brothers' and sisters' offspring. This would, of course, point to women's feelings of obligation as both *amitae* and *materterae* and illuminate the use, discussed below, of *consobrinus/a* for children of sisters or of sister and brother. Beekes, "Uncle and Nephew," 52 n. 6, observes that this ritual "points to the relation between sisters and their children in early Roman society, and perhaps in P(roto) I(ndo) E(uropean) times. In this picture fits well the existence of a very archaic PIE

The high valuation of *amitae, materterae,* and *avunculi*—all of whom a Roman would seem to have reckoned close, parentally nurturant kinfolk, all of whom were reckoned kinfolk because they were sisters to one's parents, or because one's mother was their sister—seems to have been responsible for the fact that classical Latin authors apply the term *consobrinus/consobrina* (male/female) "cousin," solely to children of sisters or of a brother and sister. Indeed, *consobrinus* derives, on good linguistic authority, from *con-sororinus,* "linked through a sister." Sons, and daughters, of two brothers were technically called *fratres,* and *sorores, patrueles,* "siblings kindred through fathers," "siblings linked through a paternal uncle."[29] To be sure, this fact permits one to deduce that such paternally linked, cousins, who would of course bear the same *gentilicia nomina* (unlike *consobrini*), were judged veritable siblings, closer kin than those related through a mother. But it need not compel one to do so. That the Romans had no original kinship term for the children of brothers, merely employing an adjective from *patruus,* the noun for paternal uncle, to distinguish such cousins, and that paternally related cousins were not

---

word for MoSi." For the festival of the Matralia generally, see H. H. Scullard, *Festivals and Ceremonies of the Roman Republic* (Ithaca, N.Y., 1981) 150-151. Bush, *Studies,* 3 n. 23, 117 n. 57, notes that Roman law forbade marriage between either a *matertera* or an *amita* and her nephew, and that Justinian, *Institutes* 1.10.5, states that both mothers' and fathers' sisters stood *in loco parentis* to a nephew; both provisions further suggest a view of aunts as special, surrogate mother figures.

[29] For *consobrinus/a,* see the *TLL* 4 (1896-1899) 473-474, Szemerényi, 63, and Ernout-Meillet, 637; see also Beekes, "Uncle and Nephew," 51-52 (who argues that the term ousted *sobrinus,* which originally meant "sister's son"). For the application of *frater/soror patruelis* to paternal uncles' children, see Szemerényi, 63; Ernout-Meillet, 252; Shackleton Bailey, "Brothers or Cousins?" *AJAH* 2 (1977) 148-150.

ritually promised the same sort of maternal care as were *consobrini* also raise another possibility: that such paternally related cousins were not originally regarded as close kindred at all.

Such an attitude toward the children of paternal uncles would tally with that postulated to explain the original meaning of and original relationships among *nepos, avus*, and *avunculus*: namely, that an early Roman *pater* considered his daughters' offspring important descendants, and viewed his sons as his surrogates in caring for the children of his daughters (as a result of which the children of his son could expect concern from their father's sister just as children of this sister could from her brother, and children of sisters could from each others' mother). Yet the existence of such an attitude might also suggest that early Roman sons could expect to be of primary concern to their own fathers, their mothers' fathers and their mothers' brothers—but not necessarily their fathers' brothers, whose obligations to offspring and *sorores*, not to mention concerns as *avunculi*, were burden enough. Such a situation would not, to say the least, tally with the agnatic system of family responsibilities legally ordained and culturally elaborated in Rome from early republican times onward; its likelihood will be more fully discussed later.

There are other reasons, to be discussed in the next section and in the concluding chapter of this study, for conjecturing that Roman children related through brothers did not expect or experience the same emotional nurturance and support from their father's male siblings that they did from his female siblings, or from their mother's siblings of either sex. There are other implications of the kinship term *consobrinus/a*, of the term *matertera*, and of the ritual pledge made each year by *sorores* at the Matralia. After all, not only these linguistic data but also this cultic practice appear to be of regal Roman vintage. The integration of the Matralia festival into the annual celebration of Vesta alone suggests as much. That the goddess worshipped at the Matralia, Mater Matuta, had a temple of sixth century B.C. date in the Forum Boarium, Rome's primitive cattle market, helps confirm the Roman view of this festival as dating back to monarchic times.[30] A linguistic emphasis on and cultic expression of the bonds between sisters and between brother and sister by the very earliest Romans, moreover, lends validity to what is reported by another, less reliable, body of evidence: the portraits of close sister-sister and brother-sister ties and the cultural importance accorded the role of sister in the legends of monarchic and early republican Rome retailed by authors of the classical period.

In addition to the stories about various brothers and sisters that we have already cited, several depict sisters as valued and important figures to one another; such stories represent sisterly ties as possessing considerable sociopolitical significance (much as the bond between brother and sister is represented in legends treating that sibling relationship). We have already looked at Ennius' passage about Romulus' mother and the prophecy she relates to her beloved sister. In this connection we should note as well that, at Livy 6.34, in the narrative about Fabius Ambustus and his underprivileged daughter, it is said that Fabia Minor was reluctant to tell her father the cause of her grief because it reflected insufficient

[30] Although the Matralia, on June 11, followed the actual festival of Vesta, the Vestalia, by two days, three days after the Matralia the refuse from Vesta's temple was swept out into the Tiber (so Ovid, *Fasti* 6.711-714); Scullard, *Festivals*, 149, also notes that the temple of Vesta was open from June 7 through 14. For the dating of the Mater Matuta temple to the sixth century B.C., see Ogilvie, 680-681; Scullard, *Festivals*, 151; and the article on Rome by E. Nash in the *Princeton Encyclopedia of Classical Sites*, ed. R. Stillwell, W. L. MacDonald and M. H. McAllister (Princeton, 1976) 768.

reverence (*nec satis piam*) toward her sister, and bestowed no great esteem upon her husband; we should recall, too, that Ambustus is said to have found the notion of two sisters receiving unequal dignity intolerable. At 1.48.7 Livy also describes the evil Etruscan Tullia (who helped dispose of her more advantaged elder sister and politically unpromising husband) as having been driven to frenzy by the furies of her sister and husband, and thus having driven her carriage over her father's corpse. Through such details he characterizes her not only as a most un-Roman daughter, but as a most un-Roman wife and sister to boot.

Lastly, that the role of parent to sisters' offspring is emphasized by the original meanings of the terms *matertera, avunculus,* and *consobrinus,* and by the promise made by sisters at the Matralia, suggests that a special bond was originally thought to exist between Roman women and their sisters as well as between them and their brothers because of their joint role in continuing their father's blood line by producing his grandchildren. In republican Roman times, however, the only grandchildren awarded similar public identification—in the form of *gentilicia nomina*—were those of their paternal grandfather's sons. We should, therefore, look at evidence on the bond between these male children and on the Roman notion of the brother's brother role to comprehend two matters more fully: why brothers' offspring were defined as partaking of a different sort of relationship than that of other Roman first cousins, and how they—Roman brothers—themselves were generally thought to have interacted with one another.

FRATER FRATERQUE

Evidence on how elite Romans of classical times defined the role and characterized the conduct of a *patruus*, the brother of a brother with children, merits our attention first. As we have observed, brothers were required by the laws of the Twelve Tables to be financially and legally responsible for one another's families, and were defined, through similar *nomen* and often *cognomen*, as somewhat similar individuals. Like the word *matertera*, moreover, *patruus* derives from the term for a biological parent—in this case the father—and signifies that parent's surrogate. A *patruus* was, therefore, the male kinsman most closely identified with one's *pater* and with the formal obligations of one's *pater*. Indeed, the paternal identity and responsibility assigned the Roman *patruus* probably provide the best evidence that the role of brother's brother was an important one to the classical Roman elite, a role whose occupants expected, and were expected, to proffer their male siblings strong support.[31]

Nevertheless, the traits evidently associated with the Roman *patruus*, important though his role may have been, contrast sharply with those thought characteristic of an *avunculus*. We have seen that several *avunculi* of Roman legend—Collatinus, the Vitellii, Numitorius— are portrayed as not merely willing to exert themselves publicly for their sister's offspring but even, in the cases of Collatinus and the Vitellii, as evincing more support and sympathy for their nephews than an actual father: Collatinus, by insisting on a less harsh punishment for his conspiratorial nephews than Lucius Brutus had for his similarly inclined sons; the Vitellii, by inspiring their nephews to embrace their own political cause—some-

---

[31] For the etymology of *patruus*, see Szemerényi, 55-56, 155, 164, who argues rather unpersuasively that it derives from *patr-awos and contains the word for "grandfather" and "uncle" (as seen in *avunculus*); the ultimate derivation of the word, however, does not seem as important as the fact that it was formed from the Latin (and Indo-European) word for "father."

thing that their father did not manage to do. We might observe as well that even though lines 682-700 of Plautus' *Aulularia* depict Lyconides as worried about how his *avunculus* Megadorus will greet his request to wed the girl who is engaged to Megadorus but pregnant by himself, Plautus does not imply that Megadorus offered much opposition to his nephew. The next time we meet Lyconides, he has obtained his wish; in introducing himself to the girl's father Euclio at lines 777-780, he even mentions his *avunculus* Megadorus prior to his *pater* Antimachus. What is more, two actual *avunculi* so prominent in our earlier discussions render these portrayals of their fictive counterparts more credible by behaving far more solicitously and supportively toward their sisters' offspring than these children's fathers: the tribune Drusus, by fostering the offspring of Caepio even though their father still lived; Marcus Brutus, by asking to be regarded as surrogate *pater* to Lepidus' offspring.[32]

Roman *patrui*, however, were apparently stereotyped as harsh, unaccommodating and censorious figures. At *Pro Caelio* 25 Cicero describes how his friend Lucius Herennius rebuked Caelius as a "parent has never rebuked a child" (*obiurgavit . . . sicut neminem umquam parens*), behaving as "an extremely severe paternal uncle, censor, school master" (*pertristis quidam patruus, censor, magister*); the apposition of *patruus* with *censor* and *magister* and the implication that the formal behavior of all three was not merely similar but more demanding and strict than that of a parent among the Roman elite deserve special note. At *Satires* 2.2.97 Horace alludes to the "angry paternal uncle" and at 2.3.88 quotes one

[32] Indeed, at *Ad Brutum* 1.12.2, the letter written in response to Brutus' appeal that he be regarded as *pater* to Lepidus' children, Cicero specifically terms Lepidus "cruel to his children" (*crudelis in liberos*).

Staberius as asking his judgmental heirs "not to play the *patruus*"; he thus indicates that a *patruus* was looked upon as *the* proverbial stern and severe relative by his Roman readership. Tacitus often speaks of Tiberius as *patruus* when relating his cruel treatment of his brother's son Germanicus—although Tiberius was technically Germanicus' *pater* by adoption. The paternal uncle of Roman legend, the evil usurper Amulius, is represented as murdering his brother Numitor's son and relegating Numitor's daughter to perpetual Vestal Virginity, and for this reason meriting murder by this daughter's sons. And sources characterize various historical figures as actually receiving far less support and solicitude from paternal than from maternal uncles: two of the brood fostered by the tribune Drusus, we should recall, had a living (and hence, according to Roman law, negligent) *patruus*; the children offered paternal care by Marcus Brutus had a living *patruus* as well.[33]

The application of *patruelis*, an adjective derived from *patruus*, to the offspring of a father's brother might well, therefore, undercut the affective force of the nouns *frater* and *soror* when they are applied to such cousins; it might imply that the parental figure providing the kindred link in this blood relationship, by reason of his reputation for strict and judgmental (if not outright cruel) conduct

---

[33] For Horace on *patrui*, see also *Odes* 3.12.3, referring to the fearsome nature of a "paternal uncle's tongue" (*patruae linguae*). For Tacitus on Tiberius as *patruus*, see *Annales* 1.33.1; 2.5.2 and 43.5; 3.3.3, 5.2, 17.2 and 31.1; I owe this observation to K. G. Wallace. For Amulius as *patruus*, see Livy 1.3.10-11 as well as the references cited above, n. 5. For the *patruus* of Cato and Porcia, see above, n. 4; for that of Lepidus' offspring, see Appian, *Bella Civilia* 4.37. For Cicero himself as harsher to Quintus (to whom he was *patruus*) than the lad's *avunculus* Atticus, see *Ad Atticum* 10.6. Other Roman sources on the negative image of the *patruus* include Manilius 5.454 and Persius 1.11.

to his brother's children, had somehow distanced them from his own. Whatever the connotations of *patruelis*, however, one must attempt to account for this persistently unsympathetic and often unsupportive cultural image of a *patruus*, particularly when compared to that of an *avunculus*. It might be argued that the parent through whom one was related, and presumably through whom one had access, to an *avunculus* was one's mother. Roman *matres*, of course, did not have formal life-and-death powers over their children, and did apparently make considerable demands upon and wield considerable influence over their brothers. We might note in this connection that Plautus portrays Lyconides' mother Eunomia as the first person to whom he discloses his paternity of the child carried by the intended of his *avunculus*; she is begged by Lyconides to tell this news to her brother, and is rightly confident that Megadorus will not refuse *her* request to let her son wed the girl.[34] But, as we will see, many Roman *matres*, particularly those rearing children without a husband's aid, and hence occupying paternal as well as maternal roles vis-à-vis their offspring, are also remembered as formidable, demanding individuals to offspring as well as to male siblings, their lack of legally sanctioned "*matria*" *potestas* notwithstanding.

Furthermore, even though Roman fathers—through whom one was related and had access to a *patruus*, and for whom a *patruus* functioned as a surrogate—were legally entitled to deal with their children as harshly as they wished, they did not tend, we have seen, to be particularly harsh and unfeeling with their accommodating daughters. Nevertheless, sources portray certain *patrui* as no less capable of harsh and unfeeling treatment to

[34] Cf. especially *Aulularia* 685-686, Eunomia's words to her son: "you know that I want to accomplish what you want, and I trust that I'll get what I want from my brother."

accommodating *filiae* than to unruly *filii fratris*. One thinks of the legendary Amulius denying his brother's only surviving child, a daughter, the possibility of continuing her father's blood line. We might observe that the emperor Claudius had his brother's daughter, and fourth wife's sister, Julia, executed on a vague charge and without any opportunity for self-defense. The emperor Domitian is reported to have seduced his brother's daughter—whom he had refused to wed—while Titus was still alive, and impregnated this niece after her father's and husband's deaths, as a result of which he forced her to undergo a fatal abortion.[35]

Roman fathers' displays of strictness and censoriousness to their sons (presumably in the hope of holding them to high standards of achievement) seem to have been far from infrequent in classical times; one might also argue that harsh and unsupportive *patrui* were merely emulating, or supposedly emulating, the conduct of the *patres* for whom they were surrogates. But enough *patrui* are characterized as outdoing *patres* in harshness to their brothers' offspring for this phenomenon to demand explanation as well. Cicero, *Pro Caelio* 25 represents *patrui* as more exacting and disapproving than *parentes*, and Tacitus depicts a cruel adoptive *pater* as revealing his true "paternal uncle's" colors. Cicero's own correspondence characterizes him as stricter toward his brother Quintus' son than Quintus was himself; Terence's *Adelphoe* even portrays a *patruus* as being a kind and indulgent parent once he adopts his brother's son and becomes the young man's *pater*.[36]

[35] For Claudius and Julia, see Suetonius, *Divus Claudius* 29.1; for Domitian and Titus' daughter, see Suetonius, *Domitianus* 22, and Pliny, *Epistles* 4.11.6-7.

[36] For Cicero and the two Quinti, see *Ad Atticum* 10.4.5-6, 10.6 (in which Cicero complains "His overly permissive father undoes

It is possible, however, that this culturally assumed, emotional and social distancing between a Roman paternal uncle and his brother's children may have some of its roots in social and emotional distancing between a Roman paternal uncle and his brother: in other words, strains in the elite Roman brother-brother bond may have made the role of *patruus*, as a second-string and strictly controlling father to the issue of an uneasily regarded brother, doubly negativized. For several of these uncompassionate and unsupportive, actual and fictive, *patrui* are specifically characterized by our sources as on uneasy terms with the fathers of these coldly or cruelly treated nephews and nieces. Suetonius, for example, states at *Tiberius* 50.1 that Tiberius once handed over to Augustus a private letter from his brother, and Germanicus' father, Drusus in which the latter discussed the possibility of pressuring Augustus to restore the republic. To Suetonius, this act qualifies as an example of Tiberius' hatred for his entire family; while one might not agree with his interpretation, and might simply construe such behavior as designed to make Tiberius look more loyal to Augustus than his more popular brother, one still cannot view Tiberius' disclosure as anything but intentionally harmful to Drusus. At *Domitianus* 2.3 Suetonius relates that Domitian told the attendants at Titus' bedside to leave, and thus presume his brother's death, before Titus had in fact died; he claims, too, that Domitian

---

all my disciplinary measures. Without him, if that were possible, I could govern the lad") and 10.11.1-3. From Terence, *Adelphoe* 59ff., it is also clear that Demea, having become his elder son's adoptive *patruus*, demands—like Cicero—far more from the lad than does his (adoptive) father. Terentian comedy, however, may not be as good evidence for Roman attitudes as Plautus' works, which more loosely adapt, and more thoroughly Romanize, their Greek originals; on this point see E. Segal, *Roman Laughter* (Cambridge, Mass., 1968) 1-14.

barely acknowledged his dead brother and even slighted Titus' memory in speeches and edicts. As we have seen, too, the legendary Amulius reportedly slew Numitor's son and tried to stop his daughter from reproducing solely out of ill will toward his brother, whose throne he had already seized.[37]

Further supporting the thesis that a Roman male's negative feelings toward his brother might underlie his harsh and even harmful behavior toward that brother's children is the fact that several *patrui* noted for special fondness for and closeness to their brothers' offspring also appear to have been especially fond of and close to their brothers themselves. The most obvious example is the emperor Claudius, who broke with Roman tradition in marrying his admired brother Germanicus' daughter. But one might do better to cite the younger Cato, devoted to his half-brother Caepio and kind to Caepio's daughter (and putative adoptive son). Or Scipio Aemilianus, who kindly gave up their biological father's estate to his brother Fabius Maximus, and was later remarked upon for his strong bonds with that brother's son.[38]

---

[37] As, e.g. *Ad Atticum* 1.17, 6.6.3-4 and 9.3, and 11.10.1 indicate, Cicero was not immune to feelings of annoyance at his own brother either, and this could not help but affect his dealings with Quintus' son.

[38] For Claudius and Germanicus, see, for example, Suetonius, *Divus Claudius* 11.2-3, and Seneca, *Ad Polybium De Consolatione* 16.3; it is only fair to reiterate, however, that Claudius had another of Germanicus' daughters, Julia, executed, albeit apparently to accommodate the wishes of his freedman and wives. For Cato, Caepio, and Caepio's offspring, see Plutarch, *Cato Minor* 3.5-6, 8.1, 11, 15.4; *Brutus* 2.1 and 3. For Scipio Aemilianus and Fabius Maximus, see Polybius 31.28.1-7; for Scipio and Fabius' son, see, for example, Valerius Maximus 7.5.1 (and n. 12 above) as well as 8.15.4. K. G. Wallace has also called to my attention the fact that Vespasian's brother, T. Flavius Sabinus, made himself responsible for the safety of Vespasian's son, Domitian, at the siege of the Capitol in A.D. 69

To be sure, strains in the bond between Roman brothers appear to have been most marked in royal families, where the question of succession to supreme authority often lay open and loomed large, and where competition between brothers was intensified. When Tacitus makes knowing reference, at *Annales* 4.60.3, to "the hatred common between brothers" (*solita fratribus odia*), he is discussing tensions in the palace, between Drusus and Nero, sons of (the late) Germanicus. Furthermore, unhelpful and unsympathetic behavior by an elite Roman to his brother does not ever appear to have gained acceptance as a tolerable or even an understandable mode of fraternal conduct. Polybius' approving citation of Scipio Aemilianus for generosity to Fabius Maximus indicates as much, as do Plutarch's descriptions of Cato's admired affection for Caepio and the similarly regarded support of their brother-in-law Lucullus and his brother for one another. Indeed, when Velleius Paterculus relates the proscribing of his brother Paullus by the triumvir (and Marcus Brutus' brother-in-law) Lepidus and of Plotius Plancus through the agency of his brother Munatius Plancus, he is quick to note that these deeds occasioned the sarcastic line *de germanis, non de Gallis duo triumphant consules* ("these two consuls triumph over brothers with whom they share two parents, not Gauls").[39]

(Tacitus, *Historiae* 3.69.4) and that Domitian obtained for this *patruus* a censor's funeral (*Historiae* 4.47): it may thus be significant that Suetonius remarks, at *Divus Vespasianus* 2.2, upon Vespasian's reluctance to compete with his brother by entering political life.

[39] For praise of Scipio Aemilianus' closeness with Fabius Maximus, see Polybius 31.28.1-7; for praise of Cato's closeness with Caepio, see Plutarch, *Cato Minor* 3.5-6, 8.1, 11, 15.4; for the Luculli, see Plutarch, *Lucullus* 1.6, 43.3. See also the roster of bereaved and grieving brothers in Seneca, *Ad Polybium De Consolatione* 14.4ff. (e.g.

We should, however, take note that the peculiar political and social circumstances of the proscriptions, which
we will discuss in the next chapter, bear little affinity to
those of a royal household. For under a monarchic government, succession—unlike political power under a republican system—is indivisible and accords its possessor
rights which those of no other citizen approximate. So,
too, the portrayal of brotherly love as something
noteworthy even by authors of the republican era such
as Polybius would suggest that brotherly animosity, or
at least brotherly indifference, was not unknown among
upper-class Roman males of this period. Various evidence corroborates such an implication. It seems, for
example, that Lucius Antonius, consul in 41 B.C., merely
purported to represent the interests of his brother Mark
Antony while championing the rights of dispossessed
Italian landowners: at *Bella Civilia* 5.54 Appian reports
that Lucius, having been praised by Octavian for devotion to his brother, immediately reassured Octavian
that this was not the case and that loyalty to Mark Antony played no part in his political decisions. To be sure,
Valerius Maximus dwells on the sorrow of one Serto-
rianus, who committed suicide after discovering that he
had slain his own brother while fighting under Pompey
in the civil conflict with Caesar, and on M. Fabius' decision to refuse a triumph because his brother had fallen

Scipio Africanus over Asiaticus, Scipio Aemilianus over his father's
youthfully deceased sons, the Luculli, Sextus over Gnaeus Pompey,
Lucius over Gaius Caesar, Mark Antony over his brother, Tiberius
over Drusus). For the proscriptions of brothers by Lepidus and Munatius Plancus, and the line they evoked, see Velleius Paterculus 2.67.3-
4; see also Livy, *Periochae* 120. At *Cicero* 10.2, when Plutarch relates
that Catiline had his brother's name placed on Sulla's proscription
list, he explains this as a ploy by Catiline to avoid prosecution for
hs brother's murder. Plutarch also lists the accusation of fratricide
along with that of deflowering his own daughter and after mentioning Catiline's other great crimes: clearly Catiline's alleged conduct horrified Plutarch, and was not well received at the time.

in the battle he claimed as his victory. Valerius also cites
the emotional conflict experienced by a censor of the
late third century B.C., Q. Fulvius Flaccus, when Flaccus
expelled his brother from the senate. Valerius even likens
the emperor under whom he wrote, Tiberius, and his
brother Drusus to the mythical Castor and Pollux because of their close fraternal bond (and thereby subscribes to a very different view of their relationship than
does Suetonius). Nonetheless, even Valerius acknowledges the plight of the brother-proscribed Plotius Plancus when enumerating *exempla* of slaves' extreme loyalty
to their masters at 6.8.5. What is more, even Valerius'
emotionally charged description of brotherly good will
(*fraterna benivolentia*) speaks of it as an obligation, twice
using the verb form *debet*, "ought," in justifying its
existence, rather than referring to it as a natural im-
pulse.[40]

Most importantly, there are the aforementioned leg-

---

[40] For Valerius Maximus on devoted brothers, see 5.5.4 (Serto-
rianus), 5.5.2 (Fabius), 2.7.5 (Fulvius Flaccus) and 5.5.3 (Tiberius and
Drusus). Valerius cites as evidence for closeness between Tiberius
and Drusus the two men's behavior at the latter's deathbed; Seneca
includes these brothers in his roster (above, n. 39) because of Tiberius' display of grief at Drusus' death. Such behavior, however,
does not rule out the existence of tensions between the two men
during Drusus' lifetime; the sentimental contexts of both Valerius'
and Seneca's descriptions should also be taken into account. For
Valerius Maximus on *fraterna benivolentia*, see 5.5; by way of contrast,
at 5.6, in discussing patriotic feelings—to which Valerius claims the
authority of parents and brotherly affection are subordinate—Valerius employs no verbs which represent them as anything but spon-
taneous. K. G. Wallace has called to my attention Tacitus, *Historiae*
3.51, where the contrast is made between an ordinary imperial soldier
who killed his brother in battle and demanded a reward and a republican soldier who killed himself after discovering that he had slain
his brother in civil conflict. One might, in fact, infer from our
evidence that *fraterna benivolentia* among brothers of all classes diminished after Rome became a monarchy, and opportunities for
public leadership diminished as well (on which point see chapter six
below).

ends about brothers in earliest Roman times and the fact
that these idealizing portraits from the classical era of
Rome's first families agree with Festus in painting *fratres*
as discordant, envious, and competitive. Admittedly,
one of these evil brothers, Tarquinius Superbus, belongs
to an Etruscan couple memorable for their desecration
of other hallowed Roman blood and affinal ties: those
between *pater* and *filia, socer* and *gener, soror* and *soror,
avunculus* and *sororis filius, frater* and *coniunx sororis*; he
is, moreover, himself implied to be an inadequate *pater*.
Nevertheless, one of the others, Amulius, comes from
the royal house of Rome's Alban forefathers, and another, Romulus, is Rome's founder himself. Additionally, unlike the fabled sister-slayer Horatius or the fabled
son-slayer Lucius Brutus, neither of these *fratres* is represented as politically provoked to, or as particularly
patriotic in, conduct destructive to his brother: Amulius
simply covets his brother's throne; Romulus simply feels
threatened by his brother's challenge to the site and
boundaries of his newly founded city. So, too, the frequent references in Latin literature from the mid-second
century B.C. onwards to the story of Romulus' more
favorable augury and subsequent fratricide suggest a
preoccupation with strains in the fraternal bond which
can best be attributed to a recognition that such strains
were a fact of elite Roman life, strains which threatened
to disrupt many a Roman upper-class family, and hence
the harmony of the Roman political order.[41]

[41] For Tarquinius Superbus' heinous treatment of all his relations,
see Dionysius of Halicarnassus 4.79-80.1 (in which Brutus notes that
he also had his mother-in-law hanged). For his inadequacies as a
pater, see Livy 1.50.9. There Tarquin gives as grounds for his own
tardiness the excuse that he was settling a dispute between a father
and son: to this the retort is made that he simply should have told
the son to obey his father; that this philosophy led to his own sons'
misbehavior is implied by Livy's following account of the corrupt

This explicit and implicit concern, displayed by various Roman authors of the classical period, with potentially harmful tensions in what was expected to be a mutually supportive bond between brothers, is significant for an additional reason. Such authors, be they depicting imaginary or reporting on actual personages, give no indication that strains might or actually did exist in the bond between sisters or the bond between brothers and their (often anything but compliant) sisters. Such tensions have already been associated with the Roman image of the paternal uncle as a figure difficult to please and presumably to get along with. An association has been suggested between strains perceived in these, agnate, and particularly male agnate bonds, and strains perceived in the Roman male agnate bond *par excellence*, that between Roman fathers and their sons. The reasons for these tensions will also be considered at length in our final chapter. But their impact and nature perhaps deserve some reflection now: after all, such strains may further illuminate a linguistic phenomenon mentioned in the previous chapter and should be further contrasted with the relatively strain-less impression sources give of non-agnate, both blood and non-blood, bonds among the Roman elite.

In the first place, our evidence for tensions in Roman agnate bonds prompts one to regard these strains as contributing to the limited, non-affective and technical,

---

conduct of Tarquin's own sons (e.g. at 53.5-54, 56.9-13, 57.6ff.). For references to Romulus' fratricide, see Ennius, *Annales* 77-96 Vahlen (for which our source is Cicero, *De Divinatione* 1.48.107ff.) and 97-100 Vahlen; Horace, *Epodes* 7.17-20; Propertius 3.9.49-50, 4.1.49-50; Lucan, *Bellum Civile* 1.95, as well as Livy, Dionysius of Halicarnassus, and Ovid (in the passages cited in n. 5 above). For the development of the Romulus and Remus legend in classical Roman times, see J. Classen, "Zur Herkunft der Sage von Romulus und Remus," *Historia* 12 (1963) 447-457.

sense of the words *agnatus* and *agnatio*. For these words not only differ in usage and connotation from their less "marked" counterparts *cognatio* and *cognatus*. Roman law, naming practice and other custom—most notably the reckoning of political achievements by earlier male agnates in a man's own political standing—gave agnate bonds priority of formal cultural emphasis over cognate ones by early republican times. Indeed, the Romans have been said, in a major anthropological work on kinship and the social order, to "think agnatically about social relations," and to have relied upon the "paradigm of patrilineal descent" as "their fundamental guide to conduct and belief in all areas of their social life." One would, therefore, expect the terms for these particular, culturally emphasized, bonds to have greater semantic flexibility and affective resonance. In determining why these words do not, therefore, one should look at these particular bonds themselves as well as those described by their more flexible and affective counterparts *cognatio* and *cognatus*.[42]

[42] For *agnatus/agnatio*, see chapter three above, n. 70. For agnate succession in the Twelve Tables, see chapter one above, n. 35. For the definition of a *novus homo*, "new man," in republican times, as the first man of a family to reach the senate, and in a special sense, to reach the consulship and hence *nobilitas*, see, e.g. the article "Novus Homo" by E. Badian in the *Oxford Classical Dictionary*[2] (Oxford, 1970) 740; see also Badian's article on *nobilitas*, 736. That "family" in republican times meant, for political intents and purposes, male agnates alone is to be inferred from the modern scholarly view that the reckoning of maternal male kin as significant antecedents does not begin until Augustus' principate (on which see chapter six below); it may also be inferred from various statements in ancient authors (e.g. that of Plutarch at *Cato Major* 1.1-2, first citing Cato's own complimentary comments about his father and paternal grandfather, then noting that Cato was called a new man owing to his lack of family distinction). For the Romans as agnatic and patrilineal thinkers about social life, see M. Fortes, *Kinship and the Social Order* (Chicago, 1969) 290-291.

Admittedly, sources document instances of unsympathetic and unsupportive conduct by upper-class Roman men to their daughters' and sisters' sons. One might cite Augustus' harsh treatment of his daughter's youngest boy Agrippa Postumus; the dictator Marius, though remembered as adopting a sister's son, is reported to have approved the decision to execute another such nephew after the latter had forced a military subordinate to submit to him sexually. Nevertheless, the mere emotional and sociopolitical strength of these male, blood, cognate ties in a formally and intensely agnatic kinship system and social organization is itself significant. No less so is the fact that these cognate blood bonds, most notably that involving the *avunculus*, appear on the whole less strained than those between male agnates.[43]

Just as striking, however, is the emotional and sociopolitical strength which one may discern in the technically de-emphasized non-blood bonds between Roman upper-class males and their daughters' and sisters' husbands. It has been argued that the evils of the Roman civil wars—when Julius Caesar opposed his son-in-law Pompey and Octavian his brother-in-law Antony—were seen at the time as a legacy of Romulus' fratricide. Support for this argument resides in the popularity of the Romulus and Remus theme in literature of and about

[43] For Augustus and Agrippa Postumus see, for example, Suetonius, *Divus Augustus* 65.1, 4; Augustus did, however, apparently grieve profoundly over the misbehavior of Agrippa, his sister Julia, and their mother and—if we are to believe Tacitus, *Annales* 1.5— secretly visited his exiled grandson for a tearful reunion before his death. For Marius' verdict that his nephew Lusius had been rightly slain, see Valerius Maximus 6.1.12. This story is also related by Plutarch, *Marius* 14.3-5. As J. Boswell remarks on 64 n. 10 of *Christianity, Social Tolerance and Homosexuality* (Chicago and London, 1980), however, Marius was expected to avenge his nephew's death. Only because he failed to do so, and hence behaved unusually for an *avunculus*, did his conduct stir comment.

the civil war period. It may also be found in Octavian's refusal to adopt the name "Romulus" and decision to select "Augustus"—with its mere Romulean reverberations—instead (and to do so at the urging of the aforementioned brother-proscribing Munatius Plancus). But should this theory be valid, it would imply a Roman view of indissoluble blood ties between male siblings as comparable to, and perhaps as no more revered than, voluntary ties between men and the husbands of their daughters and fathers' daughters: in other words, a view that these affinal ties could be as strained as those, but also should be as revered as those, between male agnates. Evidence supporting such a Roman view of affinal and agnate ties as similar in strength, from the civil war period, is in fact provided by Cicero himself at *Ad Brutum* 1.3.1. There, speaking to Brutus about Brutus' brother-in-law, the triumvir Lepidus, Cicero remarks "I believe you have already gotten a full picture from your correspondents' letters about the fickleness, irresponsibility, and unceasingly unpatriotic attitude of Lepidus, your kinsman by marriage, who ranks his in-laws just below his brother among the close kin (*proximos*) whom he hates." Cicero hence groups in-laws and brother together as close kin shamefully treated by Lepidus, implies that there is but little difference between the shameful treatment accorded by Lepidus to each, and does not seem to judge Lepidus' similar treatment of both as at all unusual. [44]

[44] For this interpretation of Romulus' fratricide as symbolizing the affinal conflicts which caused the civil wars, see Ogilvie, 54; for Augustus' refusal of the name Romulus, see Suetonius, *Divus Augustus* 7.2. An attitude similar to Cicero's may be seen at 1.145ff. of Ovid's *Metamorphoses*. Here, in describing the mythic iron age, Ovid claims that human relations had degenerated to the point that "a father-in-law was not safe from his son-in-law and good will among

The historical origins of the sociopolitical prominence and emotional strength of ties, both blood and non-blood ties, and for the most part male ties, through daughters warrant both dating and explanation: Roman society was not only patriarchal but emphatically patrilineal and agnatically oriented in its formal kinship system by the mid-fifth century B.C. As we will see, on the basis of cross-cultural and cross-periodic observation, it is quite conceivable that Romans' original kinship and social organization in monarchic times had been even more emphatically filiafocal than it was in the classical era: i.e. that the earliest Romans assigned social and affective priority of emphasis not (or not only) to bonds between fathers and sons, but (also) to those between men and their daughters' and sisters' offspring and spouses.[45] We should perhaps note in this connection

---

brothers was unusual"; by citing in juxtaposition strains in these two, affinal and agnate, bonds, Ovid also seems to equate the emotional pull and social importance of a tie created by marriage to a female blood relation with those of a tie to an actual agnate blood kinsman. Plutarch, *Cicero* 27.2-3 also equates, as equally offensive to his listeners, various Ciceronian witticisms which poked fun at various individuals on account of exiled sons-in-law, ugly daughters, and a lowly-born father.

[45] Scholars such as Goody, "The Mother's Brother," and Fortes, *Kinship*, 47ff., have concluded that the critical factor of the patrilineal avunculate is the jural status of the parties to one another. In a patrilineal and patriarchal society, they argue, the bond with the mother's brother owes its strength, and the mother's brother owes his kindly and nurturant image, to the fact that mothers' brothers have no formal authority over and no legal responsibility to and for sisters' offspring: they are technically external to the jurally controlling, respected paternal family. Such a theory would help account for the importance of the avunculate and other, affinal and blood, filiafocal bonds among the classical Roman elite. This theory does not, however, account for the discrepancy between certain aspects of the Roman jural situation and the implications of varied evidence about Roman society prior to the codification of the Twelve Tables: that is, it does not explain why the early Romans established *in the*

the implication of the late Roman jurist Ulpian that agnate guardianship and succession were instituted by the Twelve Tables and the fact that automatic guardianship of females by their male agnates was eventually abolished by the emperor Claudius; such evidence at least suggests that the Romans did not always regard male agnates as alone entitled to paternal responsibility for other kindred.[46] One might postulate—and indeed the final chapter of this study will marshal further evidence on which to do so—that the Roman practice of assigning primary cultural emphasis to ties between male agnate kindred began as a means of compensating for, if not actually replacing, a traditional Roman preference for bonding among men linked through blood and marriage by female kin. It also warrants reiterating that ties between men and their own, and fathers', daughters were not only given explicit formal emphasis by early republican Roman law and naming practices connected with male agnate bonding but also were given implicit, if more informal, recognition by Roman kinship terms, cultic behavior, and legends connected with Rome's earliest years. Such emphasis and recognition may suggest that a concern for ties with, and protection of, daughters was pivotal in any transformation of Roman kinship and society from a more emphatically filiafocal to a strongly agnatic orientation. But sociocultural factors, which will be considered in the final chapter, seem to possess greater

---

first place laws failing to accord much importance to non-agnate bonds.

[46] For the view that the Twelve Tables *introduced* agnate succession, see chapter one above, n. 35; for Claudius' abolition of agnate guardianship over women (which may, of course, be accounted for by the emperor's redefinition of the bond between *patruus-fratris filia* in wedding his own brother's daughter), see Gaius, *Institutes* 1.157, 1.171.

importance as explanations for the filiafocal character of Roman elite society in classical times.

Patterns of association among men linked through female kin are often labeled by anthropologists with the prefix matri-, since the female kin so involved often loom large in maternal roles.[47] As we have seen, elite Romans of the classical period expressed high esteem for female kin occupying maternal roles and did so in various public contexts; such expressions and other assorted evidence indicate that the role of mother commanded great respect in Roman upper-class society and that this role merits separate attention. But it bears noting first that a Roman mother's ability to command respect from offspring and society seems closely related to her intitial valuation as her father's dependent daughter and, had she a male sibling, to her subsequent valuation as her brother's rather more independent sister.

Such formidable *matres* of the republic and early empire as Cornelia, mother of the Gracchi, and Agrippina, mother of the emperor Nero, may have first attained the high regard of other men and arguably acquired their strong sense of self-worth because they were the daughters of renowned Roman leaders. But each is also remembered as the earlier recipient of favored treatment

---

[47] An example is the definition of descent units by D. M. Schneider, "The Distinctive Features of Matrilineal Descent Groups," in D. M. Schneider and K. Gough, eds., *Matrilineal Kinship* (Berkeley, Los Angeles and London, 1961) 2-3: "when kinsmen related through one sex are excluded . . . and female sex is the distinguishing criterion the principle is called *matrilineal*." Matrilocal residence, in which men and women live together in the community where their mothers, and not necessarily their fathers, reside is yet another. As the next chapter will demonstrate, however, one cannot apply such "matri-" terms to Roman social phenomena involving kinship bonding patterns without misrepresenting the nature of bonds and associations to and through women.

from her brother or his household. Polybius, as we have seen, relates that Cornelia was rapidly dowered by her brother's adopted son and surrogate, Scipio Aemilianus; Plutarch relates that Scipio took her elder son Tiberius Gracchus to Carthage for his first taste of military life, sharing his tent and soldierly wisdom with the young man. From Suetonius and Cassius Dio we hear that Agrippina's brother, the emperor Caligula, had her and her two sisters named with him in all oaths and consular motions, and awarded the three women imperial seats at the games as well as honorary Vestal Virginity; Caligula's coinage honors his three sisters by representing them as Securitas, Concordia, and Fortuna. And Suetonius also reports that when a name was chosen for Agrippina's newborn son, Caligula jokingly recommended that of their *patruus* Claudius—whereupon his sister made it quite clear that she was not amused.[48]

Furthermore, other influential and self-possessed *matres*, and aunts functioning as *matres*, during the republic and early empire appear to have wielded considerable influence with their brothers in addition to being (and probably well before becoming) formidable figures to their offspring. In such conduct they resemble Plautus' Eu-

---

[48] For Cornelia and Agrippina as daughters, see chapter two above, n. 29 and n. 30. At *Annales* 12.42.2, Tacitus refers to Agrippina as unique in being daughter of a commander (*imperatore genitam*), sister of the supreme ruler (*sororem eius, qui rerum potitus sit*), and wife and mother of emperors. He thus, however, connects her position as daughter of a powerful man to her position as sister, wife, and mother of the most powerful men in Rome. On Cornelia's dowering, see Polybius 31.27 and chapter two above, n. 13; on Scipio's training of her elder son, see Plutarch, *Tiberius Gracchus* 4.4. For Caligula's honors to his sisters, see Cassius Dio 59.3-4, 11, 24.7; Suetonius, *Gaius Caligula* 15.3; H. Mattingly, *Coins of the Roman Empire in the British Museum* (London, 1923) I pl. 28, 4 (Caligula, nos. 36ff.). On Caligula's jocular naming of Agrippina's son, see Suetonius, *Nero* 6.2.

nomia, first characterized as imperious with and accommodated by her brother Megadorus, and only later shown as appealed to by her obeisant son for advocacy of his plea with this *avunculus*. Julius Caesar is represented by Suetonius as determined to credit his mother Aurelia by winning the post of *pontifex maximus*, but as first having wangled Sulla's pardon through the intercession of the Vestal Virgins and a kinsman, Aurelius Cotta, presumably Aurelia's importuned brother. Antony's mother Julia is represented by Appian both as successfully sought for succor by her brother during the triumviral proscriptions and as successfully pressuring her son to modify a major triumviral decision regarding the taxation of females.[49]

Suetonius also attributes the praetor Gnaeus Domitius Ahenobarbus' change in policies concerning prize money disbursement to teasing by his sister, apparently Domitia Lepida, with whom he was accused of incest. After Domitius' death, this intimidating woman, mother of the empress Messalina, is also said by Suetonius to have assumed charge of educating her brother's son Nero— and to have posed such a threat to the boy's actual mother, Agrippina, in this role that Agrippina had her brought to trial and forced Nero to testify against her. Nero, significantly, is reported to have waited until he had killed Agrippina before murdering the dauntless Domitia Lepida—and as not doing so until hearing this bedridden *amita* proclaim his presentation of his beard to her the sole prerequisite for her happy death.[50]

[49] For Caesar and Aurelia, see Suetonius, *Divus Julius* 13 and 1.2; both Münzer, *Römische Adelsparteien und Adelsfamilien* (Stuttgart, 1920) 324-325, and Gruen, *Last Generation*, 77, take issue with the view that this Aurelius Cotta was Caesar's *avunculus*, and judge him Aurelia's *frater patruelis* instead. For Appian on Julia, her brother and Antony, see *Bella Civilia* 4.32 and 37, 5.52 and 63.

[50] Suetonius, *Nero* 5.2, 6.3, 7.1, 34.5; cf. also Tacitus, *Annales* 12.64.2-

The elder Servilia, noted for her lifelong influence with her maternal half-brother, the younger Cato, is described by Cicero to Atticus as also commanding the utmost deference from her son Brutus at the summit conference two years after Cato's death. One of Cicero's own letters relates that his nephew Quintus, son of Atticus' sister Pomponia, came to him despairing because his mother was displeased with him, and hence his *avunculus*—who, as we have seen, took immense pride in his lifelong concord with his *soror*—was displeased with him no less.[51] But let us now examine the role of the Roman *mater* itself and see how a well-born woman's support from male blood kin enabled her to function with confidence, and be treated with deference, in discharging her maternal duties.

---

65 (according to which Agrippina had Domitia Lepida sentenced to death prior to the death of Claudius).

[51] For the elder Servilia and Cato, see chapter two above, n. 21; for her cowing of Brutus, see Cicero, *Ad Atticum* 15.11. For Pomponia's—and hence Atticus'—displeasure with Quintus, see Cicero, *Ad Atticum* 13.42.

V

Matres Familiae

VARIED evidence testifies to the political influence, social esteem, and general cultural importance of mothers and mother-figures among the classical Roman elite: some of this evidence has been dealt with in chapter two, which discussed women's sociopolitical impact; some has also been treated in chapter four, which discussed *amitae* and *materterae*, paternal and maternal aunts. Sources from the classical era additionally ascribe influence, social esteem, and general cultural importance to *matres* in Rome's monarchic and earliest republican periods. Indeed, the influential, esteemed, and important roles assigned both actual *matres* of the classical era and their fabled predecessors of Rome's earliest days have, as we have observed in chapter one, given rise to a far from compelling but often accepted modern theory: that a matriarchal or matrilineal order existed during Rome's formative years and left discernible traces upon upper-class Roman society in much later times.

Among the evidence for the classical Romans' view of motherhood as highly valued in their own remote past is one of the *Leges Regiae*. It forbids the burial of a woman who has died during pregnancy until the offspring is first removed from her; to act otherwise was thought to destroy the hope of a living being as well as a woman. Such an ordinance assumes that the earliest Romans regarded gestation itself, and not merely parturition, with religious awe, and that a mother's role as incubator of unborn offspring was important to the earliest Romans. Legends of Rome's foundation assume a high valuation of motherhood too. They stress the maternal guidance given Aeneas by Venus, the right to kingship inherited by Romulus and Remus through their mother and her father, and the divinity also possessed by these, royal, twins through their mother's union with Mars; the Sabine women, we must not forget, are said in Livy's account to appeal to their fathers and husbands as mothers of these fathers', and these husbands', common descendants.[1]

Linguistic data, moreover, confirm the classical Romans' belief that motherhood was highly valued by their earliest ancestors. *Filius* and *filia*, early and standard Latin words for "son" and "daughter," are, to reiterate, anomalous in Indo-European kinship terminology; if, as is thought by most scholars, they technically signify "suckled," the Romans would then have originally described children in relation to parents by noting their maternal nurturance. The etymology of the word *matertera* would imply that the earliest Romans prized mothers to the extent of calling mothers' sisters, apparently because they aided mothers in childrearing, "motherlike" figures. The Latin noun *materies*, later *materia*, meaning the stuff of which an object is composed, and clearly deriving from *mater*, further suggests an early Roman view of mothers as important, primal figures.[2]

---

[1] For this royal law, see Marcellus 1.28 (*Digest* 11.8.2). For Aeneas and Venus, see in particular Vergil, *Aeneid* 1.314-417, 2.588-620, and 8.370ff.; for Romulus and Remus and their mother, see chapter three above, n. 53 and, e.g., *Aeneid* 6.778-788, and Plutarch, *Romulus* 2-3; for the appeal of the Sabine women at Livy 1.13.1-4 see chapter three above.

[2] For *filius/filia* as cognate with *felare*. "to suck" (and hence derived from Indo-European *dhē-), see, for example, Ernout-Meillet, 223, 234. For *matertera*, see chapter four above. As Szemerényi notes, 60-

Testimony on the long tradition of Roman "father-right," however, implicitly portrays Roman mothers as always much less politically powerful than Roman fathers. It certainly allows one to dispute the thesis that the Roman mother was ever culturally idolized and politically omnipotent. No less significantly, testimony on daughter valuation by fathers throughout the classical era and on the continuing cultural elaboration of the daughter role by various, patriarchal, Roman institutions in classical times distinguishes Roman kinship and society from "classically" matrifocal family organizations and social systems. For—and as was maintained previously—the Romans gave cultural emphasis to daughterhood, not only in and of itself but also as having priority over other female familial roles.[3]

To recapitulate briefly, Roman law even assigned a woman "daughter right" in relation to her husband if she had, by passing into his *manus*, relinquished her position as daughter in her family of birth; it defined all, save for a few exceptional, women as needing paternal protection through the institution of *tutela mulierum*, female guardianship. Rome's naming system and practice of specifying familial ties generally identified a woman for as long as she lived as her father's daughter

---

62, the Indo-European term for mother's sister becomes the word for stepmother in various languages. That the Romans did not follow this practice, and employed a totally different term, *noverca* (apparently from *novus*, "new"), for a father's subsequent wife, who merely succeeded one's mother, is itself significant. It suggests a high esteem for biological motherhood, and for the woman most closely akin to one's biological mother, her sister, not awarded the later marital partners of one's father. For *materies/materia*, see Ernout-Meillet, 390.

[3] For the tradition of Roman "father-right" and the efforts of Bachofen and others to disregard it, see chapter one above. For matrifocality, see N. Tanner, "Matrifocality in Indonesia and in Africa and Among Black Americans," *Woman, Culture, and Society*, 129-156, as well as chapter three above.

(and otherwise often identified her as her mother's father's daughter's daughter). Within the realm of Roman religion women could gain the greatest prestige—and unique rewards and privileges—by serving as Rome's archetypal daughter figures, the virgin priestesses of Vesta; so, too, women annually reaffirmed their roles as their fathers' daughters by pledging their commitment to the offspring of their female and male siblings at the Matralia. Roman legend, often related and regarded as ideological in its aim, accords particular prominence to females who occupy the role of father's daughter, and females whose validation in maternal roles is itself inseparable from their valuation as their fathers' daughters: one thinks of the aforementioned mothers of Aeneas and Romulus, or Ascanius' stepmother Lavinia, or the raped Sabine women.[4]

To be sure, we have seen and will see that certain features of "classical" matrifocal societies obtained among the classical Roman elite as well: most notably a strong emphasis was placed on the bond between mother and child and on the sibling relationship; the expectation seems to have been that the conjugal relationship would be less solidary and less affectively intense than either. But we have observed and will observe that women's valuation as their fathers' daughters and brothers' sisters often served as the foundation for women's esteem, influence, and self-assertive conduct in maternal roles. Roman sources have provided several examples of women memorable for their esteem, influence, and self-assertive conduct in distinctly non-maternal, for the most part daughterly and sisterly, capacities: Cloelia and the Va-

---

[4] For (invariable) "daughter right," daughter naming, the daughterly genesis of the Vestal Virgins, and Roman ideological legends featuring maternal daughters, see chapter three above; for the pledge at the Matralia, see chapter four above.

leriae of legend; the younger Cato's daughter (and Brutus' wife) Porcia, the matron eulogized in the so-called
Laudatio Turiae, and the Vestals Fonteia, Claudia, and
Junia Torquata from more plausible historical record.
Indeed, both the classical Roman definition of the daughter
role as involving self-abnegating and dependent behavior and the paternally protective or oriented nature of
various Roman practices and institutions which culturally elaborated the daughter role are consistent with the
fact that women's structural, affective, and cultural centrality in upper-class Roman kinship and society did not,
as would be the case in matrifocal organizations, invariably relate to their functioning as strong, decisive, and
independent mothers. These complementary but "sexually asymmetrical"—filiafocal and patriarchal—aspects
of Roman kinship and society also tally with the fact
that, and help explain why, the sexes did not ultimately
enjoy an egalitarian relationship in upper-class Roman
society, and women and men were not equally important actors in the Roman economic and ritual spheres;
sexual equality in society as a whole, or at least in economic and ritual activity, would, as we have observed,
theoretically obtain if the elite Romans were truly matrifocal.[5]

Legal and linguistic evidence which seems to indicate
that the Romans bestowed much less value upon the
maternal role than they did upon the role of father merits

[5] For features characteristic of matrifocal societies, see R. Smith,
"The Matrifocal Family," in J. Goody, ed., *The Character of Kinship*
(Cambridge, 1973) 140-141, also cited in chapter three above, n. 9.
For Publicola's sister Valeria and Porcia, see chapter two above; for
Cloelia, Publicola's daughter Valeria, and the Vestals Claudia and
Fonteia, see chapter three above; for Junia Torquata and the matron
of the so-called *Laudatio Turiae*, see chapter four above. For sexual
equality as a hallmark of matrifocal societies, see Tanner, "Matri-
focality," 131.

special scrutiny for a further reason. The Twelve Tables, we are told, not only preferred the issue of males as heirs but excluded those individuals related to each other through a female so strictly that a mother not in her husband's *manus* was denied the right to leave an inheritance to or inherit from her son and daughter. Various Latin words built from *mater* contrast in connotation with parallel formations from *pater* no less strikingly than do Roman maternal and paternal testamentary rights. A Roman *matrona*, for example, was not necessarily a mother; the title distinguished her merely as a respectable married woman, who—unlike a *patronus*—offered no one parental protection. *Matrimonium*, etymologically "the legal status of motherhood," refers solely to a woman's honorable wedded state; unlike *patrimonium*, it did not designate transferable property.[6]

One might choose to interpret these legal and linguistic data as proof that the Romans had at some point in their history labored to devalue motherhood relative to fatherhood, especially as the term *matrona* appears to have been employed to denote "maternal protectors of children" in other parts of Italy as late as the third century B.C. But it seems more likely that this provision and these terms attest to a Roman view of motherhood as at times basically an honorific status, automatically conferred upon a married woman so as to acknowledge her legal right to bear her husband's heirs, and so as to require her to regard herself as joined with her husband for the purpose of procreating his heirs—although she might legally remain in her family of birth, thus be

[6] For this provision in the Twelve Tables, see Justinian, *Institutes* 3.3 pr. For *matrona* and *matrimonium*, see Aulus Gellius 18.6.9; the *TLL* 8 (1936) 483ff., 474ff.; Ernout-Meillet, 389; C. W. Westrup, *Recherches sur les formes antiques de mariage dans l'ancien droit romain* (Copenhagen, 1943) 39-40.

financially independent of her husband, and pay little heed to his wishes. After all, a Roman woman could not belong to two family units simultaneously because this would have entailed appointing a male guardian and protector for her in each. If she had not passed into her husband's *manus* upon marriage, she retained the right to inherit as her father's daughter, and to bequeath and inherit as her siblings' sister, in her family of birth; she could not, therefore, additionally and equitably claim the right, of a wife in *manus*, to inherit as her husband's daughter, and to bequeath and inherit as her offspring's sister. A Roman mother's legal "alienation" from her children, therefore, resulted from the legal decision to separate rather than merge her *status* as daughter and her *role* as wife, apparently did not reflect a negative Roman notion of motherhood, and rather points to the Roman cultural de-emphasis of mere wifehood. Similarly, *matrona* would appear to describe a powerless and non-parental role in classical Latin, and *matrimonium* an insubstantial entity, precisely because both terms may be derived from *mater*, mother, but actually are concerned with women in their capacity as wives.[7]

In order to obtain a clear picture of how the upper-class Romans looked upon motherhood and the role of

[7] For the use of *matrona* outside Rome in early republican times, see the two early occurrences of *matrona* cited by Ernout, *Recueil de textes latins archaïques*[4] (Paris, 1973) 42: CIL I²378 = XI 6300 and CIL I²379 = XI 6301. They are found on votary inscriptions dedicated to the goddesses Juno Regina and Mater Matuta, respectively; that the term is applied to women who donated offerings to tutelary divinities of motherhood may suggest that the word began as a term for mothers in their roles as protectors of offspring. A similar inference might be drawn from the use of the term *matrona* as a title for the goddess Juno—cited by the *OLD* fasc. 5 (1976) 1084. I owe the idea that *matrona* and *matrimonium* point to a Roman view of motherhood as also an honorific status to J. E. Phillips; such a view of course, would qualify as another quasi-matrifocal aspect of Roman culture.

mother one must keep in mind that such women were also, and previously, defined as wives. This chapter on *matres familiae* will, in consequence, begin by examining some classical Roman assumptions about the role of *uxor*, wife, relative to her *maritus*, husband, from considering testimony on the nature of the bond between husband and wife among the Roman elite. It will then focus upon the role of *mater* itself and the bond thought to exist, and attested as existing, between a Roman woman of the classical elite and her *liberi*, male and female children. In both of these sections, moreover, this discussion will try to account for yet another paradoxical situation. Legally, and especially if a Roman woman had been married with *manus*, her ties with her husband were far stronger than those with her offspring: all issue of their union belonged to her husband, and she had no claim upon her children in the event that the marriage dissolved. Nevertheless, the emotional bonds between Roman mothers and their children of both sexes appear to have been far stronger, ideally and in reality, than those between most Roman wives and their husbands; so, too, the role of Roman wife seems on the whole to have been less culturally valued than that of Roman mother. Therefore, our examination of both Roman wifehood and Roman motherhood will concern itself with those aspects of elite Roman life in the classical era which strengthened a woman's ties to offspring at the expense of ties to spouse, and diminished the Roman esteem for wives relative to that for mothers. In so doing, we will also try to explain Plutarch's observation that mothers possessed "greater affection for their sons," and look at the mother-son relationship among the Roman elite as a complement and contrast to that between Roman fathers and their daughters.

Uxor et Maritus

Unlike the Etruscans, who were concerned with couples
and with the conjugal relationship, the Roman elite of
the classical era does not appear to have culturally elaborated or assigned cultural and affective centrality to the
role of female marital partner either in its own time or
in its past. What is more, classical authors seem to have
viewed Roman wives as figures distanced from their
husbands: necessary housemates but not necessarily
pleasant, devoted, or respected helpmates. How and why
our sources characterize elite Romans *uxores* in this way—
and in a way so unlike their characterization of *filiae,
sorores, amitae, materterae*, and *matres*—will be the focus
of this section.

Roman legends about monarchic and early republican
times in fact make a point of defining Roman wives as
possessing personal characteristics altogether antithetical
to those of their Etruscan counterparts, particularly in
their commitment to combining daughterly devotion
with uxorial obligations. Lucretia, we recall, is portrayed by Livy and other sources as, by reason of her
interest in nocturnal spinning, totally different from the
Etruscan princesses wed to her husband's military companions. She is also depicted as no less concerned about
her father's reaction to her rape than about her husband's, and as bringing sorrow and sympathy for her
father alone by her suicide. Livy, we should recall as
well, alludes to the Etruscan queen Tullia, who cruelly
placed ambitions for spouse over loyalty to sire, in the
midst of recounting the aftermath of Lucretia's death;
such allusions are clearly intended to contrast these two,
Roman and Etruscan, women as both daughters and
wives.[8]

---

[8] For the Etruscans' concern with couples, see L. Bonfante, "Etrus-

Only one "Roman" female figure in legendary lore
is memorable as a wife *per se*, Romulus' wife Hersilia.
Livy represents her, moreover, as pleading with her
husband on behalf of the raped Sabine daughters and as
begging that he pardon the girls' parents and welcome
them to Rome as valuable members of the new community. Hersilia's intervention in her spouse's public
affairs solely for the purpose of honoring and capitalizing
upon Sabine familial ties to daughters does not seem, in
Livy's account, to have prevented a full-fledged Roman-
Sabine battle, stayed by the intervention of the daughters
themselves. Hersilia's ineffectuality no less than her support of daughterly requests for family unity thus distinguishes her sharply from Livy's Tanaquil, the first intervening and advice-dispensing Etruscan wife who bulks
large in Livy's first book. After all, Livy portrays Tanaquil as pressuring her husband to leave their native
town and his mother's birthplace, and as readily obtaining her husband's compliance with her wishes.
Needless to say, Hersilia's lack of impact, and keen interest in family solidarity, additionally contrast her with
the much-heeded and familially destructive Etruscan wife
Tullia in Livy's, and in others', narratives.[9]

---

can Couples," *Women's Studies* 8 (1981) 157-187; for the Roman
portrayal of Lucretia as antithetical in her ways to Etruscan women,
see L. Bonfante Warren, "The Women of Etruria," *Arethusa* 6 (1973)
94-95; for Livy's, Dionysius' and Ovid's portrayals of Lucretia, see
chapter three above.

[9] For Livy's Hersilia, see 1.11.1-4. Dionysius of Halicarnassus, we
should note, speaks of Hersilia at 2.45.2ff. merely as a Sabine woman
who had not herself been seized by the Romans but who had remained with her only daughter after this daughter had been seized—
and who headed a successful peace-seeking embassy of Sabine daughters to their fathers. At 3.1.2 Dionysius also claims that this Hersilia
wed not Romulus, but one Hostus Hostilius, and that their son was
the father of Rome's third king, Tullus Hostilius. For other accounts
making Hersilia Romulus' wife, and other accounts pairing her with

The Romans' belief that the role of wife and the emotional bond between husband and wife had not received special emphasis in their remote past finds some corroboration in linguistic testimony. *Uxor*, the Latin word for wife, does not come from any obvious Indo-European root; it thus immediately differs from such other Latin nouns for female relatives as *soror* and *mater*. Recently scholars have tried, without much success, to construe *uxor* as the Latin cognate to the passive pendant of a Sanskrit word *uksán*, "the impregnator, bull" (a word cognate with English "ox"); they therefore interpret it to mean merely "the impregnated," "a woman employed to engender blood descendants."[10] Even the Romans themselves, when attempting to invent an etymology for *uxor*, did not delve into verbal elements referring to affect or close ties with kindred; this thus differs from their "folk" etymologizing of *amita, frater, matertera,* and *avunculus*. Two later commentators, for example, would derive *uxor* from *ungere*, "to anoint." One specifically cites the ancient Roman custom whereby a bride decorated the door-posts of her new husband's house with wool fillets, and anointed them with animal fat, before crossing the threshold; such an association hence defines a well-born Roman wife as her husband's housekeeper, *custos domi*, rather than as a prized family relation. Twice in his *Amphitruo* the playwright Plautus juxtaposes—in a contrived *figura etymologica*—the words

Hostus Hostilius, see Ogilvie, 73-74. For Livy's portrayals of Tanaquil and Tullia, see chapter three above, n. 10.

[10] For *soror*, see chapter four above; for *mater*, see Ernout-Meillet, 390, and Szemerényi, 7-10. For *uxor* as cognate with *uksán*, see V. Pisani, "*Uxor*—Ricerche di morfologia indeuropea," *Miscellanea G. Galbinati* 3 (1951) 1-38. Pisani is refuted by Szemerényi, 40-42, who would ideally like to derive *uxor* from **wik-* or **woik-*, since "that would yield 'mistress of the house.' " I am indebted for this point to J. Puhvel.

usurarius, "lent out," "for use," and *uxor*. This, admittedly punning, association may imply a view of wives as women to be borrowed for useful functions, which they in fact were in Roman society; like the association between *uxor* and *ungere*, it would not identify Roman married women in terms of their husbands' valuation of and affection for them (or credit Roman married men with valuation by and affection from their wives).[11]

That many upper-class husbands of classical Roman times did not expect or manage to enjoy mutually pleasant and emotionally fulfilling relationships with the women they wed is implied by various kinds of testimony. At 1.6.1-6 Aulus Gellius relates that Metellus Numidicus, during his censorship in the late second century B.C., made the following remark in an oration urging Roman men to wed:

> If we were able to exist without wives, fellow Romans, we would all be free from that troublesome matter; but since nature has so ordained that it is impossible to live very comfortably with them, and utterly impossible to live without them, we must consider our long-term welfare rather than our short-term pleasure.

Gellius relates that some individuals felt Metellus had undermined the purpose of his speech, and in fact discouraged those in attendance from marrying, by acknowledging the troubles and discomforts wives bring

---

[11] For *uxor* and *ungere*, see Isidorus, *Origines* 9.7.12, and Donatus, *ad Terenti Hecyram* 1.2.60. For the domestic definition of the Roman wife, see T.E.V. Pearce, "The Role of the Wife as *Custos* in Ancient Rome," *Eranos* 72, fasc. 1-2 (1974) 17-33. The symbolic association between a Roman wife and the household keys—on which see Cicero, *Philippics* 2.69, and Plutarch, *Romulus* 22.3—further points up this concept of the Roman wife as housekeeper. For *uxor* and *usurarius*, see Plautus, *Amphitruo* 498, 980-981 (as well as *Argumentum* 3); 108, with *usuram . . . corporis cepit*, and 1135 may also merit note as evidence for a Plautine, and perhaps a Roman, link between *uxor* and *usus* (specifically the procedure of *usucapio*).

in their wake. Metellus ought, they argued, to have minimized the shortcomings of marriage, maximized its joys and advantages, and blamed its problems on the individuals involved and not on the institution of matrimony itself. Gellius adds, however, that one Titus Castricius ably defended Metellus' approach by stressing that he spoke as a censor, not as an orator, and was hence duty bound "not to say anything which was not accepted as true by himself and everyone else, especially as his topic dealt with a matter of everyday intelligence and a common and well-known experience of life."

Elsewhere, at 1.17.4-5, Gellius quotes from Varro's Menippean satire "On the Duty of a Husband" what he adjudges a clever remark: "A wife's faults must be borne away with or born up with: he who bears her faults away makes his wife more agreeable; he who bears up with them improves himself." Furthermore, two passages in Cicero's *De Oratore* indicate that jokes at the general expense of wives, like admissions of wives' general defects, were as acceptable in Roman public-speech-making as they were in literary parody, and hence doubtless thought to deal with Roman elite reality. As in both passages the deliverer of the punchline is a married man who cannot bear his wife, thus these men are characterized as superior wits to, and arguably more sophisticated speakers than, the defenders of marriage they deflate; neither is Cicero's own utterance, but the *bon mot* of another man, quoted as an example of clever worldly humor appropriate to an upper-class public speaker. The first witticism, set in (and perhaps dating back to) the elder Cato's censorship of 184 B.C., has one Lucius Nasica retorting to that champion of Roman moral righteousness. Asked, "Can you swear to your satisfaction that you have a wife?" Nasica said that he indeed had a wife, but could not swear that it was to his satisfaction. The second quip, ascribed to an unnamed Sicilian, has this fellow ridicule a friend's pretensions of grief over a wife who hanged herself from a fig tree; he eagerly requests from this friend some cuttings from the tree, in the hope that its offshoot may provoke his own wife to behave similarly. Such humorous portrayals of wives as troublesome and demanding individuals also have, as we have seen, counterparts in yet another body of Latin literature, Plautine comedies such as the *Casina* and *Menaechmi*.[12]

Somewhat more seriously, Valerius Maximus' *Memorable Deeds and Sayings* contains one section "On Conjugal Love" and another "On the Devotion of Wives to Husbands." That such categories of conjugal conduct need special citation at all may well imply that they were somewhat out of the ordinary (there is no section, for instance, on devotion to sisters, the love of fathers for daughters, or the love of mothers for children, all of which Valerius and other sources establish as commonplaces of elite Roman comportment). Additionally, Valerius offers in these sections examples which may present upper-class Roman wifely behavior in the best light possible but still do nothing to prove erroneous the general assessment of wives in oratorical circles. The five Roman *exempla* in the section "On Conjugal Love," 4.6, are Tiberius Gracchus (father of the Gracchi), C. Plautius Numida, M. Plautius, Julius Caesar's daughter Julia, and the younger Cato's daughter Porcia. Whereas Valerius here characterizes the first three as husbands who *chose*

---

[12] For these Ciceronian witticisms, see *De Oratore* 2.64.260 and 69.278; it merits attention that at *Cicero* 27 Plutarch does not list any of Cicero's jokes about wives as offensive at the time, though he does mention witticisms insulting to daughters, fathers, and sons-in-law as so judged. For Plautus' *uxores*, see chapter two above and E. Segal, *Roman Laughter* (Cambridge, Mass., 1968) 23-27, 44-47.

to die with, or in lieu of, their wives, he represents the fourth as a wife who *happened* to miscarry and die at the sight of her husband Pompey soaked in blood. Valerius may, moreover, portray Porcia as a wife who committed suicide upon her husband's death; nevertheless, Valerius claims that Porcia did so in imitation of her father (*patris exitum imitata*), whose political cause her husband had at her urging continued. In other words, Valerius' male examples willingly sacrifice their lives out of conjugal love, while one of his female paradigms dies involuntarily (for physical reasons beyond her control) and the other chooses to die because her father and his political successor had done so: in truth, therefore, only the male *exempla* illustrate the phenomenon Valerius claims to describe.

Similarly, Valerius' section on the devotion of wives to their husbands, 6.7, features just three brief examples from Roman society: how Aemilia, wife of the great Scipio Africanus, not only endured her husband's liaison with a slave girl but freed the girl and married her to her own freedman after Africanus' death; how one Turia saved her husband from the proscriptions of 42 B.C. by hiding him in an attic; how Turia's contemporary Sulpicia fled, disguised as a slave, to join her proscribed husband.[13] The first of these illustrations, needless to say, hardly testifies to the conjugal devotion of this wife: if anything, it points to the kindness of a Roman slave-owner to her slave (it may not be coincidental that Valerius Maximus' following chapter, 6.8, features seven

[13] As the titles of their works indicate, both E. Wistrand, *The So-Called Laudatio Turiae* (Göteborg, 1976) 9-10, and his predecessor, M. Durry, *Éloge funèbre d'une matrone romaine (Eloge dit de Turia)* (Paris, 1950) 54ff. find the identification of the matron honored in the inscription which they study with the Turia celebrated by Valerius Maximus neither established nor very plausible.

lengthy anecdotes about the devotion of slaves toward their masters). Admittedly, the two women cited for conjugal devotion during the proscriptions were willing to risk their own lives on their husbands' account. So, too, at 2.67.2, in generalizing about the behavior of those close to the proscribed during this period, Valerius Maximus' contemporary Velleius Paterculus states that "wives showed the greatest loyalty, freedman a moderate amount, slaves some, and sons none." Nevertheless, this assertion appears to be making an ironic contrast between those over whom Roman men held absolute power, and from whom loyalty therefore might be expected—sons and slaves—and those from whom Roman men had less cause to expect such conduct. For while such wifely devotion was not unique, it was unusual enough in other eras of Roman history to warrant mention by Velleius only twice elsewhere: at 2.26.3 he relates that in 82 B.C., when Antistius was put to death, his wife Calpurnia pierced her own breast with the same sword; at 2.88.3 he likens to this Calpurnia the Servilia who killed herself upon the destruction of her husband and *consobrinus* Lepidus, unsuccessful plotter against Octavian in 30 B.C. What is more, the topsy-turvy nature of Roman society during the terror of the proscriptions—when Hortensia, a woman, delivered a successful oration to a male assemblage, and Fulvia, a woman, helped dictate the treatment of various victims—is well-known: one would be ill-advised to extrapolate normative Roman behavior in other times solely from anecdotes about this period.[14]

[14] For the suicide of Antistius' wife, see also Plutarch, *Pompey* 9, and chapter three above; Plutarch, we should recall, associates her suicide with her daughter's divorce by Pompey and does not imply that wifely devotion had very much to do with it. For this Servilia see also chapter four above, n. 14. For the loyalty of Tanusia to her proscribed husband in 42 B.C., see Cassius Dio 47.7.4-5; for other devoted wives during the triumviral proscriptions, see Appian, *Bella*

One also sees evidence for the weakness of the Roman husband-wife bond—and for the general recognition of this weakness—in the words attributed to Rome's most renowned moralist, the elder Cato. In a much-quoted fragment from an oration *De Dote*, "On the Dowry," Cato defines a husband's role when divorcing his wife as a judgmental one, comparable to that occupied in regard to the Roman people by a Roman censor; in this context he justifies a husband's killing—without penalty to himself and without trying her—a wife caught in adultery. Fragments from his speech on the Lex Voconia, as noted earlier, deplore the insubordination to husbands supposedly characteristic of independently wealthy wives. Plutarch's life of the elder Cato contains a memorable Catonian witticism which ironically diminishes wives by groundlessly aggrandizing their powers: this aphorism, purloined and adapted from the Athenian Themistocles, runs "Other men rule their wives, we rule other men, but our wives rule us."[15]

Civilia 4.39-40. That such wifely devotion was not altogether typical of behavior by elite Roman *uxores*, even in times of stress, may be inferred from these same authors: at 9.11.7 Valerius Maximus mentions the proscribed Vettius Salassus, who was betrayed and as good as slaughtered by his wife; Appian, *Bella Civilia* 4.23ff., relates the betrayal of Salassus and Septimius by their wives during the triumviral proscriptions. From Livy, *Periochae* 89, moreover, we learn that during Sulla's reign of terror one Bastia refused her proscribed husband admittance to her house, and he proceeded to stab himself at the door. For Hortensia and Fulvia, see chapter two above and the discussion below. Velleius' reference at 2.67.1 to the period of the triumviral proscriptions as "indescribably lamentable" testifies to the abnormal nature of Roman society at this atypical time; so does Appian, *Bella Civilia* 4.13ff., which introduces the proscriptions as "full of paradoxes" and claims to relate only "extraordinary and shocking events."

[15] For Cato's speech *De Dote*, see Aulus Gellius 10.23.4ff. = *ORF* pp. 89-90. For Cato's apparent misrepresentation of a cuckolded husband's rights in this instance, see the discussion below. For Cato on the Lex Voconia, see chapter three above, n. 38. For Plutarch on

Cato's public utterances appear to lay such stress on husbands' rights and failures to assert absolute authority over their wives in part because wives in his day were acting in self-assertive and non-compliant ways (although his diagnosis of widespread hen-pecking, like his censorial definition of husbandly prerogative, clearly reeks of rhetorical and comic exaggeration). But it also seems likely that Cato, shrewd orator and jokester that he was, perceived wives as the least emotionally valued of a Roman male's kinswomen, and the role of wife as the least vulnerable to male sentimentality. After all, throughout the fragments of his orations and accounts of his witticisms we find him describing women specifically as wives when he is endeavoring to diminish their power and stature, using them as symbols of Rome's moral decline, but depicting them as *matres* when acknowledging their influence and formidability. Both his belittlement of women *qua* wives and concession of maternal power are revealed in the famed Papirius Praetextatus speech, to be discussed shortly. We should, moreover, take note of a Catonian remark and deed related by Plutarch which reflect this view of mothers as meriting respect from, and because of, their offspring. Cato, Plutarch tells us, once insulted an enemy, who was reputed to have lived in an utterly disgraceful manner, with the words "this man's mother considers the wish that he survive her a dreadful curse, not a pious prayer." By acerbically imputing this *mater* with suspicions of and unhappiness over her son's matricidal motives, and so imputing her to discredit her son, Cato not only implies that she deserved totally different treatment, but also that her son deserves nothing but con-

---

Cato's other wife-diminishing utterances, see *Cato Major* 8.2-3. Cf. also Cato's other wife-jokes at 9.6, 17.7 and 20.2, which presume wifely subordination to husbands and disparage wives' self-assertiveness.

tempt for so treating her. Plutarch also emphasizes Cato's own unfailing attendance at his wife's bathing and diapering their son; as Plutarch reports in this same chapter that Cato chose this, well-born but far from well-off, bride because he expected her to be particularly obedient, this display of deferential interest in her maternal tasks seems all the more noteworthy.[16]

Curiously, Livy's rendition of Cato's speech against repealing the Lex Oppia at 34.2ff. resembles Cato's actual words about "uppity" women in directing its criticisms chiefly against women in their role as wives. In fact, the speech begins and ends with the allegation that the women participants in the protest demonstration are turning to *viri alieni*, husbands other than their own; it hence employs the same phrase Cato himself uses when describing a wife's adultery in his oration *De Dote* (*si cum alieno viro probri quid fecit*). Curiously, too, the response Livy places in the mouth of Cato's victorious opponent, the tribune Valerius, for the most part avoids references to *uxores* and husbands, sandwiches one such allusion between mentions of *filiae* and *sorores*, and concludes by entreating "that you men keep women in control and guardianship, not in slavery, and that you prefer to be called *patres* or *viros* rather than *dominos*

---

[16] For some purported instances of wives' self-assertive conduct during the heyday of the elder Cato, see, for example Livy 38.57.8, 40.37.5-7, and *Periochae* 48. The first of these passages, also cited in chapter three above, n. 80, relates Aemilia's vocal annoyance at the failure of her husband Scipio Africanus to consult her when betrothing their daughter to Tiberius Gracchus. The second (also cited in chapter two above, n. 15, and below) tells of the condemnation to death of Hostilia Quarta for the murder of her husband, consul in 180 B.C. The third notes the condemnation of Publilia and Licinia, both noble women, for murdering their consular husbands; this story is also related by Valerius Maximus at 6.3.8. For Cato's remark, and behavior, reflecting respect for motherhood, see Plutarch, *Cato Major* 8.6-7, 20.2-3.

(masters of slaves)." Testimony to the dependency and
devotion of daughters apparently made a far more moving impression upon a Roman male audience (at least as
far as Livy, and presumably his, and perhaps Valerius',
audience were concerned) than did reminders of the insubordination and ingratitude of wives.

A view of wives as low women on elite Romans' scale
of emotional priorities, women from whom they did
not count on loyalty or expect accommodating and affectionate behavior, also helps explain why disloyal, unaccommodating, and disaffected behavior on the part of
wives was evidently tolerated to a great extent by various Roman husbands of the upper classes. Quintus Cicero's twenty-odd years of enduring Pomponia's foul
disposition serves as a good case in point. So does the
decade which passed between Terentia's failure to meet
Cicero upon his return from exile and his dismissal of
her. So does the fact that the husband of Sempronia—
whose loose habits Sallust so vividly delineated in the
Bellum Catilinae—did not divorce her in spite of her
numerous infidelities.[17]

---

[17] For Quintus Cicero and Pomponia, see chapter four above, n.
18; for Cicero's neglect by Terentia on this occasion, see Plutarch,
Cicero 41.2, and chapter three above, n. 77); for this Sempronia and
her husband, see Balsdon, 48-49, and Syme, "No Son for Caesar,"
Historia 29 (1980) 428-430. Another husband of the late republican
period whose wife's unfaithfulness did not evidently disturb him or
their marriage was Cicero's client T. Annius Milo, wed to Sulla's
daughter Fausta; see E. S. Gruen, *The Last Generation of the Roman
Republic* (Berkeley, Los Angeles and London, 1974) 151. Titinius,
husband of Fannia, serves as an example of like conduct from the
next-to-last republican generation: see Plutarch, *Marius* 38.4.

Some upper-class Roman husbands were not, of course, as tolerant
as others. We should recall the fabled self-justification for divorcing
Papiria attributed to Lucius Aemilius Paullus by Plutarch at *Aemilius
Paullus* 5.2 and *Coniugalia Praecepta* 22, and Balsdon's paraphrase of
the account at 211-212. "Because she was sensible, rich and lovely,
his friends criticized him for divorcing her. In reply, he stretched

At the same time the low emotional priority assigned Roman wives in general makes sense out of the younger Cato's decision to divorce his own apparently accommodating and pregnant wife rather than break up his daughter's marriage when his friend Hortensius requested to wed one of his kinswomen. That upper-class Roman husbands would not expect much in the way of emotional fulfillment from their marriages also renders more comprehensible both Cornelia's failure, in Propertius 4.11, to avow any affection for her husband and the fact that Murdia's son, as noted earlier, cites her love for and from her children but says nothing about affection between her and either of her husbands. Furthermore, it accounts for the assumption that Roman men of the upper class acted inappropriately when they appeared to make a large emotional investment in their wives: such an assumption is illustrated in imaginative literature by Mercury's contemptuous address to Aeneas as "wife-devoted," *uxorius*, at 4.265-267 of Vergil's *Aeneid*; it appears, too, in the criticism voiced of the emperor Claudius as a result of his indulgent fondness for his wives.[18]

The emotional distance and lack of strong mutual

out his leg and said, 'This shoe of mine is nice and new—but it pinches, just where, none of you can tell. So it is a mistake for a woman to rely on her wealth, her breeding and her looks; she should think more of the qualities which affect her husband's life, of those traits of character which make for harmony in domestic relationship. Instead of being impassive or irritating in everyday life, she must be sympathetic, inoffensive and affectionate. . . .' "

[18] For the younger Cato's divorce from Marcia, see Plutarch, *Cato Minor* 25. 4-5, also cited in chapter two above, n. 31. For Cornelia and Murdia, see chapter two above; for the love between Murdia and her children, see especially line 5 ("her maternal love, from the dearness of children . . . ," *amor maternus caritate liberum . . .*) and line 27 (calling her *carissima mihi mater*). For criticism of Claudius' uxoriousness, see Suetonius, *Divus Claudius* 25.5, 29.1.

loyalties seeming to characterize the elite Roman husband-wife bond also accord with the relatively limited
influence various Roman wives seem to have exerted
over their spouses. To be sure, such figures as Livia and
the younger Agrippina are depicted by Tacitus as influ-
encing their husbands (and hence Roman political developments), and as thus cut from the same mold as the
legendary Etruscan queens Tanaquil and Tullia. Plutarch
represents Sulla as eager to please his wife Caecilia Metella in all things and as inflicting savage treatment upon
the captured Athenians for shouting obscene jokes about
her; it was to Caecilia, Plutarch also maintains, that the
Romans applied for recall of Marius' exiled supporters
when Sulla opposed their return. Yet evidence suggests
that even upper-class Roman women noted for political
activity and self-assertive conduct possessed more clout
with brothers and sons than with spouses: the younger
Cato's sister and Brutus' mother Servilia may have had
considerable say with them, and with her lover Julius
Caesar, but she is not remembered for working her will
on either of her two husbands; Brutus' own wife Porcia
is depicted as resorting to self-mutilation and obsessive
behavior merely to convince her husband to regard her
as a worthy political supporter. In the years following
Caesar's assassination, Servilia's daughter, wed to the
triumvir Lepidus, may have enlisted her half-brother
Brutus' aid on her children's behalf, and evidently inspired her son to take up Brutus' political cause, but she
did not manage to convert Lepidus to her family's anti-
Caesarean sympathies. Plutarch himself portrays several
wives as pleading with their husbands to change their
course of public action and going tragically unheeded.
Gaius Gracchus is alleged to have turned a deaf ear to
his wife, Licinia, when she entreated him not to enter
the forum on the day of his death. Julius Caesar's final

wife Calpurnia is credited with forebodings of her husband's assassination, which were corroborated by consultation with seers; these premonitions were, however, disregarded after Decimus Brutus predicted that harm would befall Caesar's reputation if he were thought to take his wife's dreams seriously. Pompey's final wife, Cornelia, is represented as vehemently questioning her husband's decision to call for her in Lesbos after his defeat at Pharsalia, and take her with him in his flight; Pompey's subsequent, fatal, decision to seek refuge in Egypt is ascribed to his wife's presence in his entourage.[19]

Even Fulvia, the one formidable female figure of the late republic who does not seem to have owed her political influence to male blood kin, but rather to Clodius, Curio, and Mark Antony, her three powerful husbands, is portrayed as on one occasion less influential with the last of these three spouses than kinswomen pressing claims on a son and brother. At *Bella Civilia* 4.32-34, Appian precedes his account of Hortensia's speech to the triumvirs on behalf of her harshly taxed upper-class women

---

[19] For Tacitus' Livia and her influence on Augustus, see *Annales* 1.3.3; for Tacitus' younger Agrippina, and her influence on Claudius, see, for example, *Annales* 12.41.3-42. We should, however, note again Tacitus' admission that even the younger Agrippina felt especially threatened by her former husband's sister, foster-mother to her own son Nero and maternal grandmother to Claudius' children (*Annales* 12.64.2-65.1, cited in chapter four above, n. 50). For Caecilia Metella's respect from and influence with Sulla, see Plutarch, *Sulla* 6.12. For the elder Servilia and Porcia as politically active and self-assertive, see chapter two above; for Servilia's daughter, her apparent influence with her half-brother Brutus and son Lepidus, and evidently unsuccessful attempts to mediate between the "republicans," led by her blood kin, and her husband Lepidus, see chapter two above, n. 23, chapter four above, n. 14 and Cicero, *Ad Atticum* 14.8. For Plutarch on Licinia, Calpurnia and Cornelia—and their husbands' disregard for their wishes, see *Gaius Gracchus* 15.4, *Caesar* 63.6-64.3, and *Pompey* 74-75.1, 76.6-77.1.

friends by retailing how these women first besought the triumvirs' own womenfolk. Although they were greeted with kindness by Octavian's sister Octavia and Antony's mother Julia, Antony's wife Fulvia rudely repulsed them. Appian claims, moreover, that Hortensia commenced her address by describing this rebuff. Additionally, as Appian says that a day elapsed between Hortensia's speech—which had infuriated and antagonized the triumvirs at the time—and the triumvirs' positive response to her appeal, we may deduce that consultation by the triumvirs with Octavian's sister and Antony's mother, and disregard for Antony's wife, brought about this decision.

It may also be of relevance in this context that Valerius Maximus 8.3, on "Women Who Pleaded Cases Before the Magistrates On Their Own Or Others' Behalf," featuring Hortensia as the last of the three *exempla*, pays lavish tribute to her performance here as displaying her "father's eloquence" and as bringing her father back to life "through his female issue and the words of his daughter." Nevertheless, the woman in the preceding example, one Gaia Afrania, is introduced as the wife of the senator Licinius Bucco and does not receive such flattering treatment. Valerius refers to her name as proverbial for female immorality, to her as a monster, and to her death date as more fittingly recorded than that of her birth. One might conclude from these contrasting characterizations that the classical Roman elite, or at least Valerius, could not justify public behavior by women in their role as *uxores* as readily as similar conduct performed as part of daughterly devotion. Such a conclusion is strengthened, of course, by the fact that a woman such as Porcia commanded Valerius' respect for her political support of her husband because her deeds primarily redounded to the credit of her father.

The early marriage age for Roman elite women, the average nine-year age difference between Roman women and their husbands, and the fact that women's husbands were chosen by their fathers (and other, elder, male and female kin) for reasons other than mutual emotional compatibility warrant emphasis at this point. These facts do much to account for the affective weakness in the bond between husband and wife. Nevertheless, that a Roman husband had in all probability been selected by his bride's deferred-to father, possessed a substantial advantage over her in years (and hence worldly knowledge and experience), and acquired paternal responsibility for his wife if theirs was a marriage with *manus* warrants emphasis as well. These facts do little to account for the unaccommodating behavior apparently so characteristic of and tolerated in many upper-class Roman wives. Admittedly, the role of husband as all-superior father-surrogate may explain why Roman upper-class wives do not seem to have exerted much influence on their husbands. But by all rights it should have additionally ensured the total compliance and obedience so praised in wives by diverse Roman sources.[20]

The legal complications of both *manus* and non-*manus* marriage may, however, have contributed to emotional distancing between elite spouses, and thus may have encouraged wifely indifference to doing what a husband bade. After all, a Roman wife did not have to belong legally to her husband's family at all. Furthermore, a husband (or his *pater*) legally owned his children in both

[20] For Roman women's age at marriage, and the average age difference between them and their husbands, see M. K. Hopkins, "The Age of Roman Girls at Marriage," *Population Studies* 18 (1965) 309-327. For idealized wifely traits see G. Williams, "Some Aspects of Roman Marriage Ceremonies and Ideals," *JRS* 48 (1958) 25; even Livia, we should note, is referred to by Tacitus at *Annales* 5.1.3 as a "compliant" (*facilis*) wife to Augustus.

types of marriage, whereas a wife not in her husband's *manus* had no legal claims upon them, and a wife in *manus* was merely numbered among them. Extrafamilial legal status and the invariable legal disregard for a wife's equal involvement in the producing and rearing of offspring could easily have alienated women emotionally from the men with whom they resided and for whom they bore issue, and thus discouraged women from fashioning their ways to suit their husbands' satisfaction.[21] Concomitantly, a Roman woman's legal status and lifelong role as her father's daughter and brothers' sister might undermine her own bond with and subservience to her husband, especially if he and these kinsmen did not see eye to eye.

Most importantly, an elite Roman conception of the affective bond between husbands and wives as relatively weak, and of the wife as a distanced and often indifferent figure, cannot be unrelated to the possibility for and increasing prevalence of divorce among the ancient Roman aristocracy. Since remarriage of at least one partner customarily followed such divorces, we should also keep in mind the fact that a Roman wife could legally be replaced in as well as legally and biologically ousted from her role, while blood kinswomen could not be removed

[21] As this state of affairs would also tend to distance mothers legally from their own offspring, it might also have encouraged them to bond more closely with the children of their brothers and sisters, and thus further helps explain the prominence, discussed in the preceding chapter, of women in their roles as *amitae* and *materterae*. In contrast to the "legal distancing" between Roman spouses, however, this "legal distancing" of mothers from children does not appear to have had much of an emotional impact; the following section of this chapter, in fact, will point out several instances of children born to the same mother by different fathers whose closeness to and support for one another must betoken an original, and strong, bond with their common parent. For the "legal distancing" between Roman mothers and children, see also Westrup, *Recherches*, 39ff.

from or succeeded in theirs. An observation by Plutarch
in chapter seven of his life of the younger Cato attests
that elite marital schisms and recouplings were both
frequent and far from unusual during the classical period. There Plutarch cites the once-married Laelius (whose
floruit was nearly a century before that of the much-wed
younger Cato), as "rather fortunate, more fortunate than
the younger Cato, for having known only one woman,
the wife of his youth"; he hence implies that however
much well-born Romans of the classical era may have
admired those who married only once, many did not
themselves enjoy such marriages, and those that did
were considered to enjoy special luck.

To be sure, many elite Roman divorces occurred—as
did many elite Roman marriages and remarriages—for
strictly political reasons: the shifting alliances among
elite Roman males. But the Roman view of the marital
union as dissoluble in the service of political aims, be
they of the husband or his wife's male kin, is itself significant. It shows that other, non-family, ties could possess more importance than those of the marital partners
to one another; it hence illustrates the weakness of the
elite Roman husband-wife bond still further.

In light of the younger Cato's marital failures (his first
wife, Atilia was dismissed as unchaste) and the aforementioned endurance of such marriages as that between
Sallust's Sempronia and her cuckolded husband, it is
additionally important to note that up until the passage
of Augustus' *Lex Julia de Adulteriis Coercendis* in 18 B.C.,
a Roman wife's infidelity does not appear to have been
viewed as a particularly grave offense. A husband divorcing his wife for acknowledged adultery had the right
to retain but one-sixth of her dowry, only one twenty-
fourth more than he could claim for other types of marital misbehavior. So, too, by the late republic adultery

seems to have caused little moral outrage among the elite: even Cicero's harshest invective does not level charges that a well-born man is not his father's son (though accusations of murder, incest, and homosexual degradation figure among the attacks in his speeches).[22]

It is true that the elder Cato is reported to have labeled a wife's adultery not only a capital crime but one for which a husband could slay her on the spot with impunity. But the discrepancy between what Cato asserts to have been a wronged husband's rights and what other sources indicate to have been the customary courses of action in such cases may readily be explained; first by the fact that Cato made this statement in an oration "On the Dowry"; second, by the conjecture that Cato, disturbed by women's independent wealth and its uses, was arguing, unsuccessfully, for an increase in the dowry percentage a man was entitled to retain after divorcing an adulteress. For at *Annales* 3.24.2, Tacitus characterizes both Augustus' exile of his adulterous daughter and granddaughter and the severe punishment of their alleged lovers as extreme and unprecedented behavior: Tacitus refers to adultery itself as a "common misdeed between men and women" (*culpam inter viros ac feminas*

---

[22] On the younger Cato's divorce from Atilia, see Plutarch, *Cato Minor* 24.3. For a republican Roman husband's rights to retain an additional but small portion of a wife's dowry *propter mores*—a point called to my attention by R. E. Fantham—see Ulpian, *Regulae* 6.12, and P. E. Corbett, *The Roman Law of Marriage* (Oxford, 1930) 193. For adultery as a way of late republican noble life, and questionable paternity as a non-subject in Ciceronian invective, see Syme, "No Son," 424. At *Cicero* 26.6-7 Plutarch recalls that Metellus Nepos, who kept asking Cicero "Who is your father?" received the response that Metellus' mother had made that question difficult to answer. Cicero's remark, however, was delivered as a witty retort and not as public invective; Cicero's bilingual *bon mot*, reported by Plutarch at 25.4, alluding to one Crassus' supposed fathering by one Axius, was not part of a public attack either.

vulgatam) which Augustus solemnly labeled sacrilege and treason; he then claims that Augustus' treatment of these adulterers went beyond the "forgiving attitude of earlier generations" (*clementiam maiorum*) as well as his own laws. In other words, forgiveness rather than harshness seems to have been regarded as the republican *mos maiorum* when elite Roman wives were discovered to have strayed, and it is by no means clear that whole-hearted and successful efforts at discovery were invariably made.

Furthermore, Augustus' legislation does not appear to have put an end to adultery among the Roman upper classes nor to elite men's (and Roman society's) toleration of their wives' infidelities. Historical sources suggest that the Lex Julia was irregularly applied; first century A.D. rhetorical exercises abound in cases of adultery. During the Julio-Claudian period, even after the punishment of Augustus' daughter and granddaughter, several women belonging to the publicly conspicuous imperial household itself are reported to have engaged in extramarital affairs which their husbands overlooked: this would in particular indicate that, in spite of its illegality, adultery by a wife did not automatically result in punitive action. To judge from the unfavorable comparison of Roman to German marital morals in Tacitus' own *Germania*, other and later adulterous Roman wives often avoided the disgrace and pariahdom such behavior was supposed to bring.[23] Needless to say, tolerance of

[23] On Augustus' penalties for a wife's adultery, see again A. E. Richlin, "Approaches to the Sources of Adultery at Rome," *Women's Studies* 8 (1981) 226-229, and Pomeroy, *GWWS*, 159-160; on Augustus' moral legislation generally, see L. F. Raditsa, "Augustus' Legislation Concerning Marriage, Procreation, Love Affairs and Adultery," *Aufstieg und Niedergang der Römischen Welt* II.13 (1980) 278-339, and G. K. Galinsky, "Augustus' Legislation on Morals and Marriage," *Philologus* 125 (1981) 126-144. On the irregular application of the Lex Julia, and the frequent rhetorical treatments of

and minimal infractions for wives' infidelity goes hand in hand with Roman husbands' low emotional expectations of the marital relationship and with elite Roman society's view of wives as under no great obligation to be loyal and compliant to their spouses.

To be sure, elite Romans of the classical era were apparently as uncomfortable with the emotional strains in the husband-wife bond as they were with those affecting the ties between brothers. Efforts to strengthen the relationship and to inspire wives to accommodating and devoted comportment may be perceived as early as the second century B.C., when the elder Cato not only rallied husbands to exert stricter controls over their wives but reportedly stated, "the man who strikes his wife or child lays his hands on the most hallowed sacred things." The well-known epitaph of one, presumably aristocratic, Claudia, from slightly later in the same century (and perhaps a woman of those Claudii into whom Tiberius Gracchus married?) asseverates that "she loved her husband with her heart." Julius Caesar's unprecedented *laudatio funebris* of his young wife in 68 B.C. merits citation as part of this same endeavor. Augustus' moral legislation accorded even greater cultural prominence to the role of wife by upgrading the rewards for virtuous and fecund *uxores* and intensifying the punishments for errant ones; Augustus' own final words were, according to Suetonius, directed at his own wife, Livia, enjoining her to "live mindful of their marriage."[24]

---

adultery, see Richlin, 230-234, 236-237. For Julio-Claudian wives whose adultery was overlooked by their husbands, see Tacitus, *Annales* 4.3.3-4 (Drusus' wife Livilla), 12.65.2-3 (the younger Agrippina before the death of Claudius), 13.45.3-4 (Nero's second wife Poppaea Sabina). For Tacitus' insinuations in the *Germania*, written at the end of the first century B.C., about the prevalence of adultery at Rome, see 18.1, 19.1-2 (also to be discussed in chapter six below) and Richlin, 234.

[24] For Cato's remark, see Plutarch, *Cato Major* 20.2-3. For this

Augustus' concern with promoting marriage, particularly among the Roman upper classes, may account for
the public profusion of uxorious sentiment by the bereaved husband who dedicated the so-called *Laudatio
Turiae* in the last decade of the first century B.C., and
who attests both to his dead wife's loyalty to him and
to his grief and longing over her loss. Augustus' efforts
to strengthen the marital bond may also explain the
proliferation of loyal wives under the Julio-Claudians:
one thinks of the elder Agrippina, Seneca's wife Pompeia
Paulina, Artoria Flaxilla, Egnatia Maximilla and Arria
in Tacitus' *Annales*; Mutilia Prisca in Cassius Dio. The
younger Pliny praises several women of the mid- and
late first century A.D. for their singular devotion to their
husbands, most notably the mother and daughter of the
Arria described by Tacitus. The latter of these, Fannia,
is remembered for following her husband twice into
exile and for suffering banishment a third time when
she commissioned one Senecio to write his biography.
The former, also named Arria, is celebrated by Martial
in 1.13 as well as by Pliny for not merely joining her
husband Paetus in suicide but even stabbing herself first
and passing the sword to Paetus with the words "It does
not hurt." At the start of his *Historiae* (1.3.1), Tacitus
claims that the troubled period which he is about to
chronicle, beginning in A.D. 69, did not fail to exhibit

Claudia, see CIL I² 1211-VI 15346, discussed by Ernout, *Recueil*,
77-78. For Tiberius Gracchus' marriage into the Claudii, see, for
example, Plutarch, *Tiberius Gracchus* 4.1-3 and chapter three above.
For Caesar's *laudatio* of Cornelia, see chapter two above, n. 9. For
Augustus' moral legislation, see the preceding note and *Acta Divi
Augusti*, Part I (Rome, 1942) 112-118; for his last words, see Suetonius, *Divus Augustus* 99.1. We should also note in this context the
Roman idealization, in epitaphs (and hence in a literary work such
as Propertius 4.11), of women who died having known only one
husband; for this idealization, and the putative cultic distinctions of
univirae, see Pomeroy, *GWWS*, 161, 207-208.

examples of admirable conduct. Such behavior, he spec-
ifies, included the accompaniment of fugitive offspring
by mothers, and of exiled husbands by wives, as well
as loyalty by kinsmen, sons-in-law, and slaves; the *Historiae* subsequently feature several wives who displayed
signal devotion to their spouses.[25]

Nevertheless, even the mourning dedicator of the so-
called *Laudatio Turiae* makes a point of remarking that
in their day "marriages of such long duration, not dissolved by divorce, but terminated by death alone, are
indeed rare." Tacitus' *Annales* also contain several disloyal, or at least embarrassing, *uxores*: Vistilia, who reg-
istered as a prostitute and thus forced her husband to
explain why he had not punished her; Piso's wife Plancina, who conspired with him to dispose of Germanicus,
swore she would die with him afterwards, but appealed
to Livia and managed to obtain a separate, successful,
defense; Claudius' third wife, Messalina. The mere publication of a literary work like Juvenal's Sixth Satire,
which inveighs against marriage in general and exco-
riates upper-class wives for their selfish, immoral, de-
ceitful, and cruel conduct, shows that the image of wives

[25] For this *laudatio*, ILS 8393, see also chapter three above, n. 36,
and chapter four above, n. 26. For Tacitus' accounts of the devotion
of these women to their husbands, see *Annales* 1.33ff. (the elder
Agrippina), 15.63-64 (Pompeia Paulina), 15.71.3 (Artoria Flaxilla
and Egnatia Maximilla), 16.34 (Arria). For Cassius Dio on Mutilia
Prisca, see 58.4.6. I owe the Cassius Dio reference to R. MacMullen.
For Pliny on the Arriae and Fannia, see *Epistles* 3.16, 7.19; for Pliny
on other devoted wives, see 6.24, 8.5, 18. For loyal wives in Tacitus'
Historiae, see 1.47.2 (Verania's burial of Piso), 4.42 (Sulpicia Prae-
textata's readiness to avenge her husband Crassus), 4.67 (Epponina's
devotion to Sabinus); the first two of these passages, however, emphasize just as strongly the devotion displayed by a daughter (Cris-
pina, who buried Vinius) and brothers (Scribonianus who aided his
sister-in-law in burying Piso; Vipstanus Messalla's pleading for Aquilius
Regulus). I owe these references from Tacitus' *Historiae* to K. G.
Wallace.

as troublesome burdens to their husbands so memorably articulated in the second century B.C. still had some literary currency in the early second century A.D.[26]

MATER ET LIBERI

An upper-class Roman woman of the classical era may not, therefore, have or have been expected to receive much emotional sustenance from her husband nor to make much of an emotional investment in him. It appears, moreover, that such a woman was not guaranteed much influence in her role as wife. Nevertheless, evidence suggests that she could look to her children to help sustain her emotionally, and that they repaid her bountifully for making them a major emotional focus of her existence. So, too, it indicates that she wielded considerable emotional and social influence, and commanded immense respect, in her role as a mother. The sense of self-worth and ease at self-assertion required to function in the formidable Roman maternal fashion were, this study has argued, to a large extent acquired through previous and simultaneous interactions with male blood kin, fathers and brothers, who greatly valued (and in the case of the latter set great store by getting along with and pleasing) their daughters and sisters. But the actual deference and affection shown to a mother by her children deserves special and separate scrutiny because they were not, legally, her children but her husband's and she was not, legally or culturally, assigned much power or importance as a wife. Scipio Aemilianus' devotion to

[26] For Tacitus' accounts of these women's disloyalty to their husbands, see *Annales* 2.85 (Vistilia), 3.15 (Plancina), 11.2ff. (Messalina). I owe these examples to K. G. Wallace. On Juvenal's sixth satire, see W. S. Smith, "Husband vs. Wife in Juvenal's Sixth Satire," *CW* 73 (1980) 323-332.

Papiria, which made her the envy of her female contemporaries, is noteworthy in part because Scipio's biological father had long since divorced her and by all
rights should have estranged her from her son. Scribonia's accompaniment of Julia into exile, thirty-seven
years after her divorce from Augustus and separation
from their daughter, is remarkable for the same reason.[27]

Just as striking, though, are the close ties that appear
to have existed between various Romans of the upper
classes who were the offspring of the same mother but
different fathers: their dissimilar names no less than their
dissimilar patrilinies might have been expected to keep
them from regarding one another as true siblings, but
obviously they did not. The family solidarity displayed
by such maternal half-brothers and sisters seems to reflect strong bonding with and high regard for their common parent. Such figures as Valerius Maximus' Afronia,
who did not wish to dispute their mother Aebutia's
testamentary partiality to her half-sister Pletonia in court
for fear of behaving in an unseemly manner toward her
sister, and Propertius' Cornelia, who claims that her
mother Scribonia's subsequent husband viewed her as a
worthy sister to his daughter Julia, illustrate the pull of
sisterly ties among women who shared a mother, but
not a father. A strong bond may also be inferred between
Cicero's wife Terentia and her maternal half-sister, the
Vestal Fabia. Mucia's support from the Metelli indicates
that different paternity did not prevent Roman men from
furnishing fraternal aid to their mother's female chil-

[27] On Papiria, see Plutarch, *Aemilius Paullus* 5 (also cited above,
n. 14) and Polybius 31.26 (also discussed in chapters two and three
above). On Scribonia, see Velleius Paterculus 2.100.5, Cassius Dio
55.10.14-15, and E. F. Leon "Scribonia and her Daughters," *TAPA*
82 (1951) 168-175. Pomeroy, *GWWS*, 158, also notes the closeness
between Scipio and Julia and their divorced mothers.

dren. Probably the best examples of maternal half-siblings whose bonds equalled—indeed exceeded—those
between offspring of the same father in their solidarity
and affective strength occur in the family of the younger
Cato. Cato himself, as we have observed, was extolled
for his devotion to his maternal half-brother Servilius
Caepio and evinced impressive concern for the welfare
of the two Serviliae: in particular, he functioned as a
caring and inspiring *avunculus* to the children of these
half-siblings. The elder Servilia's own son Brutus, as
we have pointed out, proved a no less devoted *frater* to
his mother's daughters by her second marriage: the wife
of Lepidus has been cited for relying upon this half-
brother's help in protecting her children's financial interests; both her son and the daughter of another sister
have been cited for continuing (and dying in the name
of) this *avunculus*' political cause. In a letter of June 43
B.C. to Atticus, moreover, Brutus concludes by promising to do gladly what Atticus seeks and adds that his
sisters make the same request: their commitment to their
brother's aim suggests that they reciprocated his devotion to them as best they could.[28]

[28] On Afronia and Pletonia, see chapter three above, n. 39, and
chapter four above, n. 26. On Cornelia and Julia, see chapters two
and four above. For Terentia and Fabia as sisters, see Plutarch, *Cato
Minor* 19.3, and Asconius 82 K-S; on the Vestal Virgins' favorable
omens for Cicero's undertakings in 63 B.C.—and their conveyance
of this message through Terentia—see Plutarch, *Cicero* 20.1.2: presumably Fabia's inclusion in this body is not unrelated to Terentia's
key role in this incident. On Mucia and the Metelli, see chapter two
above, n. 26, and chapter three above; for problems involving their
relationship, and mother's identity, see T. P. Wiseman, "Celer and
Nepos," *CQ* n.s.21 (1971) 180-182, and D. R. Shackleton Bailey,
"Brothers or Cousins?" *AJAH* 2 (1977) 148-149.

For Cato, Servilius Caepio and the Serviliae, see chapter two above,
chapter three above, nn. 82, 83, and chapter four above, n. 38. For
Brutus and the Juniae, see chapter four above, nn. 7, 14, as well as
n. 14 above; for his pledge of their support to Atticus, see *Ad Brutum*

As we have noted, the close ties between an elite Roman mother and her *male* offspring, as well as her influence over them, in particular aroused comment and prompted commemoration by various ancient authors. Plutarch remarks that mothers have a greater affection for their sons because of their sons' presumed helpfulness (the antithesis of a daughter's helplessness, which Plutarch finds, and other evidence implies to have been, so appealing to a Roman father). Other literary testimony to the elite Roman emphasis on the mother-son bond has been surveyed previously: the popularity of the legend about Coriolanus' capitulation to his mother; the idealization in Tacitus' *Dialogus* of such republican matrons as Cornelia, Aurelia, and Atia for taking charge of their highly achieving sons' upbringing and education; the recurrent and prominent characterization in historical writings of various Roman mothers—Livy's Hostilia Quarta, Tacitus' younger Agrippina, Appian's Cornelia—as murdering their own husbands or close kin for the political advancement of their sons. This and other evidence, however, suggests that the ability of well-born Roman mothers to obtain their sons' help did not stem from mere maternal helplessness. Rather, it implies that elite Roman mothers could demand their sons' help in recompense for their own labors in their sons' rearing, and for their own resourceful efforts, often with male kinsmen, in their sons' interests; such evidence also represents Roman *matres* as for this reason

---

1.17.7. Other examples of close bonding and mutual support by maternal half-siblings include the activity of Faustus Sulla on behalf of M. Aemilius Scaurus at the latter's trial in 54 B.C., discussed by Gruen, *Last Generation*, 334; see also chapter four above, n. 12, on the similar activity of C. Memmius, son of Scaurus' maternal half-sister Fausta. I owe this point about the close ties between maternal half-siblings to E. Badian.

exacting deference and loyalty from their *filii* much as Roman *patres* did from their *filiae*.[29]

Plutarch's *Lives*, for example, represent two of the elite Roman mothers just mentioned as single-handedly rearing and educating their sons, one of these women as successfully enlisting the support of a male relation on her sons' behalf, and not only these two but also a third mother as instilling in their sons both deep devotion to them and a fearful desire not to disappoint them. In retailing the life of the legendary Coriolanus, Plutarch explains his awe of and zeal to please his mother Volumnia by stating that she had been widowed when Coriolanus was young, managed his rearing by herself, dictated his marriage arrangements, and continued to reside with him even after he and his wife had themselves become parents. Plutarch's more factually based life of Tiberius Gracchus claims that his mother Cornelia did such an impressive job of parenting and educating her sons that she justified her husband's decision to die in her stead, and earned for her sons—by common consent the most naturally gifted of all Romans ever—the reputation of owing their virtues more to nurture than to nature. Plutarch notes later in this same life that Tiberius' first position abroad was under Scipio Aemilianus, adopted son of his mother's late brother and later hus-

---

[29] For Plutarch on mother-son bonding, see chapter three above, n. 1; for Roman renditions of the Coriolanus legend, see chapter two above, n. 8; for Tacitus on Cornelia, Aurelia, and Atia at *Dialogus* 28 see also chapter one above; for the motif of the murdering mother, see chapter two above, n. 15. P. Numminen, "Severa Mater," *Arctos* 3 (1962) 143-144, furnishes further testimony for the Roman image of the demanding mother: e.g. Horace, *Epistles* 1.1.20-22; Cicero, *Tusculan Disputations* 3.64. Asconius' phrase *materna auctoritas*—describing the elder Servilia's influence over the younger Cato (on which see chapter two above, n. 22)—also points to a Roman view of mothers as exerting considerable control over their sons.

band of Tiberius' sister; as Plutarch relates that Tiberius'
brother Gaius also served as a young man under this
same maternal kinsman, one may infer that Scipio had
become mentor to Cornelia's sons, and perhaps even
spouse of her daughter, out of devotion to Cornelia
(who was also his *consobrina*) herself. On the other hand,
Plutarch makes it clear that Cornelia exacted a steep price
for her self-sacrificing maternal nurturance. He asserts
that she was blamed by some for Tiberius' death because
she often reproached her sons that the Romans still referred to her as the mother-in-law of Scipio but not yet
as the mother of the Gracchi. Plutarch further reports
that Gaius admitted to having withdrawn a law affecting
the former tribune Marcus Octavius at the request of
Cornelia; he adds that Gaius publicly attacked an enemy
for insulting his mother by contrasting this man's barren
and homosexual promiscuity with Cornelia's fecund and
monogamous chastity. Like Suetonius, moreover, Plutarch states that Julius Caesar was kissing Aurelia farewell when he swore to her that if he did not return that
day as *pontifex maximus* he would not return at all: Plutarch hence links mother-love and mother-fear in Caesar's case as well.[30]

As further examples of reverential Roman sons, and

[30] For Coriolanus and his maternal upbringing, see *Coriolanus* 4.3-
4; for Cornelia, the Gracchi, and Scipio Aemilianus, *Tiberius Gracchus*
1.4-5, 4.4, 13.1-2, 8.6, as well as *Gaius Gracchus* 4.2-4. For Caesar's
farewell to Aurelia on this occasion, see *Caesar* 7.2-3, as well as
Suetonius, *Divus Julius* 13 (also cited in chapter four above, n. 49).
On these three mother-son relationships, see also Africa, 602-605.
Another, widowed, mother of illustrious sons who boasted (and
presumably relied upon the connections of) a father distinguished in
warfare and a brother distinguished in politics, and who sarcastically
chided her younger son into entering public life was Vespasia Polla,
mother of the emperor Vespasian (so Suetonius, *Divus Vespasianus*
1.3-2.2); she, however, is said to have entrusted Vespasian's rearing
to her husband's mother.

mothers who could rely upon these sons' help as a result of endeavoring to help them, one might, of course, cite Brutus and Servilia, and the impression which one gets of their relationship from Plutarch, Cicero, and Brutus himself. Helvia and her three sons, who included the younger Seneca, provide a later instance of the same phenomenon. Seneca, we might note, contrasts his mother favorably with "other mothers who use their sons' power with womanly lack of self-restraint, who—because they cannot themselves hold office—satisfy their own ambitions through their sons, who drain and hope to inherit their sons' legacies, and wear out their sons' eloquence in putting it at the service of others." Seneca thus indicates that well-born Roman mothers were perceived as capable of exploiting their sons' potentially helpful gifts and opportunities, and of exploiting their sons' gifts to compensate for their own lack of opportunities.[31]

This perception of well-born Roman *matres* also emerges in a speech given by the elder Cato to an assemblage of Roman soldiers in 167 B.C. He facetiously attributes the prohibition against Senate attendance by young boys to an episode involving one such attendee, the ostensibly deferential youth Papirius, and his demanding mother. According to Cato, the lad returned home from the Senate one day only to be pressured by his mother to reveal to her its proceedings, which he had sworn to keep quiet. He decided to tease her and reported that they had debated over whether a man should have two wives or a woman two husbands. Immediately the mother spread the story to other Roman matrons: the next morning they thronged to block access to the senate house, crying hysterically, "It must be two husbands to

---

[31] For Brutus and Servilia, see chapter two above, and Africa, *passim*; for Seneca, his brothers and Helvia, see Seneca, *Ad Helviam Matrem De Consolatione* 14.2-3ff.

one wife and not vice-versa!" Young Papirius' eventual explanation of this upheaval was, Cato tells us, accepted by the Senate, and his (arguably sadistic) cleverness rewarded: he thereupon received the title *Praetextatus* to denote his precocity. Nevertheless, sobered by the realization that most Roman boys were no less susceptible to maternal importuning, and far less adroit in handling it, the senators also resolved to discontinue the practice of allowing them to be present at their meetings.[32]

Scholars generally question the plausibility and historicity of this tale; also suspect are the similarities between its scenario—with its greedy women, eager for "husbands other than their own"—and that of Livy 34.1ff., describing Cato's reaction to and interpretation of the protest demonstration over the Lex Oppia. But the speech, paraphrased by Aulus Gellius and Macrobius, seems genuinely Cato's. As such, it not only shows that his ridiculing of women as wives did not rule out his simultaneous acknowledgment, albeit an apprehensive one, of the control which Roman mothers exerted over their sons, and of a mother's feeling that she was entitled to her son's aid and cooperation. It also shows that Cato, and by extension his audience, presumed the existence of intimacy between elite mothers and sons and the desire of such sons to gratify their mothers' wishes.[33]

Intimacy of this sort, and the emotional investment

---

[32] For this speech, see Aulus Gellius 1.23 and Macrobius, *Saturnalia* 1.6.19 = *ORF* pp. 67-69.

[33] For scholarly suspicions about this tale, see, Balsdon, 203 ("if the story is to be believed"). Both he and Malcovati, *ORF* p. 68, note the theory of C. Cichorius that the boy's name was Sulpicius (as Praetextatus is an attested *cognomen* of the Sulpicii). That a new fragment of the Capitoline Fasti attests to a Papirius Praetextatus is, however, noted in the article on Papirius Praetextatus by Münzer, *RE* 18.3 (1949) 1073-1074.

in a son by a mother and emotional commitment by a son to a mother which such intimacy implies, requires explanation as well. No doubt it was fostered by the mother's actual and increasing dependence on her son as her ostensible male protector and link to male society, for he would normally outlive her father, husband(s) and—should she have them—brothers. During the youth of an upper-class Roman male, moreover, he was likely to find his father (or stepfather) and maternal male kinsmen temporarily away from Rome on military or political business. He was also not unlikely—especially in the troubled times of the late republic—to witness his mother suffer the permanent loss of her husband and/ or male blood relations; as a result of such circumstances, many Roman mothers must have been forced to function in both paternal and maternal roles vis-à-vis their growing sons, and many immature Roman males must have functioned as emotional (and perhaps at times social) surrogates for their elder, missing, male kin. Under these conditions both Roman mothers and youthful sons would tend to be more solicitous of one another than would have been the case if both had not been deprived of other male ties during the son's formative years; such, at least, seems to be the supposition of various ancient sources on various strong mother-son relationships. Plutarch, for example, states that the legendary Coriolanus always believed he ought to bestow upon his widowed and evidently brotherless mother all the filial affection which would have ordinarily been lavished on his father. Seneca portrays the husbandless, brotherless, and long fatherless Marcia as blessed with a son—who was under the care of guardians until the age of fourteen and hence presumably without a father on hand—unwilling to leave his mother's household despite the fact that he had one of his own. Seneca remarks that the youth persisted in sharing his mother's entire existence (*contubernium*) even after he had reached an age when "most male children can barely endure sharing their lives with their fathers," and even refused military service so as not to leave her. Tacitus asserts that the long-divorced mother of Sextus Papinius, who had unwittingly driven her elder son to suicide by assenting to his extravagances, was punished by ten years' exile from Rome—until her younger son had passed the perilous period of youth (and no longer stood in danger of falling victim to her indulgent ways).[34]

But intimacy between a well-born Roman mother and her son would also have initially arisen—as intimacy between a Roman father and his daughter would probably not—from the closeness in age between many Roman women and their male children. Indeed, as Roman women were generally married while in their early teens to men in their early twenties, the age difference between a mother and her son would not be much greater than that separating her from her husband. In some instances—e.g. between Cornelia, mother of the Gracchi, and her devoted sons—this age difference would be even less. The sexual dimensions of this phenomenon deserve, and will receive, separate discussion; suffice it to say now that adolescent sons might well form strong libidinal attachments to mothers in their late twenties and early thirties; one scholar ascribes Brutus' psychological makeup in part to the fact that he reached maturity when Servilia was still at the height of her physical prime (and recently remarried after a long widowhood). This issue of sexual attraction aside, proximity in age alone guarantees that Roman mothers and sons could

[34] So Plutarch, *Coriolanus* 4.4; Seneca, *Ad Marciam De Consolatione* 24.1-2; Tacitus, *Annales* 6.49.

expect to spend more of their lifetimes together than fathers could with their offspring. Furthermore, as a son would marry several years later than a female child, a Roman mother did not have to start sharing her son's time and affection with his spouse and children anywhere near as soon as mothers and fathers would have to start sharing those of daughters.[35]

It is thus not surprising that upper-class Roman males also could look to their mothers to share major burdens of various sorts. In the *Historiae* Tacitus respectfully cites *matres* for following fugitive sons. Seneca consoles Marcia by praising a similar figure of the early first century B.C.: Rutilia, who accompanied her son Aurelius Cotta into political exile. The tribune Drusus seems to have been aided in the rearing of his sister's children by his own mother Cornelia, who apparently survived her own daughter. Even the aging emperor Tiberius' deferential reliance upon his aged mother Livia can to some extent be rationalized (as the young Nero's reliance on his mother Agrippina cannot) by the fact that she had known, guided, and supported him far longer and better than had any other living human being.[36]

The expectation that well-born Roman mothers and

[35] For the age of Roman girls (and that of their husbands) at marriage, see again Hopkins; for Cornelia's age, see chapter two above, n. 16: her husband was augur in 204 B.C. (so Livy 29.38.7) and hence already a mature man at the time of her birth. Other Roman women apparently closer in age to their sons than to their husbands include Augustus' daughter Julia and—after her marriage to her *patruus* Claudius—Nero's mother Agrippina. For Brutus' sexually based obsession with Servilia, see Africa, 612.

[36] For Rutilia, see Seneca, *Ad Helviam Matrem De Consolatione* 16.7; for her son see also chapter four above. For the tribune Drusus and his mother, see the article on (his sister) Livia by Münzer in *RE* 13 (1926) 900 and Seneca, *Ad Marciam De Consolatione* 16.4. For Tiberius' deferential reliance on his mother Livia, see Tacitus, *Annales* 5.1.3-4 and 3.1.

sons would enjoy and become accustomed to one another's company longer than fathers would enjoy their
offspring of either sex warrants note for another reason.
It would help account for the sentimentalized representations by various Roman authors of aristocratic republican and early imperial Roman matrons who did not
merely spur and witness their sons' adult achievements
but outlived their adult sons; such women are accorded
sympathy reminiscent of that given fathers, such as Julius Caesar and Fundanus, bereaved of grown daughters.
Plutarch's description of Cornelia, mother of the Gracchi, at the end of his life of her younger son Gaius,
serves as a good case in point: he notes that her ability
to speak of her dead sons without any show of emotions
stirred admiration; he credits her ability to bear misfortune with equanimity to her nature, ancestry, and upbringing. Seneca's emotionally charged descriptions of
two women bereaved of sons—Cornelia, mother of the
tribune Drusus, and Augustus' sister Octavia, mother
of the much-lamented Marcellus—serve as well. Both
Seneca and the *Consolatio ad Liviam* make much of the
loss suffered by Augustus' wife Livia on the death, some
thirty years before her own, of her younger son Drusus.
Valerius Maximus, *inter alios*, makes as much of the loss
suffered by Drusus' own widow, Antonia Minor, upon
the death of her elder son, Germanicus.[37]

---

[37] Seneca's sympathetic portrayal of Julius Caesar's bereavement
of Julia at *Ad Marciam De Consolatione* 14.3 merits special attention
here, inasmuch as Seneca is here likening the loss of a female child
by a Roman father to the loss, by other Roman fathers, of male
children—and all of these paternal losses to that of a mother; on this
point see also chapter six below. On Pliny's sympathy for Fundanus,
see chapter three above. For Plutarch on Cornelia, *mater Gracchorum*,
see *Gaius Gracchus* 19; for Seneca on Cornelia, *mater Drusi*, Octavia,
and Livia, see *Ad Marciam De Consolatione* 2.3-4, 3.1-5, 16.4 (also
cited above, n. 36); for Valerius Maximus on Antonia Minor, see
4.3.3.

Antonia Minor, who died before her younger son Claudius had managed his major adult achievements, was formally commemorated by Claudius once he had become emperor and could redeem her reputation: her hateful grandson, Germanicus' son Caligula, had by this time done much to tarnish it. It is worth emphasizing that the portrait busts of Antonia Minor posthumously erected by Claudius depict her realistically, as an old woman. For there existed two popular, one idealized and one realistic, portrait types of her in her youth (dating from her days as a young matron in Augustus' court); according to the conventions of imperial portraiture, both idealistic and realistic youthful representations could have easily been employed by Claudius. Perhaps he wished to create an image of his mother, who never remarried after losing her husband in Claudius' babyhood, different from that of Antonia as "imperial daughter figure" or "Drusus' widow." Whatever Claudius' motivations, his decision indicates that the sexual impression made on a growing Roman boy by a youthfully appealing, widowed mother need not be an indelible one; other factors must be weighed into account for the lifelong closeness between so many Roman sons and their *matres*.[38]

"Sexual" attachments of young Roman men to their not much older mothers may, however, manifest themselves in situations involving the attachments, both intra- and extra-marital, of such mothers to men other than their sons (and these sons' fathers). The resentment by youthful Roman males of their mothers' second (or later) husbands and lovers is frequently suggested, and justified, by a variety of sources. That a mature woman's

[38] For the portraits of Antonia Minor after her death, see K. P. Erhart, "A Portrait of Antonia Minor in the Fogg Art Museum and Its Iconographic Tradition," *AJA* 82 (1978) 193-212. For Antonia's apparent "late" marriage (at ca. 20) to Drusus and failure to remarry, see the article by Groebe in *RE* 1 (1894) 2639.

investment of emotions in a man other than her sons
struck not only her sons but supposedly detached ob-
servers as a violation of her maternal obligations also
indicates the strength and nature of the ties expected to
bind Roman mother and son. Livy's account of the 186
B.C. Bacchanalian scandal merits particular mention in
this connection. Livy, as we have seen, blames young
Aebutius' mother Duronia for her son's initiation into
the orgiastic and subversive cult: he ascribes her desire
to corrupt her son to her intense devotion to her second
husband, the youth's stepfather, who wished to get his
hands on Aebutius' patrimony. Additionally, Livy contrasts the wickedness of Duronia, who did not hesitate
to side with her spouse rather than her son, with the
benevolence of Aebutius' *amita* Aebutia, an older woman
without sexual entanglements of her own, and thus able
to aid her nephew, and the Roman state, in combatting
the Bacchanalian menace.[39]

At *Annales* 4.40, Tacitus relates that Tiberius rejected
Sejanus' request to wed his son's widow (and Sejanus'
mistress) Livilla in part because it might upset her son,
and the sons of her sister-in-law Agrippina (to whom
Livilla was *amita*). So, too, in 2.34 Martial labels a woman
named Galla, who pampers her lover while mistreating
her sons, a *mater* more vile than the son-poisoning Pon-
tia. The accolades heaped on Cornelia, mother of the
Gracchi, to some extent stem from her reported refusal
to wed a Ptolemy, and her complete absorption in the
rearing of her children. Murdia's son actually praises his
mother for not slighting him, emotionally or financially,
even though she had wed and borne offspring to another
man; such praise may imply that the second marriages
of Roman women were thought liable to shortchange

---

[39] See Livy 39.9ff. and the discussion in chapter two above.

their children by the first. One might also adduce in this context Octavian's disagreement with his devoted mother Atia and her second husband Philippus over whether he should assume the name of Caesar; Velleius Paterculus defends Octavian's conduct in this matter by stating that Octavian preferred to trust a maternal uncle who was Caesar than a stepfather where his own situation was concerned (. . . *avunculo et Caesari de se quam vitrico credere*). One might further note Cicero's indictment of Antony for emulating his stepfather rather than his (actual) *avunculus*. Octavian's behavior and its defense suggest that a Roman son need not pay much heed to his stepfather; Cicero's attack that he should not.[40]

Paradoxically, one does not get a sense that such strains as frequently complicated the bond between young Roman females and their stepmothers. Admittedly, Seneca extends sympathy to his own mother Helvia, for losing her mother at birth, remarks that she grew up under a stepmother, and acknowledges that "even a good step-

[40] On Cornelia, see again Plutarch, *Tiberius Gracchus* 1.4-5 and *Gaius Gracchus* 19, as well as Pompey, *GWWS*, 49-152. The famous anecdote, cited by Valerius Maximus 4.4, on Cornelia's reference to her sons as the equivalent of another more ostentatious matron's jewels also depicts her as preferring the joys of devoted motherhood to the material rewards presumably offered by a wealthy spouse. For Murdia, see chapter two above, n. 11, and n. 18 above. For Augustus, Atia, and Philippus, see Velleius Paterculus 2.60.1-2, Suetonius, *Divus Augustus* 8, Appian, *Bella Civilia* 3.10, as well as Tacitus, *Dialogus* 28; Caesar was, of course, technically Octavian's *magnus avunculus*. At *Cicero* 44.1, Plutarch relates that both Philippus and Octavian's brother-in-law, Marcellus, came with Octavian to Cicero and helped arrange a compact between the two. Yet it may have been Cicero's friendship with these two men rather than Octavian's devotion to his stepfather that occasioned their presence: at *Philippics* 3.17 Cicero defends the lineage of Octavian's mother by noting the marriages between Philippus and herself and between Marcellus and her daughter. For Cicero on Antony and his stepfather, see chapter four above, n. 3.

mother comes as a great boon to no one." Nevertheless, we should also keep in mind Seneca's observation that Helvia's daughterly virtues in actuality forced this *noverca* to become a veritable *mater*. As evidence that stepmothers and stepdaughters were expected to be on intimate terms one might cite Plutarch's statement that Cicero divorced his adolescent second wife, Publilia, solely because she had displayed insufficient grief over her stepdaughter Tullia's death. As evidence that stepmothers and stepdaughters could be on good terms, one could cite the strong ties between Octavia and Antony's offspring Cleopatra Selene, and the younger Agrippina and Claudius' daughter Octavia (for as long as Nero's mother was alive, he dared not injure his own stepsister and wife). Our testimony on the images, and behavior, of elite Roman stepparents may, therefore, permit a further conclusion: that, despite their legal distancing from their offspring, Roman mothers of growing sons may have encountered difficulties in forming sexual attachments with other men, difficulties which Roman fathers of daughters, despite their legal ties to their children, did not experience in forming such attachments with other women. Again, however, such factors as the smaller difference in age between most *matres* and *filii* than between *patres* and *filiae*, the later marriage age of Roman boys than girls, and the strong likelihood of adult males' deaths or absences from Rome would figure no less significantly in this state of affairs than would a son's libidinal attraction for his mother.[41]

[41] For Seneca on Helvia's stepmother, see *Ad Helviam Matrem De Consolatione* 2.4; his remark here that even a good stepmother comes at a low cost to no child should, however, be considered along with Tacitus, *Annales* 1.33.3 (where Tacitus speaks of Livia's "stepmotherly motivations" to be on less than good terms with the elder Agrippina), as evidence for the negative aspects of the stepmother's image. For strong bonding, both prescribed and actual, between stepmothers and daughters, see Plutarch, *Cicero* 4.5 (Publilia's di-

An elite Roman daughter could, apparently, rely upon her mother's affection and support, although mothers—as a result of their daughters' less extensive public involvement and earlier marriage age—could rely less upon their female children for help than they could upon their sons. A recent study of the involvement of historical Roman mothers in the lives of their adult daughters examines evidence on the relationships between various Roman women of the classical period and their female offspring: e.g. Cornelia, *mater Gracchorum*, and Sempronia; Terentia and Tullia; Octavia and her female children. This study emphasizes that a well-born Roman woman expected and was expected to help decide whom her daughter would marry—and that the bond between daughter and mother might, at times, be accorded greater importance by both than the bond between this daughter and her husband. The study further observes that mothers customarily shared their daughters' concerns even when they did not condone their daughters' behavior. It cites, for example, Tacitus' claim that Domitia Lepida overlooked her differences with her adulterous daughter Messalina during the latter's final hours so as to be with her and to urge that she end her life as honorably as possible by suicide.[42]

---

vorce), and *Antony* 87.1 (Octavia and Cleopatra Selene); Tacitus, *Annales* 14.1-2, 64.1 (the younger Agrippina and Claudius' daughter Octavia). In *Annales* 4.71.4, Tacitus relates the kindness shown by Livia to her stepdaughter's daughter Julia; on this point see also J. E. Phillips, "Roman Mothers and the Lives of Their Adult Daughters," *Helios* 6.1 (1978) 75-76. Of further interest may be Pliny, *Epistles* 6.33, about his speech on behalf of a woman whose father had disinherited her ten days after he had taken a new wife. Pliny notes the great expectations of *patres, filiae,* and *novercae* when the verdict, in the daughter's favor, was announced; that women could not expect to replace their husbands' daughters by earlier marriages in these husbands' wills (and perhaps hearts) would, of course, cause them to be more agreeable to these female stepchildren.

[42] Phillips, "Roman Mothers and Daughters"; for Tacitus on Domitia

In addition to the strictly historical cases of the second centuries B.C. through A.D. dealt with by this particular study, others found in Latin poetic contexts (and hence of a more fictional nature) nonetheless impart the same impression about Roman notions of the mother-daughter bond. Ennius' *Annales* seemingly represents the mother of the legendary sister-slayer Horatius as killing herself out of grief at the loss of her daughter. Propertius represents Cornelia as, to be sure, describing the prospect of her husband's remarriage as potentially disturbing to her sons, and as saying nothing about its possible repercussions for her daughter (as it happens, the younger Marcella, to whom Augustus was *avunculus*, and to whom Cornelia's half-sister Julia was also *consobrina*, became her sons' *noverca*, and would seem to have been of political benefit to them). Nevertheless, Propertius has her address her own mother Scribonia affectionately as *dulce caput*, take pride in never having hurt her, and note that she is praised by her mother's tears, *maternis lacrimis*.[43]

Historical evidence about the relationships between elite Roman mothers and their daughters also indicates that daughters often regarded their mothers as models for their own conduct, to be emulated as closely as was feasible. The story of the younger Arria provides a good case in point: at *Annales* 16.34.2 Tacitus depicts her as

Lepida, see *Annales* 11.37-38; for Domitia Lepida see also chapter four above, nn. 15, 50 as well as n. 19 above. Plutarch's association of the suicide of Antistius' widow with her daughter's divorce from Pompey at *Pompey* 9, though not cited by Phillips, may be of relevance as well.

[43] For Horatia's mother, see Ennius, *Annales* 131 Vahlen; for the context, see E. H. Warmington, *Remains of Old Latin I* (Cambridge, Mass., 1967) 47. For Cornelia, her daughter and her mother, see Propertius 4.11.85-90 and 55-58. For Paullus' subsequent remarriage to Marcella Minor, see Syme, *The Roman Revolution*, 378, 421-422, and Table I; for an explanation of Cornelia's failure to worry about possible tensions between her daughter and a *noverca*, see n. 41 above.

eager to follow her mother's example and commit suicide with her husband when he was forced to end his
life as her own father had. Many other Roman women
singled out for unusual behavior, both disreputable and
admirable, had mothers noted for similar comportment.
In the former category Augustus' adulterous granddaughter the younger Julia and Nero's adulterous wife
Poppaea Sabina might be cited; in the latter the elder
Servilia's daughter Junia Tertia, Octavia's daughter Antonia Minor, and Fannia, daughter of the younger Arria
herself.[44]

The special closeness a Roman mother seems to have
enjoyed with her daughter was not unlike the intimacy
of the bond between two sisters (and a woman married
with *manus* was, as remarked upon earlier, legally the
"sister" of her children; as her male issue thereby acquired the same responsibilities for her as were assigned
to brothers, her female offspring arguably assumed the
commitments belonging to sisters, of a woman not in
her husband's *manus*). Augustus' mother Atia in fact may
well have arranged the marriage between her stepson
Lucius Marcius Philippus and her younger sister Atia so
as to strengthen her bond with this sister by placing her
in this "daughterly" role. In the so-called *Laudatio Turiae*, the speaker tells us that his childless wife and her
sister together reared several of their female *propinquae*,
near kin, in their homes, furnishing these young women
with generous dowries at their own expense. He also

---

[44] For the younger Arria, see also Phillips, "Roman Mothers and
Daughters," 76-77. For the younger and elder Juliae, see the articles
by Fitzler in *RE* 10 (1918) 896-908. For the Poppaeae Sabinae, see
chapter three, n. 51, the discussion in the following chapter, and the
articles by Hanslik in *RE* 22 (1953) 84-91. For Junia Tertia, see in
particular the article by Münzer in *RE* 10 (1918) 1114. For Octavia
and Antonia Minor see also chapter two above, n. 19, chapter four
above, n. 15, and nn. 37, 38 above.

furnishes more poignant evidence for the emotional and social needs a daughter must have filled for a woman of the classical Roman elite. Although he claims that his wife's inability to bear children did not matter to him, he immediately adds that it would have been fairer for his wife not to have predeceased him, but for him to have died first, and to have left her with a daughter.[45] At least one Roman male, it would appear, was not selfish about the affections of a female child.

[45] For the Atiae, see Syme, *History in Ovid* (Oxford, 1978) 144-145, and Table I. We should note that Wistrand, *The So-Called Laudatio Turiae*, 59ff., interprets the phrase *orbitat[i f]ilia mihi substituta* at line 63 differently, as the husband's wish to have predeceased his wife because he then might have adopted her in his will "so that on his death she would have been legally his daughter and would have taken on his family name." Nevertheless, Wistrand is able to cite only one instance of a wife's testamentary adoption by her husband—that of the empress Livia, whose situation, as mother of Augustus' previously adopted successor, is hardly analogous to the subject's; the speaker has, moreover, earlier attested to his wife's and her sister's actual rearing and dowering of younger female kinswomen and daughter surrogates. Thus I prefer to assume that the husband is here regretting their failure to beget a biological daughter (who, in this period, could apparently perpetuate her father's name by giving it to her own children; on this point see chapter four above, n. 9, and chapter six below). Needless to say, this compliment to the female sex (for one might expect regret over the absence of "children," or even of a son, rather than of a female child alone) attests to the husband's esteem for his wife and for her excellence as his family's representative; it perhaps bespeaks, too, a more general regard on the part of aristocratic Roman men and women for female children.

VI

SOME CULTURAL PERSPECTIVES
ON ANCIENT ROMAN
FILIAFOCALITY

IN SEEKING an explanation for the so-called paradox of upper-class Roman women's perceived social significance and political influence during the classical period, we have investigated women's roles in the socially significant and politically influential upper-class Roman family. We have argued that women were not only valued, and hence likely to become formidable and respected figures, in their families of birth (and for that reason those in which they gave birth) but also valued initially and primarily in Roman society as their fathers' daughters. The term "filiafocal" has been coined to describe the manifestations of this Roman phenomenon: affection and other indications of value accorded by Roman fathers to individual female children; cultural importance assigned the role of daughter itself; emphasis on ties of blood and marriage through daughters and fathers' daughters—chiefly ties of and through such males as daughters' and sisters' sons, maternal grandfathers and maternal uncles, and fathers-in-law, sons-in-law, and brothers-in-law.

In this configuration of sentiment and conduct, moreover, we have found that individual mothers and maternal aunts were highly valued and that their roles in general were considered important. Such women's positions as their fathers' daughters, of course, provide the link between an individual and maternal male kinsmen. Under such circumstances, we should also expect maternal grandmothers, and their role, to receive value and emphasis. Testimony on the positive significance ascribed by daughters' children to and to daughters' children by *maternae aviae* does not disappoint these expectations: one might recall the honor accorded Julius Caesar's deceased sister by her daughter's son (the future emperor Augustus), the activities by the elder Servilia on behalf of her daughter's children, and the cherished example of female heroism bequeathed her daughter's daughter Fannia by the elder Arria.[1] Our discussion has also observed that in this indisputably patriarchal society the importance assigned by individual males to bonds with their fathers' daughters occurs in connection with general cultural emphasis on the role of sister as revealed in Roman linguistic practices, cultic behavior, legal provisions, and ideological legend. Individual and cultural valuation of and by daughters and sisters also seems to have helped ensure a valuation of and by fathers' sisters, *amitae*, who—like a man's own daughters and sisters— were publicly identified by the feminine form of one's father's family name.

Our discussion has additionally pointed out that the elite Romans of the late third century B.C. through the early second century A.D. seem to have differed from the much imitated Etruscans and Athenians of the sixth through fourth centuries B.C. in this matter of individual daughter valuation, and in the strong Roman cultural

[1] For the esteem accorded Augustus Caesar's maternal grandmother, see chapter two above, n. 11; for Servilia and her daughter's offspring by Lepidus, see chapter two above, n. 23; for the elder Arria and her daughter's daughter Fannia, see chapter five above, n. 25.

emphasis on the role of daughter and ties through daughters. More speculatively, this study has even put forward the hypothesis that the Romans originally, in the monarchic era of the mid-eighth to late sixth centuries B.C., not only accorded special importance to daughters and the daughter role but may have accorded priority to ties of blood and marriage through daughters. If such a hypothesis is valid, we would then have to view as a later cultural development the strongly agnatic orientation of republican Roman kinship first articulated in the Twelve Tables of 451/450 B.C.—in which paternal grandfathers and uncles have jural and other sorts of priority over maternal grandfathers and uncles, brothers' and sons' offspring have priority over those of sisters and daughters, and in-laws count for little.

This discussion has, however, in no way meant to imply that the elite Romans of the classical era were unique among the ancients in their filiafocal practices and sentiments. Indeed, various Greek and Latin literary texts familiar to the Romans of the classical era, and information about the elite segments of other ancient Indo-European societies from these texts and other sources, merit scrutiny in this connection. They indicate that some of these same practices and sentiments obtained, or were thought—and thought by the classical Romans themselves—to obtain in other actual and fabled places in the ancient world. An examination of this evidence for similar patterns of belief and behavior in other ancient Indo-European societies and a consideration of the sociopolitical contexts in which these patterns occur should provide us with a fuller understanding of the larger cultural factors in the ancient world which cohered with and contributed to these patterns generally. In particular, these two efforts should help clarify whether a monarchic system of government like that of earliest

Rome does in fact promote what we have been terming a more filiafocal as opposed to a more agnatic emphasis in kinship ties.

The very fact that several classical Roman authors draw on some of this evidence in their own literary works and emphasize the filiafocal aspects of these non-Roman societies is, however, revealing about these authors and their audiences. Inasmuch as these are patterns of kinship observable in actual elite Roman practice during the classical era, and attributed to Rome's early past, Roman emphases on such patterns in other cultures may acknowledge affinity in this regard. Details furnished by such Roman writings about other aspects of non-Roman societies may, moreover, prove especially illuminating about the cultural bases for the Romans' own kinship attitudes and practices.

In undertaking such a cross-cultural examination, we must also be sensitive to differences between these other societies and that of Rome in both the classical and the pre-classical eras: in part because cultural factors peculiar to upper-class Roman life also seem to account for the Roman view of daughters, the daughter role, and the bonds of kinship created through daughters, in part because this view, regardless of when and in what sociopolitical circumstances it began, held strong currency during a period of several centuries and substantial political change at Rome itself. By reflecting upon Roman and non-Roman sociopolitical contexts of filiafocality, we are, of course, returning to the sociopolitical concerns of our first two chapters. This time, however, we are looking into why the patriarchal and yet filiafocal elite Roman family—which enabled its female members to function and be thought to function as socially significant and politically influential individuals—functioned as it did.

FILIAFOCAL ELEMENTS IN OTHER ANCIENT
INDO-EUROPEAN CULTURES

Several societies, both real and imagined, in the ancient Indo-European world are represented by ancient sources and were apparently known to and at times portrayed by the Romans themselves as displaying filiafocal characteristics: assigning importance to female children and to the role of daughter, stressing the bonds between fathers-in-law and sons-in-law (and brothers-in-law), strongly linking men with both their fathers' daughters and these sisters' children. Certain of these societies, located in Greece and Asia Minor, are first described in works which antedate Rome's classical period by several centuries, and are described by them as existing in an even more remote past. Such particularly ancient sources and some selected classical Roman portrayals of the same societies they depict warrant our attention first. Most obviously, such sources ascribe filiafocal practice and sentiment to an era earlier than the founding of the Roman republic; they therefore resemble Roman legends on the Roman monarchic period in this regard. No less importantly, the fact that these sources predate by many centuries those Roman works of the classical era which draw on them renders such sources, unlike some accounts to be mentioned shortly, independent evidence for earlier sentiment and practice, evidence to which we can observe later Roman sources reacting, and not merely evidence filtered through classical Roman eyes.

Homer's *Iliad* attributes various filiafocal male bonding practices and sentiments to the legendary Trojans, Rome's putative ancestors. At 6.242ff., not only the sons but also the sons-in-law of King Priam are said to reside in his palace; earlier, at 5.473-474, one of these sons, Hector, is said to have claimed that he could hold Troy with his brothers and sisters' husbands alone. At 16.17 Apollo appears to Hector in the shape of his mother's brother so as most effectively to persuade him. Priam's kinsman Anchises is noted at 13.429-430 for specially cherishing his eldest daughter Hippodamia, because she surpassed all the girls of her age in beauty, works, and wit; Hippodamia's outstanding features are in turn credited, at 432-433, with her marriage to the most outstanding man in Troy, Alcathous. And at 463ff. Priam's son Deiphobus urges Anchises' son (and Rome's forefather) Aeneas to avenge this fallen brother-in-law, in whose house he had been nourished as a child, "if the bond of kinship has any effect."[2]

That Homer's Roman readers took particular notice of and identified with these Trojan bonding patterns seems especially likely from the portrayal of Trojan kinship sentiments and ties in Rome's literary masterpiece. Vergil's *Aeneid* also assigns filiafocal conduct and attitudes to the Trojans, perhaps in a conscious effort to render them as similar as possible to their Homeric models and at least with the effect of rendering them far from dissimilar. Like Naevius, Vergil characterized Aeneas' mother Venus as above all a dutiful and precious daughter to the king of the gods. So, too, he expends much of his narrative on Aeneas' involvement in a bloody conflict over the hand of Lavinia, daughter of Latium's king, and on Aeneas' determination to partake of the *socer-gener* bond with this man. To be sure, some similar notions of important kinship ties are ascribed by Vergil

---

[2] I owe these observations on Priam's sons-in-law, Hector's brothers-in-law, and Hector's mother's brother to Szemerényi, 205; Lacey, 39; and J. Bremmer, "Avunculate and Fosterage," *JIS* 4 (1976) 67. Significantly the line claiming that the father and lady mother of Hippodamia specially cherished her (*tēn peri kēri philēse patēr kai potnia mētēr*) is never found anywhere else in the Homeric poems.

to the Carthaginians Aeneas visits and the Rutulians he must fight: Dido is portrayed by Vergil (and hence subsequently Ovid) as immensely close to her sister Anna; Turnus as no less close to his like-named sister Juturna. But these non-Trojan peoples are also represented by Vergil as exhibiting some distinctly non-Trojan, and non-Roman, conduct toward their kindred. Dido, and the husband she so adored in life and after death, are portrayed as cruelly treated by her own brother Pygmalion; Turnus is depicted as rousing destructive passions in his mother-in-law-elect.[3]

Vergil's Trojans additionally combine strong daughter-centered ties of kinship with close bonds to male agnates. At *Aeneid* 3.343 Andromache inquires after Aeneas' son Ascanius and asks whether "his *avunculus* Hector also inspires him to excellence of old and manly courage"; when this line is repeated, at 12.440, it is spoken by Aeneas himself in urging Ascanius to emulate both this *avunculus* and his *pater*. Aeneas' decision to flee Troy with his father and son was previously ascribed to a spectral visitation from and enjoinder by Hector, his

---

[3] For Venus and Jupiter in the *Aeneid*, see chapter three above, n. 41, and *Aeneid* 1.223-304 (especially 256 *oscula libavit natae* . . .), 10.1-62; I owe this observation about Jupiter and Venus to Arnold Pallay. For the conflict over Latinus' daughter and Aeneas' efforts to become Latinus' *gener*, see *Aeneid* 7.45-106 (especially 98-101 *externi venient generi qui sanguine nostrum/nomen in astra ferant, quorumque ab stirpe nepotes/omnia sub pedibus* . . . *vertique regique videbunt*, "sons-in-law from another nation will come destined to raise our name to heaven by their blood, and grandchildren from whose stock will see all things roll and be ruled beneath their feet"), 249-273, 313-322, 358-372, 385-434, 475-601; 12.10-70, 222-256, 783-886; emphasis on Aeneas as *gener* is also found at Ovid, *Fasti* 4.879-900. For Dido, Anna, Sychaeus, and Pygmalion, see chapter four above, n. 25, and *Aeneid* 6.450-474. For Turnus and Juturna, see *Aeneid* 10.439-440; 12.138-160, 222-256, 448-499, 623-683, 843-886; see also Ovid, *Fasti* 1.463-464 (addressing Juturna directly as *Turni soror*). For Turnus and Amata, see *Aeneid* 7.56-57, 341-405; 12.593-611, 659-660.

wife's brother; prior to that decision, amid Aeneas' futile endeavors to defend his native city, Vergil has his hero remark upon the aid proffered by Priam's prospective *gener* Coroebus, the struggle to rescue Priam's daughter Cassandra, and the seeking of shelter by Queen Hecuba and her other daughters. This account, in Book II, of Troy's destruction stresses the bond between Priam, his son Polites, and his son's son Astyanax as well as Aeneas' own agnate ties to males; indeed, Aeneas, Vergil's narrator here, pays more attention to these male agnate bonds than he does the marital ties of Priam to Hecuba (whose reaction to her husband's death is never mentioned) and of himself to Creusa (whom he loses in the course of bearing his father and guiding his son from Troy's ruins). The mere fact that Aeneas' bond with his brother-in-law and Priam's daughters and future son-in-law are mentioned in this context seems significant, reflecting classical Roman concerns as well as an apparent effort at Homeric ambiance.[4]

[4] For Aeneas' recollection of Hector's ghost, see *Aeneid* 2.270-297; for Aeneas' remarks on Coroebus, Cassandra, and Priam's other daughters, see 2.338-346, 402-452, 515-517. For Aeneas' emphasis on his own and Priam's male agnate bonds, see 2.455-457, 526-566, 594-600, 634ff.; for Priam's death (and Aeneas' failure to mention Hecuba's reaction to it), see 2.518-558; for Aeneas' loss of Creusa, see 2.735-795.

Oddly enough, in view of Aeneas' own devotion to both his father and his son, Turnus' plea at *Aeneid* 12.931ff. that Aeneas have pity on his aged *pater* Daunus (whom Turnus likens to Anchises) and hence spare Turnus himself does not move Aeneas; this may, however, be related to Vergil's consistent portrayal of all fathers in the *Aeneid* as unable to help their sons—on this point see M. O. Lee, *Fathers and Sons in Vergil's Aeneid: Tum Genitor Natum* (Albany, 1979). Notably, too, the Rutulian Drances, who bitterly opposes Turnus and his military plans, is said, at *Aeneid* 11.340-341, to be noble on his mother's side alone; of significance may be the claim by the Trojan youth Euryalus at 9.284-286ff. that his mother, from the family of Priam, is his greatest concern and Ascanius' promise that he will cherish and take care of Euryalus' mother as if she were

Homer's *Iliad*, however, also portrays Troy's allies and kindred cities in Asia Minor as assigning considerable importance to daughters and ties of kinship through daughters. The work opens with Apollo's punishment of the Greeks for Agamemnon's seizure of his priest Chryses' daughter; toward the end of the book—at lines 446ff.—the work paints Chryses' joy when the Greeks return the girl to him in his home town near Troy. In Book VI a speech by the warrior Glaucus asseverates that half the kingdom of Lycia was given, along with the hand of the king's daughter, to the hero Bellerophontes. Homer represents Glaucus as son of Hippolochus, whose parents were the king's daughter and Bellerophontes, and of royal blood for that reason; he has Glaucus claim that Bellerophontes had gone to Lycia initially because another of the king's daughters, angry when she could not seduce him, told her husband that Bellerophontes had made advances to her, and because her husband had in turn sent Bellerophontes away to his father-in-law. Homer's Glaucus also states that Bellerophontes suffered a sad and lonely end owing to the deaths of his own son and daughter. Later in *Iliad* VI, Hector's wife Andromache relates that her own mother was a "ruling power" (*basileuen*) in her native city and was "struck down by Artemis in her father's halls"; it has been argued that her mother's anomalous royal prerogatives and residence (as a mature woman with children) in her father's halls are not unrelated, and that Andromache's mother was assigned her queenly position because she was the daughter of a king.[5] Finally, at

his own. Such details, of course, also involve notions of kinship—de-emphasis of male agnate ties and stress on the son's bond with his mother and her male blood kin—prominent in elite Roman society of Vergil's time.

[5] For Bellerophontes, see Homer, *Iliad* 6.191-211. For the Lycians

11.221ff., Iphidamas, fighter for the Trojan cause, is said to have been reared in Thrace by his maternal grandfather.

Nevertheless the Homeric poems posit filiafocal customs and notions among real and imagined Greek as well as Asian peoples. The *Odyssey* depicts Alcinous' succession to the throne of the fictive Phaeacia as resulting from his roles as brother to the late king and husband to this king's daughter Arete. Arete's situation superficially resembles that of the Athenian *epiklēros*—marriage to her father's closest male kin, with the expectation that her sons will inherit her father's kingdom. Unlike an *epiklēros*, however, Arete is honored and assigned administrative responsibilities in her own right (in fact it is Homer's portrayal of both Arete's situation as daughter of the late king and her "royal" position among her people which gives rise to the aforementioned conjectures on the regal role assigned Andromache's mother). In Book IX of the *Iliad* Agamemnon promises to honor Achilles equally with his son Orestes by giving him one of his three daughters in marriage,

---

and their tradition of valuing daughters and maternal male ancestry, see Herodotus 1.173 and S. Pembroke, "Last of the Matriarchs," *Journal of the Economic and Social History of the Orient* 8 (1965) 217-247, and "Women in Charge. The Function of Alternatives in Early Greek Tradition and the Ancient Idea of Matriarchy," *Journal of the Warburg and Courtauld Institutes* 30 (1967) 1-35. For Andromache's mother, see *Iliad* 6.425-428; on her "ruling powers," see Pomeroy, "Andromaque; un exemple méconnu de matriarcat?" *Revue des études grecques* 87 (1975) 16-19. A lecture at Wellesley College in October 1976 by M. B. Arthur, "Matriarchy in the *Odyssey: Basilea, Basileuein* and *Basileus*," also treated the anomaly of the ruling powers ascribed to Andromache's mother, relating her situation to that of Arete in the *Odyssey*. The examples of Bellerophontes' in-laws and Andromache's mother (as well as those of Meleager's mother and Odysseus and his maternal male kin) are also cited by Lacey, 44, in observing that daughters in the Homeric world kept in contact with their families after marriage.

seven citadels by the sea in Argos, and subjects who will revere his rule as if he were a god. Book III of the *Odyssey* represents Nestor's daughters and their husbands as residing in Pylos with him, and as taking part—along with Nestor's sons—in Telemachus' hospitable welcome.[6]

Besides featuring these portrayals of daughters who facilitate closer political ties between men and enable their husbands to obtain power in their own right, the Homeric poems identify several mythic heroines as both their fathers' daughters and figures of considerable significance (often although not always because they gave birth to renowned sons). In Book XI of the *Odyssey*, while describing his visit to the underworld, Odysseus begins to enumerate the heroines he saw with the words "such as were the wives and daughters of outstanding men"; he concludes his list of heroines with the remark that he cannot name "as many as were the wives or daughters of heroes" whom he saw. Five of the women he cites are referred to as daughters of the men who sired them (as well as or instead of being referred to as wives and sexual partners); these women include Salmoneus' daughter Tyro, who bore Pelias and Neleus to Poseidon, and Aeson, Pheres, and Amythaon to the mortal Cretheus; Asopus' daughter Antiope, who bore Amphion and Zethus to Zeus; Chloris, daughter of Amphion, who bore Neleus, Nestor, Chromius, Periclymenus, and a daughter Pero; Minos' daughter Ariadne,

---

[6] For Arete in the *Odyssey*, see 7.61-77; the relationship between her situation and that of Andromache's mother was called to my attention by Arthur (n. 5 above). For the *epiklēros* see chapter three above. For Agamemnon's promise to Achilles, see *Iliad* 9.141-157, 283-299; of interest, too, is Achilles' response at 389-400 and his insistence on wedding a *daughter* of a man from his native region. For Nestor's daughters, see *Odyssey* 3.387, 464-468 (on the bath given Telemachus by Nestor's youngest daughter Polycaste).

abandoned by Theseus and slain, at Dionysus' command, by Artemis. In its enumeration of heroines past and its mode of identifying them, moreover, this passage resembles surviving fragments of Hesiod's *Eoeae*; from such descriptions one gets the sense that daughter-status was given special prominence in an entire, separate, Greek epic tradition (and thus in the societies which promoted and preserved that tradition). Hesiod's fully extant *Theogony*, in fact, seems to represent this "heroinic" tradition in its emphasis on various female deities in their role as daughter. For the most part such divinities are thusly characterized to stress their subordination to male rule. But lines 409-452 merit special note. There Hesiod pointedly speaks of Hecate as both Perses' daughter and her mother Asterie's only child while depicting her as an honored goddess; in so doing, however, he characterizes her as powerful in such male realms as statecraft, military combat, and athletics.[7]

In addition to portraying ties of marriage through daughters and the role of daughter as significant to Greek peoples, the Homeric epics represent certain Greeks as according importance to ties of blood through and to daughters. Both *Iliad* and *Odyssey* also contain episodes involving Greeks which assign prominence to the roles of maternal uncle and grandfather. At lines 529-605 of *Iliad* IX, for example, Phoenix relates the story of Meleager and the Caledonian boar as a parallel to and paradigm for Achilles' plight. The narrative portrays Meleager as having incurred the fatal enmity of his own

[7] For the catalogue of women in the *Odyssey*, see 11.225-330; I am grateful to B.M.W. Knox for calling my attention to this passage and its relationship to Hesiod's *Eoeae*. For Hecate as one of "a proliferation of daughters" in the *Theogony* itself, and for the narrative of the *Theogony* as "privileging the role of (subordinate) daughter," see Arthur, "Cultural Strategies in Hesiod's *Theogony*: Law, Family, Society," *Arethusa* 15 (1982) 71ff.

mother Althaea because he had slain her brother. At the same time, it makes prominent reference to the role of daughter by identifying Meleager's wife Cleopatra as daughter of Marpessa and Idas and by recalling how this Idas fought Apollo for his wife (who is pointedly described as a precious daughter to her parents, especially her mother). Boar hunting also figures in the Odyssean episode which attributes special strength to ties with maternal uncles and grandfather. At *Odyssey* 19.392ff., Homer reports that Odysseus received his name from his maternal grandfather Autolycus. The narrative then proceeds to relate that Odysseus was initiated into manhood with a feast, a boar hunt on Mount Parnassus, and the presentation of gifts, all organized by this grandfather and his sons.

Various Latin literary texts indicate that Homer's Trojans are by no means unique figures and that Vergil's similarity to his Greek epic model in representing the bonds of kinship emphasized by the Trojans is by no means a unique phenomenon. For other authors refer to some of the non-Trojan characters, both Asian and Greek, in the Homeric and Hesiodic poems whom we have just cited for valuing daughters and the kinship ties created through daughters; when referring to these characters, and at times when treating the larger episodes in which these characters exhibit filiafocal conduct and sentiment, such authors also emphasize the filiafocal aspects of these characters' identity and behavior. An obscure remark at lines 11-12 of *Priapea* 68, an extended, learned, and bawdy Homeric parody ascribed to the late first century B.C. or early first century A.D., serves as a case in point. At lines 11-12 the poem states that "if the male organ of the Tantalid (i.e. Agamemnon) had not been notorious, there was nothing about which the old man Chryses would have complained"; it thus ridicules, for an informed audience, the opening scenes of the *Iliad* by poking fun at the fateful appropriation of Chryses' daughter by the Greek commander-in-chief. At 7.74 of his *Metamorphoses* Ovid refers to the altar of Hecate, and in so doing terms Hecate "the daughter of Perses": he hence alludes eruditely to the description of the goddess in Hesiod's *Theogony* solely by acknowledging her paternity. Ovid's *Metamorphoses* also contains not merely an account but an elaborate and lengthy treatment of the story about Meleager and the boar hunt at 8.260-541. There, following a tradition found in the fifth-century B.C. Athenian poet Bacchylides, Ovid doubles the number of Meleager's murdered *avunculi*; furthermore, Ovid says nothing about Meleager's wife Cleopatra (and in fact represents Meleager as smitten by his boar-hunting colleague Atalanta) and makes much of Althaea's conflict between sisterly and maternal roles. That the tragedy of this story's hero occurs because he antagonized his mother by destroying her brother(s) may explain Ovid's decision to treat it so dramatically and lengthily; similarly, Ovid's decision to depart from the Homeric version of the tale in certain details and to follow Homer in others may be connected with the notions of important kinship ties held by Ovid's Roman readers.[8]

These legends reflecting early Greek kinship patterns were, then, familiar to the Romans of the classical period

---

[8] For the dating of the *Priapea*, see J. P. Hallett, "*Perusinae Glandes* and the Changing Image of Augustus," *AJAH* 2 (1977) 165, n. 23. For the tradition of more than one *avunculus* slain by Meleager, see Bacchylides 5.115-129; of further interest is the fact that Ovid's story ends—and has its thematic justification in—the lament and metamorphosis of Meleager's own sisters. On the evolution and transformation of the Meleager-myth after Homer, see also G. W. Most, "Of Motifemes and Megatexts: Comment on Rubin/Sale and Segal," *Arethusa* 16 (1983) 203ff."

from a literary tradition beginning with the writings, still extant today, of Homer and Hesiod; they were arguably selected (and altered) for various Latin literary purposes because they already involved or might further involve kinship patterns dear to the Romans' own hearts. They, moreover, purportedly reflect the sentiments and practices of an era in Greek history long before the eighth century B.C., when the Homeric (and perhaps also the Hesiodic) poems are thought to have been composed—and the city of Rome is said to have been founded: one might, in fact, compare the Homeric poems to the first books of Livy's history as both our earliest surviving and our earliest complete source for the Greeks' notions about their own and their close neighbors' remote past. To be sure, the Homeric epics cannot be accepted as fully reliable historical testimony to sentiment and practice in the era which they depict; so, too, by reason of their setting in a time considerably earlier than their composition, they may not even accurately represent those of the time when they were written. Nevertheless, they can command our credence and deserve attention more fully—owing to their date of composition alone—than can similar portrayals of early Greek kinship practice by such authors of the classical Roman period as Pausanias, Plutarch, and Apollodorus. Such authors, we should observe, depict filiafocal ties as important in archaic Sparta and represent mothers' fathers as rearing Theseus, Hippolytus, Neoptolemus, and other mythic heroes of the era celebrated by Homer and Hesiod. Such authors, we must grant, draw upon literary sources, no longer extant today, which date back to a period far earlier than the classical Roman era. Yet the huge chronological and cultural distance which divides such authors from their subjects as well as the possibility that the former two authors may have absorbed the elite Roman assumptions of their intellectual milieu and revised their accounts accordingly (much as Ovid seems to alter the Homeric account of the Meleager story in rendering it for his audience) limit their value as objective evidence for kinship patterns in earlier Greek society.[9]

[9] For the value of the Homeric poems as independent sources of history, see most recently W. Donlan, "Reciprocities in Homer," *CW* 75 (1982) 172ff., and M. I. Finley, *Early Greece, the Bronze and Archaic Ages* (New York, 1970) 82ff. Donlan observes that even if the society depicted by Homer is a fictional construct, it is an internally logical one, whose complexities form an intelligent and coherent pattern; he would, however, identify the society described by Homer as that of the tenth and ninth centuries B.C. rather than that of the earlier Bronze age or the eighth century B.C.

For Plutarch on (filiafocal) archaic Spartan kinship practices, see *Lycurgus* 3.3 and its implication that all Spartan female children were reared (on which practice see also Pomeroy, *GWWS*, 36) and 3.5, which cites the influence of the queen mother with her brother, and maternal uncle of the king-to-be, Leonidas. For Plutarch as a source on Sparta generally, see F. Ollier, *Le mirage spartiate* (Paris, 1943) II. 165-215, and E. N. Tigerstedt, *The Legend of Sparta in Antiquity* II (Stockholm, 1974) 226-264. Ollier also comments, at 171-172, on efforts to stress similarities between Sparta and Rome by both Plutarch and Dionysius of Halicarnassus; though various similarities (e.g. gerontocratic and militaristic orientation) are striking, these sources' cultural and chronological distance from early Sparta and potential susceptibility to Roman biases diminish their reliability on this particular matter. For the rearing of Theseus, Hippolytus, and Neoptolemus by their maternal grandfathers—as Plutarch (*Theseus* 4), Pausanias (1.22.2), and Apollodorus (*Epitomes* 5.11) report—see Bremmer, "Avunculate and Fosterage," 68. Bremmer's subsequent study on "The Importance of Matrikin in Archaic and Classical Greece and Early Byzantium," *Zeitschrift für Papyrologie und Epigraphik* 50 (1983) 173-186, enumerates other examples of fosterage by maternal grandfathers among Bronze Age figures (e.g. of Adrastus, Aepytus, and the son of Perseus); he also lists instances of supportive, paternal behavior to sisters' sons attributed to men of this era (e.g. Holaeus to Aepytus, Adrastus to Hippomedon). Yet our sources on such individuals are, again, largely from Roman times. By considering the way in which Greek mythology portrays similar or related institutions as background for these institutions during historical

Relatively contemporary sources do, however, represent some of these same filiafocal practices and attitudes as manifesting themselves in the conduct and assumptions of certain Greeks from later historical periods, men whose laws explicitly defined the bond between agnate male kin as more important than other kindred ties and who were not governed by hereditary monarchies. At 6.121-131, for example, Herodotus reports that in the sixth century B.C. Cleisthenes, tyrant of Sicyon, staged a rigorous competition among the distinguished suitors for his daughter's hand. Such a screening process calls to mind several such contests in sagas about Greece during the heroic age: in these tales, marriage to the king's daughter ensures succession to his throne; there, too, maternal male kin are portrayed as possessing political importance to the children of their successors.[10]

---

periods, Bremmer adopts the methodology of L. Gernet, who is concerned with institutional development. Such an approach is not, however, suited to my purpose here of comparing, as far as possible, "un-Romanized" and early accounts of kinship patterns elsewhere with clearly "Romanized" versions of the same story, and these kinship patterns elsewhere with those of the Romans themselves.

[10] On such stories of fabled Greek Bronze Age monarchies, in which marrying the king's daughter secures the throne—even though the daughter in question may have brothers—see Pomeroy, *GWWS*, 18-20. The mythic tradition of the Theban throne, noted by Pomeroy here, relates to the portrayal of Jocasta's and Oedipus' daughter Antigone as both a publicly visible and active figure (on which see chapter three above) and as betrothed to the son of Jocasta's brother (and Oedipus' successor) Creon. As it is the *husbands* who change residence—to the kingdoms of their wives (and wives' fathers)—under such a system, I would dispute Pomeroy's description of this pattern as "matrilocal" and prefer "uxoripatrilocal" (Szemerényi's term) or my own "socerilocal." I also question her use of the term "matrilineal" for these situations, since the son-in-law rules in his own right and does not (as would be the case in matrilineal societies) succeed his maternal uncle or have his sister's son as his successor. The significance of women in such tales lies in their role as daughters (many, such as Atalanta, whom Pomeroy herself cites, are not re-

The issue of Cleisthenes' daughter (and the man who
won her, the Athenian Megacles) became an important
political figure in his father's Athens and seems to have
had little to do with his mother's Sicyon. Nevertheless,
he was named Cleisthenes after his maternal grandfather;
at 5.69, moreover, Herodotus states that the younger
Cleisthenes imitated this kinsman to whom he was
namesake by renaming the tribes of his own city.

Of similar interest is the law code of Gortyn, a Dorian
city in Crete, which dates from the seventh or sixth
centuries B.C. It contains two columns about the *patrōïōkos*, a fatherless girl without brothers, and her role
in guaranteeing that her father's estate does not leave
her paternal grandfather's family. Like the Athenian
epiklēros, a *patrōïōkos* was expected to wed one of her
father's close male relations (her paternal uncles had first
rights to her hand, then their sons). But the code entrusts
the maternal uncles of a *patrōïōkos* with her upbringing;
it is noteworthy, too, that in Gortyn, as in Rome, freeborn women could possess, control, and inherit property.[11]

membered as mothers at all): hence the use of terms derived from
mater in relation to them appears highly misleading. For a critique
of Pomeroy's use of the term "matrilineal" in this context, and the
suggestion that these stories "illustrate the institution of the uxori-
local son-in-law" who repairs "breaches in an otherwise patrilineal
and patrilocal" edifice, see Arthur's review essay on Classics, *Signs*
2 (1976) 386.

[11] For the Gortynian code, see R. F. Willetts, *The Law Code of
Gortyn. Kadmos*, Supplement 1 (1967); D. Schaps, *Economic Rights of
Women in Ancient Greece* (Edinburgh, 1979) 44-47; and Pomeroy,
GWWS, 39-42. Citing Willetts' assertion that the provisions regarding a *patrōïōkos* reflect an earlier period when the laws of inheritance were based on the principle of female succession, C. J. Thomas,
"Matriarchy in Early Greece: The Bronze and Dark Ages," *Arethusa*
6 (1973) 178, states that in this code "the matriarchal elements appear
to be losing ground to the principle of male succession"; for a critique
of such an imprecise and confused use of the term "matriarchal,"

Several important historical figures in classical Greek culture, moreover, are remembered—albeit by later authorities—for sharing professional interests with, and thus educating, their sisters' sons. The poets Simonides and Bacchylides are said to have been maternal uncle and nephew; the same blood tie is said to have existed between the Athenian philosopher Plato and Speusippus, his successor as head of the Academy, and between the Athenian sculptor Phidias and his assistant Panaenus. The fifth-century B.C. lyric poet Pindar offers contemporary, and thus perhaps more reliable, evidence for the key role played by maternal uncles in Greece at that time. Twice—in his eighth Pythian and fifth Nemean odes—Pindar mentions boys who gained major victories in the same contest at the great games as their mothers' brothers; in the fourth Nemean ode Pindar relates that one Timasarchus requested him for an ode on his deceased maternal uncle Callicles.[12]

---

see S. K. Dickison, "Forum," *Arethusa* 9 (1976) 119-120. Although Pomeroy, *GWWS*, 41, also refers to the maternal uncle's responsibility for the *patrōïōkos* as a "matrilineal element in a patrilineal tradition," I would even question the use of the term "matrilineal" for this practice. After all, this obligation stems from the fact that the maternal uncles and mother of the *patrōïōkos* were sons and daughters of one father (totally unconnected with the father and paternal estate of the *patrōïōkos*), and has nothing to do with the long-term tracing of descent or the actual succession to property through the maternal line. Schaps, moreover, stresses that the girl, cared for by her mother and/or maternal relatives, was herself in charge of her father's property if there were no claimant on the paternal side; he notes, too, that her right to sell or mortgage property so as to pay off the estate's debts is one without parallel for an unmarried girl anywhere else in Greece (and thus, if anything, testifies to Cretan "daughter-right").

[12] For the relationship between Simonides and Bacchylides, see Strabo 10.6 and the Suda s.v. Bacchylides; for Bacchylides' own portrayal of maternal uncles in his fifth ode, see n. 8 above. For the relationship of Plato and Speusippus, see Diogenes Laertius 4.1; for that of Phidias and Panaenus, Strabo 8.30. The elder Pliny, *Natural History* 35.54, differs from Strabo in making Panaenus Phidias' brother.

Further and final evidence on filiafocal kinship patterns in the ancient Indo-European classical world occurs
in Tacitus' *Germania*. This ethnographic monograph was
written, about the Germans of Tacitus' own day, toward
the end of the Roman classical period in the late first
century A.D. Its use as a source for contemporary German kinship patterns does not, therefore, involve the
problem of chronological distance between author and
literary subject confronted in using the Homeric epics
as a source for kinship sentiments and practices of the
Greek Bronze Age, or of using authors from the classical
Roman era as sources for that same period and archaic
Sparta. Yet its use entails other difficulties. In the first
place, Tacitus has not attempted to research his subject
at first-hand: rather, he bases his discussion on the reports
of other writers. Second, since personal bias has been
detected even in Tacitus' writing about Roman events
and personages in the era immediately before his own,
one might expect to encounter it in a treatise about a
foreign and never-visited land. Third, one cannot help
but be struck by the moralistic purpose propelling the
Germania, and by various tendentious statements (some
to be noted shortly) made in it.[13]

For Pindar on athletes emulated by their sisters' sons, see *Pythian*
8.35-37 and *Nemean* 5.41ff.; for Pindar on Timasarchus' request, see
Nemean 4.79-81. I am indebted to J. Bremmer for all of these references.

[13] For the background and moralistic purpose of the *Germania*, see
Syme, *Tacitus* (Oxford, 1958) 1.46-47, 126-128, and Pomeroy, *GWWS*,
212. A. E. Richlin, "Approaches to the Sources on Adultery at
Rome," *Women's Studies* 8 (1981) 234-235, regards Tacitus' portrayal
of German marriage at *Germania* 18-19 as an indirect critique of the
Lex Julia and its inappropriateness. One might observe in the *Germania* as well a critique of the situations common to Latin love elegy
and thus an attack on Roman literature's deleterious effect on Roman
life. For Tacitus' biases elsewhere, see Syme, *Tacitus*, I. 204-211,
306-308, 418-419, 421, 431-432, 434; II. 481-486, 498, 513-514, 553,
610, 623.

One has, therefore, good cause to suspect Tacitus' prejudices of coloring his narrative point of view in this work generally; one may in particular harbor the suspicion that Tacitus' personal assumptions about what constitute important bonds of kinship may have affected his portrayal of kinship ties and familial conduct among the Germans. It is hence salutary to consider Tacitus' other writings to determine what these assumptions might be. In the *Agricola*, as we have seen, Tacitus emphasizes—and portrays with sympathy—the closeness between his wife and his father-in-law Gnaeus Julius Agricola; his own deep reverence for this *socer* is made clear in the course of this work as well. Chapter four of this monograph notes the distinctions of Agricola's father and paternal grandfather; at the same time, however, it observes that his maternal *avus* held the same procuratorial office as his paternal, and praises his mother as a woman of singular virtue (*rarae castitatis*) who supervised his education with solicitude (*indulgentia*) and good sense (*prudentia*). In chapter 28 of his *Dialogus De Oratoribus*, as we have also remarked, several Roman leaders of an upbringing similar to Agricola's are approvingly cited (albeit by a speaker other than Tacitus himself). Tacitus counted among his friends the younger Pliny, who was adopted by, publicly known by the same name as, and immensely admiring of his own *avunculus*; indeed, the writings of this *avunculus* served as a major source for Tacitus' *Germania* itself. A recent study of kinship terms in Tacitus' works has in fact concluded that he conceives of all Roman familial relationships as "predominantly strong and beneficial" and of the bond between father and daughter as especially close-knit.[14]

---

[14] For Tacitus on Agricola's close ties with his own daughter and son-in-law, see *Agricola* 6.2 (describing his wife as *subsidium* and *solacium*, "support and consolation" to her father after the death of her only sibling, a brother), 43.4, 44.4, 45.3-5. In chapters 6.1, 43.4,

If, then, Tacitus were representing German kinship patterns in a biased fashion, his personal assumptions about important kinship ties would be those we have also encountered in other writers belonging to his elite Roman milieu; he is, moreover, representing German patterns of kinship to an elite Roman audience. We must, in consequence, consider the likelihood that Tacitus' portrayal of German kinship sentiment and practice at *Germania* 20.2 reflects not German reality, but the projection of Roman notions and behavior already familiar to us from numerous sources. And it is a strong likelihood, inasmuch as he testifies to the peaceful coexistence among the Germans of powerful emotional bonds between *avunculi* and nephews, financial obligations of their own *patres* to the latter, and priority of succession to all property by male agnates—*fratres* and *patrui*:

Sisters' sons are no less esteemed by their mothers' brothers than they are by their own fathers. Indeed, some judge this blood tie as more sacred and binding than that between father and son, and demand sisters' children as hostages, as if these kin have a stronger hold on the emotions and a wider impact on the family. Nevertheless a man's own offspring are his heirs and successors, and in cases of intestacy—should there be no children—the next to succeed to the property are a man's

---

and 45.3, Tacitus also emphasizes Agricola's close relationship with his wife Domitia Decidiana; in the first of these passages, however, he characterizes their mutual concern and harmony as remarkable (*mira concordia*) and seems to characterize wifely excellence as unusual and commendable (*in bona uxore tanto maior laus, quanto in mala plus culpae est*). For Tacitus and the two Plinii see Pliny, *Epistles* 1.6 and 20, 4.13, 6.9, 16 and 20, 7.20 and 33, 8.7, 9.10 and 14 as well as Syme, *Tacitus* I. 112-120, II. 542 and 615-616. Pliny's high valuation of the bond between *avunculus* and *sororis filius*—noted at e.g. *Epistles* 2.9.4, 4.4—is also worth noting. For Tacitus' view of family ties generally, see K. G. Wallace, "Kinship Terms in Tacitus," delivered at the meeting of the Women's Classical Caucus held in conjunction with the American Philological Association, December 29, 1976.

brothers, then his father's brothers, and then his mother's brothers.

Yet it seems significant that Tacitus takes pains, when discussing the German institutions of marriage and child-rearing, to imply that the Germans differ from the Romans of his day and readership in these two matters—and differ in a way that any moral and sensible Roman ought to find commendable. At the start of chapter 18 Tacitus specifically asserts, with the second-person singular verb form *laudaveris*, "*you* would praise," that his Roman audience would be more likely to applaud the strictness of the German marital code than any German custom (*quamquam severa illic matrimonia, nec ullam morum partem magis laudaveris*). Inasmuch as subsequent remarks in the *Germania* indirectly attest to the casualness with which many Roman wives and husbands of his day regarded their marital commitments, Tacitus here evidently assumes that the German state of marital affairs would strike all Romans as unlike those at Rome and would meet with the approval of any Roman with any decent standards of behavior.[15]

At the start of chapter 20 Tacitus makes a similar comment as prologue to his observation that German mothers suckle their own children and do not leave their rearing to maids and nurses: namely, that the Germans have the robustness of body which "*we* ourselves deem remarkable," (*miramur*). That Tacitus even calls attention to this particular child-rearing practice suggests—as does other testimony, including our much adduced passage from his own *Dialogus*—that it was not a custom commonly followed by upper-class Romans. But that he also connects this child-rearing practice with the

[15] On this passage and the more oblique criticism of Roman marital *mores* at 19.1-2, see chapter five above, n. 23.

physical size and strength admired in the German people
by his Roman readers and himself may imply, albeit
somewhat subtly, something further: that the regretted
physical weakness of many a Roman naturally followed
from Roman mothers' relegation of nursing and child
care to slaves and hired help—and that the Germans
might profitably be emulated in this regard by Romans
eager to render their young more impressive physical
specimens.[16]

Tacitus, therefore, at least attempts to indicate that
German and Roman practices and sentiments differ in
certain regards. By so indicating, and in a way which
presumes his audience's attitudes as well as revealing his
own, Tacitus allows us to infer that he was perfectly
capable of acknowledging that the Germans' notions of
valued kinship ties were not those of his Roman milieu
if his own sources had said as much. It is thus striking
that Tacitus' description of German practice and sentiment in this particular regard offers no such acknowl-

[16] On the upper-class Roman preference for hiring wet nurses, and
on this particular passage, see Pomeroy, *GWWS*, 168, 212. Other
passages in the *Germania* contrast, even more subtly and implicitly,
German and Roman mores; 8.2 (contrasting the Germans' veneration
of various women with "adulating and turning women into goddesses," clearly a reference to Roman practice); 19.2 (stating that it
is considered disgraceful among the Germans to limit the number
of offspring and kill an agnate relation, and that among the Germans
good *mores* have more force than good *leges* elsewhere; clearly "elsewhere" is Rome, and what the Germans consider disgraceful is, by
his implication, not infrequent Roman conduct); 20.1 (where Tacitus
uses the second person singular from *dignoscas*, "you would discern,"
to contend that German slaves and freeborn individuals are altogether
indistinguishable from one another in their upbringing; Tacitus clearly
implies that Romans of free and servile status, unlike their German
counterparts, can be physically told apart). On chapters 17.2-19 as
presenting "Tacitus' views concerning the comparison of the more
primitive, yet better, customs of the Germans and the present mores
of the Romans," see H. W. Benario, *An Introduction to Tacitus* (Athens, Georgia, 1975) 34-35.

edgment. Tacitus may, of course, be assuming a congruence in kinship patterns between Romans and Germans without any authority or justification for so doing; his positive view of Roman familial ties—as opposed to his low estimation of Roman marital and child-rearing *mores*— might also explain his failure to differentiate German kinship practice and sentiment from those of his Roman milieu. On the other hand, that Tacitus does appear to distinguish German from Roman marriage and child-rearing might argue against his unfounded assumption of such a congruence, however strong his personal biases and however inadequate his researches into German culture. In that case, we would ourselves be justified in accepting scholarly consensus and in judging Tacitus' description as independent evidence on the kinship patterns of another non-Roman society.[17]

[17] For a discussion of this passage, *Germania* 20.2, see also Bremmer, "Avunculate and Fosterage," 69, and Szemerényi, 186-187. That Tacitus is accurately representing German patterns of kinship is accepted not only by these scholars but also by studies of women and the family in prefeudal Europe. For the former, see K. Sacks, *Sisters and Wives: The Past and Future of Sexual Equality* (Westport, Connecticut, 1979) 244, who notes recent discussions on this passage as evidence for high female status in prefeudal Europe by J. McNamara and S. Wemple, *Clio's Consciousness Raised*, ed. M. Hartman and L. Banner (New York, 1974) 103-104, and V. Muller, "The Formation of the State and the Oppression of Women," *Review of Radical Political Economics* 9 (1977) 7-21. For the latter, placing Tacitus' description in the context of Gallic practice, see G. Guastella, "I Parentalia come testo antropologico: l'avunculato nel mondo celtico e nella famiglia di Ausonio," *Materiali e discussioni per l'analisi dei testi classici* (= MD) 4 (1980) 97-124. Guastella observes that the Gallic inscriptional references to *avunculi* are far more frequent, and affectionate, than those to *patrui*; he contrasts these Gallic inscriptions to Roman epigraphical material in CIL VI studied by S. G. Harrod: these contain fifteen references to *avunculi* and ten to *patrui* (neither set of references, however, involves terms of endearment; Harrod's and Guastella's studies, moreover, are not necessarily limited to elite families and therefore have a limited bearing on this study). Guastella

Notwithstanding problems with its reliability as independent evidence, we now turn from Tacitus' description of German kinship to consider some related information which Tacitus furnishes in the *Germania* about the cultural context of these kinship patterns. In chapter 8 Tacitus claims that the militaristic Germans so prize the female sex that they rally to women's battle cries, that they carefully heed women's counsels, and that they deem the inclusion of noble maidens among a party of hostages an effective means of binding a state's loyalty. Like Gortyn, therefore, Germany is said to have accorded women certain important rights and social significance in conjunction with emphasizing the claims of women's offspring on their brothers. More abstractly speaking, Tacitus paints German society as minimizing the distinction between the domestic sphere to which it assigned women and the public sphere which was dominated by men. Warfare, by Tacitus' account the Germans' most valued male public activity, evidently integrated and treasured the contributory efforts of noncombatant females. In addition to remarking that the Germans are inspired by women's battle cries and regard maidens as effective hostages, Tacitus states at 7.2 that the Germans have their womenfolk and other close kin near them whenever they fight, are most desirous of the praise of these witnesses, and turn to mothers and wives—who have no trepidation about counting and comparing their male relations' injuries—for first aid and food. Tacitus also says that German women give and receive military weapons as marriage presents—in order that "a

additionally postulates strains in the Gallic father-son relationship which contrast to the warmth and affection characterizing bonds with maternal uncles, and thus defines the avuncular relationship as a complement to that of father and son in the Gallic system of behavior. I owe the Guastella reference to J. Bremmer.

woman may not think herself outside thoughts of manly virtues and outside the risks of warfare." And a German wife, Tacitus reports at 18.2-3, is reminded at her wedding ceremony as well as by these gifts that she had allied with her husband "to endure and dare in peace and in war"; she is, moreover, expected to pass these gifts on, intact, to her children so that her daughters-in-law may pass them on to their children in their turn.

Whether the other non-Roman societies we surveyed prior to Tacitus' Germany are imaginary or actual, and whether the accounts of their kinship practices and attitudes are objective and accurate or subjective and somewhat misrepresentative, the portrayals of these societies—by Homer and early Greek as well as later classical Roman sources—warrant further attention at this point. All similarly provide information on the cultural conditions contributing to, or at least viewed as connected with, the importance of the daughter role, the valuation of daughters as individuals, and the emphasis on the ties of blood and marriage formed through female children. Consideration of what features these disparate societies have in common with one another and with Tacitus' Germany will then better enable us to determine whether these filiafocal kinship patterns were likely to have existed in earliest monarchic Rome and to understand why these patterns persisted among the classical Roman elite.

These societies have been chosen for discussion here largely because they share an Indo-European heritage, a heritage also shared by the ancient Romans. Parallels to these filiafocal sentiments and practices have been perceived in other Indo-European cultures with which the classical Romans were not familiar; hence we might assume that all of these societies, and ancient elite Roman society itself, have simply retained attitudes and customs

from their parent culture.[18] But although the classical
Athenians can also claim an Indo-European heritage,
they, to reiterate, do not appear to have accorded daughters, or most of the bonds created to and through daughters, much particular or general value; other cultural
factors obviously play a large part in filiafocality too.[19]

[18] For the Indo-European heritage of these societies, and the assumption that Latin kinship terms—like details about patterns of
residence from the Homeric epics—primarily serve as evidence for
the family and tribal structures of the Indo-Europeans, see Szemerényi, 149-206. For parallels in other, unfamiliar, earlier and later
Indo-European cultures to Roman kinship patterns, see G. Dumézil,
Déesses latines et mythes védiques (Brussels, 1956) 1-43, on the Matralia,
and *Mariages indo-européens* (Paris, 1979), as well as Guastella, "Parentalia," and R. H. Bremmer, Jr., "The Importance of Kinship:
Uncle and Nephew in 'Beowulf,'" *Amsterdamer Beiträge zur Alteren
Germanistik* 15 (1980) 21-38; I owe the Dumézil references to J. Puhvel.
As noted below, I have not considered kinship patterns of various
Hellenistic monarchies (e.g. the Egyptian Ptolemies) in this section—
largely because their relation to the Indo-European cultural complex
is hard to determine, their similarities to monarchic Roman society
notwithstanding.

[19] Evidence on the valuation and conduct of individual Athenian
female children in upper-class families may warrant consideration in
this context, inasmuch as the discussion on the Athenian view of
daughters in chapter three dealt exclusively with the culture-wide
image of the daughter role. Such evidence suggests, as chapter three
has argued, that neither the close, mutually caring relationship assumed to exist between elite Roman fathers and their daughters nor
the Roman concept of female offspring as sharing in fathers' worldly
goods and political commitments seems to have obtained in upper-
class Athenian life. At 6.59.3, for example, Thucydides quotes the
epitaph—from her husband's city of Lampsacus—of Archedice,
daughter of "the greatest man in Greece of his day," the Athenian
tyrant Hippias. Its second couplet seems to distinguish Archedice
from her father, husband, brothers, and sons in "never displaying
reckless cruelty"; it thus allows the inference that she was publicly
honored and identified as her father's daughter (and kinswoman to
her other male relations, tyrants all) precisely because she so differed
in nature from the males of her family. At 151-152 and 159-160
Lacey discusses Demosthenes 41 and Lysias 32: in the first speech,
Lacey observes, the daughters are said to "take part in administering

The importance assigned to bonds between male agnates by the classical Athenians should not necessarily, as should by now be apparent, rule out the culture-wide valuation of daughters, the cultural significance of the role of daughter, or the cultural prominence of blood and marriage ties through daughters. Coexistence of agnate and filiafocal emphases is possible and logical, a phenomenon found in many modern societies as well as in classical Rome and, if we are to trust Tacitus, ancient Germany; its manifestations in these ancient societies hence merit explanation.[20]

---

the family property" (i.e. be present at the making of their father's will), but Lacey adds that they may be atypical (as they have no brothers); in the second, Lacey notes, a daughter is recalled as indignantly appealing to her father at a family council for mistreating her—and his own brother's—children. In other words, even such testimony to the public visibility of one, unusual, Athenian daughter and to daughters' involvement in family dealings does nothing to refute the generalizations about the devaluation of Athenian daughterhood made earlier in this study. To be sure, as J. Bremmer's article on matrikin points out, maternal uncles do seem to play a significant role in the lives of various Athenian men: at Demosthenes 39.32 we hear that one Boeotus was named after his maternal uncle; in 2.78 Aeschines cites the political conduct of both his father and mother's brother to the jury; Isaeus 3 notes that Pyrrhus' maternal uncles claimed to have witnessed his marriage; Lysias 3.6 relates that the speaker's sister and her daughters had lived under his roof; as we have indicated in n. 12 above, Plato and probably Phidias were occupational role models for their sisters' sons. Yet the fact that brothers were likely to assume *kyrieia* for a divorced or widowed sister if their father were deceased and the necessity of guardianship for all citizen women are significant here; so are other cultural factors (such as a large age discrepancy between husband and wife) conducive to a woman's relying upon her brothers to socialize her sons.

[20] That cooperation between men and matrikin and affines occurs in modern societies with patrilineal descent and agnatic inheritance is a point to be emphasized, and one which has been emphasized to me by S. C. Humphreys. This point is made throughout anthropological literature as well: the importance of matrikin in patrilineal societies was most memorably noted in A. R. Radcliffe-Brown's "The Mother's Brother in South Africa," reprinted in *Structure and*

Most strikingly, the circumstances of the Homeric
Lycians, Phaeacians, Argives, and Pylians as well as the
Homeric and Vergilian Trojans indicate that a hereditary
monarchy or chieftainship restricting rulership to males
is highly conducive to the formation of close ties between its ruler and his daughter's husband; such ties also
evidently tend to be forged, by way of imitation, between fathers and sons-in-law among the ruling aristocratic class that provide additional leadership in societies of this sort. A kingdom in which the monarch
or chief has a female child but no son to succeed him in
particular lends itself to the promotion of strong bonds
between fathers and sons-in-law. That certain of the
ancients seem to have reckoned male kingliness a hereditary trait, and hence able to be passed on by a king's
daughter to her sons (and, in the instance of Homer's
Arete, displayed by her outright), apparently also added
to the value possessed in the eyes of his wife's father by
the father of these sons.[21]

Function in Primitive Society (London, 1952) 15-31; the importance of
affines is stressed by such scholars as Sacks, *Sisters and Wives*, 146ff.
(on the South African Lovedu). Yet the degree to which cooperative
filiafocal bonds are emphasized relative to agnate ones varies; that
many of the modern societies noted for these joint emphases are
more "primitive"—or at least less urban—than Rome in the classical
period and that such societies are not necessarily elite groupings make
cross-cultural comparison difficult, desirable though it is.

[21] On the early Greek view of daughters' sons as natural successors
rather than serious threats to kings, see also Herodotus 1.107ff. He
describes the dream-inspired fear of the Median king Astyages that
the offspring of his daughter Mandane would prove threatening to
him and his consequent decision to wed her to a Persian. Herodotus
then proceeds to relate Astyages' subsequent dream that a vine grew
from Mandane's private parts and spread all over Asia; as the Magi
(correctly) interpreted this dream to mean that Astyages' daughter's
son would usurp his throne, Astyages tried to dispose of the boy,
the future king Cyrus. Herodotus portrays Astyages as a harsh ruler,
and hence meriting the misfortune he encountered when Cyrus rose
against him; Herodotus also notes that his conquering grandson

Political benefits did of course accrue to kings' sons-in-law; political security was obviously afforded a monarch by the assurance of a hand-picked male adherent in the next generation and the prospect of a biologically kindred successor in the generation after that. These advantages of father-in-law and son-in-law bonding should not be underestimated in this situation. But these patterns of male bonding depend to some extent on a concept of daughters as biological extensions and extenders of their fathers' vital selves and on a concept of the daughter role as central in forging valued ties between men. Inasmuch as we have mentioned the Sicyonian tyrant Cleisthenes, his strenuous endeavors to choose a son-in-law, and the similarly named son of his daughter who emulated him as evidence for "monarchic-style" filiafocal bonding among Greeks of historical times, it is perhaps also relevant to note that several other archaic Greek tyrants formed close ties with one another through marriages of one tyrant to another's daughter. Herodotus, for example, represents Procles of Epidaurus as allied thus with Periander of Corinth at 3.50.2 and 52.7, and Terillus of Himera as allied thus with Anaxilas of Rhegium at 7.165. The formation of such alliances by men who had not themselves been bequeathed hereditary thrones suggests their eagerness for legitimation through imitating the hereditary monarchs of an earlier era. It also shows that a hereditary monarchic tradition was viewed in the ancient classical world itself as associated with the close and public bonding, through daughters, of fathers-in-law and sons-in-law.[22]

---

treated Astyages kindly and kept him at his court until he died: the implication may be that this, barbarian, monarch should have welcomed the advent of such a worthy successor rather than oppose it.

[22] On these tyrants, see also A. Andrewes, *The Greek Tyrants*

We have observed the lack of a sharp distinction between the domestic and public/military spheres in German society as Tacitus represents it in *Germania*. Such
a "commingling of the spheres," as we pointed out in
the first two chapters of this study, is thought to ensure
a higher valuation of all women than that which characterizes societies marked by sharp differentiations between domestic and public activity. The distinction between domestic and public spheres also seems somewhat
blurred in some of the other societies surveyed in this
section. Women in Gortyn were involved in their society's economic life through their rights to possess,
inherit, and bequeath property. The "palace" societies
of Homeric Ithaca, Phaeacia, Pylos, and Sparta as well
as those of Homeric and Vergilian Troy also unite domestic and politically related activity under one roof. In
several of these societies, too, the family functions as an
important social, economic, and political institution, and
women occupy a structurally central position: one thinks,
in particular and again, of the Homeric "palace" societies: there female royalty play active decision-making
roles and some part in economic matters; in doing so,
both have an impact upon their societies no less than
upon their immediate families.[23]

(London, 1956) 49ff., 132; Lacey, 67-68; Gernet, *Anthropologie de la
Grèce antique* (Paris, 1968) 344-359. Significantly, at 3.53 Herodotus
also depicts Periander of Corinth as relying upon his own daughter
to effectuate a reconciliation between himself and his estranged younger
son.

[23] For Homeric Sparta, see in particular *Odyssey* 4.1ff. There the
king Menelaus does not, however, plan on bequeathing the kingdom
to the husband of his daughter by his wife Helen, but rather begets
a son by a slave woman for that very purpose. For women's structural
centrality in the families who rule Homeric palace societies, see, for
example, Homer's portrayals of Penelope, Helen, and Arete. Pertinent passages include *Odyssey* 2.85-137 (especially the final eight
lines, in which Telemachus fears the wrath of his mother's father if

Nevertheless, many of the societies we have discussed are additionally represented as promoting cooperative male bonding activities which exclude women, activities which serve an educational purpose for young men by initiating them into behavior deemed both culturally important and the province of responsible adult males. In the case of the Germans the cooperative masculine activity promoted most avidly is of course military combat. Tacitus reports in chapter 13.1 of the *Germania* that the first public distinction conferred upon a male youth is that of a shield and spear, presented by one of the chieftains, the youth's father, or some other male kinsman; this distinction, he says, is the equivalent of the Roman male youth's first donning the politically symbolic toga. Among the peaceful Phaeacians young men are portrayed as joining together in seafaring pursuits: although the royal princes are depicted as partial to competitive athletics, their father graciously accepts Odysseus' show of physical superiority to them and insists

he sends her back to him and worries about furies summoned by his mother's parting curse), 4.120-146, 219-305, 561-569; 6.304-315; 7.67-77, 139-152, 233ff.; 8.419-445, 11.335-346; 15.172-181; 17.488-588; 18.158-303; 19.53ff. My point about the blurring of domestic and public in Homeric palace societies is also made by H. P. Foley, "The Conception of Women in Athenian Drama," *Reflections of Women in Antiquity*, ed. H. P. Foley (London, 1981) 150, "the aristocratic women of early Greece had some share in the political life of the community and the division between the domestic and public spheres was less radical." For the (eventually heeded) plea of Aeneas' wife Creusa that her husband protect his family rather than die in combat with the Greeks, see Vergil, *Aeneid* 2.675-678. In "The Women of Greece in Wartime," *CP* 77 (1982) 193-213, Schaps remarks upon the public self-assertion ascribed to women in various parts of Greece, during various historical periods, when their cities were under military attack. His evidence makes it clear that the circumstances of wartime, and especially nearby combat, also help to break down the division between domestic and public; it does much to explain the blurring of this distinction not only in besieged Homeric and Vergilian Troy but in Tacitus' Germany as well.

that they demonstrate for their guest their prowess at dance and song; eschewal of the "agonistic" mentality by the daughter-respecting Phaeacians may suggest—as would the agonistic orientation of male activity in classical Athenian society—that some incompatibility exists between high cultural valuation of youth-oriented competitive male activities and filiafocal bonding patterns. Odysseus' own maternal grandfather and uncles, we should recall, are said to have marked his entry into manhood by including him in a feast and boar hunt, then showering him with magnificent gifts. Ovid's account of the Meleager story, moreover, emphasizes the pursuit of the dread Calydonian boar by Meleager and a "chosen band of youths" (*lecta manus iuvenum*).[24]

Such cooperative male bonding activities, needless to say, can better be undertaken by a young man if he is introduced to and trained for them by an experienced elder male role-model, who enlightens him in the techniques and values required by the activity in question, and encourages him to function in the way that other adult males do when performing this activity. The ob-

---

[24] For youthful male pursuits among the Phaeacians, see Homer, *Odyssey* 8.26-55 and 100ff.; for the "agonistic" orientation of male activity in classical Athenian society, see A. W. Gouldner, *The Hellenic World: A Sociological Analysis*, part I of *Enter Plato: Classical Greece and the Origins of Social Theory* (New York, 1969 [originally published 1965]) 45-60. For Odysseus' initiation into manhood through the boar hunt sponsored by his maternal uncles, see J. Bremmer, "Heroes, Rituals and the Trojan War," *Studi Storico-Religiosi* 2 (1978) 15ff., and R. Lonis, *Guerre et religion en Grèce a l'époque classique* (Paris, 1979) 202. For Meleager and his fellow hunters, see Ovid, *Metamorphoses* 8.300ff. In line 304, in fact, Ovid lists the *duo Thestiadae*, Meleager's maternal uncles, as among this band of youths and hence distinguishes them from Meleager's father Oeneus—who does not take part in hunting the boar—as well as classing them among Meleager's contemporaries; for proximity in age to sisters' children as contributing to maternal uncles' involvement in their preparation for adult activity, see the discussion below.

vious male to serve in this, initiating and educating, capacity would be a young man's father. But a biological father might be deceased or absent or lacking in the physical strength needed if the activity were strenuous. A father's personal and financial obligations to, and investments in, male children might well militate against his altruistic nurturance of their adult individuality in this pursuit. Furthermore, if one's mother were considerably younger than one's father—a situation that we often find in these ancient societies—her younger or even slightly elder brothers would seem a particularly attractive alternative to a father in this mentorial role. Chances were greater that they would outlive, or at least be in more robust physical condition than, her sons' father. Chances were smaller that their own sons would be as old as, and hence competitive with, their sister's. This likelihood that an *avunculus* would be closer in age to his sisters' sons than the sons' own fathers were, and the unlikelihood that an *avunculus* would be identified and compared with his sisters' sons to the extent that the sons' own fathers were (by these fathers and sons themselves as well as by others) would also prompt an *avunculus* to be regarded as an ideal socializing figure to his sister's sons, capable of guiding them into adult behavior in an affectionate yet selfless fashion impossible for these young men's fathers.[25]

The suitability of a maternal uncle for this task of social initiation, in lieu of an absent or even a present father, and in important pursuits involving collaborative

[25] That the Spartans and Germans were exceptional in supposedly wedding girls for the first time when they were in their late teens to men approximately the same age (and thus that a large age disparity between the brides and grooms usually prevailed in the ancient classical world) is implied by Plutarch, *Lycurgus* 15.3, and Tacitus, *Germania* 20.2. For marriage ages in the ancient Greek world, see also Lacey, 71-72, 106-107, 162-163, 212.

and often physically demanding exertions by males, would thus accord with the reported sponsorship of Odysseus' first hunting expedition by his mother's brothers, the ill-fated participation by Homer's and Ovid's Meleager alongside of his mother's brother(s) in a similar boar hunt, and the close bond Tacitus ascribes to German warriors and their sisters' sons; regard for maternal uncles as role models explains Pindar's portraits of athletic victors as emulated by sisters' sons as well as the fact that various Greek males (even in classical Athens, where other aspects of filiafocality are not particularly prominent) seem to have followed their mothers' brothers in their chosen, skilled, professions of poetry-writing, sculpture, and philosophy. The willingness of a maternal uncle to perform this task of social initiation, and his initial selection for it, would, however, be greater if prompted by prior regard for his sister as a valued fellow offspring of their father (and mother). We should therefore not be surprised to discern this pattern of bonding between men and their sisters' children attributed to circumstances—such as those of Odysseus—in which brothers are furnishing aid to their own father in nurturing the offspring of his valued daughter; no less surprising is its attribution to a society such as Tacitus' Germany, where the sexes reportedly share concerns and realms of activity, and to Meleager's Aetolia, which both Homer and Ovid depict as like Germany in according women respect as significant individuals.[26]

[26] For Autolycus' sons as aiding their father in initiating his daughters' son, see, for example, *Odyssey* 19.409-418 and 455-466. For Tacitus' portrayal of German men and women as sharing interests and pursuits and Homer's portrayal of Meleager's wife and her mother as—like Meleager's own mother—valued by their male kinfolk, see the discussions above. For Ovid's depiction of various women as prominent and respected individuals in Meleager's milieu, see, for example, *Metamorphoses* 8.380-395 (Meleager's appreciation of Ata-

FILIAFOCALITY AND THE ANCIENT ROMAN ELITE:
SOME CULTURAL FACTORS

As a means of accounting for the filiafocal elements in the patrilineal, agnatically-oriented society of elite Rome during the classical period, we have suggested that Rome of the early monarchic era emphasized daughters, the role of daughter, and ties of blood and marriage through daughters more than it did in republican times, and more than it did sons, the role of son, and blood relationships through males. Such an assumption would, of course, require that the agnatic orientation of classical Roman kinship and society be a later development in Rome's history. Such an assumption, needless to say, agrees with the implications of the legends previously cited about Rome in the monarchic era; it finds actual corroboration from more reliable evidence, also discussed in earlier chapters, about Rome in monarchic times. The bond between father-in-law and son-in-law is portrayed in legendary lore as a key one, especially but not exclusively among supposedly hereditary kings, during this regal period: in the stories of the Roman-Sabine merger, of Titus Tatius' succession by Numa Pompilius, of Tarquinius Priscus and his selection of a successor, and of Servius Tullius and Tarquinius Superbus; in the characterization of Lucretia's husband Collatinus as deferential first to the grief and later to the wishes of her father. High valuation by, or succession to the powers

---

lanta's skill, which is contrasted with the resentment of such talents in a woman by an Arcadian man), 425-436 (Meleager's insistence that Atalanta share the hunting honors, which is contrasted with his uncles' fatal opposition to her receiving the spoils), 451-532 (Althaea's emotional conflict over whether or not to let her son live unavenged, and the destruction to her city wrought by her decision), and 533-546 (the mourning by Meleager's sisters, and the reward of metamorphosis granted them by the goddess Diana).

of, a maternal grandfather figures in the legend of the peace between Romans and Sabines brought about by the abducted Sabine daughters and their offspring, in Romulus' claims to royalty through Numitor, and Ancus Marcius' claims through Numa Pompilius. Females defined solely or memorably as daughters—Lavinia, Rhea Silvia/Ilia, the Sabine women, Tarpeia, Horatia, Tullia, and Lucretia—loom larger in these tales than women in any other kinship role. Bonds between male agnates are invariably portrayed in these legends as strained and weak: the sole *patruus*, Amulius, is depicted as a cruel and heartless figure; royal brothers such as Amulius and Numitor, Romulus and Remus, and Tarquinius Superbus and his *frater* display destructive enmity to one another; no Roman monarch—even those with male issue—is succeeded by his son.[27]

More importantly, we have seen that archaeological and cultic investigations establish the Vestal Virgins as having begun in Rome's monarchic times, most probably as daughters of Rome's priest-king; they hence give us further cause to believe that the father-daughter bond and the daughter role received special religious and cultural elaboration in this early era. Similar conclusions can be reached by analyzing survivals from the cult of Mater Matuta, in which ties to and ties as fathers' daughters were annually reaffirmed. There seem to survive from Rome's regal past, however, no cultic practices which place such emphasis on the role of father's son or on male agnate bonds. Arguments from silence are of course far from incontrovertible; nevertheless, these

[27] For these stories of succession by sons-in-law and daughters' sons as well as these tales of daughters, see chapter three above; for these strains in the bonds between male agnates of legend, see chapter four; see these same chapters for the cultic and linguistic data cited in the following paragraph.

male agnate ties may be regarded as lacking in strength
at this period from the testimony of various linguistic
data: the primal association of the term *avus* with a maternal rather than a paternal uncle; the affective resonance
of the words *cognatus* and *cognatio* lacking in *agnatus* and
agnatio; the limitation of the term *consobrinus/a* to offspring of siblings other than two brothers.

Our cross-cultural glimpse of filiafocal kinship patterns in other ancient Indo-European monarchic societies adds to the credibility of this hypothesis about the
origins of and priority given filiafocal attitudes and practices in earliest monarchic Rome. More compelling evidence still for this theory may be adduced from historical
developments in Rome of the classical era itself, from a
"cross-temporal" consideration of emphases in kinship
practice and sentiment after Rome ceased to function as
a republic and became a hereditary monarchy. Admittedly, we may ascribe these emphases on daughters, the
daughter role, and daughter-centered bonds in part to
the personal plight and example of one individual Roman instrumental in precipitating the later conversion
from republic to imperial principate, Julius Caesar. As
we have seen, his family claimed descent, through a
Trojan prince, from the goddess-daughter of Rome's
major male divinity; Julius Caesar took special pride in
his father's maternal ancestry, a line originating with a
king indebted for his throne to his own maternal grandfather. We have observed that Caesar evinced this pride
when publicly displaying his devotion to his father's
sister Julia, that he rated notice by Tacitus for his upbringing by his mother Aurelia and, most notably, that
he invested himself emotionally and politically in his
daughter (to the extent that he was later portrayed in
Latin literature as the archetypal *socer* who broke faith
with his *gener*). We might also note that Caesar's close

bonds with his sisters resulted in political prominence for the son of one, Quintus Pedius, as well as pre-eminence for the son of another's daughter. One scholar has even called attention to the fact "Julius Caesar's immediate family was composed almost exclusively of women—he had virtually no close male family ties during his lifetime."[28]

Yet Caesar's adopted son and heir Augustus, who established a new form of monarchic government and forever laid the Roman republic to rest, continued to emphasize the same bonds of kinship accorded special importance by his *magnus avunculus* Caesar: those between *pater* and *filia, frater* and *soror, socer* and *gener, avunculus* and *amita* and their nephews and nieces, *maternus avus* and *nepotes*. Personal circumstances also played a large part in Augustus' emphasis on these ties of kinship. Deprived of a father at an early age and lacking brothers, Augustus is cited for enjoying nurturance from his mother Atia much like that given Caesar by Aurelia. His public début, speaking in honor of his mother's mother (and Caesar's sister) seems modeled on Caesar's funeral oration in praise of his *amita*; his devotion to his

---

[28] For Julius Caesar, his ancestry and female kin, see chapters two and three above, especially n. 19 of the former and n. 43 of the latter. Of special interest may be Plutarch's report, at *Caesar* 14.4-5, that the younger Cato criticized Caesar's marital alliance—through Julia— with Pompey, since it "degraded the government" and permitted advancement in military and provincial posts through women; political advancement through women is, of course, a hallmark of monarchic government and alliances of royal fathers and daughters' husbands therein. For Quintus Pedius, see Suetonius, *Divus Julius* 83.2, Appian, *Bella Civilia* 3. 22, 23, 94, 96, as well as the discussion of E. S. Gruen, *The Last Generation of the Roman Republic* (Berkeley, Los Angeles and London, 1974) 205-206. For Caesar's bonds with Augustus see Suetonius, *Divus Julius* 83 and *Divus Augustus* 8, as well as the discussion below. For Caesar's almost exclusively female family ties, see M. Deutsch, "The Women of Caesar's Family," *CJ* 13 (1918) 502.

sister and her children calls to mind Caesar's conduct as well. He, too, produced a politically exploited *unica filia*, though his daughter Julia proved far different in character from her similarly named kinswoman listed by Valerius Maximus among those displaying memorable examples of conjugal love. Nonetheless, Augustus contrasts with his adoptive father personally in endeavoring, concertedly and throughout his lifetime, to form and strengthen *male* family ties, and not merely relying on female relations for support in his public endeavors. One need only look at his own *Res Gestae* for corroboration of this statement; this account of his career does not even mention his female kin, but constantly refers to all manner of male relatives—adopted father, the nephew, stepson, and third son-in-law appointed as his heirs, the grandsons he made his sons and supposed successors. The marriages which Augustus engineered and contracted also illustrate his eagerness to make his political associations with males into male family ties and *vice-versa*: those of his colleague Mark Antony to his own sister; of his elder stepson Tiberius to the daughter of his friend (and son-in-law) Agrippa; of his sister's daughter to his younger stepson Drusus; his own marriages to Antony's stepdaughter and the *amita* of Sextus Pompey's wife.[29]

[29] For Augustus and his female blood kin, see, for example, chapter two above, n. 19, and Suetonius, *Divus Augustus* 34.2, 63-64, Plutarch, *Antony* 31.1, 53.5, and Tacitus, *Dialogus* 28. On Augustus' failure to mention any of his female relations in the *Res Gestae*, see T. Mommsen, *Res Gestae Divi Augusti*[2] (Berlin, 1883) V; for Augustus' references to all manner of male "kin," see *Res Gestae Divi Augusti* 2, 8, 10.2, 14, 20.3, 21, 22.3, 27, 30.2. On Augustus' own, and Octavia's marriages, see Suetonius, *Divus Augustus* 62-63; on his marriage of Tiberius to Vipsania Agrippina, see Nepos, *Atticus* 19.4; on his marriage of Drusus to Antonia Minor, see Suetonius, *Divus Claudius* 1, and chapter five above, n. 38, as well as the discussion below.

Consequently, it appears all the more significant that under Augustus' monarchic rule filiafocal practices and sentiments became increasingly important. Augustus' own conduct merits attention first. His initial choice as heir was Marcellus, to whom he was *avunculus*; Antonia Minor and Marcella Major, to whom he was *avunculus* as well, received special distinctions from him, including privileged treatment of their sons. Augustus so prized his daughter as to turn a blind eye to her indiscretions for over a decade, until they threatened him politically, and then manifested greater sorrow over her misbehavior than over his adopted sons' deaths. He cherished these youths, her two elder sons, as his own offspring, and doted on Julia's daughters (until Julia's namesake turned into a moral and political liability); he even, as we have seen, is said to have cared deeply for his stepdaughter. Augustus clearly felt special reverence for the bond between *socer* and *gener*; that he desired to avoid violating it as his adoptive father had done is reflected in his choice of men already close to him, by blood, marriage or friendship, as his sons-in-law.[30]

---

[30] For Augustus and Marcellus, see Vergil, *Aeneid* 6.86off.; *Res Gestae Divi Augusti* 21; Tacitus, *Annales* 1.3.1, Cassius Dio 50.30.5; Suetonius, *Divus Augustus* 29.4, 63.1, as well as chapter three above, n. 48. For Augustus' insistence that his stepson Tiberius adopt Antonia Minor's son Germanicus, and his naming Germanicus as an heir in the second degree to his own estate, see Tacitus, *Annales* 3.5, Suetonius, *Tiberius* 15, *Divus Augustus* 101.2, and *Divus Claudius* 1.5. Even though Antonia Minor was still of childbearing age when widowed by Drusus, she did not wed again, presumably because Augustus had exempted her from his legislation requiring her to do so: on this legislation, see Suetonius, *Divus Augustus* 34.1. For Augustus' treatment of the elder Marcella's son after the suicide of his father Iullus Antonius, see Tacitus, *Annales* 4.44.3; Iullus took his life when disgraced by charges of adultery with Augustus' daughter Julia (as Velleius Paterculus reports at 2.100.4). For Augustus' initial disregard of, and later reaction to, Julia's affairs, see Macrobius, *Saturnalia* 2.5; Suetonius, *Divus Augustus* 65; Pliny, *Natural*

During Augustus' principate, moreover, filiafocal practices and sentiments received greater cultural elaboration in Roman law, political life, linguistic convention, and literature. The moral legislation associated with his principate and name, as observed earlier, assigned a father ultimate authority over the punishment of an adulterous daughter. These laws also prohibited the daughter of a senator—or of a senator's male agnate descendants—from becoming affianced or wed to a freedman, actor, or son of an actor; they thus sought to prevent the daughters of Rome's senatorial houses just as they did the sons of Rome's senatorial houses from marrying into Rome's lowest classes. In this period, the descendants of a republican consul's female children as well as those of his male children apparently acquired the right to claim *nobilitas* for themselves. In this period, too, the offspring of a man's daughters as well as those of his sons began to be called by his *gentilicium*.[31] Fur-

---

History 21.9; Seneca, *De Beneficiis* 6.32; Cassius Dio 55.10-12; and Balsdon, 82-87. For the republican political connections of the men involved in her downfall, including Mark Antony's son Iullus, see Pliny, *Natural History* 7.149, and Seneca, *De Brevitate Vitae* 4.6; see also A. E. Ferrill, "Augustus and His Daughter: A Modern Myth," *Studies in Latin Literature and Roman History* II. *Collection Latomus* 168 (1980) 332-346, who argues against the popular "conspiracy" theory. On Augustus' close ties to Gaius and Lucius Caesar, see chapter three above, n. 51, as well as Suetonius, *Divus Augustus* 64; on Augustus and the younger Julia, see Suetonius, *Divus Augustus* 65.1, Tacitus, *Annales* 4.71.4 as well as Balsdon, 88, and Syme, *History in Ovid* (Oxford, 1978) 206ff. For Cornelia, see Propertius 4.11 and chapter two above; for Augustus and his *generi* after Marcellus, see chapter three above, n. 48.

[31] For Augustus' moral legislation and its provisions regarding daughters, see *Acta Divi Augusti*, Part I (Rome, 1942) 166-198, as well as chapter three above, n. 79. For the reckoning, in the imperial era, of *nobilitas* by maternal as well as paternal ancestors, see M. Gelzer, *The Roman Nobility*, transl. R. Seager (Oxford, 1969) 143ff. Of interest, too, is Vergil's statement (cited in n. 4 above) about Drances— to whom nobility of maternal ancestors (*materna . . . nobilitas*) gave

thermore, it was under Augustus that Livy, Dionysius
of Halicarnassus and Ovid composed and published their
respective works which attribute so much importance
to daughters and ties of blood and marriage through
daughters during Rome's formative, monarchic and early
republican, years. The significance ascribed by Vergil
in the *Aeneid* to daughters and such bonds of kinship
not only among Rome's Trojan ancestors and Latin forbears but even among her Carthaginian and Rutulian
foes deserves notice again at this juncture—for this work,
this Homeric-style epic, was inspired by Augustus' principate itself.[32]

Under the monarchies of Augustus' Julio-Claudian
and Flavian successors, expressions of regard for daughters and stress on daughter-centered ties continued to be

a proud lineage—at *Aeneid* 11.340-341: it indicates that this reckoning
had commenced early in Augustus' reign, before Vergil died in 19
B.C. For the use, in this period, of the maternal rather than the
paternal grandfather's *gentilicium* and *cognomen* (or form of the maternal grandfather's *gentilicium* as *cognomen*, see chapter three above,
chapter four above, n. 9, and B. Doer, *Die Römische Namengebung*
(Stuttgart, 1937) 95-118. Doer sees the beginning of this practice in
the elder Cato's differentiation between his sons by Licinia and Sa-
lonia through the fourth names of Licinianus and Salonianus, respectively (so Aulus Gellius 13.20.6ff.), and views it as an "Italian"
innovation.

[32] For Vergil's emphasis on filiafocal kinship patterns and the role
of daughter in the *Aeneid*, see notes 3 and 4 above. Of further significance may be Vergil's depiction, at *Aeneid* 5.568-569, of Iulus'/
Ascanius' beloved Trojan friend Atys as ancestor of the Latin Atii.
These are, of course, Augustus' maternal male kin: as Suetonius notes
at *Divus Augustus* 4, Augustus' mother Atia was daughter of Marcus
Atius Balbus, himself a praetor and land commissioner, and of prominent senatorial background; for Cicero's defense of this man's lineage (impugned by Antony), see chapter five above, n. 40. Vergil's
allusion to the Atii, like his many allusions to the Julii—family of
Augustus' mother's mother—would thus reflect his, and Augustus',
emphases upon these ties to illustrious houses through these houses'
daughters.

conspicuous. At 25.4 of his life of *Caligula*, Suetonius reports that this emperor carried his baby daughter around to the temples of all the goddesses before entrusting her to Minerva for nurture and education; in so doing Caligula recalls Vergil's portrayal of King Metabus and his dedication of his infant daughter Camilla to Diana at *Aeneid* 11.557ff. Suetonius also claims, at *Divus Vespasianus* 14, that the emperor Vespasian arranged a splendid marriage for the daughter of his ex-foe and predecessor Vitellius, even providing her with a dowry and other material goods. Caligula's successor Claudius was able to break with Roman law and precedent in making the younger Agrippina his wife—with the approval of the Roman senate and people—because, although he was Agrippina's *patruus*, she was the daughter of the beloved Germanicus. Claudius, as has been noted, wed his own daughter Octavia to his new wife's son Nero, revealing that he shared the feelings of his *magnus avunculus* Augustus about the bond between *socer* and *gener*, and wished to link his apparent heir more intimately to him through marriage. Mature daughters of emperors may not have been numerous after the principate of Augustus, but cherished and/or devoted female offspring of aristocratic households were. Many are remembered for the protection they received from, and their loyalty to, their own fathers: we have alluded frequently to Seneca's consoled Marcia and Tacitus' Servilia and Antistia Pollitta, these latter two characterized as latter-day versions of the fabled self-sacrificing daughters of Rome's earliest years. Another aristocratic daughter prominently protected by a powerful father during these years was Aemilia Lepida, *filia* of Marcus Aemilius Lepidus, himself son of Propertius' Cornelia and friend to the emperor Tiberius: as long as her father lived, she was not prosecuted for her adultery and vile treatment of her royal husband, the son of Germanicus and the elder Agrippina.[33]

The bond between a brother and his father's daughter and the tie between men and their sisters' children are also accorded cultural emphasis, and emphasis of a new sort, in these monarchic times. We might note again the honors—including the status of Vestal Virgins and mention in official edicts and oaths—lavished by Caligula upon his sisters and the interpretation of his behavior in this regard as imitating the conduct of Hellenistic kings. We should note as well that in this period the term *avunculus* is applied by various authors to men occupying roles other than that of maternal uncle. Germanicus, whose mother Antonia Minor had Augustus as *avunculus*, is nevertheless said by Tacitus at *Annales* 2.43.5 and 53.2 to have been himself distinguished owing to

[33] For the marriage of Claudius and the younger Agrippina, see chapter four above, n. 10; both Tacitus, at *Annales* 12.1.2 (with *Agrippinam Germanico genitam*) and 5.1 (with *fratris filiae*) and Suetonius, *Divus Claudius* 26.3 (introducing Agrippina as *Germanici fratris sui filia*) stress her role as daughter to Germanicus in accounting for their union. As M. Arthur has called to my attention, the relationship between Claudius and Agrippina is identical to that of King Alcinous and Queen Arete in the *Odyssey*; it perhaps further marks Claudius' principate as "conventionally" monarchic, strengthening the ruler's hold on the throne through an alliance with the daughter of a previous ruler or "royally significant" individual (as Germanicus had been in his role as Augustus' and Tiberius' appointed successor). For Claudius' affectionate feeling toward his own daughter Octavia, see Tacitus, *Annales* 12.4.3 (*caritate filiae*). To be sure, Claudius himself is held responsible for the bereavement of his elder daughter Claudia Antonia (on whom see chapter one above, n. 15) since he had her husband Gnaeus Pompey stabbed to death while in bed with a boy favorite. Nevertheless, at *Divus Claudius* 29.1-2, Suetonius attributes the original motives for this execution—like that of Germanicus' daughter Julia—to Claudius' freedmen and wives; for this Julia's execution, see chapter four above, n. 38. For Marcia, Servilia, and Antistia Pollitta, see chapter three above; for this Aemilia Lepida, see Tacitus, *Annales* 6.40.3.

his "*avunculus* Augustus." Seneca evidently uses the term *avunculus* for the esteemed husband of his *matertera* at *Ad Helviam Matrem de Consolatione* 19.4. As we have observed, Velleius Paterculus speaks of Julius Caesar as Octavian's *avunculus* at 2.60.2—though technically Caesar stood in the relation of maternal great-uncle to Octavian just as Octavian later would to Germanicus.[34] One may conjecture that the word *avunculus* was at this time employed for men who did not strictly qualify as such because the role it described was assumed to be a protective and supportive one, and the word itself thus resounded with positive connotations.

It would not, therefore, be altogether implausible for the high Roman valuation of individual daughters, the Roman cultural elaboration of the daughter role, and the Romans' emphasis on ties of blood and marriage through daughters to have begun, and prevailed, in Rome's earliest, monarchic, era. But we must now explain the equally important fact that daughters, the role of daughter, and bonds created to and through daughters possessed considerable cultural significance under a long-lived republican form of government in which women played no formal part, and which the early Roman empire tried to resemble as closely as possible. We should,

[34] For Caligula's treatment of his sisters, see chapter four above, n. 48; for its Hellenistic monarchic antecedents, see the article on "Gaius" by Balsdon in the *Oxford Classical Dictionary*[2] (1970) 452; for such conduct among the Hellenistic monarchs of Egypt, see Pomeroy, *GWWS*, 123-125. For Tacitus' use of the term *avunculus* in its correct sense of "mother's brother," see, e.g. *Annales* 2.41.3 (where he speaks of Germanicus as having Marcellus as his *avunculus*); for Velleius', see 2.67.3, where he speaks of Antony as proscribing his *avunculus* L. Caesar: that both apply the term to non-*avunculi* does not, therefore, suggest confusion as to its meaning but rather desire to widen its range of reference. On this wider meaning of *avunculus*, see also A. C. Bush, *Studies in Roman Social Structure* (Washington, D.C., 1982) 109 n. 20.

therefore, attempt to account for the strong filiafocal
elements in Roman republican culture despite the patrilineal, male agnatic, orientation of the political system
which operated and the laws which were strictly adhered
to for centuries after this republican form of government
came into being.

Two previously mentioned elite Roman cultural phenomena of the classical era deserve notice as possible
explanations at this point in our discussion, as does the
Romans' much-noted reverence for ancestral custom and
strikingly tradition-bound nature. For the Roman commitment to perpetuating the ways of earlier generations
may in fact explain both of these phenomena: namely,
the social, economic, and political importance of the elite
Roman family—in which women occupied a structurally central position; the consequent blurring of a distinction between domestic and public spheres of elite
Roman life. After all, both of these phenomena also
characterize the various Indo-European hereditary monarchies which we have surveyed as well as the monarchic
Roman imperial principate. They also occur in the monarchic societies of various Hellenistic kingdoms in close
contact with Rome of classical times; these kingdoms
have been excluded from the discussion of kindred ancient cultures in the first section of this chapter (because,
inter alia, these kingdoms may not warrant being ascribed membership in the Indo-European cultural complex, and because the classical Roman elite generally
made it a point to define themselves as utterly different
from and superior to such alien societies, a fact which
creates problems in using classical Roman authors as
sources for these societies) but furnish relevant points
of cross-cultural comparison nonetheless. Both of these
phenomena, consequently, may represent survivals from
Rome's monarchic past at the same time that they il-

luminate the presence of filiafocal elements in the agnatically emphatic society of republican Rome. That both
the early Roman monarchy and later republic seem to
have flourished in an aristocratic society warrants note
in this context no less, since this particular sociopolitical
development would represent yet another enduring survival, and would itself cohere with these two phenomena.[35]

What is more, our analysis of the elements common
to other fictive and factual ancient Indo-European societies which exhibit filiafocal features has suggested a
further explanation for the importance there attributed
to daughters and especially to ties of kinship through
daughters among males: the promotion by these societies of masculine activities demanding cooperative effort and associated with adult male competency and elite
status. Promotion of such pursuits is said to occur in

[35] For the blurring of domestic and public spheres and the structural centrality of women in the families of the Hellenistic kingdoms,
see Pomeroy, *GWWS*, 121-130. For the Romans' efforts to differentiate themselves and their "superior" values from those of the
Hellenistic monarchies, see, for example, Livy, 40.8.15ff., on the
strife between the Macedonian prince (and later king) Perseus and
his brother: Livy characterizes their father Philip as citing several
Roman paradigms of mutual fraternal devotion—the Quinctii, Publius and Lucius Scipio and their *pater* and *patruus*; as his portrayal
of Rome's earliest brothers in his first book indicates, Livy seems to
regard ill will between brothers as behavior marking more primitive
and more monarchic societies than that of republican Rome. That
Rome's kings ruled an aristocratic society, and hence that there seems
to be an unbroken development from the gradual emergence of an
aristocracy in the regal period to its assertion of hegemony in republican times is a point I owe to K. Raaflaub. He has also suggested
to me that women in aristocratic societies tend to occupy structurally
central roles within leading families and that such societies generally
blur the distinction between public and domestic: this suggestion is
borne out by the findings of L. Bonfante, "Etruscan Couples," *Wom-
en's Studies* 8 (1981) 157-187, as well as by the situation obtaining in
various aristocratic societies portrayed in the Homeric poems.

cultures such as Tacitus' Germany and Homer's Phaeacia, Aetolia, and Ithaca, which emphasize the bonds between male agnates as well as those formed through
daughters; promotion of such pursuits in fact appears to
encourage close ties between male participants and the
sons of their fathers' daughters regardless of what particular kinship bonds were customarily emphasized by
the society in question. The strength of ties through
daughters among the upper-class males of the Roman
republic, amid the legal and general cultural stress placed
on male agnate bonds, may then derive in part from the
promotion and valuation of male bonding in both political and military endeavors, endeavors which doubtless intensified and expanded after Rome's early monarchy fell and a republican government extremely keen
on military expansion took its place. After all, a representative political system in which different men were
supposedly elected to office each year, and which required a large number of military officers to carry out
expansionistic and defensive campaigns, afforded more
men a vital part in the governing and administrative
processes than they would have had under a system such
as that said to exist in early monarchic Rome. In a system
of that sort, one man reportedly ruled for life, aided by
male appointees who served him officially for as long
as he wished (and perhaps by unofficial advisers, who
might be kinswomen as well as men). Under Rome's
early kings, moreover, the waging of war does not seem
to have been conducted on the large scale of republican
Roman military operations.[36] So, too, after a change

[36] On the apparent increase in positions of political leadership (for
both patrician and plebeian males) in fifth-century-B.C. Rome, see
R.E.A. Palmer, *The Archaic Community of the Romans* (Cambridge,
1970) 220ff.; for Rome's apparent expansion of military operations
in this period, see, for example, Ogilvie, 234, 283-289, 302, 307-
309, 314-321, 353-366, 390-411, 521-525, 567-574, 584-589, 597-606,
620-632.

from monarchy to representative republic, accidents of birth and alliances through marriage would no longer serve as the sole determinants in securing, or at least would not guarantee, positions of leadership. More opportunities would exist not only for participating but also for excelling in political activity.

Needless to say, under the Roman republic, a man's public service was thought to redound to the credit of his family, particularly those with whom he shared a name. As we have observed, previous political and military accomplishments by male agnate kin conferred singular distinction and status on an individual in republican times; this view that similarly named male agnates contributed, by their recognized achievements, to a kinsman's repute and likelihood for similar success is inseparable from the greater formal emphasis assigned by elite Roman republican society to male agnate ties than to bonds of blood and marriage through daughters. One would thus logically presume that under this system male agnates, particularly fathers, would also introduce youthful male kin to, and train them for achievement in, public speaking and jurisprudence as well as actual statecraft and warfare; such political and military activities were, by all accounts, the endeavors which elite Roman males were expected to make the focus of their adult existence and through which they were expected both to reflect in and add to the luster of their similarly named male kin.[37]

37 For the view that public service redounded to the credit of one's (agnate) family, see such mid-republican epitaphs as CIL I²10 (that of Scipio Aemilianus' adoptive father) and CIL I²15 (that of M. Cornelius Scipio Hispanus); these are discussed by A. Ernout, *Recueil de textes latins archaïques²* (Paris, 1973) 18-21. The view that public accomplishments by male (and often female) agnate kin contributed to an individual's high repute and likelihood for similar success is implied by various sources of the republican era. One might in particular note Cicero's enumeration of Clodia's similarly named

Our survey of comparable ancient societies in the first
section of this chapter has, however, warned us against
automatically making such a presumption, logical though
it is. Various aspects of elite male existence in republican
Rome also merit note in this context. First of all, the
activities of warfare and provincial administration demanded that participants undergo long separations from
their kinfolk at Rome as well as numerous personal haz-
ards. Second, Romans of the upper classes tended to
favor, or at least produce, small families: Lucius Aemilius Paullus may have fathered seven children, but he
gave up two of his four sons for adoption; Metellus
Macedonicus is hailed as felicitous for being survived
by four adult sons. A relatively high mortality rate and
low life expectancy characterize all pre-industrial societies, even in times of peace. Such factors must have
combined to create a strong likelihood that a well-born
Roman male youth might have no male agnate kinsman
on hand or able to function in a mentorial capacity. In

---

illustrious ancestors as a means of browbeating and shaming her at
Pro Caelio 33ff. (no mention, however, is made by Cicero of her
maternal ancestors). For this view see also chapter four above and
the discussion of D. C. Earl, *The Moral and Political Tradition of
Rome* (Ithaca, N.Y., 1970) 12ff.

That public speaking and jurisprudence as well as statecraft and
warfare served as the customary focus of upper-class Roman male
education during the republic, and that the family itself provided
such training, are indicated by various sources. See, for example,
Polybius 6.53 (on the oratory and symbolic display of the upper-
class Roman funeral, about which Polybius says, at 9-10 "that for
a young man desirous of high repute and excellence there is no sight
more beautiful and ennobling") and 31.29 (on how Scipio Aemilianus' unorthodox pursuit of "Macedonian" hunting functioned as a
superior substitute for speaking in the law courts and won him a
reputation for courage without vexing others); see, too, Cicero, *De
Oratore* 2.55.226 (criticizing Brutus for his neglect of the law, military
camp, eloquence and the assembly—and for failing his family by so
doing). On this point, see also chapter four, above, and the discussion
of Earl, *Moral and Political Tradition*, 26ff.

such instances, the brothers of his mother might well be enlisted instead. As close contemporaries of a young man's mother, herself generally several years his father's junior, these might well, in fact, be more youthful, energetic, and interested in performing mentorial duties than a male agnate even if one were available. In the event that one's mother had no male kinsman for this task either, a father-in-law might have filled in: one recalls young Aelius Tubero's inclusion by Lucius Aemilius Paullus in the fighting against Perseus, after which Paullus so handsomely rewarded his son-in-law; one remembers, too, the political guidance proffered the young and fatherless Tiberius Gracchus by his *socer* Appius Claudius Pulcher after his split with his mother's kinsman Scipio Aemilianus.[38]

The political prominence of a similarly named Roman *pater* or *patruus* or *frater* publicly reflected upon a young man in a way that eminence of a dissimilarly named *avunculus* or *socer* did not; it is thus possible that it was easier for an *avunculus* or *socer* to furnish help in the pressured and generally competitive elite Roman political environment, since they had less face to lose if their protégés proved wanting.[39] At least among the elite re-

[38] For Paullus' decision to give up two of his four sons, see Polybius 31.28.1-2 and chapter three above, n. 21; for Metellus Macedonicus and his supreme felicity, see Valerius Maximus 7.1.1 (also cited in chapter three above, n. 47). The speech delivered by Metellus Numidicus cited by Aulus Gellius 1.6, and discussed in chapter five above warrants mention in this context as well; entitled *De Prole Augenda*, "On Increasing the Number of Offspring," it was presented to raise the low birthrate of the senatorial class. For Paullus and Tubero, and Appius Claudius Pulcher and Tiberius Gracchus, see also chapter three above, n. 47. Like Paullus, Claudius Pulcher had a son of his own; thus neither of these men needed these younger males as substitutes for male offspring, "surrogate fathers" though they may have been.

[39] That the similar *nomina* of agnate kin were perceived as rendering

publican Roman *avunculi* who helped socialize sisters' sons, we have encountered some—such as the legendary Vitellii and the historical Atticus and Brutus—who helped to socialize nephews with living fathers and male agnates as well as others—such as the younger Cato—who clearly substituted for deceased male agnate kin of their sisters' sons. The fact that republican fathers-in-law did at times function in this same socializing capacity further indicates that the *socer-gener* bond, although perhaps originally prized by the Romans because it facilitated monarchic succession by biological kindred, remained an important educational as well as political relationship even if republican *soceri* and *generi* may have harbored different expectations of one another than those holding the reins of state in monarchic societies.

Nevertheless, we should not forget that the elite Roman emphases on both the *avunculus-sororis filius* and the *socer-gener* bond seem to have coexisted with an initial recognition of daughters and fathers' daughters as significant individuals, biological links to allies, protectors, and protégés in the all-important aristocratic republican realms of politics and warfare, if not invariably as individuals whose own interests and wishes deserved consideration. Nor should one forget that fathers' biologically based recognition of daughters as significant transmitters of their blood line seems to underlie the

---

those of earlier generations "an act to be followed" by their successors seems clear from such Ciceronian passages (cited in n. 37 above) as *Pro Caelio* 33-34 and *De Oratore* 2.55.225-226. It may also be inferred from, e.g., Suetonius' reference—when describing various of Tiberius' Claudian ancestors at *Tiberius* 1-2—to these male and female forbears' conduct as *exempla*. Such a perception, of course, need not limit the exemplary elder agnates to the deceased; the Roman funerary practice—cited by Polybius at 6.53—of wearing ancestors' death masks and hence "revivifying" them points to a blurring of the distinction between the living and the dead.

emphasis on the bonds between *socer-gener* and *maternus avus-nepos* under a monarchic system. And this brings us to the question of why both elite monarchic and republican Romans valued female children themselves not only as links to and biological perpetuators of male kin but also as precious offspring emotionally.

These cross-cultural comparisons strikingly distinguish the classical, and in all probability the pre-classical, Roman elite from other ancient peoples we have cited for valuing daughters, for culturally emphasizing the role of daughter, and for stressing ties of kinship through daughters in that these other peoples do not seem to invest the father-daughter bond with anywhere near as intense an affect as do the Romans. At *Iliad* 1.106-120 Homer's Chryses may ask Agamemnon and the Achaeans to return his daughter, but it is Agamemnon and not Chryses who details his affection for the girl. Homer's Agamemnon may later—at *Iliad* 9.142-147—claim to honor his son Orestes and promise to honor Achilles equally as a son-in-law, but he says nothing about honoring or valuing any of the three daughters he offers Achilles in marriage. Although at *Odyssey* 6.67-71 Alcinous tells his daughter Nausicaa to her face that he cannot deny her anything she asks, he later, at 7.299-307, criticizes her behind her back to Odysseus and forces Odysseus to defend her conduct with him. It may in fact be significant that Anchises, whom Homer specifically cites for specially cherishing his eldest daughter Hippodamia, is also the father of Aeneas, and hence regarded by the classical Roman elite as their own mythic ancestor. Hesiod may speak of the honor awarded to Hecate by Zeus, gods and men, but he makes no mention of love for Hecate on the part of her father Perses. While Tacitus' *Annales* may conclude with two moving portrayals of fathers' devotion to and from their daughters, his *Germania* does not point out any examples of comparable caring for daughters by German men who are said to esteem their own and their sisters' sons. We must, in consequence, now try to account for the fond Roman fatherly feelings about female children evinced in so many of our sources, feelings which seem to account for fond Roman brotherly and sisterly feeling about female siblings, and adoration as well as respect for Roman mothers by their offspring.

It has been argued that in a primitive stage of Roman cultural development the complexities of marriage patterns were such that a man's daughters and other blood kin would occupy more than one kinship role. This state of affairs would perhaps tend to increase a daughter's emotional value to her father, and those of other kinswomen to blood kinsmen. These arguments were, however, advanced primarily to account for peculiarities of Latin kinship terminology: in particular the fact that the word *avunculus*, mother's brother, is unmistakably a diminutive of *avus*, grandfather, and the consequent implication that mothers' brothers were somehow regarded as lesser versions of grandfathers. These arguments were, moreover, advanced by two British classicists, H. J. Rose and G. D. Thomson, who evolved elaborate and generalizing anthropological theories on earliest Roman kinship. Rose postulated that the Romans must have originally grouped themselves in agnatic, exogamous blood clans; Thomson, a social evolutionist and Marxist as well as a matriarchalist, hypothesized a universal stage of cross-cousin marriage.[40] Yet neither Rose nor Thomson had any evidence for the existence of the

---

[40] H. J. Rose, *Primitive Culture in Italy* (London, 1926) 159-169; G. D. Thomson, *Studies in Ancient Greek Society: The Prehistoric Aegean* (New York, 1949) 78-99. See also chapter three above, n. 68.

social organizations they posited. In addition, one should note the recent study by O. Szemerényi, which scrutinizes Indian, Iranian, Greek, and Latin kinship terminology in its attempts to determine the kinship orientation of Indo-European society, and which makes extensive use of current anthropological theories and findings; it has persuasively demonstrated the flaws in these and other, ultimately oversimplifying, structural models.[41]

Just as importantly, Szemerényi stresses the need to adopt the "principle of multiple causation" rather than single cause to explain the organization of kinship. In reasserting the "patriarchal nature" of all Indo-European society, he also issues the caveat that "this term comprises a bundle of highly variable components": although "patriarchal" means that a society is basically "patrilineal, patrilocal and to a considerable extent patripotestal," other "individual" factors would seem to influence other matters.[42] Szemerényi's insistence on the significance of both multiple and individual factors in kinship organization has particular relevance to our investigation of the Roman elite family: the powerful ties of sentiment therein to daughters, and by extension to all blood kinswomen valued as fathers' daughters, appears to be a no less crucial determinant in the organization

[41] Szemerényi, 158-206, dismisses the theories of Thomson and Isačenko, refutes the theories of Benveniste and Lounsbury, and demonstrates the limitations in the theory of Lévi-Strauss.

[42] Szemerényi, 195, 206. See also Sacks, *Sisters and Wives*, 122, who makes the point that economic factors (in this case the existence of a corporate owning group) allow women's roles as "sisters" and "wives" to receive different emphases "even in patrilineal, patrilocal corporations, often conceived of as necessarily patriarchal"; though evidence does not permit us to consider in any detail the economic bases for elite Roman notions of valued kinship ties, Roman women's claim to their family's property gives Sacks' point special pertinence.

of Roman patriarchal kinship than other cultural factors and is apparently interconnected with these factors as well. Furthermore, since we have already examined cultural features shared by elite Rome with other similar societies displaying filiafocal kinship patterns, and since attempts at generalizing anthropological classifications of Roman society do not appear fruitful in illuminating the intensity of affect invested by the Romans of the upper classes in the father-daughter bond (or, for that matter, in embracing all the complexities of Roman kinship), it seems appropriate to try and explain elite Roman feelings about fathers and daughters through a different avenue of approach. That is, by considering some of the other ways in which the classical Roman elite individuated itself in practice and assumption from the other cultures we have surveyed, and by assessing how the Romans defined themselves as a distinctive culture.

Let us begin with our observation that the elite Roman valuation of daughters by fathers and the elite Roman cultural emphasis on the daughter role appear closely linked with the special valuation of daughters' offspring, sisters and sisters' children, and mothers, maternal grandfathers, and *avunculi*. This situation immediately suggests one possible explanation for the affective intensity of Roman filiafocality and points up one distinctive aspect of elite Roman society, namely that such individuals could more safely be presumed blood kin, and parents of blood kin, than could male agnates; after all, kinship studies have often associated cultural emphasis on bonds with females, and kindred related through females, with the phenomenon of uncertain paternity. The classical Romans themselves even made literary capital of the fact that biological paternity is far harder to prove than maternity in the famed, ideological, legend of Verginia: both Livy's and Dionysius of Halicarnassus'

accounts present Verginius' adversaries as charging that
he was not his daughter's father; the latter even has him
vindicated by proof of his late wife's pregnancy and
lactation. For this reason, we might hypothesize that,
once an elite Roman male had acknowledged paternity
of a daughter, he might feel more secure about his consanguinity with her children than he might about that
with those of a similarly acknowledged son. In like fashion, a man whose father had accepted both him and his
sister as offspring might automatically assume consanguinity with her children, whereas such an assumption
could not be made as confidently about a brother's—or
his own—offspring. So, too, the "double leaps" of biological faith required to reckon one's self descended
from one's father's father, or kindred with one's father's
brother, were unnecessary in relating one's self to one's
mother's father or one's mother's brother.[43]

The extent to which upper-class Roman men of the
classical period (and earlier) experienced uncertainties or
anxieties over their actual siring or ability to sire offspring cannot be determined. That paternity was an individual and cultural concern, however, is implied by
various evidence. This testimony, moreover, allows certain inferences about close ties between men linked
through blood kinswomen, and hence about close ties
between men and these blood kinswomen themselves:
namely, that such secure ties through and to females
were apparently associated with and regarded as anti-

---

[43] For the theoretical link between uncertain paternity and cultural
emphasis on kinship ties through females, see chapter one above, n.
26; and D. M. Schneider in D. M. Schneider and K. Gough, eds.,
Matrilineal Kinship (Berkeley, Los Angeles and London, 1961) ix, 13.
For Livy and Dionysius on the legal certification of Verginia as her
parents' child (established, in the latter's account, by proving Nu-
mitoria's maternity), see Livy 3.44.9ff. and Dionysius of Halicarnassus 11.34ff.

thetical to the insecurities men felt about their consanguinity with their offspring and male agnates.

For one thing, Roman society provided a *pater* with religious and legal mechanisms for disowning, or having disowned, a child not believed to be his. Newborn babies were placed on the ground at their father's feet so that he could acknowledge paternity by picking them up, or could disavow it by not doing so. The Twelve Tables evidently prohibited a child born more than ten months after his or her father's death from being admitted into a legal inheritance. In addition, legends about Rome's early past portray both concerns over paternity and security about consanguinity through females as evidently affecting men's conduct with kindred males. We should recall that the usurper Amulius is represented as evil not merely for slaying his brother King Numitor's son, but also for refusing Numitor's daughter the opportunity to continue her father's line by bearing children. So, too, we should note that Verginius is represented as not merely assailed by the charge of not having fathered his beloved *filia unica*, but also as forming alliances with the Numitorii—kinsmen of the daughter's late, and biologically "certified" mother—to protect the girl from Appius Claudius' lust and to oppose the despotism of the decemvirs.[44]

Historical figures of the classical period merit mention in this connection as well. It is striking that the morally upright younger Cato is remembered both for divorcing his first, adulterous, wife—who bore two children dur-

---

[44] For the custom of acknowledging paternity by picking up the newborn child, see Suetonius, *Nero* 6.1; for the Twelve Tables' prohibition against admitting children born more than ten months after their father's death to inheritances, see Ulpian, *Digest* 38.16, 3, 9, 11 (also cited in chapter one above, n. 34). For Amulius, see chapter three above, n. 53 and chapter four above, n. 5; for Verginius, see the preceding note.

ing the marriage—and for prominently emphasizing his kindred bonds with the offspring of the two Serviliae, siblings with whom he shared a mother but not a father. Inasmuch as the elder Servilia was suspected of having an extramarital liaison with Julius Caesar at the very time she conceived her son Brutus, and as the younger Servilia was divorced for unchastity by her husband Lucullus, Cato's security about his blood ties to the sons of his *sorores* may well underlie his willingness to overlook conduct on the part of these women which he would not tolerate in the woman who had born him offspring. Tacitus' *Annales* also tell of a well-born woman whose husband's avowed anxieties over his paternity of her child did not deter her brother from aiding her publicly, and who looked to maternal, and hence more consanguineal, kin for support and self-affirmation. This is another Aemilia Lepida: during Tiberius' reign she was outlawed because her former husband Quirinius claimed that she had falsely represented a child as his; she was subsequently defended at her trial by her brother Manius Aemilius Lepidus. Aemilia Lepida's (and Lepidus') descent—through their mother—from Sulla and Pompey was made much of by Lepida and a throng of lamenting noblewomen at the games in Pompey's theater which occurred during her trial, particularly her descent from Pompey himself, whose daughter was the mother of her mother.[45]

In this context one might also consider Augustus' marriage to Livia when she was six months pregnant with Drusus (or, by some accounts, already delivered

[45] For the younger Cato's divorce, and support of his sisters, see chapter two above, n. 22, and chapter five above, n. 22. For the conduct of Cato's sisters, see also Suetonius, *Divus Julius* 82.2-3, and Plutarch, *Lucullus* 38.1. For this Aemilia Lepida, see Tacitus, *Annales* 3.22ff., and Tables V and VI.

of him). For by this bizarre and much-commented upon act, he may have hoped to foster the impression that he, and not Livia's husband, was the child's father. Were this to have been his motivation, his behavior would rank as another instance of Roman paternity anxiety, and may explain his later privileged treatment of Drusus and Drusus' son, especially his effort to link Drusus and this son more closely to him in the way that he did. To be sure, any implied admission of paternity on Augustus' part did not go unchallenged at the time of Drusus' birth: Livia's ex-husband Nero claimed and initially reared the boy. Nevertheless, after Nero's death, when Drusus joined Augustus' household rather than that of a male agnate, this challenge substantially weakened. And eagerness to be regarded as Drusus' sire renders more comprehensible why, after choosing and losing his sister's son Marcellus as an intended successor, Augustus wed Drusus, and not Drusus' elder brother Tiberius, to a daughter of his sister Octavia. It renders more comprehensible as well why, after the death of Drusus and Augustus' adoption of Tiberius, Augustus forced Tiberius to adopt Drusus' son Germanicus—whose kinship to Augustus was guaranteed since his mother Antonia Minor was Augustus' own *sororis filia*.[46]

Whatever Augustus' reasons, political and sexual, for marrying the pregnant Livia and for his later, special,

---

[46] At *Divus Claudius* 1.1 Suetonius reports that the birth of Drusus within three months after Livia's marriage to Augustus did arouse suspicions of Augustus' paternity. For the view that Drusus' birth occurred three days before Augustus' and Livia's marriage, see Balsdon, 68. For Drusus' initial rearing by Nero, see Cassius Dio 48.44.4-5; for Nero's death in 33 B.C., when Drusus was only five, see, for example, Suetonius, *Tiberius* 6.3. See also chapter five above, n. 38, and nn. 29, 30, above, for Augustus' loss of Marcellus, Drusus' marriage to Antonia Minor, and Augustus' insistence that Tiberius adopt Drusus' son.

concern for her offspring then *in utero*, certainly Augustus' and the early imperial modification of Roman naming practices deserves renewed attention. From his own personal circumstances and those of other individuals we have reason to judge that the secure assumption that the children of a man's daughters were his biological descendants played some part in the custom of naming children after a maternal grandfather rather than their father. At least Augustus, who was associated with this custom not only because of his daughter's sons, whom he adopted and identified as Julii Caesares, but because of his daughter's daughter named Julia as well, was known to be related to his daughter's offspring, whereas their resemblance to his son-in-law Agrippa occasioned astonishment. That the mature society beauty Poppaea Sabina, daughter of the illustrious Gaius Poppaeus Sabinus, evidently killed herself rather than have suspicions of her sexual misconduct come to light may be significant too, explaining why her daughter went by the feminine form of Sabinus' *nomina* no less than does the political disgrace suffered by Poppaea's one-time husband.[47]

Elite Roman males of the republican and imperial era may, therefore, have been rightly concerned about their own and other men's paternity. But despite concern and uncertainties, they did not seem to demand female chastity as strictly and uncompromisingly as Tacitus claims the Germans did. The Romans themselves thought that

[47] For doubts about Agrippa's paternities, see Macrobius, *Saturnalia* 2.5.9; for Julia's adultery with Sempronius Gracchus while Agrippa's and Tiberius' wife, see Tacitus, *Annales* 1.53.3-4; for Julia's adulteries as contributing to Agrippa's early death, see Pliny, *Natural History* 7.46. For the circumstances of the elder Poppaea Sabina's suicide, see Tacitus, *Annales* 11.2; for the disgrace of her husband T. Ollius as the pretext for naming her daughter after her father, Tacitus, *Annales* 13.45.1.

lengthy separations of distance and time between men
fighting and governing abroad and their wives back in
Rome promoted wives' adultery. Thus it is significant
that in the *Germania* Tacitus intimates that German women
do not experience similar separations, inasmuch as they
proudly witness their menfolk fighting; it is significant,
too, that in the *Annales* Tacitus portrays Valerius Messalla Messalinus as alluding to the temptations of grass
widowhood in the capital to justify a fairly late development in Roman "imperial" living arrangements, the
accompaniment of provincial governors by their wives
to their posts.[48]

The early age of marriage for Roman women in general, the considerable seniority of their spouses, and the
ever-present possibility of divorce and remarriage for a
well-born Roman female furnish further reasons for
wifely infidelity. No less significantly, therefore, at *Germania* 20.2 Tacitus points out, in another implicit contrast between German and Roman *mores*, that German
women wait to wed until they are fully mature, then
wed men of their own age and, in some tribes, once
wed never marry again. Furthermore, we should not
forget the facts that adulterous conduct did not, in pre-
Augustan times, substantially reduce the amount of her
dowry that a divorcee was entitled to retain (the impressions afforded by the elder Cato notwithstanding) and
that even Augustus' legislation did not put an end to
men's toleration of their wives' extra-marital affairs. Such
facts imply that many elite Roman males did not view
lapses in female chastity as the wholly shameful social

---

[48] Tacitus, *Germania* 7.2, *Annales* 3.33.2 (on the earlier prohibition
against wives' accompanying husbands to provinces), 34.5. See also
chapter two above, n. 35, and the article by A. J. Marshall cited
therein.

and moral transgressions which Tacitus reports them to
have been among the Germans. There, Tacitus says, an
adulterous wife's husband cuts off her hair, strips her
naked and—in the presence of her kinsmen—turns her
out of the house and flogs her all through the village;
she receives no compassion, and neither good looks,
youth, nor wealth can find her another husband. There,
too, Tacitus earlier claims, cases of adultery are *paucis-
sima*, most uncommon.[49]

Indeed, we may deduce the elite Roman male acceptance of female marital infidelity as a bearable if regrettable fact of life from observing that even men such
as the younger Cato who could not always bring themselves to accept it from their wives nevertheless overlooked it in their blood kinswomen. The practice of
forgiveness by a wayward woman's blood kinsmen possessed some impressive Roman legendary paradigms: in
the example of the once and future king Numitor, whose
daughter's Vestal Virgin status and illicit motherhood
did not, in various versions of his story, keep him from
recognizing and closely bonding with her twin sons (or
them from helping him regain his throne); in the display
of compassion and understanding by the later father of
Lucretia.[50] In fact, one might conclude that readiness to

[49] Tacitus, *Germania* 19.1-2. Richlin, "Approaches," 234, percep-
tively observes that the Romans reserved for slaves what the Germans supposedly did to punish adulteresses. By way of contrast, the
Spartans' celebrated unfamiliarity with the concept of adultery is
thought to stem from their widespread promotion of "wife sharing"
to keep up the birthrate: see Lacey, 199.

[50] For Numitor, see, for example, Livy 1.5.6-6.2 and Dionysius
of Halicarnassus 1. 81.4-84; for Lucretius, see Livy 1.58.9. For the
republican and imperial Roman elite male tolerance of adultery which
may have encouraged even the moralistic Livy to characterize these
men as he did, see chapter five above, nn. 22, 23. Of further interest
is the report, by Plutarch at *Cato Minor* 52.3ff., that the younger

forgive the sexual transgressions of daughters, sisters, and mothers might occur among well-born Roman males—as it seems to have occurred in the individual case of the younger Cato—because guaranteed consanguinity with these women and their offspring functioned compensatorily for widespread insecurities about blood bonds with their own and their male agnates' issue.

To be sure, an elite Roman father might not as willingly assume consanguinity with his infant daughter as that father's acknowledged son might with a mature woman always acknowledged as his sister. But initial paternity anxiety and life-long fraternity security themselves help explain why, as we have seen, the fathers of Roman women placed a higher premium on their chastity than did their brothers.[51] What is more, the notable fathers of legend (such as Numitor and Lucretius) and the equally notable fathers of history (such as Augustus and Marcus Aemilius Lepidus) who overlooked daughters' sexual indiscretions warrant attention along with the general Roman upper-class male recognition throughout (and perhaps prior to) classical times of uncertain paternity as a strong and frequent possibility in their milieu: such individuals and such a perception render more understandable the persistent emotional distancing between and among male agnates which we have noted. It is not altogether improbable that the practices of using the same *nomen* for, assigning rights of succession to, and estimating political status by the achievements of agnate kin themselves began as compensatory behavior, providing formal links to bolster an uncertain blood tie. Nor is it implausible that a Roman *pater*'s acquiescence

---

Cato remarried his former wife Marcia after Hortensius' death, even overlooking the fact that she had borne offspring to another man in his zeal to have her return to his household and to their children.

[51] On this point, see the discussion in chapter three above.

in the fact that his and his sons' supposed children might not truly be his sons' or his own biological descendants emotionally facilitated the Roman practice of adopting male heirs.

Finally, to take a broader and less speculative view of this Roman cultural situation, we should be aware that several of the phenomena discerned in Roman elite society of the classical and perhaps pre-classical period are also cited as the hallmarks of societies with matrilineal descent groups: e.g. uncertainty over (or indifference to) paternity, the consequent assumption of paternal responsibility by the maternal grandfather and uncle, and the "phrasing" of this concern for a sister's children by the display of interdependence by male and female siblings.[52] In other words, what we seem to find among the aristocratic Romans are expressions of "matrilineal" sentiment and matrilineally organized family bonding patterns in a patriarchal and patrilineal society. In addition, the blood kinfolk with whom Roman men seem to have felt especially secure about their consanguinity were often females and those who were kindred through females, a phenomenon compatible with matrilineal kinship patterns as well. Yet it bears emphasis that the women with whom such secure consanguinity was felt had not necessarily given birth to offspring (or, if they had, did not necessarily owe their support from male blood kin to their having given birth); this fact calls into question the suitability of using the verbal element *matri-* to describe such sentiment and bonding patterns among the Roman elite. Such women were, however, invariably daughters and at times sisters: we have just noted the support allegedly proffered by father and maternal male kin to and over the legendary maiden Verginia,

[52] See Schneider, *Matrilineal Kinship*, 1-29.

and similar aid awarded the historical Aemiliae Lepidae by their respective *frater* and *pater*. We might better, therefore, regard this Roman male blood security as stemming from and further accounting for a special feeling of closeness to a daughter (and hence one's father's daughter), a woman who had a potential for becoming the mother of kin indisputably related to her male blood kin, but who would be valued by these kinsmen whether she did so or not.

Rome was, moreover, always a gerontocratic as well as patriarchal society. Her first monarchs, and later emperors, ruled for life; unlike Homer's Ithaca, Rome did not retire living leaders in favor of their more robust sons. Membership in the *senatus*, Rome's governing assembly in both republican and imperial times, required advanced age and considerable experience in public life as well as certain property qualifications; it expired only when the senator himself did. Unlike various Homeric societies where the relatively youthful military combatants, often men with living fathers such as Hector and Achilles, are said to have complete control over the conduct of war-waging, Rome delegated to her noncombatant elder *senatores* a major role in the running of her military enterprises.[53] In fact, when confronted with the infiltration of contrary values imported from the

[53] For the life-tenure of early Roman kings, see Dionysius of Halicarnassus 4.74.2-3; for Laertes' retirement from the Ithacan throne, see Homer, *Odyssey* 15.351-360, 24.205ff. For the Roman senate, and its role in the conduct of military affairs, see, for example, Polybius 6.15 and the article in the supplement to *RE* (1935) 660-800 by O'Brien Moore. For Peleus' farewell to his son Achilles (in which he dispenses far less advice on war-waging than does the father of Achilles' subordinate Patroclus) and his need for his son as a protector, see, for example, Homer, *Iliad* 11.785-803, 24.486-492. For Priam's lack of involvement in military decisions, see Homer, *Iliad* 18.243-314, 22.25-92.

Greeks, and particularly the Athenians, whose obsession with male youth portended to weaken the sway of Roman *senes*, the aging Cicero penned an essay on old age to remind Romans of their traditional ways; he also dedicated to his son a treatise on duties which stresses the necessity of youthful deference to elders.[54]

Since, however, Roman society combined its gerontocratic organization with a strong military orientation, it also placed a high premium on youthful male physical powers. Under such circumstances, and particularly among the elite providing military leadership in such a society, a powerful elder male's mature son, capable of performing in warfare at a physical level which his father could no longer attain, might threaten his father's self-esteem and authority. A well-known example from classical times illustrates this phenomenon among the Romans during their regal phases: the envy ascribed to the aging emperor Tiberius, who had distinguished himself in soldiery as a younger man, of the popularity and competence possessed by his adopted son Germanicus (and perhaps even of the leadership efforts displayed by his biological son Drusus). Rome's legends

[54] For criticisms of Greek, and especially Athenian, culture in the *De Senectute*, which centers on the life and achievements of the elder Cato, and is addressed to the Hellenophile Atticus, three years Cicero's senior, see 45 and 63. For Cicero on the necessity of youthful deference, see *De Officiis* 1.33.122; of significance as well is his farewell enjoinder to Marcus at 3.33.121, in which he states that Marcus will become dearer to him (*multo cariorem*) if Marcus finds pleasure in his own ideas about human obligations. For the Roman paternal obsession with keeping sons in their place, see also, for example, Aulus Gellius 2.2.7, 15, as well as Tacitus, *Annales* 3.31.3-5. On Roman son-subordination generally, see M. Reinhold, "The Generation Gap in Antiquity," in S. Bertman, ed., *The Conflict of Generations in Ancient Greece and Rome* (Amsterdam, 1976) 48-54; on father-son conflict, see P. Veyne, "La famille et l'amour sous le haut-empire romaine," *Annales* ESC 33 (1978) 36.

about her early monarchy, in which the successful running of military endeavors characterized the reigns of
most kings, and no king is actually succeeded by his
son, may even express a common fantasy of Rome's
male senior citizens, and at least would suggest resentment of subordinate sons by aging fathers.[55]

Sources also, and more unequivocally, attest to resentment by grown, well-born Roman sons of their
subordination to senescent *patres*; such resentment has
marked cultural acknowledgment and impact in republican as well as in imperial times. The annual religious
festival of the Argei, dating back to the monarchic period
but unceasingly celebrated throughout the classical era,
featured the symbolic practice of throwing what were
thought to be straw effigies of old men off the Pons
Sublicius, Rome's oldest bridge, into the Tiber. A much-
mouthed Latin proverb—*sexagenarios ex ponte*—alluded
to this practice. The long-lasting popularity of Plautus'
comedies, a great many of which portray sons' rebellion
against paternal authority, surely implies that Plautus'
elite Roman public recognized as realistic, and to some
extent sympathized with, sons' efforts to overthrow pa-

[55] For war as a (if not the) major adolescent and adult experience
of the Roman aristocratic male until very late in the second century
B.C., see W. V. Harris, *War and Imperialism in Republican Rome 327-
70 B.C.* (Oxford, 1979) 10ff.; the foreign and civil wars of the subsequent two centuries also bulked large in the lives of Rome's male
elite. For Tiberius' envy of Germanicus (and his offspring), see, for
example, Tacitus, *Annales* 1.33 and 52; 2.5.1, 26.4-5, 43.5-6, 82.1-
3; 4.12. For his reported envy of his own son Drusus, see Tacitus,
Annales 1.76.3-4, 4.10. The fact that legends of early Rome also
represent the brothers of rulers as few in number, and brothers as
destructively competitive figures—on which see chapter four above—
should be noted again here, and perhaps ascribed to Roman male
wishful thinking as well: as we have observed, however, monarchy
seems particularly conducive to strains in the fraternal bond.

ternal authority. At *De Officiis* 3.31.112, a work dedicated to his own son Marcus, Cicero relates an episode from the life of Titus Manlius Torquatus: both Cicero here and other sources also remember this Torquatus, a figure of the mid-third century B.C., for having his own son executed when he disobeyed orders and attacked the Latins (despite the fact that this maneuver resulted in a Roman victory). Cicero recounts that one Pomponius, a tribune indicting Torquatus' own father for, *inter alia*, banishing Torquatus himself to the country, received Torquatus alone in his bedroom on the assumption that Torquatus was about to bring some new evidence against his father. Pomponius' assumption was proven false when the young man drew a sword and threatened to kill the tribune if he did not withdraw his suit; nevertheless, Cicero's assertion that this man merely made such an assumption indicates recognition of a Roman son's potential for hostile behavior toward an authoritarian father.[56]

---

[56] For the Argei, see Ovid, *Fasti* 5.621ff.; Dionysius of Halicarnassus 1.38; L. A. Holland, *Janus and the Bridge* (Rome, 1961) 313-331; and J. P. Hallett, "Over Troubled Waters: The Meaning of the Title *Pontifex*," *TAPA* 101 (1970) 223-226. For the proverb, and notion behind, *sexagenarios de ponte*, see Cicero, *Pro Roscio Amerino* 100; Ovid, *Fasti* 5.623-624; Varro, apud Nonium 523.21ff.; and Festus, p. 450-452 Lindsay and 66 Lindsay (for *depontani: senes appellabantur, qui sexagenarii de ponte deiciebantur,* "from-the-bridge men: old men in their sixties who are thrown from a bridge are so called"); see also J. P. Neraudau, "*Sexagenarii de ponte*," *Revue des études latines* 56 (1978) 159-174.

For sons' rebellion against paternal authority as a basic, and reality-rooted, Plautine comic theme, see E. Segal, *Roman Laughter* (Cambridge, Mass., 1968) 15-19, 27-28; for Plautus' immense popularity, see Segal, 2-3. The elder Torquatus is also discussed as a paradigm of the harsh Roman *pater* by Segal on 18; Torquatus' behavior toward his son is treated by Livy 8.7 and by Valerius Maximus at both 5.8 and 2.7.5. One might also recall in this context Seneca's aforemen-

Such potential was, at times, translated into actual hostile behavior. Velleius Paterculus, as we have seen, reports that sons showed the least loyalty of all to endangered men during the proscriptions. At *De Clementia* 1.15, Seneca tells of Tarius Rufus' discovery, during Augustus' principate, that his son was plotting against his life. Tacitus, at *Annales* 4.28-29, depicts the accusation of a father by his son, Vibius Serenus, during the reign of the son-threatened Tiberius. But this episode redounded to the son's disgrace and resulted in his flight from Rome, while turning out favorably for the accused *pater*. For Roman fathers usually had both general sentiment and revered tradition on their side: we have already mentioned the tales of son-slaying by fathers of the republican era (Valerius Maximus has five, but only four of paternal leniency); we should, perhaps, also recall the time-honored legal provision for surrendering a son three times into bondage.[57]

The potential for strains in the bond between elite Roman fathers and their sons would have placed daughters' husbands in a favorable position. Sons-in-law were chosen by fathers-in-law on the basis of talent and prom-

---

tioned remark to Marcia (on which see chapter five above, n. 34): that her son persisted in sharing her life even after he had reached an age when "most male children can barely endure sharing their lives with their fathers."

[57] For Velleius' remark, see chapter five above. For the outcome favorable to Serenus' father, see *Annales* 4.30.1: there Tacitus relates that, despite sentiment to execute Serenus père in accordance with the *mos maiorum*, Tiberius refused so as to mollify ill will. For son-slaying and the law on selling sons into bondage, see above chapter one, n. 33, and chapter three. Seneca also reports at *De Clementia* 1.15.1 that a Roman knight Tricho who had flogged his son to death was stabbed, with writing styluses, by a mob in the forum; this may suggest that "popular" notions of proper paternal conduct conflicted with those of the mature Roman males who served as spokesmen for the upper classes.

ise as well as pedigree and connections; sons-in-law whose conduct did not meet with the approval of their fathers-in-law could be disposed of simply, through divorce: the problem of having to endure or execute unsatisfactory *filii* did not exist with *generi*. What is more, a son-in-law, who appreciates, rather than assuming as a birthright, any share in a patriarch's assets, often presents far less of a threat than does a son when those assets are needed to obtain or maintain political power. Lucius Aemilius Paullus' generosity to his *gener* Tubero, a man of humble means less likely to take such munificence for granted than Paullus' own more advantaged male children, may be so explained, particularly in the light of Paullus' giving up his two elder sons for adoption. Had Paullus' decision been economically motivated—to postpone undertaking the financial burdens of launching a grown son into public life—surely he would have seen to it that his own sons profited from the spoils of his conquest no less than his son-in-law; one may more safely conjecture that Paullus wished to distance himself from two young men perceived as in political competition with himself. Favor shown to sons-in-law who did not have to vie with sons is only to be expected, although a man with more than one daughter may have played *generi* off against one another: at least Cicero reports, at *Brutus* 101, that the great orator Gaius Laelius, consul in 140 B.C., did as much with his sons-in-law Fannius and Quintus Mucius Scaevola. There may also have been some competition for a son-in-law from the sons of his *socer*'s sisters: the younger Cato's son-in-law Bibulus, for example, certainly took a back seat to his sister's son Brutus. Thus the possibility of making a sister's son one's son-in-law, as Cato did posthumously and Augustus did during his lifetime, must

have been attractive as a means of avoiding such conflict.[58]

Nevertheless, an aging *pater* might lessen tensions between himself and his sons, if not totally deter his sons
from trying to diminish his powers and resources, by
encouraging sons to channel their energies into activities
supportive of rather than competitive with paternal interests. And this a *pater* might easily do by emphasizing
his sons' bonds to their blood family, and his own and
his sons' joint attachments to his daughters and the offspring of his daughters. Because of the earlier marriage
age for Roman women, these daughters' children would
tend to be born prior to these sons' children; so, too,
sons could safely assume these offspring of their sisters
to represent the continuation of their own bloodline.
Such an emphasis on sons' ties to sisters and their offspring might result in sons' efforts to educate *filii sororum*
in the pursuits of elite male public life rather than to
seek public distinctions themselves, at great expense to
their fathers and their fathers' familial and political au-

[58] For Paullus, his son-in-law, and his sons, see chapter three above,
nn. 21, 47, as well as n. 38 above. We might also note the tradition—
which was questioned by the early Roman historian L. Piso on
chronological grounds (so Dionysius of Halicarnassus 4.7) and acknowledged by Livy at 1.46.4—that the husbands of Servius Tullius'
daughters were sons of Servius' predecessor Tarquinius Priscus, and
were rejected in favor of his son-in-law Servius as their father's
successor. On this tradition, see T. N. Gantz, "The Tarquin Dynasty," *Historia* 24 (1975) 543-544, who postulates that Priscus' own
son suffered an untimely death and that the husbands of Servius
Tullius' daughters were this man's sons. For Bibulus, see Plutarch,
Cato Minor 25.1-3 and *Caesar* 14.6, Suetonius, *Divus Julius* 19.1,
Asconius 31 K-S. We should not forget, moreover, that the younger
Cato had a son of his own (see, for example, Plutarch, *Cato Minor*
73, and Velleius Paterculus 2.71, the latter of whom reports that
Cato's nephew Lucullus as well as his own and Hortensius' sons fell
at Philippi).

thority. It would also set a behavioral pattern for the son which would continue after the *pater*'s death, and hence achieve a posthumous perpetuation of the *pater*'s interests as well.

Such kindness to her husband by her *pater*, and such filial dutifulness by her *frater*, however, would additionally benefit the upper-class Roman daughter and her offspring. She would personally benefit from the father-son tensions fostered by a gerontocracy of military orientation in other ways too. She was under no pressure to leave Rome for military service or provincial administration, and thereby to do her male agnates and *patria* credit. The likelihood that she would die before her father, despite the dangers of childbirth for Roman women, was probably not as great as that of her brother's losing his life: hence her father could more readily count on both her proximity and availability to him. Her exemption from the public responsibilities and strains which loomed so large in the lives of elite Roman males defined her as a figure strikingly different from her father, and thus arguably a more comfortable companion than his male kin. Constant comparisons with and obligations to living and dead male blood kin, not the least of whom were his own offspring and siblings, and responsibilities to male in-laws must have proven somewhat of a burden and source of resentment to an elite Roman male. Furthermore, as a *pater* did not demand the total emulation from a daughter which he might from a son, so she would not—as her brother often might—pose a threat or be perceived as a competitor to him. These advantages would, moreover, also work in a daughter's favor by strengthening her ties with her father's son—since she, as Festus noted, would differ from another brother in her comportment as well as in being more accessible to her brother and in not being publicly perceived as in competition with him.[59]

Still, even though her sex, age, and lack of formal political and military duties and opportunities differentiated a well-born Roman daughter from her father, she was regarded by him and by others as no less his biological extension and, more importantly, his personal and familial continuation into the future, than were his male offspring. Limited in her potential leadership of government and warfare she may have been, but she was also limited in her potential to mishandle important matters of state and military craft (and hence disgrace both country and kindred). Immense, moreover, was a daughter's presumed potential for sustaining the public identity and reputation of her father and blood kin, especially if opportunities for achievements ordinarily regarded as masculine should arise.

This view of upper-class Roman *filiae* as fully capable of displaying their father's, and blood family's, unique nature and talents, and often doing so in an impressive manner recognized publicly by outsiders, manifests itself in diverse Roman authors from the classical period. Cicero, for example, refers to Tullia as the image (*effigiem*) not only of his appearance (*oris*) but also of his speech and mind (*sermonis, animi mei*)—the source of his public greatness. Cicero describes the conversation of Laelia as imbued with the elegance of her father Laelius' words, and as passed on to her two daughters and their daughters; Cicero then characterizes one such granddaughter,

---

[59] For death in childbirth by Roman women, see, for example, Seneca, *Ad Helviam Matrem De Consolatione* 2.4; Pliny, *Epistles* 4.21; and Pomeroy, *GWWS*, 169. For the expectation that elite Roman sons would emulate *patres* and *maiores* in their public careers, see, for example, Cicero, *De Officiis* 2.32.116ff. (especially 33.121, *imitandos esse maiores*) and the aforementioned *De Oratore* 2.55.225-226.

Licinia, as especially pleasant to hear since she was the daughter of the esteemed orator Lucius Licinius Crassus (who in turn adopted one of her oratorically gifted sons). Valerius Maximus, as we have seen, joins Cicero in portraying the daughters of memorable public speakers as carrying on their fathers' achievements when he depicts Hortensia's eloquent speech to the triumvirs as "causing her father to live again in the female line and breathe in his daughter's words."[60]

Tacitus' characterization of the elder Agrippina in the *Annales* is another case in point. At 1.69 he relates the heroic way in which she prevented the demolition of a bridge over the Rhine by German columns; in so doing, he speaks of her as "great of spirit" (*ingens animi*) and as taking on the "duties of a general" (*munia ducis*). Earlier, at 1.41.2, Tacitus observes that Agrippina's very appearance summoned up for the Roman soldiers memories of her father Agrippa and (maternal) grandfather Augustus. Inasmuch as even earlier, at *Annales* 1.3.1, Tacitus had described Agrippa as a good ally in soldiery and victory to Augustus, both his account of her heroic conduct and his observation on her appearance seem to imply that Tacitus regards Agrippina as having continued her father's high-quality service to the *princeps*, and as having inherited her father's gifts for leadership in battle. Tacitus depicts Tiberius as deeply suspicious of and threatened by Agrippina's "unfeminine" behavior, contrasting him unfavorably with his predecessor Augustus and with Augustus' appreciation of similar behavior by Agrippina's father; such a contrast, moreover,

---

[60] For Cicero on Tullia as his image, see *Ad Quintum Fratrem* 1.3.3 and the discussion of T. Carp, "Two Matrons of the Late Republic," *Women's Studies* 8 (1981) 197. For Cicero on Laelius' and Crassus' daughters, see *Brutus* 211-212. For Hortensia, see Valerius Maximus 8.3.3 (also cited in chapter two above, n. 32, and chapter five above).

heightens Tacitus' portrayal of Agrippina as, like her husband Germanicus, a tragic and victimized figure.[61]

The younger Pliny also remarks on the perpetuation, by daughters, of their fathers' attributes and publicly recognized aptitudes. In addition to asserting that Fundanus' daughter was her father's exact living image in appearance and ways, he notes that the girl worked at her books studiously and intelligently, and that her father is a man of great learning and sense. Pliny's statement in *Epistles* 7.19 that Fannia possesses courage and spirit worthy of her husband Helvidius Priscus, and father Thrasea Paetus gains greater impact from his reference to the latter as a man most humane and for that reason also exceedingly great (*mitissimus et ob hoc quoque maximus*). Pliny even asseverates that the death of this Helvidius Priscus' daughters in childbirth concerns him because of his love for their late father, and means that Helvidius' sole surviving offspring—a son—is now the sole prop and stay of a family which not long ago had many members to sustain it.[62]

Seneca's *Consolatio ad Marciam* warrants final and special mention again in this context. Here Seneca makes no distinction between the untimely loss of sons by aristocratic Roman fathers and mothers, and Julius Caesar's loss of his daughter. He answers the possible objection that his male *exempla* have no relevance to the plight of a grieving female by asserting that Roman

[61] Also of note is *Annales* 3.4.2, the praise (which so rankled in Tiberius' heart) of Agrippina as *decus patriae, solum Augusti sanguinem, antiquitatis specimen*, "distinction to her father-country, the only true descendant of Augustus, a model of traditional behavior": these, politically charged, terms are no less applicable to males than to females. I owe this point about Tacitus' characterization of Agrippina to W. Avery.

[62] For Pliny on Fundanus' daughter, see *Epistles* 5.16.3ff. (also cited in chapter three above); for Helvidius Priscus' daughters, see *Epistles* 4.21.

women have as much strength (*vigor*), propensity for honorable conduct (*ad honesta . . . facultas*) and capacity for endurance of sorrow and struggle (*dolorem laboremque . . . patiuntur*) as their menfolk. Significantly, too, he cites two legendary daughter-figures, Lucretia and Cloelia, as proof of this latter claim.[63]

By way of contrast, sources on the other ancient societies which we have cited for exhibiting filiafocal features do not represent daughters as prominently displaying and passing on to their offspring their fathers' and male blood kindred's distinctive traits and talents. At the most these sources imply a regard for daughters as biological continuations and continuators of their father's blood-line and as individuals who may incidentally display characteristics given esteem by males; these characteristics are not, moreover, necessarily ascribed to their fathers. Homer's *Odyssey*, for example, may introduce Arete as daughter of Rhexenor and enumerate her special excellences—the general honor in which she is held, her grace, her wisdom and her skill at arbitrating men's quarrels fairly—but does not say that her father shared these outstanding attributes. Similarly, Hesiod's *Theogony* does not impute to Hecate's father Perses any of his daughter's gifts for aiding men in governance, military victory, athletic contests, horsemanship, seafaring, or herding and pasturage. The notion of female offspring as resembling male blood kin and, after their

---

[63] Seneca, *Ad Marciam De Consolatione* 12.4-15.3. The aforementioned characterization, by such authors as Cicero and Suetonius, of both male and female agnates as important public behavioral exemplars to both male and female descendants also testifies to this view of women as possessing their father's and blood kinsmen's special qualities; see n. 39 above. See, too, the honorific association of elite males with illustrious Vestal ancestors discussed in the third chapter. Significantly, Suetonius states at *Caligula* 25.5 that Caligula was reassured of his daughter's paternity when she displayed fierceness (by attacking the faces and eyes of her fellow infants).

deaths, visibly carrying on their special, publicly valued, traits into later generations is a far cry from the Greek concept—expressed in the aforementioned Herodotean and Polybian obituary notices—that only male issue deserve the linguistic label of "surviving children," and that daughters belong to a separate, biologically bound, category; this notion also accords with the Roman linguistic practices of assigning forms of paternal *gentilicia* and using fathers' *praenomina* to identify children of both sexes.[64]

The reckoning by elite Roman patriarchal society of female issue as somewhat different from but nonetheless "continuative" offspring of their *patres* in character and publicly displayed talents warrants emphasis for a further reason. The classical Roman elite greatly prized continuity, unbroken tradition and the display of individual talent for the public weal; such a view, therefore, additionally helps to account for daughters' preciousness, their emotional appeal to their fathers. These perceptions of daughters by fathers, and society at large, need not, moreover, be unique to the classical Roman elite. Comparable perceptions of female children, particularly by men of the upper classes in later, militarily stressful, cultures and eras, should be sought elsewhere; they should prove of value in future anthropological and historical efforts to investigate and determine the cultural impact of the so-called and much neglected "father-daughter dyad" (and "brother-sister dyad") in other societies.[65]

---

[64] For Homer on Arete, see n. 6 above. For Herodotus' and Polybius' use of Greek terms for children to mean sons alone, see chapter three above, nn. 20, 21.

[65] On these "dyads"—and the more closely scrutinized father-son, husband-wife, and brother-brother dyads—see, for example, *Kinship and Culture*, ed. F.L.K. Hsu (Chicago, 1971) 1-29. I am grateful to my colleague D. McCall for directing my attention to this entire concept.

"Daughters," says one of the two *filiae* at line 96 of
Plautus' *Stichus*, "can never care for their father too much."
In focusing on the cultural elaboration and cultural ramifications of the Roman father-daughter bond, this study
has concentrated exclusively on its representation by
men belonging to or writing for classical Roman elite
circles, although not necessarily by men who were
themselves fathers of daughters. Attitudes of Roman
women, all of whom were of course daughters of fathers, do not lend themselves so readily to documentation. Like so many remarks in Plautus' comedies, this
avowal of daughterly devotion cannot be taken at face
value, but must be understood in context: here a typi-
cally topsy-turvy one in which iron-willed young women
manipulate a soft-hearted old *pater*. Plutarch's characterization of the younger Cato's daughter Porcia, Tacitus' portrayals of Antistia Pollitta and Servilia, and
Pliny's recollections of Fundanus' daughter presumably
constitute more reliable evidence of how elite Roman
daughters could, in certain situations, behave toward
and out of regard for their fathers. But the fact remains
that no testimony which we can safely assume to be "by
a woman writ" survives to tell us the elite Roman
daughter's side of the story. We cannot know, for example, whether Hortensia intended her much-touted oration as a credit to her dead father (which our male
sources evidently infer to be the case) or as a purely self
assertive "masculine" act (like the conduct which these
and other male sources impute to the less illustriously
fathered Fulvia, who rebuffed Hortensia on this occasion, or to Hortensia's predecessor in female oratory,
Gaia Afrania).[66]

---

[66] For Fulvia's masculine image, see J. P. Hallett, *"Perusinae glandes,"*
157; for Gaia Afrania, see again Valerius Maximus 8.3.2 and chapter
five above. K. G. Wallace has, however, called to my attention the
fact that the sole kinship term which appears in the poems of the

This lack of evidence from elite Roman women prevents us from investigating many other important questions and verifying many other tantalizing hypotheses. It appears, for instance, that Roman women deprived of their fathers before bearing children were more likely than those with living fathers to be deeply involved in promoting the careers of their sons. The elder Servilia, the empress Livia, Antonia Minor, the younger Agrippina and Cornelia, *mater Gracchorum*, had all lost their fathers before becoming mothers, and likewise are remembered for their efforts on behalf of their male children. Perhaps, therefore, the formidable and demanding maternal conduct we have noted on the part of so many upper-class Roman matrons, and noted for its impact on Roman public life, required that a Roman woman first assume a mature and independent self-image incompatible with the role of deferential daughter to one's father. But we can go no further than sheer speculation in these matters of how well-born Roman women felt about *being* daughters or with what affective and libidinal dimensions women personally invested their bonds with their fathers (and sons and brothers): the necessary data for theorizing are simply not there.

There are, however, still many questions pertaining to ancient Roman kinship attitudes, and their cultural expression, which may be reasonably answered as well as asked; there are, moreover, many issues of importance in the fields of Latin literature and Roman studies which findings on male views about important kinship ties may illuminate. This discussion has tried as far as possible to refrain from adducing as documentation for Roman elite

---

Augustan female elegist Sulpicia is *filia* (when she identifies herself as *Servi filia Sulpicia* at 4.10.4); Sulpicia's guardian Messalla, to whom she refers as "solicitous of me" at 4.8.6, is generally thought to be her *avunculus* as well.

sentiment and practice the portrayal of daughters, sisters, wives, and mothers in Augustan Latin poetry (the prominent family and political connections of Propertius' Cornelia render the elegy in her honor a key exception). Such literature presents particular problems as a source for notions of valued kinship ties; not only elegy and lyric verse but also Horace's *Satires* and Ovid's *Metamorphoses* (and even Vergil's poems) seem more concerned with the dynamics of extramarital erotic attraction and attachment than with those of kindred relationships (this concern is not, obviously, unrelated to the relatively low emotional investment apparently made by upper-class Romans in their marital attachments). Yet a study of how Roman attitudes about important kinship ties appear to influence Ovid's treatment of Greek myths in the *Metamorphoses* or *Heroides* would be feasible, particularly in the light of our earlier observation that Ovid differs from Homer in key details when portraying the tragedy of the mythic Meleager; a study of how Ovid's more conscientiously Roman *Fasti* compare and contrast in their depiction of valued kinship bonds with the more "Hellenistic" *Metamorphoses* warrants undertaking too. The representation of various familial roles and ties of kinship in both the tragedies of Seneca and the Athenian works which served as their models merits close scrutiny as well. Finally, both the tensions ascribed in this study to male agnate bonds among the classical Roman elite, and the strength attributed to ties of blood and marriage through daughters, might be taken into account in future analyses of actual Roman political behavior, particularly during the mid- and late republic: greater caution may need to be exercised in postulating alliances among men who share the same *gentilicia*; greater ingenuity in establishing if kindred relationships of a non-agnate nature underlie alliances among those dissimilarly named.

We have, therefore, much still to discover about how
the elite Romans' view of kinship, and Roman women's
place therein, are manifested in Roman forms of literary
entertainment and political conduct. We might, though,
conclude our foray into the manifestations of Roman
filiafocality itself, in everyday life, with a further—and
perhaps rather obvious—observation about elite Roman
fathers and their daughters. A daughter was the one
kinswoman for whom a Roman *pater* invariably occupied a unique male role. After all, it was often the case
that his mother had more than one male offspring, and
his sister(s) more than one male sibling; he might well
have been preceded, or be succeeded, as husband to his
wife. He could reasonably expect that his daughter might
bear more than one son, or wed more than one man;
often a daughter would have several *fratres*, or *patrui*, or
avunculi. But no other man would ever be her father,
although Roman law insisted that one man always formally function in such a way. To imagine the deep, and
unique, devotion a Roman pater could rightfully assume
in a female child, we might recall Cordelia's words to
her father in Shakespeare's *King Lear*:

> You have begot me, bred me, lov'd me: I
> Return those duties back as are right fit,
> Obey you, love you, and most honor you.

And we might also make serious use of a phrase from
a Cole Porter song, and conclude that his unique role
in his daughter's life gave a Roman *pater* good cause not
merely to regard her as most honoring him, but also to
regard her heart as, first and foremost, belonging to
daddy.[67]

[67] *King Lear*, Act I, scene i, 98-100; Cole Porter, "My Heart Belongs to Daddy," from *Leave It To Me* (1938).

SELECTED BIBLIOGRAPHY

MOST, although not all, of the modern works cited in the text have been included here. Articles in A. Pauly, G. Wissowa, and W. Kroll, *Real-Encyclopädie der classischen Altertumswissenschaft* (1893-), and entries in the *Thesaurus Linguae Latinae* (1900-) and the *Oxford Latin Dictionary* (1968-1982) are not listed; entries cited in the *Oxford Classical Dictionary*² (1970) and *The Princeton Encyclopedia of Classical Sites* (1976) are listed by author of the individual article. The articles by L. Bonfante, T. Carp, C. Dewald, and A. Richlin in *Women's Studies* 8 (1981) also appear in *Reflections of Women in Antiquity*, ed. H. P. Foley (New York, 1981) at 323-342, 343-354, 91-125 and 379-404, respectively. References to passages in Cicero, the Greek tragedians, Herodotus, Homer, Horace, Livy, Pindar, Plautus, Propertius and Vergil generally follow the Oxford Classical texts of those authors; references to Suetonius and Tacitus follow the Teubner texts. References to Cicero's *De Divinatione, De Officiis,* and *De Oratore* provide fuller chapter data than those to his other works.

Africa, T. W., "The Mask of an Assassin: A Psychohistorical Study of M. Junius Brutus," *Journal of Interdisciplinary History* 8 (1978) 599-626.

Alföldi, A., *Early Rome and the Latins* (Ann Arbor, 1965).

Alfs, G., *Adoptionen in der Zeit der römischen Republik bis auf die des Caesar Octavianus* (Cologne dissertation, 1950).

Arthur, M. B., "Cultural Strategies in Hesiod's *Theogony*: Law, Family, Society," *Arethusa* 15 (1982) 63-82.

Arthur, M. B., " 'Liberated' Women: The Classical Era," in *Becoming Visible: Women in European History*, ed. R. Bridenthal and C. Koonz (Boston, 1979) 60-89.

———, "Matriarchy in the *Odyssey: Basilea, Basileuein* and *Basileus*" (unpublished lecture, Wellesley College, October 1976).

———, "Review Essay, Classics," *Signs* 2 (1976) 382-402.

Astin, A. E., *Cato the Censor* (Oxford, 1978).

———, *Scipio Aemilianus* (Oxford, 1967).

Babcock, C. L., "The Early Career of Fulvia," *AJP* 86 (1965) 1-32.

Bachofen, J. J., *Gesammelte Werke*. Vol. VI. *Die Sage von Tanaquil: eine Untersuchung über den Orientalismus in Rom und Italien*, ed. K. Meuli (Basel, 1943).

———, Vol. VIII. *Antiquarische Briefe* (Basel, 1966).

Badian, E., "Nobilitas," *Oxford Classical Dictionary*² (Oxford, 1970) 736.

———, "Novus Homo," *Oxford Classical Dictionary*² (Oxford, 1970) 740.

Balsdon, J.P.V.D., "Gaius," *Oxford Classical Dictionary*² (Oxford, 1970) 452-453.

———, *Roman Women: Their History and Habits* (London, 1962).

Bamberger, J., "The Myth of Matriarchy: Why Men Rule in Primitive Society," *Woman, Culture, and Society*, ed. M. Z. Rosaldo and L. Lamphere (Stanford, 1974) 263-280.

Beard, M., "The Sexual Status of Vestal Virgins," *JRS* 70 (1980) 12-27.

Beauvoir, S. de, *The Second Sex*, transl. H. M. Parshley (New York, 1952).

Beekes, R.S.P., "Uncle and Nephew," *JIS* 4 (1976) 43-63.

Benario, H. W., *An Introduction to Tacitus* (Athens, Georgia, 1975).

Best, E. E., Jr., "Cicero, Livy and Educated Roman Women," *CJ* 65 (1970) 199-204.

Benveniste, E., *Le vocabulaire des institutions indo-européennes* I (Paris, 1969).

Bonfante, L., "Etruscan Couples," *Women's Studies* 8 (1981) 157-187.

Bonfante Warren, L., "Etruscan Women: A Question of Interpretation," *Archaeology* 26 (1977) 242-249.

———, "The Women of Etruria," *Arethusa* 6 (1973) 91-101.

Boswell, J., *Christianity, Social Tolerance, and Homosexuality: Gay People in Western Europe from the Beginning of the Christian Era to the Fourteenth Century* (Chicago, 1980).

Bosworth, A. B., "Tacitus and Asinius Gallus," *AJAH* 2 (1977) 173-192.

Bowra, C. M., *Sophoclean Tragedy* (Oxford, 1944).

Bremmer, J., "Avunculate and Fosterage," *JIS* 4 (1976) 65-78.

———, "Heroes, Rituals and the Trojan War," *Studi Storico-Religiosi* 2 (1978) 5-38.

———, "The Importance of Maternal Uncle and Grandfather in Archaic and Classical Greece and Early Byzantium," *Zeitschrift für Papyrologie und Epigraphik* 50 (1983) 173-186.

———, "Plutarch and the Naming of Greek Women," *AJP* 102 (1981) 425-426.

Bremmer, R. H., "The Importance of Kinship: Uncle and Nephew in 'Beowulf,' " *Amsterdamer Beiträge zur Alteren Germanistik* 15 (1980) 21-38.

Briffault, R., *The Mothers: A Study of the Origins of Sentiments and Institutions* (New York, 1927).

Brown, F. E., "New Soundings in the Regia: the Evidence for the Early Republic," *Les origines de la république romaine. Entretiens Hardt* 13 (Geneva, 1967) 47-64.

―――, "La protostoria della Regia," *Rendiconti della Pontificia Accademia di Archeologia* 47 (1974-75) 15-36.

Burkert, W., *Structure and History in Greek Mythology and Ritual* (Berkeley and Los Angeles, 1979).

Bush, A. E., *Studies in Roman Social Structure* (Washington, D.C., 1982).

Butler, H. E., and Barber, E. A., *The Elegies of Propertius* (Oxford, 1933).

Carney, T. F., "Prosopography: Payoffs and Pitfalls," *Phoenix* 27 (1973) 156-179.

Carp, T., "Two Matrons of the Late Republic," *Women's Studies* 8 (1981) 189-200.

Classen, J., "Zur Herkunft der Sage von Romulus und Remus," *Historia* 12 (1963) 447-457.

Corbett, P. E., *The Roman Law of Marriage* (Oxford, 1930).

Crawford, M., *Roman Republican Coinage* (Cambridge, 1974), 2 vols.

Crook, J., *Law and Life of Rome* (Ithaca, N.Y., 1967).

―――, "Patria Potestas," *CQ* n.s. 17 (1967) 113-122.

Degler, C. N., "Women and the Family," in *The Past before Us. Contemporary Historical Writing in the U.S.*, ed. M. Kammen, (Ithaca, N.Y., 1980) 308-326.

Deutsch, M., "The Women of Caesar's Family," *CJ* 13 (1918) 502-514.

Dewald, C. "Women and Culture in Herodotus' *Histories*," *Women's Studies* 8 (1981) 93-127.

Dickison, S. K., "Forum," *Arethusa* 9 (1976) 119-120.

Diner, H., *Mothers and Amazons: The First Feminine History of Culture*, ed. and transl. J. P. Lundin (Garden City, N.Y., 1973).

Dixon, S., "The Family Business: Women and Politics in the Late Republic," *Classical et Medievalia* 34 (1983) 91-112.

Doer, B., *Die Römische Namengebung* (Stuttgart, 1937).

Donlan, W., "Reciprocities in Homer," *CW* 75 (1982) 137-175.

Dumézil, G., *Déesses latines et mythes védiques* (Brussels, 1956).

———, *Mariages indo-européens* (Paris, 1979).

Durry, M. ed., *Éloge funèbre d'une matrone romaine (Éloge dit de Turia)* (Paris, 1950).

Earl, D., *The Moral and Political Tradition of Rome* (Ithaca, N.Y., 1967).

———, "Political Terminology in Plautus," *Historia* 9 (1960) 234-243.

Erhart, K. P., "A New Portrait Type of Octavia Minor(?)" *The J. Paul Getty Museum Journal* 8 (1980) 117-128.

———, "A Portrait of Antonia Minor in the Fogg Art Museum and Its Iconographic Tradition," *AJA* 82 (1978) 193-212.

Ernout, A., *Recueil de textes latins archaïques*[4] (Paris, 1973).

Ernout, A., and Meillet, A., *Dictionnaire étymologique de la langue latine*[4] (Paris, 1967).

Eving, L., *Die Sage von Tanaquil* (Frankfurt, 1933).

Ferrill, A., "Augustus and His Daughter: a Modern Myth," *Studies in Latin Literature and Roman History* II, ed. C. Deroux. *Collection Latomus* 168 (Brussels, 1980) 332-346.

Finley, M. I., *Early Greece, the Bronze and Archaic Ages* (New York, 1970).

Foley, H. P., "The Conception of Women in Athenian Drama," in *Reflections of Women in Antiquity*, ed. H. P. Foley (New York, 1981) 127-168.

———, "The 'Female Intruder' Reconsidered: Women

in Aristophanes' *Lysistrata* and *Ecclesiazusae*," *CP* 77 (1982) 1-21.

Fortes, M., *Kinship and the Social Order* (Chicago, 1969).

Fortsch, B., *Die politische Rolle der Frau in der römischen Republik* (Stuttgart, 1935).

Furneaux, H., *The Annals of Tacitus*. Vol. II: Books XI-XVI² (Oxford, 1907).

Fustel de Coulanges, N. D. de, *The Ancient City: A Study on the Religion, Laws, and Institutions of Greece and Rome*, with a new foreword by A. Momigliano and S. C. Humphreys (Baltimore and London, 1980).

Gabba, E., "Considerazioni sulla tradizione letteraria sulla origini della Repubblica," *Les Origines de la république romaine*. *Entretiens Hardt* 13 (Geneva, 1967) 135-174.

Galinsky, K., "Augustus' Legislation on Morals and Marriage," *Philologus* 125 (1981) 126-144.

Gantz, T. N., "The Tarquin Dynasty," *Historia* 24 (1975) 539-554.

Geiger, J., "The Last Servilii Caepiones of the Republic," *Ancient Society* 4 (1973) 143-156.

Gelzer, M., *The Roman Nobility*, transl. R. Seager (Oxford, 1969).

Gernet, L., *Anthropologie de la Grèce antique* (Paris, 1968).

Gjerstad, E., "The Origins of the Roman Republic," *Les origines de la république romaine*. *Entretiens Hardt* 13 (Geneva, 1967) 1-43.

Goodwater, L., *Women in Antiquity: An Annotated Bibliography* (Metuchen, N.J., 1975).

Goody, J. ed., *The Character of Kinship* (Cambridge, 1973).

———, *Comparative Studies in Kinship* (Stanford, 1969).

Gould, J., "Law, Custom and Myth: Aspects of the Social Position of Women in Classical Athens," *JHS* 100 (1980) 38-59.

Gouldner, A. W., *The Hellenic World: A Sociological Analysis* [Part One of *Enter Plato: Classical Greece and the Origins of Social Theory*] (New York, 1965).

Gruen, E. S., *The Last Generation of the Roman Republic* (Berkeley, Los Angeles, and London, 1974).

———, "Macedonia and the Settlement of 167 B.C.," *Philip II, Alexander the Great, and the Macedonian Heritage*, ed. W. L. Adams and E. N. Borza (Washington, D.C., 1982) 257-267.

———, *Roman Politics and the Criminal Courts 149-78 B.C.* (Cambridge, Mass., 1968).

Guastella, G., "I parentalia come testo antropologico: l'avunculato nel mondo celtico e nella famiglia di Ausonio," *Materiali e discussioni per l'annalisi dei testi classici* (=MD) 4 (1980) 97-124.

Hallett, J. P., "Over Troubled Waters: The Meaning of the Title *Pontifex*," *TAPA* 101 (1970) 219-227.

———, "*Perusinae Glandes* and the Changing Image of Augustus," *AJAH* 2 (1977) 151-171.

———, "The Role of Women in Roman Elegy: Counter-Cultural Feminism," *Arethusa* 6 (1973) 103-124.

Harris, W. V., *War and Imperialism in Republican Rome 327-70 B.C.* (Oxford, 1979).

Harrison, A.R.W., *The Law of Athens: The Family and Property* (Oxford, 1968).

Herrmann, C., *Le rôle judiciaire et politique des femmes sous la république romaine* (Brussels, 1964).

Heurgon, J., *Daily Life of the Etruscans*, transl. J. Kirkup (New York, 1964).

———, "Valeurs féminines et masculines dans la civilisation étrusque," *Mélanges d'archéologie et d'histoire de l'École Française de Rome* 73 (1961) 139-160.

Holland, L. A., *Janus and the Bridge* (Rome, 1961).

Hommel, H., "Vesta und die frührömische Religion,"

Aufstieg und Niedergang der Römischen Welt I.2 (1972) 397-420.

Hopkins, M. K. "The Age of Roman Girls at Marriage," *Population Studies* 18 (1965) 309-327.

Hsu, F.L.K., ed., *Kinship and Culture* (Chicago, 1971).

Humphreys, S. C., *Anthropology and the Greeks* (London, 1978).

Hunter, V. J., "Review of M. Lefkowitz and M. Fant, *Women in Greece and Rome*," *Helios* n.s. 7.1 (1979-80) 82-95.

Immerwahr, H. R., *Form and Thought in Herodotus* (Cleveland, 1966).

Johnston, P. A., "*Poenulus* 1, 2 and Roman Women," *TAPA* 110 (1980) 143-159.

Just, R., "The Conception of Women in Classical Athens," *Journal of the Anthropological Society of Oxford* 6 (1975) 153-170.

Kajanto, I., "On the Chronology of the Cognomen in the Republican Period," *L'onomastique latine*, Colloques Internationaux du Centre National de la Recherche Scientifique (Paris, 1977) 63-70.

———, "On the First Appearance of Women's Cognomina," *Acts of the Sixth International Congress on Greek and Latin Epigraphy* (Munich, 1972) 402-404.

———, "On the Peculiarities of Women's Nomenclature," *L'onomastique latine*, Colloques Internationaux du Centre National de la Recherche Scientifique (Paris, 1977) 147-158.

———, "Women's Praenomina Reconsidered," *Arctos* 7 (1972) 13-30.

Kierdorf, W., *Laudatio Funebris. Interpretationen und Untersuchungen zur Entwicklung der Römischen Leichenrede, Beiträge zur Klassischen Philologie* 106 (Meisenheim am Glan, 1980).

Kluckhohn, C., *Anthropology and the Classics* (Providence, R.I., 1961).

Koestermann, E., *Cornelius Tacitus Annalen* 11-13 (Heidelberg, 1967). 3 vols.

Lacey, W. K., *The Family in Classical Greece* (Ithaca, N.Y., 1968).

Latte, K., *Römische Religionsgeschichte* (Munich, 1960).

Lee, M. O., *Fathers and Sons in Vergil's Aeneid: Tum Genitor Natum* (Albany, 1979).

Leon, E. F., "Scribonia and Her Daughters," *TAPA* 82 (1951) 168-175.

Lonis, R., *Guerre et religion en Grèce á l'époque classique* (Paris, 1979).

MacCary, W. T., and Willcock, M. M., *Plautus' Casina* (Cambridge, 1976).

Malcovati, H. ed., *Oratorum Romanorum Fragmenta*[3] (Turin, 1967).

Marshall, A. J., "Roman Women and the Provinces," *Ancient Society* 6 (1975) 109-127.

Mattingly, H., *Coins of the Roman Empire in the British Museum* (London, 1923).

McDermott, W. C., "The Sisters of P. Clodius," *Phoenix* 24 (1970) 39-47.

Momigliano, A., *Secondo contributo alla storia degli studi classici* (Rome, 1960).

Mommsen, T., *Res Gestae Divi Augusti*[2] (Berlin, 1883).

Most, G. W. "Of Motifemes and Megatexts: Comment on Rubin/Sale and Segal," *Arethusa* 16 (1983) 199-218.

Murray, M., "Royal Marriage and Matrilineal Descent," *Journal of the Royal Anthropological Institute of Great Britain and Ireland* 45 (1915) 317-325.

Nash, E., "Rome," *The Princeton Encyclopedia of Classical Sites*, ed. R. Stillwell, W. L. MacDonald, and M. H. McAllister (Princeton, 1976).

Neraudau, J. P., "*Sexagenarii de ponte*," *Revue des études latines* 56 (1978) 159-174.

Nisbet, R., *Cicero: In L. Calpurnium Pisonem Oratio* (Oxford, 1961).

North, J. A., "Religious Toleration in Republican Rome," *Proceedings of the Cambridge Philological Society* 25 (1979) 85-103.

Numminen, P., "Severa Mater," *Arctos* 3 (1962) 143-166.

Ogilvie, R. M., *A Commentary on Livy Books I-V* (Oxford, 1965).

———, "Review of J. Poucet, *Recherches sur la légende sabine des origines de Rome*," *CR* 18 (1968) 327-329.

Ollier, F., *Le Mirage Spartiate* (Paris, 1933 and 1943), 2 vols.

Pais, E., *Ancient Legends of Roman History*, transl. M. Cosenza (Freeport, N.Y., 1971).

Pallottino, M., "The Origins of Rome: A Survey of Recent Discoveries and Discussions," in *Italy before the Romans: The Iron Age, Orientalizing and Etruscan Periods*, ed. D. and F. R. Ridgway (New York, 1979) 197-222; this is a translation of "Le origini di Roma: considerazioni critiche sulle scoperte e sulle discussioni piu recenti," *Aufstieg und Niedergang der Römischen Welt* I.1 (1972) 22-47.

Palmer, R.E.A., *The Archaic Community of the Romans* (Cambridge, 1970).

Pearce, T.E.V., "The Role of the Wife as Custos in Ancient Rome," *Eranos* 72 (1974) 16-33.

Pembroke, S., "Last of the Matriarchs: A Study in the Inscriptions of Lycia," *Journal of the Economic and Social History of the Orient* 8 (1965) 217-247.

———, "Women in Charge: The Function of Alternatives in Early Greek Tradition and the Ancient

Idea of Matriarchy," *Journal of the Warburg and Courtauld Institutes* 30 (1967) 1-35.

Phillips, J. E., "Roman Mothers and the Lives of Their Adult Daughters," *Helios* n.s. 6.1 (1978) 69-80.

Pisani, V., "Uxor—Ricerche di morfologia indeuropea," *Miscellanea G. Galbinati* (1951) 3.1-38.

Pomeroy, S. B., "Andromaque: un exemple méconnu de matriarcat?" *Revue des études grecques* 88 (1975) 16-19.

——, *Goddesses, Whores, Wives, and Slaves: Women in Classical Antiquity* (New York, 1975).

——, "The Relationship of the Married Woman to Her Blood Relatives in Rome," *Ancient Society* 7 (1976) 215-227.

Poucet, J., *Recherches sur la légende sabine des origines de Rome* (Louvain, 1967).

Radcliffe-Brown, A. R., "The Mother's Brother in South Africa," reprinted in *Structure and Function in Primitive Society* (London, 1952) 15-31.

Raditsa, L. F., "Augustus' Legislation Concerning Marriage, Procreation, Love Affairs and Adultery," *Aufstieg und Niedergang der Römischen Welt* II.13 (1980) 278-339.

Randolph, R. R., "The 'Matrifocal Family' as a Comparative Category," *American Anthropologist* 66 (1964) 628-631.

Rapp, R., "Review Essay, Anthropology," *Signs* 4 (1979) 497-513.

Redfield, J., *Nature and Culture in the Iliad: The Tragedy of Hector* (Chicago, 1975).

Reinhold, M. R., "The Generation Gap in Antiquity," in *The Conflict of Generations in Ancient Greece and Rome*, ed. S. Bertman (Amsterdam, 1976) 15-54.

Riccobono, S. ed., *Fontes Iuris Romani Antejustiniani*[2] (Florence, 1941).

Richardson, E. H., *The Etruscans: Their Art and Civilization* (Chicago and London, 1964).

Richlin, A., "Approaches to the Sources on Adultery at Rome," *Women's Studies* 8 (1981) 225-250.

Rix, H., "Zum Ursprung des römische-mittelitalischen Gentilnamensystems," *Aufstieg und Niedergang der Römischen Welt* I.2 (1972) 700-758.

Rosaldo, M. Z., "The Use and Abuse of Anthropology: Reflections on Feminism and Cross-Cultural Understanding," *Signs* 5 (1980) 389-417.

———, "Woman, Culture and Society: A Theoretical Overview," in *Woman, Culture, and Society*, ed. M. Z. Rosaldo and L. Lamphere (Stanford, 1974) 17-42.

Rose, H. J., "Die Virginibus Vestalibus," *Mnemosyne* 2nd ser. 54 (1926) 448-449.

———, "Iterum de Virginibus Vestalibus," *Mnemosyne* 2nd ser. 56 (1928) 79-80.

———, "Mother-Right in Ancient Italy," *Folklore* 31 (1920) 93-108.

———, *Primitive Culture in Italy* (London, 1926).

Sacks, K., *Sisters and Wives: The Past and Future of Sexual Equality* (Westport, Connecticut, 1979).

Schaps, D., *Economic Rights of Women in Ancient Greece* (Edinburgh, 1979).

———, "The Women of Greece in Wartime," *CP* 77 (1982) 193-213.

———, "The Woman Least Mentioned: Etiquette and Women's Names," *CQ* n.s. 27 (1977) 323-330.

Schneider, D. M., and Gough, K., *Matrilineal Kinship* (Berkeley, Los Angeles, and London, 1961).

Scholz, U. W., *Studien zum altitalischen und altrömischen Marskult und Marsmythos* (Heidelberg, 1970).

Scullard, H. H., *Festivals and Ceremonies of the Roman Republic* (Ithaca, N.Y., 1981).

———, *From the Gracchi to Nero*[3] (London, 1970).

Segal, C. P., "The Menace of Dionysus: Sex Roles and Reversals in Euripides' *Bacchae*," *Arethusa* 11 (1978) 185-202.

Segal, E., *Roman Laughter. The Comedy of Plautus* (Cambridge, Mass., 1968).

Shackleton Bailey, D. R., "Brothers or Cousins?" *AJAH* 2 (1977) 148-150.

———, *Cicero* (London, 1971).

———, *Two Studies in Roman Nomenclature* (New York, 1976).

Singer, M. W., "Octavia Minor, Sister of Augustus: A Historical and Biographical Study." Unpublished Ph.D. dissertation, Duke University, 1945.

Skinner, M. B., "Pretty Lesbius," *TAPA* 112 (1982) 197-208.

Slater, P., *The Glory of Hera: Greek Mythology and the Greek Family* (Boston, 1968).

Slotty, F., "Zur Frage des Matriarchates bei den Etruskern," *Archiv Orientálni* 18 (1950) 262-285.

Smith, R., *The Negro Family in British Guiana* (London, 1956).

Smith, W. S., "Husband vs. Wife in Juvenal's Sixth Satire," *CW* 73 (1980) 323-332.

Soliday, G. L., ed. (with T. K. Hareven, R. Vann and R. Wheaton), *History of the Family and Kinship: A Select International Bibliography* (Millwood, N.Y., 1980).

Sommerstein, A. H., "The Naming of Women in Greek and Roman Comedy," *Quaderni di Storia* 11 (1980) 393-409.

Sorum, C. E., "The Family in Sophocles' *Antigone* and *Electra*," *CW* 75 (1982) 201-211.

Stone, L., "Prosopography," *Daedalus* 10 (1971) 46-79. Reprinted in *Historical Studies Today*, ed. F. Gilbert and S. Graubard (New York, 1972) 107-140.

Syme, R., "The Historian Servilius Nonianus," *Hermes* 92 (1964) 408-414. Reprinted in *Ten Studies in Tacitus* (Oxford, 1970) 91-109.

———, *History in Ovid* (Oxford, 1978).

———, "No Son for Caesar?" *Historia* 29 (1980) 422-437.

———, "Princesses and Others in Tacitus," *G and R* 28 (1981) 40-52.

———, *The Roman Revolution* (Oxford, 1939).

———, *Tacitus* (Oxford, 1958). 2 vols.

Szemerényi, O., *Studies in the Kinship Terminology of the Indo-European Languages with special reference to Indian, Iranian, Greek and Latin. Acta Iranica* 17 (Tehran-Liège, 1977).

Tanner, N., "Matrifocality in Indonesia and in Africa and Among Black Americans," *Woman, Culture, and Society*, ed. M. Z. Rosaldo and L. Lamphere (Stanford, 1974) 129-156.

Thomas, C. J., "Matriarchy in Early Greece: The Bronze and Dark Ages," *Arethusa* 6 (1973) 173-195.

Thomson, G. D., *Studies in Ancient Greek Society: The Prehistoric Aegean* (New York, 1949).

Tigerstedt, E. N., *The Legend of Sparta in Antiquity* II (Stockholm, 1974).

Townend, G. B., "Some Flavian Connections," *JRS* 51 (1961) 54-61.

Treggiari, S. M., "Consent to Roman Marriage: Some Aspects of Law and Reality," *Classical Views* 26 n.s.1 (1982) 34-44.

Vermeule, C. III, and Comstock, M. B., *Greek, Etruscan and Roman Art: The Classical Collections of the Museum of Fine Arts, Boston* (Boston, 1972).

Vernant, J. P., "Hestia-Hermès: sur l'expression religieuse de l'espace et du mouvement chez les Grecs," in *Mythe et pensée chez les Grecs* (Paris, 1969).

Veyne, P., "La famille et l'amour sous le haut-empire romaine," *Annales* ESC 33 (1978) 35-63.

Vollmer, F., *Laudationum funebrium Romanorum historia et reliquiarum editio, Jahrbucher für classische Philologie*, Supplement-Band 18 (1892).

Walbank, F. W., *A Historical Commentory on Polybius* III (Oxford, 1979).

Walde, A., and Hofmann, J., *Lateinisches Etymologisches Wörterbuch³* (Heidelberg, 1954).

Wallace, K. G., "Kinship Terms in Tacitus," delivered at the meeting of the Women's Classical Caucus held in conjunction with the American Philological Association, December 1976.

Warmington, E. H., ed. and transl., *Remains of Old Latin*. I: *Ennius and Caecilius* and III: *Lucilius and Laws of the Twelve Tables* (Cambridge, Mass., 1967).

Watson, A., *Roman Private Law Around 200 B.C.* (Edinburgh, 1971).

———, *Rome of the XII Tables* (Princeton, 1975).

Weinrib, E., "The Family Connections of M. Livius Drusus Libo," *Harvard Studies in Classical Philology* 72 (1967) 247-278.

Westrup, C. W., *Recherches sur les formes antiques de mariage dans l'ancien droit romain* (Copenhagen, 1943).

Wieacker, F., "Die XII Tafeln in ihrem Jahrhundert," *Les origines de la république romaine. Entretiens Hardt* 13 (Geneva, 1967) 291-362.

Willetts, R. F., *The Law Code of Gortyn. Kadmos*, Supplement 1 (1967).

Williams, G. W., "Some Aspects of Roman Marriage Ceremonies and Ideals," *JRS* 48 (1958) 16-29.

Wiseman, T. P., "Celer and Nepos," *CQ* n.s. 21 (1971) 180-182.

———, *Cinna the Poet and Other Essays* (Leicester, 1974).

Wiseman, T. P., "Lucius Memmius and His Family," *CQ* n.s. 17 (1967) 164–167.

Wistrand, E., *The So-Called Laudatio Turiae* (Göteborg, 1976).

Zeitlin, F. I., "The Dynamics of Misogyny: Myth and Mythmaking in the *Oresteia*," *Arethusa* 11 (1978) 149–184.

APPENDIX:
GENEALOGICAL TABLES

WITH the exception of Table VII, each of these tables has been adapted from recent scholarly work on the family concerned. None of these tables attempts to be a complete representation of a given family; they are intended merely to aid readers in visualizing the relationships between and among individual members of the major families treated in this study. These families are presented here in the order of their introduction in the second and third chapters of the text. Dates of consular office are provided for men who held that position. For most of those men who did not attain the consulship, dates of either the highest office held or death are supplied. The following abbreviations are employed: d. = died; cos. = consul; cos. suff. = consul suffectus; tr. pl. = tribune of the plebs; pr. = praetor. Unless otherwise indicated, all dates are B.C.; dotted lines are used to signify adoptive relationships. Annotation to each table furnishes further information about various individuals represented therein: that furnished for Tables I–VI is largely concerned with kindred and marital ties not noted on the tables, but also includes the dates for the principates of Rome's Julio-Claudian emperors; that furnished for Tables VII and VIII includes the dates ascribed to the reigns of Rome's legendary kings, and key details from the legends themselves.

Grateful acknowledgment is extended to the Oxford University Press for permission to adapt genealogical tables from R. Syme, *The Roman Revolution* (1939) I–V; A. E. Astin, *Scipio Aemilianus* (1967) 357; T. P. Wiseman, "*Celer and Nepos,*" CQ n.s. 21 (1971) 182. Acknowledgment is also extended to the journal *Historia* for permission to adapt a genealogical table from T. N. Gantz, "The Tarquin Dynasty," 24 (1975) 551.

TABLE I: THE FAMILY OF JULIUS AND AUGUSTUS CAESAR.
Adapted from Syme, *The Roman Revolution*, Table III.

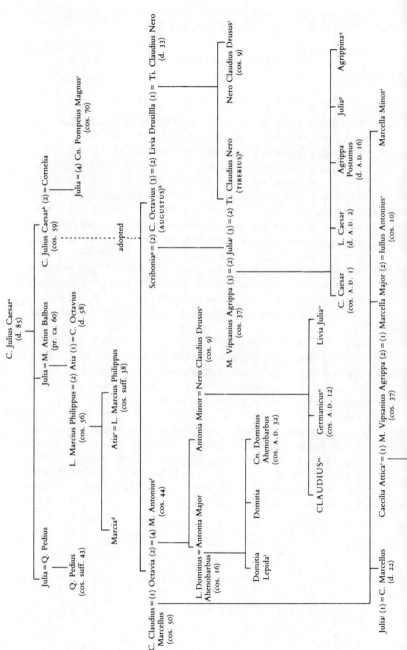

a Son of C. Julius Caesar and Marcia; brother of Julia, who was married to the dictator Marius. His own wife Aurelia came from the house of the Aurelii Cottae.

b His third wife was Pompeia; his fourth wife Calpurnia, daughter of L. Calpurnius Piso Caesoninus, consul in 58 B.C. He adopted his sister's grandson C. Octavius, later the emperor Augustus, in his will; hence the name Octavian.

c (Pompey the Great.) For his other marriages, see Tables III and V.

d Second wife of M. Porcius Cato (the Younger); subsequently married to Q. Hortensius (cos. 69) and Cato again. For her husbands, see Table IV.

e Sister of Atia who was wife to L. Marcius Philippus (cos. 56), her own husband's father.

f (Mark Antony). He was earlier married to Fulvia. For her, see also Table III. One of Fulvia's daughters by her first marriage to P. Clodius was the first wife of Octavian.

g For her family, see Table V; for her marriage to P. Cornelius Scipio (cos. suff. 35) and children, see Table VI.

h Known as Octavian from 44 to 27 B.C., and Augustus thereafter until his death in A.D. 14.

i Conceived by Livia when she was still married to Tiberius Claudius Nero, but not born until after she had wed Octavian. The name Drusus honors Livia's own family.

j Exiled in 2 B.C. for her adulteries with, e.g., Iullus Antonius (cos. 10). For her half-sister and brother, see Table VI.

k Consul in 13 B.C., he was emperor from A.D. 14 to 37. By his first wife Vipsania, he had a son, Drusus Caesar (cos. A.D. 15); he also adopted his brother's son Germanicus (cos. A.D. 12).

l Wife of M. Valerius Messalla Barbatus, she was the mother of Messalina, the third wife of the emperor Claudius; she also helped to rear her brother's son, the future emperor Nero (A.D. 54–68).

m Emperor of Rome from A.D. 41 to 54. By his second wife, Aelia Paetina, he had a daughter Claudia Antonia; by his third wife Messalina, he had a son Britannicus and a daughter Octavia. His fourth wife was his brother's daughter (the younger) Agrippina.

n Married to (the elder) Agrippina, daughter of M. Vipsanius Agrippa (cos. 37) and Augustus' daughter Julia. Their children include the emperor Caligula (A.D. 37–41), Drusilla, Julia Livilla and the younger Agrippina.

o Wife of Drusus Caesar (cos. A.D. 15), who was the son of the emperor Tiberius.

p Wife of L. Aemilius Paullus (cos. A.D. 1). For his family and their children, see Table VI.

q The elder Agrippina, wife of Germanicus (cos. A.D. 12); her daughter the younger Agrippina was first married to Cn. Domitius Ahenobarbus (cos. A.D. 32) and later wed to the emperor Claudius. This daughter's son by Ahenobarbus became the emperor Nero.

r Daughter of T. Pomponius Atticus, who received the name Caecilius from a maternal uncle who had adopted him.

s Son of Marcus Antonius (cos. 44) and his third wife Fulvia; reared by his stepmother Octavia.

t One of her husbands was Paullus Aemilius Lepidus, who had previously been married to Augustus' stepdaughter Cornelia; for this marriage, see Table VI. Another husband was M. Valerius Barbatus Appianus; by him she had a son who married Domitia Lepida and a daughter who married P. Quinctilius Varus (cos. 13).

TABLE II: THE FAMILY OF SCIPIO AEMILIANUS.
Adapted from A. E. Astin, *Scipio Aemilianus*
(Oxford 1967)

A) THE FAMILY OF L. AEMILIUS PAULLUS

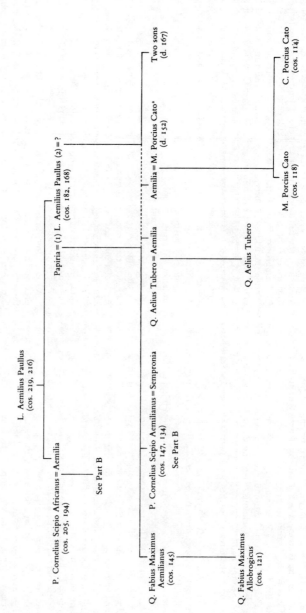

B) THE FAMILY OF P. CORNELIUS SCIPIO AFRICANUS

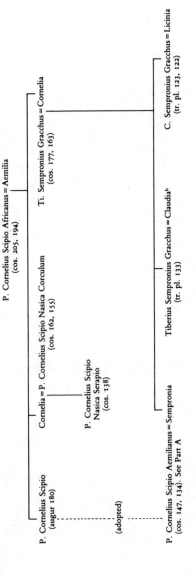

a Son of M. Porcius Cato (The Elder) (cos. 195) and Licinia
b Daughter of Appius Claudius Pulcher (cos. 143); sister of Vestal Claudia

TABLE III: SOME DESCENDANTS OF Q. METELLUS MACEDONICUS.
Adapted from Syme, *The Roman Revolution*, Table I;
T. P. Wiseman, "Celer and Nepos," *CQ* n.s.21 (1971) 182;
D. R. Shackleton Bailey, "Brothers or Cousins?"
AJAH 2 (1977) 148–150.

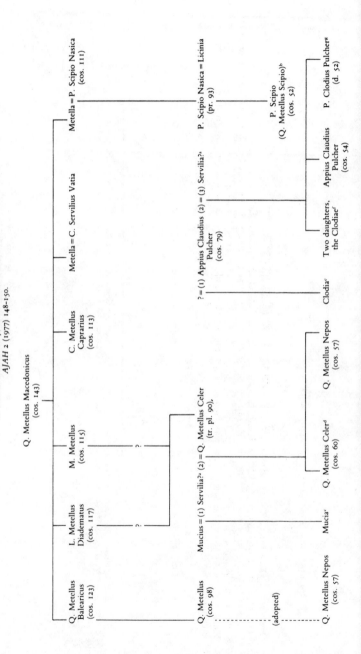

ᵃ Daughter of Q. Servilius Caepio, consul 106 B.C. (and hence *amita* to the elder Servilia, mother of Marcus Junius Brutus).

ᵇ Father of Cornelia, who was the fifth wife of Pompey the Great (Cn. Pompeius Magnus, cos. 70).

ᶜ Third wife of Pompey the Great, she was later married to M. Aemilius Scaurus.

ᵈ Husband of Clodiaᵉ.

ᵉ Wife of Q. Metellus Celerᵈ.

ᶠ One was married to L. Licinius Lucullus (cos. 74); the other to Q. Marcius Rex (cos. 68).

ᵍ Husband of Fulvia, who was later married to Mark Antony (M. Antonius, cos. 44).

TABLE IV: THE FAMILY OF MARCUS JUNIUS BRUTUS.
Adapted from Syme, *The Roman Revolution*, Table II as well as Table III above

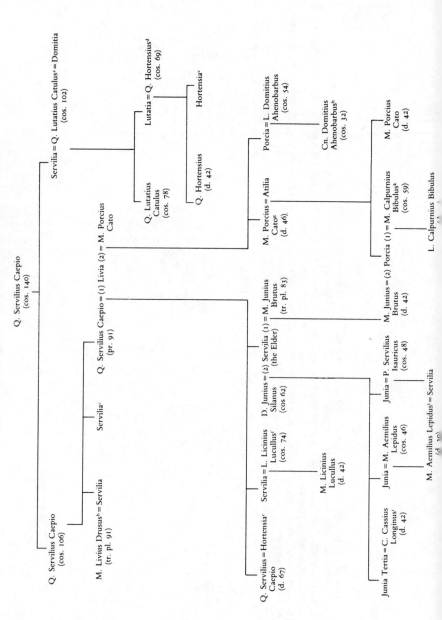

a Son of Popilia, for whom he delivered the *laudatio funebris*—the first ever given in honor of a woman.

b His wife Servilia was sister of Q. Servilius Caepio, who was married to Drusus' own sister Livia. His adopted son, M. Livius Drusus Claudianus, was father of the empress Livia. For her descendants, see Table I.

c On this woman, see Table III. It is conjectured that she was married to a Mucius, Appius Claudius Pulcher (cos. 79) and Q. Metellus Celer.

d Later married to Marcia, second wife of M. Porcius Cato (The Younger).

e Married to Q. Servilius Caepio, maternal half-brother of M. Porcius Cato (The Younger).

f Previously married to a Clodia, daughter of Appius Claudius Pulcher (cos. 79). See Table III.

g Cato The Younger. Later married to Marcia, daughter of L. Marcius Philippus (cos. 56). See Table I.

h For his son, L. Domitius Ahenobarbus (cos. 16), and his son's descendants, see Table I.

i Assassin—along with his brother-in-law Marcus Junius Brutus—of Julius Caesar in 44 B.C.

j Perhaps adopted by his mother's half-brother, Q. Servilius Caepio. Assassin—along with his brother-in-law C. Cassius Longinus—of Julius Caesar in 44 B.C.

k Consular colleague in 59 of Julius Caesar.

l Although his father was triumvir along with Octavian and Mark Antony from 43–36 B.C., he is remembered for carrying on the pro-republican cause of his maternal uncle Marcus Junius Brutus: in 30 B.C. he was executed for attempting to assassinate Octavian. His wife Servilia, whose mother was also a half-sister of Brutus, followed him in death. For his paternal family, see Table VI.

TABLE V: POMPEY AND HIS DESCENDANTS.
Adapted from Syme, *The Roman Revolution*, Table V.

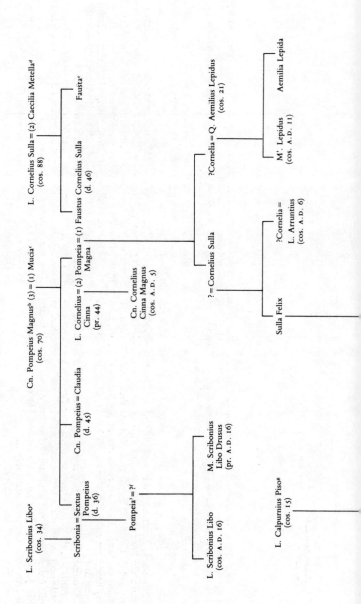

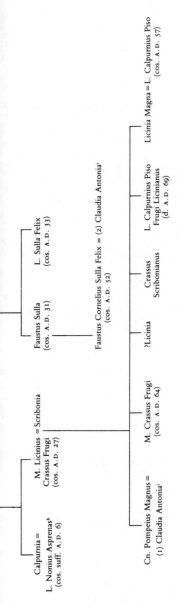

Calpurnia =
L. Nonius Asprenas[b]
(cos. suff. A.D. 6)

M. Licinius = Scribonia
Crassus Frugi
(cos. A.D. 27)

Faustus Sulla
(cos. A.D. 31)

L. Sulla Felix
(cos. A.D. 33)

Cn. Pompeius Magnus =
(1) Claudia Antonia[i]

M. Crassus Frugi
(cos. A.D. 64)

?Licinia

Faustus Cornelius Sulla Felix = (2) Claudia Antonia[i]
(cos. A.D. 52)

Crassus
Scribonianus

L. Calpurnius Piso
Frugi Licinianus
(d. A.D. 69)

Licinia Magna = L. Calpurnius Piso
(cos. A.D. 57)

a His sister, Scribonia, was wed first to a Cornelius Scipio, to whom she bore Cornelia, wife of Paullus Aemilius Lepidus (cos. 34), and P. Cornelius Scipio (cos. 16); she then wed Octavian, to whom she bore Julia. For her marriages, see Tables I and VI. Libo may have been either the father or the brother of M. Livius Drusus, consul in 15.

b (Pompey the Great). His first wife, Antistia, was daughter of P. Antistius, the praetor who presided over Pompey's trial for embezzlement in 86 B.C.; his second, Aemilia, was stepdaughter of Sulla (consul in 88) and daughter of Caecilia Metella. For his fourth wife, Julia, daughter of Julius Caesar, see Table III. For his fifth wife, Cornelia, see Table III.

c For her family, see Table III.

d She had been previously married to M. Aemilius Scaurus, consul in 115; their children were Aemilia, second wife of Pompey the Great, and M. Aemilius Scaurus, who married Pompey's third wife Mucia after she and Pompey were divorced.

e She was married, in turn, to C. Memmius and T. Annius Milo.

f Her husband is often—and doubtless erroneously—thought to be L. Scribonius Libo, her mother's brother.

g From the names of his son, M. Licinius Crassus Frugi, and his son's daughter(s) Licinia, it is conjectured that his wife was a Licinia from the house of the Crassi.

h Son of a Quinctilia, he served with distinction under his mother's brother P. Quinctilius Varus, consul in 13 B.C.

i Daughter of the emperor Claudius and Aelia Paetina.

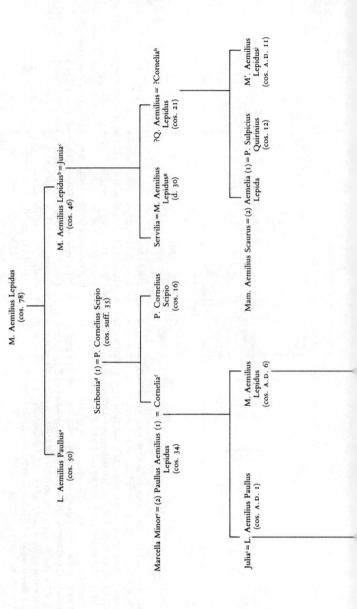

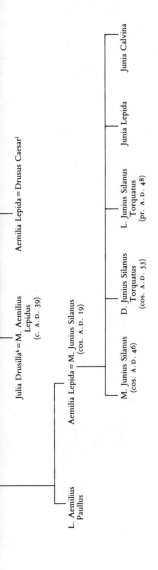

Julia Drusilla* = M. Aemilius Lepidus (c. A.D. 39) Aemilia Lepida = Drusus Caesar[l]

L. Aemilius Paullus Aemilia Lepida = M. Junius Silanus (cos. A.D. 19)

M. Junius Silanus (cos. A.D. 46) D. Junius Silanus Torquatus (cos. A.D. 53) L. Junius Silanus Torquatus (pr. A.D. 48) Junia Lepida Junia Calvina

a Proscribed, along with his son Paullus Aemilius Lepidus (cos. 34), by his brother, the triumvir M. Aemilius Lepidus, in 43 B.C. See also Table IV.

b Triumvir with Octavian and Mark Antony from 43-36 B.C. See also Table IV.

c Sister of Marcus Junius Brutus, Caesar's assassin, and of Junia Tertia, who was wed to Brutus' co-conspirator C. Cassius Longinus. See Table IV.

d Later married to Octavian, the future emperor Augustus, she was sister of L. Scribonius Libo, consul in 34. See also Tables I and V.

e She was the daughter of Octavia, sister to the emperor Augustus, and C. Claudius Marcellus, consul in 50. Also married to M. Valerius Barbatus Appianus, consul in 12; see Table I.

f Also the mother of an unnamed daughter.

g He was married to the son of his mother's sister; both he and his wife died after his unsuccessful attempt to assassinate Octavian. See also Table IV.

h See also Table V.

i She was the daughter of Julia and Agrippa (M. Vipsanius Agrippa, cos. 37), and hence granddaughter of the emperor Augustus. See also Table I.

j For Aemilius and his sister, who claimed descent from both Sulla and Pompey through their mother, see Table V.

k Daughter of Germanicus (cos. A.D. 12) and the elder Agrippina: see also Table I.

l Son of Germanicus and the elder Agrippina: see also Table I.

TABLE VII: THE LEGENDARY RULERS OF EARLIEST ROME

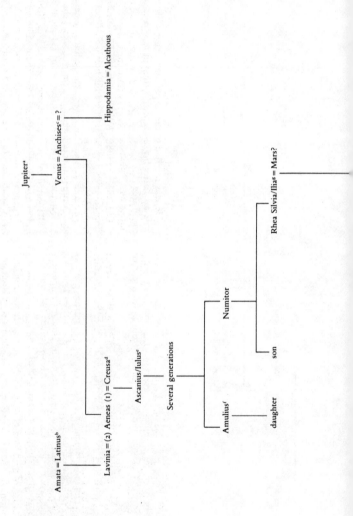

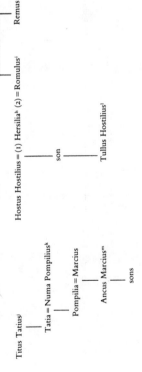

Hostus Hostilius = (1) Hersilia[h] (2) = Romulus[i]   Remus

son

Titus Tatius[j]

Tatia = Numa Pompilius[k]

Pompilia = Marcius

Ancus Marcius[m]

Tullus Hostilius[l]

sons

[a] King of the gods. Father of Mars—who allegedly sired Romulus and Remus—as well as of Aeneas' mother Venus.

[b] Legendary king of Latium. He had earlier promised his daughter Lavinia in marriage to Turnus, prince of the Rutulians; as a result, Turnus waged war on Aeneas and the Trojans.

[c] Trojan noble. Said to have fathered Aeneas on the goddess Venus when he was pasturing herds on Mt. Ida. Also said to be the father of daughters by a mortal woman.

[d] Reported to have been a daughter of the Trojan king Priam and sister of the leading Trojan warrior Hector.

[e] Supposed founder of both Alba Longa, Rome's parent city, and the Julian family.

[f] Claimed to have deposed his elder brother Numitor from the throne of Alba Longa; killed Numitor's son and made his daughter a Vestal Virgin. Eventually killed by this daughter's sons Romulus and Remus, who restored the kingdom to Numitor.

[g] Said to have cast her infant sons—on the order of Amulius—into the flooding Tiber river. After drifting ashore, the babies were sup- posedly suckled by a she-wolf and reared by the royal herdsman and his wife.

[h] Abducted Sabine woman, a widow with children of her own when she came to Rome. According to some sources, one of these children was father of Rome's third king, Tullus Hostilius.

[i] Legendary founder of Rome in 753 B.C. and subsequently its first king; he is said to have killed his brother Remus for violating the boundaries of his city.

[j] Claimed to have been king of Sabine town; supposed to have shared the kingship of Rome with Romulus after the merger with the Sabines.

[k] Reported to have been Rome's second king (from 715-673 B.C.), and to have received counsel from the nymph Egeria.

[l] Legendary Rome's third king (673-642 B.C.); battle of Horatii and Curiatii said to have occurred during his reign.

[m] Said to have been Rome's fourth king (642-617 B.C.) and to have founded the Marcian family.

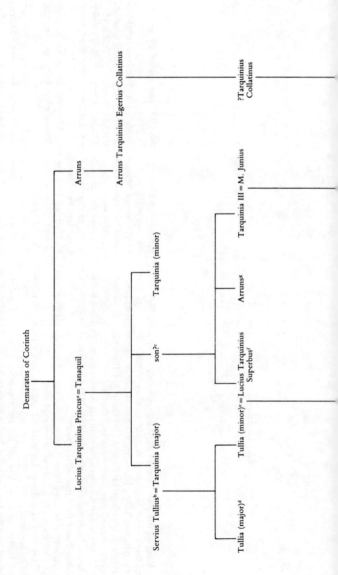

TABLE VIII: THE TARQUIN DYNASTY.
Adapted from T. N. Gantz, "The Tarquin Dynasty,"
Historia 24 (1975) 551.

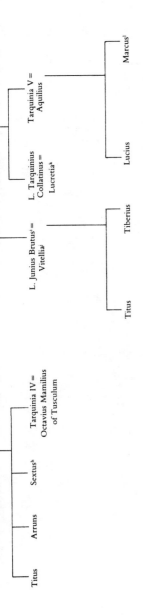

Titus Arruns Sextus[h]

Tarquinia IV = Octavius Mamilius of Tusculum

L. Junius Brutus[i] = Vitellia[j]

L. Tarquinius Collatinus = Lucretia[k]

Tarquinia V = Aquilius

Titus Tiberius

Lucius

Lucius Marcus[l]

---

[a] Traditionally the fifth king of Rome (616–579 B.C.). Said to have emigrated from Tarquinii in Etruria at the insistence of his wife Tanaquil. At Rome became guardian to the sons of King Ancus Marcius; later reportedly murdered at their instigation.

[b] Traditionally the sixth king of Rome (578–535 B.C.); helped to accede to the throne by his predecessor's wife Tanaquil. Died at the hands of his son-in-law, Tarquinius Superbus, who had been driven to this crime by his second wife, Servius' younger daughter Tullia.

[c] Perhaps Cn. Tarquinius/Cneve Tarchunies Rumach of the François Tomb.

[d] First wife of Tarquinius Superbus; said to have died at the hands of her younger sister, so that this ambitious sister and Superbus might wed.

[e] First married to Arruns; he was then slain—at her urging—by his brother Tarquinius Superbus; her sister, Superbus' wife, was slain too. After wedding Superbus, goaded him into killing her father; these deeds supposedly recalled when Tarquins ousted in 510 B.C.

[f] Traditionally the seventh and last king of Rome (534–510 B.C.); also known as Tarquin the Proud.

[g] First husband of Tullia (minor); killed, at her urging, by his brother, Tarquinius Superbus.

[h] His rape of Lucretia, wife of his cousin L. Tarquinius Collatinus, and her subsequent suicide, reportedly led to the Tarquins' expulsion from Rome.

[i] Traditional founder of the Roman republic; had his own sons executed when they took part in a conspiracy to overthrow the republic and reinstate the Tarquin monarchy. Celebrated as ancestor of Marcus Junius Brutus, who slew Julius Caesar; see Table IV.

[j] Sister of the Vitellii, who involved her sons in an abortive conspiracy against the republican form of government founded by their father.

[k] Daughter of Spurius Lucretius Tricipitinus; avenged by L. Junius Brutus.

[l] Fellow-conspirators of L. Junius Brutus' sons. Their mother's brother L. Tarquinius Collatinus supposedly left Rome rather than have his nephews suffer the same punishment as Brutus' sons.

INDEX OF
ANCIENT SOURCES

Index of Historical
and Legendary Persons

INDEX OF SUBJECTS

Roman sisters to brothers, 146-147

senes (old men), 55-56, 142, 143, 330-333

senex (old man), *see senes*

sexual behavior, Roman female: brothers' expectations of sisters', 147-148, 322-323, 327-330; fathers' expectations of daughters', 141-142, 327-330; husbands' expectations of wives', 227-240, 327-330. *See also* adultery, Roman

sisters, *see sorores*

slaves, 199, 225-226

sobrinus/sobrina (kindred through a sister), 186 n29

socer (father-in-law), its form and meaning, 104 n7, 131-132, 178

soceri (fathers-in-law): historical and legendary Roman, 50, 54, 55-56, 57-58, 100, 101, 102-108, 111-113, 116-117, 119-120, 140, 144, 156, 174, 203-204, 263, 265, 283, 299, 301, 302, 304, 307, 315, 316-317, 325, 334-336; in Greek literature and society, 272-273, 279-280 n10, 292-293, 298; in Vergil, 268, 270

socerilocality, 279 n10

sons, *see filii*

sons-in-law, *see generi*

soror (sister), its meaning, usage and derivatives, 148, 178, 186-187, 189

sorores (sisters): historical and legendary Roman, 12, 31-34, 42, 43, 44, 45, 46-54, 66, 72 n12, 78, 80, 82, 92 n36, 93, 94, 100, 114-115, 121-122, 127-129, 130, 131, 141, 143, 147-149, 150-194, 200-201, 207-210, 214-215, 217, 229, 232, 244-245, 260-262, 264, 320-323, 328-329, 336-337, 345; in cross-cultural perspective, 319

n42; German, according to Tacitus, 284-285; in Greek literature and society, 72-73, 75, 267-268, 271, 279 n10, 281 n12, 297-298; in Vergil, 181, 269

soror patruelis (father's brother's daughter), 122 n53, 186-187, 192-193

Spartans, 162 n10, 277, 278 n9, 294, 297 n25, 327 n49

stepfathers, 54, 100, 141, 154, 181, 255-257, 303, 323-324

structural centrality, *see* centrality

Thetis, 98

trinoctium (annual separation of Roman spouses for three nights so as to prevent *manus* through *usus*), 124

Trojans, 16, 42, 98, 121, 181, 212, 267-270, 272, 275, 292, 295 n23, 306, 317

Twelve Tables, 22-23, 27, 86, 90, 123-127, 131 n70, 145, 179, 190, 202 n42, 205 n46, 206, 216, 265, 322

tyrants, 293

uncles, *see avunculi* and *patrui*

univirae (women married only once), 241 n24

uxor (wife), its derivations, 221-222

uxores (wives): historical and legendary Roman, 9, 11 n15, 12, 14, 15, 22, 23, 30 n46, 35 n1, 38-40, 41, 43, 44, 45, 46 n15 and n16, 47, 49 n49, 50-61, 66, 79, 85-87, 93, 100, 102, 104, 105, 106-107, 113, 116-117, 120-121, 123-126, 136-137, 139, 140-141, 142, 148, 158, 159, 162, 166, 168, 171-173, 175-177, 179-180, 182, 184, 194, 196, 216-218, 219-243, 244, 246, 247, 249, 250, 252, 255, 256, 258, 260-262, 283, 303,

Library of Congress Cataloging in Publication Data

Hallett, Judith P., 1944-
    Fathers and daughters in Roman society.

    Bibliography: p.   Includes index.
    1. Women—Rome—Social conditions. 2. Fathers and
daughters—Rome—History. 3. Family—Rome—History.
4. Rome—History. 5. Upper classes—Rome—History.
I. Title.
HQ1136.H35 1984   305.4'2'0945632   83-43074
ISBN 0-691-03570-9 (alk. paper)
ISBN 0-691-10160-4 (pbk.)